A Concise Survey of Western Civilization

Supremacies and Diversities throughout History

VOLUME 1: PREHISTORY TO 1500

Third Edition

BRIAN A. PAVLAC
King's College

ROWMAN & LITTLEFIELD
Lanham • Boulder • New York • London

Executive Editor: Susan McEachern
Editorial Assistant: Katelyn Turner
Senior Marketing Manager: Kim Lyons

Credits and acknowledgments for material borrowed from other sources, and reproduced with permission, appear on the appropriate page within the text.

Published by Rowman & Littlefield
An imprint of The Rowman & Littlefield Publishing Group, Inc.
4501 Forbes Boulevard, Suite 200, Lanham, Maryland 20706
www.rowman.com

6 Tinworth Street, London SE11 5AL, United Kingdom

Copyright © 2019 by The Rowman & Littlefield Publishing Group, Inc.
First Edition 2011. Second Edition 2015.

British Library Cataloguing in Publication Information Available

Library of Congress Cataloging-in-Publication Data

Names: Pavlac, Brian Alexander, 1956– author.
Title: A concise survey of western civilization : supremacies and diversities throughout history / Brian A. Pavlac, King's College.
Description: Third edition. | Lanham, MD : Rowman & Littlefield, [2019] | Includes bibliographical references and index.
Identifiers: LCCN 2018059659 (print) | LCCN 2018059913 (ebook) | ISBN 9781538112519 (electronic) | ISBN 9781538112540 (v. 1 electronic) | ISBN 9781538112571 (v. 2 electronic) | ISBN 9781538112496 (cloth : alk. paper) | ISBN 9781538112502 (pbk. : alk. paper) | ISBN 9781538112526 (v. 1 : cloth : alk. paper) | ISBN 9781538112533 (v. 1 : pbk. : alk. paper) | ISBN 9781538112557 (v. 2 : cloth : alk. paper) | ISBN 9781538112564 (v. 2 : pbk. : alk. paper)
Subjects: LCSH: Civilization, Western.
Classification: LCC CB245 (ebook) | LCC CB245 .P38 2019 (print) | DDC 909/.09821—dc23
LC record available at https://lccn.loc.gov/2018059659

Printed in the United States of America

Brief Contents

Contents

Diagrams, Figures, Maps, Primary Source Projects, Sources on Families, Tables, and Timelines

DIAGRAM

FIGURES

MAPS

PRIMARY SOURCE PROJECTS

SOURCES ON FAMILIES

TABLES

TIMELINES

Acknowledgments

I was interested in history from a young age, as most kids are. Too often, as they grow older, kids lose their fascination with the past, partly because it becomes one more thing they have to learn rather than a path of self-understanding or even just "neat stuff." Wonderful teachers taught me history through the years, and partly inspired by them, I foolishly went on to study history in college. Before I knew it, history became my intended profession. Since then I have been fortunate to make a living from history.

In teaching courses over the years, I found my own voice about what mattered. Instead of simply sharing my thoughts in lectures, I produced this book. Former teachers, books I have read and documentaries I have viewed, historical sites I have visited, all have contributed to the knowledge poured into these pages. Likewise, many students, too many to be named, have sharpened both words and focus. I owe thanks to the many readers whose suggestions have improved the text. For their help to me in getting this project as far as it has come, I have to thank a number of specific people. I appreciate my editor, Susan McEachern, who gave the book her time and consideration and offered a third edition, and her associates Katelyn Turner and Jehanne Schweitzer. Various people have offered useful suggestions for this edition: Cristofer Scarboro, Charles Ingram, Nicole Mares, Megan Lloyd, and especially the two readers, Ian Crowe and John Williams. Finally, most of all, my spouse, Elizabeth Lott, has sustained me through all the editions and permutations. Her skills in grammar, logic, and good sense have made this a far better book.

The final version is never final. Every new history source I read makes me want to adjust an adjective, nudge a nuance, or fix a fact. With every edition of this text, I find room for improvement. Should any inaccuracies or errors have crept in, please forgive the oversight and contact me with your proposed corrections.

How to Use This Book

Learning is difficult. If it were easy, everyone would be educated. In this age of multimedia, reading still remains one of the best ways to learn something. Of course, reading well is not always easy. You cannot read a nonfiction informative work such as this in the same way as you would a Harry Potter novel. Those novels, though, are full of information with strange new terms, from *muggles* to *Hogwarts*, that people learn easily and absorb into their knowledge. The same can be true of learning history once it interests you.

The pictures on the covers of the various editions of this textbook illustrate people in the past writing something. They have produced the sources that we use today to understand our heritage and ourselves. History is a product of people, by people, and for people. We create it, preserve it, and share it. The purpose of this text is to help you integrate the history of the Western past into your meaning of life.

I hope to make learning history as enjoyable as possible, even to those who are not in love with the past. As a survey, this book offers one person's opinion about what is good, bad, useful, and wasteful to know about our wider civilization. This book does cover the minimum historical information that educated adults should know—just compare it to other texts. Also, in the author's opinion, it offers a tightly focused narrative and interpretive structure, in a sometimes quirky style.

This text's distinctive approach applies major themes of conflict and creativity. The phrase *supremacies and diversities* describes the unifying theme through which this text evaluates the past. Supremacies focus on the use of power to dominate societies, ranging from ideologies to warfare. Supremacy seeks stability, order, and amalgamation. Diversities encompass the creative impulses that concoct new ideas, as well as people's efforts to define themselves as different. Diversity produces change, opportunity, and individuality. A tension, of course, arises between the "supremacy" desire for conformity and the "diversity" idea of individuality. This interaction has clearly driven historical conflict and change. Other approaches might be equally valuable. Indeed, to be truly educated, you should be looking at a variety of views about the past. History is rarely simple. This version merely provides a foundation for learning more.

Fulfilling the survey function, this narrative examines political, economic, technological, social, and cultural trends, depending on the historical period. The book does not much emphasize the everyday-life aspects of people in the past. For more on this, and art and literature, see the website. Five main topical themes regularly inform how this text looks at change: technological innovation, migration and conquest, political and economic decision making, church and state, and proposals about the meaning of life. These topics have significantly altered history and are still influential in the present.

How could you best learn from this book? Read well. This time-tested advice applies to anything you might want to learn thoroughly for the rest of your life. Here are a few steps:

1. Read the text in a space and at a time conducive to reading—not in the few minutes before class, not where others will interrupt, not with television or music blaring.

2. Prudently mark up, underline, highlight, and otherwise annotate your text as you study. Use the margins for notes, questions, comments, and marks to remind yourself of some important point.

3. Critique the book as you read; enter into its conversation. You might comment in the margins or on blank pages on the following points:

    connections between themes, ideas, or subjects;
    ideas you agree with;
    ideas you disagree with;
    reactions provoked by the text;
    material of particular interest to you; and
    material you would like to know more about.

4. At the end of each section, jot down notes or write a brief comment about what you have just read. The review question at the end of each section and the space provided for a response encourage this learning skill.

5. Each chapter provides a primary source project to help you think like a historian while determining your own perspective on the past and present. In the Primary Source Projects you can compare and contrast the ideas in the sources (or in a few cases within one source). Topics include the different roles of government, the power of religion, perceptions of good or bad leadership, the role of the individual, and social values. The Sources on Families present different views on the nature and experience of that basic social unit, further described in chapter 2. Important aspects of such sources are property, choice in forming a family, sexuality, social status, raising children, breaking spousal relationships, religious support, and alternatives to the "traditional" family. Answering the given questions for the sources in the space provided will help you understand and remember them. The sources have usually been lightly edited from their cited printed versions for spelling, grammar, clarity, and length (being the only correction noted by ellipses [. . .]). More versions, questions, and information

about these sources are available at the website http://www.concisewesternciv.com/sources. A list of suggested readings of primary sources is at http://www.concisewesternciv.com/sources/suggested.html. They are largely primary sources that provide essential points of view or capture the spirit of their times, sometimes at great length.

6. A common question students have about history is "How important is it to know dates?" Understanding dates is essential. History is all about what happens before (which can affect causation), what events are happening at the same time (which adds to context), and what happens after (which may show results). The more dates connected with historical change you know, the better you will be at historical explanation. At least attempt to memorize the dates of the major periods (although different approximate dates may be offered for the same large periods—historians do not always agree on exact beginnings and ends). The book presents dates in chapter subtitles, on most maps, throughout the text, and in the block timelines toward the end of the text. Use these block timelines to review and structure your knowledge according to theme or time period. The most important terms in the text appear in **boldface** and are listed in the block timelines. Additionally, terms representing significant ideas and ideologies are defined both in the text and again in the glossary at the back of the book; these terms are set in ***boldface italics***.

7. To further help you learn dates, names, and terms, on the last page of each chapter is a "Make your own timeline" feature. Use the terms in boldface italics from what you have just read and those in the block timelines toward the end of this text. See the sample timeline at the end of chapter 1 for an example of how you can make your own.

8. As is clear from the above, even more information is provided on the website: **ConciseWesternCiv.com**. The website offers more study guides, questions, outlines, summaries, all the maps in color, diagrams, tables, many of the figures (pictures), a history of art relevant to each chapter, and links to many more websites and primary sources. All of these materials can reinforce and expand on what you learn from the text.

Finally, connect what you learn here to the rest of your experience. The more you know, the more you can know. And according to the liberal arts credo, the more you know, the better will be your decisions about your life.

CHAPTER 1

History's Story

"N ow" is over and done with. It can never take place again. Each moment is surrendered to the past, whether forgotten or remembered. In our personal lives, we treasure or bury memories on our own. Our larger society, however, has historians to preserve and make sense of our collective recollection. Historians recapture the past by applying particular methods and skills that have been nurtured over the past few centuries. Although such processes are not without challenges, the work done by historians has created the subject of this book you are reading: **Western civilization**.

THERE'S METHOD

"How do we know anything?" is our starting point. As **humans**, some of our knowledge comes from instinct: we are born with it, beginning with our first cry and suckle. Yet instinct makes up a tiny portion of human knowledge. Most everything we come to know we learn in one way or another. First, we learn through direct experience of the senses. These lessons of life can sometimes be painful (fire), other times pleasurable (chocolate). Second, other people teach us many important matters through example and setting rules. Reading this book because of a professor's requirement may be one such demand. Third, human beings can apply reason to figure stuff out.[1] This ability enables people to take what they know, then learn and rearrange it into some new understanding.

The discipline of **history** is one such form of reasoning. History is not just knowing something—names, dates, facts—about the past. The word *history* comes from the Greek word ιστορία for "inquiring," or asking questions. The questioning of the past has been an important tool for gaining information about ourselves. Indirectly, it helps us to better define the present.

---

1. This approach assumes we can correctly understand the world. When the title character in Shakespeare's play *Hamlet* pretends insanity in order to discover truth, another character rationally concludes that though "this be madness; yet there is method in it."

Quite often authorities, the people in charge, have used history to bind together groups with shared identities. For many peoples, history has embodied a mythology that reflected their relationship to the gods. Or history chronicled the deeds of kings, justifying royal rulership. History also sanctioned domination and conquest of one people over another. Most people are raised to believe that their own country or nation is more virtuous and righteous than those others beyond their borders. The history of Western civilization abounds with examples of these attitudes.

Then, about two hundred years ago, several men began to try to improve our understanding of the past. These historians began to organize as a profession based in the academic setting of universities (at which they did not allow women to study at that time). Historians imitated and adapted the scientific method (see chapter 10) for their own use, renaming it the **historical method** (see table 1.1). In the scientific method, scientists pose hypotheses as reasonable guesses about explanations for how nature works. They then observe and experiment to prove or disprove their hypotheses. In the historical method, historians propose hypotheses to describe and explain how history changes. The two main problems historians have focused on are **causation** (how something happened) and **significance** (what impact something had). History without explanations about how events came about or why they matter is merely trivia.

Unlike scientists, historians cannot conduct experiments or run historical events with different variables.[2] Historians cannot even obtain direct observational evidence of events before their own lifetimes—there are no time machines. Instead, historians have to pick through whatever evidence has survived. They call these data **sources**. At first, historians sought out sources among the written records that had been preserved over centuries in musty books and manuscripts. Eventually historians learned to study human-made objects, ranging from needles to skyscrapers.

Obviously, not all sources are of equal value. Those sources connected directly with past events are called **primary sources**. These are most important for historical investigation. Reading them, one encounters history in the raw.[3] When evaluating these primary sources, historians face two predicaments. For one, evidence for many events has not survived at all or remains only in fragments. Much of history is never recorded in the first place and dies with people's memories. Even for recorded sources, some are eaten by rats and rot, while others are obliterated in war or trashed on purpose (such as the records of the British Empire in Operation Legacy, where officials purged files to keep them out of the hands of their colonial successors). For another, some people have forged sources, in whole or in part. Much of historical research involves questioning human character, deciding who is honest or deceitful, trustworthy or undependable. Then, through careful examination and questioning, historians try to write the most reliable and accurate explanation of past events, carefully sifting and then citing their sources.

2. Alternative histories are an increasingly popular genre of fiction. Similar to science fiction's guesses about the future, alternative histories are based on "what if" issues of the past: what would have happened differently if, for example, some leader had not been killed.

3. The "Primary Source Projects" and "Sources on Families" offer opportunities to wrestle with such primary sources. For more explanation, see "How to Use This Book."

Table 1.1.   The Historical Method

1. Find a problem.

2. Form a hypothesis (a reasonable or educated guess to the solution).

3. Conduct research into sources.

Questions to ask of sources:

    A.   External: Is it genuine? Is it what it says it is?
          When and where was it made?
          How did it get from its original recording to the present?
          Who is the author?
          How was the author able to create the source?
          Are there any interpolations, emendations, or insertions by others?

    B.   Internal: What is its meaning? How is it significant?
          What is the source's ostensible or intended purpose?
          How accurate is the author (any competence, bias, prejudice)?
          What is the source's content?
          How does it compare with other reliable sources?
          What do modern scholars say about the source?

4. Make the argument and conclusions, usually in written form.

5. Share the knowledge, usually through publication.

Note: The step-by-step process of the historical method rigorously questions sources in order to reconstruct the best version of the past.

As the last and most important part of the historical method, professional historians have shared their information with one another. They produce **secondary sources**, usually books and articles.[4] At academic conferences and in more books and articles, historians learn from and judge one another's work. They debate and challenge one another's arguments and conclusions. Often a consensus about the past emerges. Generally, agreed-on views begin to appear in **tertiary sources**, such as encyclopedias, handbooks, or this very textbook. Although tertiary sources are several steps removed, these sources offer convenient summaries and overviews but usually lack citations to sources.

Because the past is so vast, historians have always divided it up into smaller, more convenient chunks. All history is about selection, choosing what to examine. Professional historians usually specialize, becoming experts in one small slice of the past. Since so many historians publish scholarship today, hardly anyone can ever read all that has been written about any single subject. New books and articles emerge each year, especially about popular topics such as the American Civil War or Hitler. The history of even one day covered in any detail would be long and confusing; the novel *Ulysses* by James Joyce, about the events of 16 July 1904, is an

---

4. A good secondary source has footnotes (at the bottom of the page) or endnotes (at the end of each chapter or the whole book or article) that cite the other primary, secondary, and tertiary sources. The footnotes in this text merely add some tangential commentary.

interesting example. Whether writing many volumes or a slim book, it is impossible to cover every detail on even a small subject. Something is always left out.

Therefore, historians prioritize to make the past manageable. They select certain events or places as more important than others. For example, in one person's life, a onetime decision, such as which college to attend, would probably be more essential to include in her biography than a description about what she chose to eat for breakfast on the day the decision was made. The former probably deserves more attention, since that choice can change a life. The quality of a unique, decisive historical moment is usually more interesting than a quantity of mundane events. However, the description of breakfast choice might be valuable if, for example, years of eating too much bacon and eggs led to heart disease or a dose of poison killed a person. Few readers, though, would want to read a close description of every repeated meal. Selection and generalization prevent us from becoming either overwhelmed or bored.

Historians can select only a few bits of the past, leaving out the vast majority of human activities. They then categorize or organize their selections into sensible stories and arguments. For example, eating breakfast differs a lot from choosing a college or waging a war. Politics—kings, wars, treaties, and rebellions—was once considered by historians as the only important human activities worthy of investigation. Within the past century, however, historians have broadened their interests to include a wider range of human pursuits. These days, many historians examine social manners: family, sex roles, food, and fashion.[5] Even a shift in breakfast habits from waffles and bacon cooked by Mom to a drive-in processed Egg McMuffin can illustrate something about a **society**, a coherent group of people.

Historians categorize the past in three main ways. The first and most obvious division is **chronological**, using time as dividing points. The most natural division of time is the day, with its cycle of sunlight and darkness. This cycle regulates us all. Some particular days, like those on which battles are waged or a notable inspiration is put to paper, can change the course of history. A larger natural unit of time is the year, especially important for people in temperate climates who experience the change of seasons. Finally, the basic human experience stretches, for each of us, over a lifetime. Some lives are short and others seem long, but all end in death. Yet history marches on.

Aside from natural portions of time, historians divide up history into manageable blocks. In the largest artificial division, historians split the past into two periods: **prehistory** and history. Prehistory includes everything humans did up until the invention of writing about five thousand years ago in the Middle East and East Asia. We can examine human activity before writing only through physical remains and artifacts, such as bones and shaped stones.

Technology (the use of raw materials to make tools), ideology, and narrower political movements also define different eras. Many of the commonly used historical labels, terms such as *antiquity*, *medieval*, and *Renaissance*, were not drawn from the sources and lives of past people; instead, historians later coined those

---

5. For interesting perspectives on marriage, children, and sex and gender, see the "Sources on Family" for each chapter after this one.

terms. The names for the Stone Age or the Iron Age are based on the use of those materials for making tools during those times. The term *Middle Ages* draws on the perceptions of politics and culture that fall between the ancient and modern epochs. The titles of the ages of Renaissance and Enlightenment derive from artistic and intellectual achievements. Sometimes a country's dynasty or ruling family provides a useful marker, such as Victorian England. Given our preference for round numbers, a century fits into historical schemes, especially the more recent nineteenth or twentieth centuries. Historians apply such divisions to the past to show both what the people within a period shared in common and what they have to teach us. Acts of naming may simplify the complexities and contradictions of any given time period, but without choosing such terms we cannot have a discussion.

While chronology applies time to divide up the past, **geographical** divisions, where events took place on our planet, are equally common. The largest unit for human activity is world or global history (with the minor exception of recent space exploration). Historians are increasingly finding connections and continuities among civilizations around the planet. By the twentieth century, people were clearly bound together worldwide. At the opposite end of size, the smallest unit could be a town, a college, or even a home. Historians usually focus somewhere between these two extremes, most frequently dealing with a country, nation, or state. Indeed, history became a profession in modern times as academics constructed national stories for the modern nation-states.

The third method that historians use to slice up the past is a **topical** approach, separating the wide range of human activities into smaller groupings of human enterprise. For example, historians today often specialize in areas of intellectual, social, constitutional, gender, literary, diplomatic, or military history.

The timelines at the back of this book group historical activities into six different columns. First is *science* and technology: how we understand the universe and build tools to cope with it. Second is **economics**: how we create and manage the distribution of wealth. Third is **politics**: how people create systems to organize collective decisions. Fourth is **social structures**: the units and hierarchies (such as families and communities) within which people place themselves and the humble activities of daily life. Fifth is **culture**, especially those works and activities that people fashion in order to cope with, understand, or simply share their experiences of the world. Culture includes music, **art** (largely visual creations), **literature** (compositions of words read or performed), and recreation (acts ranging from sports to hobbies). Finally are both *philosophy* and *religion*: how people understand the purpose of life and the meaning of death, which usually involves the supernatural, or beliefs in a reality beyond our senses. These six topics essentially embrace all human accomplishments.

Historians, and this text, define a *civilization* as a coherent, large collection of peoples in a specific time and place who establish particular approaches to political, social, and cultural life, especially around their cities. The concept remains slippery, however. Where any civilization began (or ended), whether in time, geographic boundary, or membership, depends on who defines it and by what criteria. And generalizations of what holds a society together often ignore contradictions and minority movements. Sometimes a civilization is dominated by one powerful people or idea (Chinese or Muslim civilizations), while Western civilization developed from the interaction of several cultures. Most people have historically tended to view the world from their own vantage points. Historians naturally tend to focus on the history of the political states in which they live. Whether in the Americas, Europe, Asia, or Africa, historians have too rarely gazed across borders and boundaries to see how often and in what ways people have believed and acted in common.

This particular text reviews a civilization defined by many historians as "Western." As an academic subject it originated about one hundred years ago, after the United States had risen to become a world power. Many American historians saw a shared Western past with other European nations that had also risen to global power status. If Americans learned only US history without understanding how the United States fits into the larger culture of competing European powers, they argued, Americans would misunderstand their own heritage and the challenges of the future. The founders of classes on Western civilization deliberately wove together American with European history, showing the common origins of so much that Americans, and Europeans, took for granted. Thus, Western civilization courses and texts multiplied until a few years ago, when other historians argued in favor of world or global history courses, which try to cover all societies on planet Earth. An even newer trend is the "Big History," which covers material from the "big bang" origin of the universe through our current human predicaments.

Western civilization is worth studying because it organizes a large portion of interrelated history that is relevant to today's problems in a world dominated by Western industrialized states and ideologies. The West is not necessarily better in creativity or virtue than many other civilizations that arose around the world, even if many past and even present historians have thought so (for more about studying Western Civ, see the epilogue). This text will often point out where the West borrowed knowledge and when its moral virtue fell short of its proclaimed ideals. It also developed deeply contradictory ideas within itself, many of which still battle with each other today. Undoubtedly, the West became more powerful, becoming the dominant society of the contemporary world. To understand it is to comprehend how many of the globe's institutions, practices, and ideologies came to function as they do, for good or ill.

The word *Western* obviously reveals a strong geographical component. The name separates it from what might be considered northern, southern, or Eastern civilizations. While historians have not created a category for northern or southern civilizations, they used to apply the term *Eastern* (or *Oriental*, from the Latin for where the sun rises) to what they now prefer to call Asian civilizations (China and India, for example). Just as the name of the "Orient" comes from the place of the rising sun over the Eurasian landmass, the old-fashioned name for the West, the "Occident," derives from where the sun sets.

This book's narrative will show how a civilization that can be called "Western" began in the specific geographical area of **western Europe**, the northwestern extension of land from the vast landmass of Eurasia and Africa, bordered by the North Sea, the Mediterranean Sea, and the Atlantic. Its first inspirations lay in the

Middle East, the region including the river systems of the Tigris and Euphrates and the Nile. The core of its culture next developed around the Mediterranean Sea, until it shifted north into western Europe between fifteen hundred and a thousand years ago. There the key components of Western civilization finally jelled. About five hundred years ago, bearers of Western civilization began to conquer much of Eurasia and many overseas territories. The interactions of the West with other peoples around the world will decide the questions of where the West begins, endures, changes, or ends.

Just as geography defines the West, so does its chronology. Setting an exact starting date presents as many difficulties as setting its contemporary borders. One self-defining moment in Western tradition appears in its calendar, today accepted by many people around the world. The Western chronology has traditionally divided history into two periods, labeled with the initials **BC** and **AD**. These large periods mark the founding of Christianity by Jesus of Nazareth about two thousand years ago (see chapter 6). Most people can readily say BC means "before Christ," but fewer can explain that AD is the abbreviation for *anno Domini*, which means "in the year of the Lord" and refers again to Jesus of Nazareth. Many current history writers, apparently uncomfortable with the religious roots of our calendar, have switched to using the terms BCE and CE, meaning "before the common era" and "common era." These terms lack any historical content other than being placeholders for political correctness. No other event changed history around two thousand years ago to make any civilization more "common." This book's use of the terms BC and AD is not intended to privilege Christianity but merely recognizes the actual origins of our dating system.

Rather than this simple duality centered on Christianity, historians more sensibly divide the Western past into three or four periods. Ancient history (which includes prehistory) usually ends around AD 500. The Middle Ages then follow, ending any time between 1300 and 1789, depending on the historian's point of view. Then early modern history might begin as early as 1400 or as late as 1660 and last until either the modern or contemporary periods take over in the past few centuries. The year 1914 seems useful as a starting point for contemporary history because of the first modern world war. To make the past still more manageable, this book divides up the past into fifteen parts, or chapters (including this introduction and an epilogue to both sum up and point forward). The above dates and eras, of course, make sense only in relation to the history of Europe. Other civilizations need other markers, although historians often try to impose Western categories on world history.

This survey assigns the beginning of Western civilization to between fifteen and eleven hundred years ago, as western Europe recovered from the disaster of the collapse of its part of the Roman Empire. Understanding how this civilization built on previous human experiences, however, requires our reaching back beyond the fall of Rome to humanity's beginnings. Therefore, this particular book covers prehistory and the West's deep roots in the Middle East and Mediterranean regions. Sometimes coverage overlaps between chapters, and it certainly intensifies as it approaches the present, because recent events impact our lives more directly.

Chapter 2 lightly skims over several million years, while chapter 14 covers only a few decades.

Covering much of Western history in fifteen chapters requires careful selection of the most resonant information. This narrative touches on the basic topics of politics, economics, technology, society, culture, and intellectual cultural trends, depending on the historical period. This story does not deal as much with the everyday-life aspects of people in the past, such as how families lived in their homes, or what they ate. Five main topical themes regularly guide the flow: (1) control over nature through technological innovation, (2) the rise and fall of communities through migration and conquest, (3) disagreements about political and economic decision making, (4) conflicts about priorities in religion and government, and (5) proposals about the ultimate meaning of life. These topics have significantly affected the past and are still influential in the present.

This book, then, covers a lot of time, over a large part of the world, involving many human events. As a concise history, it necessarily leaves out a great deal. Historians are always making choices about what they want to study, what approach they take, and what stays in. As you learn more about history, you can choose for yourself what else to learn. For a beginning, this text should ground you in the basics of this civilization called the West.

Review: How do historians study and divide up the past?

Response:

WHAT IS TRUTH?

History is a human production. Every idea, institution, painting, document, movement, war, or invention originated with a human being. People believe in, fight for, kill for, and die for ideas. While natural forces such as floods, drought, and disease affect people and may influence the course of history, the survivors still must choose how to react to those disasters. No "force" works by itself to change history.

True power comes from people joined together. People usually organize themselves so that a few lead and most follow. Motivations for forming larger groups could include love, favoritism, hunger, greed, blood loyalty, defense of hearth and home, and cruelty. The variety of human experiences guarantees different points of view. The challenge for historians is to sort through those views and reach the best explanation of how history changes and what it should mean to us.

People write history. In this text's version of history, choices about what to include or exclude are shaped by the broad culture of the modern West, the personal judgment of recent professional historians, and the author. In today's modern culture, factions of citizens sharply disagree about politics, economics, science, and even the meaning of words.[6] Cultural guardians argue over which sets of facts and interpretations today's citizens and students should be required to learn. Communities disagree on how to honor or mourn the past with markers, statues, and memorials. Some differences are inevitable. The vast amount of possible information imposes selection, as do individual perspectives and agendas. As imperfect people select what goes into their history, the accounts will differ from one another.

Degrees of ***subjectivity*** versus ***objectivity*** affect any accurate version of the past. Objectivity is seeing events and ideas in an impartial way, while subjectivity involves a view ranging from **bias** (inclination toward a particular point of view) all the way to **prejudice** (dismissal of other points of view). Even the historian Herbert Butterfield referred to the "magnet in men's minds" that attracts only information that already aligns with a person's political and social inclinations. No one can entirely escape being somewhat subjective. Good historians strive toward objectivity, aware of their own inclinations. Historical relativism goes so far as to claim that no objectivity exists: actual truth is impossible to find. While most history has an agenda of supporting the dominant culture, relativists would promote better knowledge of oppressed and ignored people. Unfortunately for us all, few people really learn from history; most people use history only to confirm what they already believe.

This lack of perspective has always shaped or reflected the values of whole cultures. Different societies have seen their past according to shared grand concepts, sometimes called paradigms. In our Western civilization, the ancient Greeks, Romans, and Germans believed in both the intervention of divine beings and a powerful role of unchangeable fate. The rise and fall of people, or nations, followed according to the will of the gods. The Jews saw themselves as being chosen by one all-powerful God who reserved for them a special place in history. The Christians of the Middle Ages supposed that they were caught in a battle of good versus evil. They condemned to hell their enemies, even if those enemies were fellow Christians. Intellectuals during the Enlightenment reasoned that history obeyed unalterable laws of nature. In reaction, social Darwinists and nationalists embraced the jungle's competition of claw and fang and cheered on peoples warring against one another for supremacy. All of these versions of history's purpose made perfect sense to people at the time. Their histories usually glorified their own achievements and diminished their flaws. Nor are we in our time exempt from the limitations of our own points of view, which may one day seem quaint or even wrongheaded.

As for our view of the past today, the historical method gives us much of what actually happened, as much as it can be known. The trustworthiness of history

---

6. US president Bill Clinton (r. 1993–2001) famously responded to a question about knowledge of his extramarital affair: "It depends on what the meaning of 'is' is."

depends on whether it presents **fact**, **opinion**, or **myth**. Facts are those pieces of historical information that all reasonable people agree upon. They are the data of history, drawn from a serious examination of the sources. Once proved by historians, hard facts are the most reliable and least arguable information available. They come closest to anything we can call truth.

In recent years the entire concept of truth has come even more into question. Historians used to find it self-evident that our empirical observation of the world through our senses, the scientific and historical methods, and reasoned debate of various viewpoints would arrive at indisputable truth. The challenge of historical relativism was followed by the "linguistic turn" in philosophy and literature. Their ideas insisted that a source may be read one way superficially and officially, but when deconstructed it reveals hidden signs, meanings, and systems of discourses that explain both power and resistance to it.

These postmodern approaches seemed to question whether anything could be known for certain about history. Even more, modern neuroscience seems to indicate that an individual human brain cannot tell the difference between real or false memories. As these ideas filtered into the popular culture, those with political agendas have created their own historical discourse. Revisionism used to mean a good critical reexamination of sources and historical arguments in order to improve our understanding. Now it can mean attacking accepted historical events, such as those who deny the Holocaust or the moon landing or claim that Elvis is alive or that earth has been visited by space aliens.[7] Conspiracy theories are spread and fed by social media through the Internet. Most recently, even partisan government spokespeople deny obvious lies and errors with claims of "fake news" and "alternative facts."

Yet even those facts that are agreed upon as true mean little by themselves. Only when they have been selected and interpreted do they explain historical causation and significance. Facts become what people make them into. People may blow them out of proportion or neglect them into nonexistence. To use a metaphor, facts are the bricks of historical work. Hard and rough, they can be used to frame a hearth or build a wall, but they can also be tossed aside or thrown through a window. Because of gaps in historical preservation, many details will be missing. A historian who bothers to contemplate an ancient ruin has incomplete information, since bricks have been lost, destroyed, or perhaps never even made in the first place. In contrast, a historian reviewing recent history may have too much information, piles upon piles of construction materials. Either way, we cannot really see behind the façade of the source (see figure 1.1). We try to read the minds of people in the past, attempt to see through their eyes, but perfect clarity is impossible.

Historians construct opinions choosing from whatever sources are available. These opinions are their arguments and explanations about history. Almost all history writing today consists of opinions, which historians form as they challenge one

---

7. To be clear: there exists substantial and conclusive evidence that (1) Nazis during World War II carried out the systematic murdering of millions of Jews and others, and (2) American astronauts personally explored the lunar surface between 1969 and 1972. There exists no evidence that (1) Elvis Presley did not die partly from an overdose in 1977, and (2) almost no good evidence that extraterrestrials have buzzed the skies in flying saucers, landed on earth in their chariots of the gods, or are kept in Area 51.

Figure 1.1.   What appears to be a random pile of stones in the
foreground is clearly organized in the background as a cairn or burial place.
Four thousand years ago at Clava, now in Scotland, people stacked the
foundations of these tombs and set up the standing stones in the
background for a few of their dead. The doorway is oriented to face the
rising sun on the first day of winter. What beliefs they associated with
death, we do not know.

another about interpretations of the past. Opinions reveal the significance of the
details and show how they mattered to people in the past or to us now. Arguments
among historians with differing opinions help to keep them honest. To extend the
metaphor, a historian may say that one set of bricks belongs to a palace, yet another
historian, looking at the same bricks, might say they come from a fortress. Who is
correct?

Without conclusive evidence (blueprints, foundations, illustrations, eyewitness
accounts), disputes may remain tangled. Usually the weight of public opinion leans
one way or another. People will choose facts and opinions written by respectable
historians or adopt positions that flatter their belief systems. Sometimes, new
insights might lead to an alternative suggestion, such as a compromise—a palace-
fortress. Good historians are ready to change their opinions, given solid evidence
and cogent argument. This author might conceivably rewrite and improve every
sentence of this book to respond to new information in the future. Every new
source provides new nuance. This changeableness is not inconsistency, dodging, or
flip-flopping, but rather a result of sound judgment.

To provide some coherence to what would otherwise be only a string of facts,
historians build themes around what they think changes the course of history.
These paradigms, theories, or grand narratives help history give meaning, making

sense of the past. Story arcs explain causation and significance in terms of the rise or decline of societies, crises or stability, the primacy of foreign or domestic policy, sex or power, or any number of drives and choices. Yet they can also obscure, simplify, and mislead.

Different historians offer competing narratives about specific points in the past and the grand sweep of time. This book's themes of supremacies and diversities help to explain our complex past. Supremacies focus on how the use of power dominates societies. Those who want *supremacy* usually seek stability, order, and consolidation. They also often seek to expand their power over others by using anything from warfare to ideologies. People react to such power by accommodating and transforming themselves in compliance or by resisting in public or covert ways. Power may flow from the top down, from rulers to subjects, or from the bottom up, from the masses to the leaders. *Diversity*, on the other hand, reflects the creative impulse that produces new ideas, as well as people's efforts to define themselves as different. Those who promote diversity create change, opportunity, and individuality.

These two trends do not necessarily oppose each other. They are not a version of dialectical materialism (see chapter 11). The opposite of supremacy is inferiority; the contrary of diversity is conformity. Nonetheless, both trends involve people excluding others who do not belong to the group. People who want supreme power usually demand *universalism*, applying the same beliefs and practices to everyone. They would promote **acculturation**, where one ethnic group conforms its culture to another. Likewise, people's frequent tendency toward diversity often encourages *particularism*, requiring that various ideas and activities differ according to location. In addition, the mixture of cultures may result in *syncretism*, where elements of one join or blend with another. A tension thus may arise between the supremacy desire for conformity and the diversity push for variety, or the two may align together. One or the other, or both, intermingle in different societies and ages. Whether applied to politics, culture, or society, supremacies and diversities offer a structure in which to illustrate historical conflict and change. They are not the only way to understand history, just this book's attempt to help make sense of facts and opinions about the past.

Explanations based on these facts and opinions can sometimes mutate into myths, which then complicate a historian's task. Myths are stories that give meaning to a society's existence. Because myths obscure the facts they draw on, they complicate understanding the past. People embrace myths as true because they make sense of a confusing world. Passed on from generation to generation, myths stubbornly exist beyond rational proof (see figure 1.2). These stories justify both the worst and the best behavior of individuals, societies, and states. The myths inherent in religion and the so-called lessons of history are problematic because they shape the meaning of life. Even religion, however, may not always offer clarity. For an example with real specifics (see chapter 6 for more context), in the Gospel of John, chapter 18, verse 37, translated from the Greek, the Roman procurator Pontius Pilate asks Jesus, "What is truth?" and does not get an answer.

Figure 1.2.   This round stone disk is now called the Bocca della Verità (Mouth of Truth). Historians suggest that it was a sculpture representing Oceanus, ancient god of the seas, made during the Roman Empire, and served as a drain cover. In the Middle Ages someone brought it to a church in Rome, where it now serves as a tourist attraction (cinematically seen in the movie *Roman Holiday*). If one lies while putting one's hand in the mouth, the hand gets bitten off. How can that be true?

In striving for objectivity, many modern historians try not to favor one religion or belief system as being more true than any other. Indeed, the rational and empirical historical method cannot assert any religion's validity or falsity. Religion draws on the ***supernatural***, which is beyond the limits of nature, to which historians are confined. Perhaps a religion might be true. But no one religion has ever objectively been proven real in all its supernatural aspects; otherwise most people would be convinced. Faith is there for those willing to believe, or not. The historian instead examines what the followers of any religion believed and, based on those beliefs, how they affected history.

People also want to believe good things about their own society. Thus, myths are often disguised as lessons learned from history. One should be cautious about them, since such myths are often too full of comforting pride. In particular, historical figures are often mythologized into heroes. Our own society promotes potent myths about figures such as Christopher Columbus, or George Washington, or Robert E. Lee that resist change in the face of reality. Most of Columbus's contemporaries knew the world was a globe; good evidence is lacking that Washington chopped down a cherry tree and confessed it to his father. These men might be notable, but their significance should not be based on stories that mislead. Even more tricky, from opposing points of view the heroes are switched to villains. For some Native Americans, Columbus began genocide. Washington is considered a traitor by some of the British, and some Americans believe Lee committed treason. Accurate portrayals of such figures require subtlety. Cracking open myths and examining their core is essential to learning from history.

The best history makes us self-critical, not self-congratulatory. Too often, someone's victory and satisfaction is someone else's defeat and suffering. Everyone joins in to take collective credit for victories, but resulting atrocities are blamed on isolated others. The American philosopher George Santayana wrote in 1905, "Those who cannot remember the past are condemned to repeat it." Since then, many have tried to learn from history but have nonetheless committed the same mistakes as their predecessors. While those who make history could not foresee the consequences of their actions, they should at least have been aware of contemporaries whose belief systems contradicted theirs. Learning history is dangerous, especially when opinions sprout into myths.

This text will regularly offer "basic principles," clear statements of obvious common historical behavior. They are not so much "lessons" of history as contradictions of common myths and suppositions (although there are always exceptions). They should challenge you to test them against historical experience. The first basic principle is:

> **There is no such thing as the "good ol' days," except in a limited way for a few people.**

People like to believe that there was once a golden age to which we should aspire to return. Whether in first-century Rome or eighteenth- and nineteenth-century Virginia, social elites have always proclaimed myths of their own supremacy to justify their status and power. Both Rome and Virginia, of course, benefited from enslaved people who did not enjoy the same luxuries as their masters. Plenty of privileged people have always led lives of comfort and calm. If they lost those privileges, then they could legitimately claim that a way of life once was better. A limited number of people in some places did benefit from the so-called good ol' days. Yet this good life of the few has often been based on the exploitation of a much larger number of other people.

From a broader perspective, looking at the entire sweep of human history, most people have always faced difficulties. We all face our own mortality. There has probably never been a day when one individual did not kill another somewhere or when one people did not fight against another people. Disease, hunger, natural disasters—these caused and still cause much misery. If people successfully confronted one moral dilemma, they failed in another. Each age has had its trials and tribulations, as well as its ecstasies and excitements.

The challenge for this book is making sense of the Western past for someone unfamiliar with its history, through the words of one particular author and the few translated voices of people from the past. As should be clear from the above discussion, no single view can be true for everyone, everywhere, forever. This historical account will regularly note the disputes, gaps, and disagreements of modern historians about specific interpretations. Like a reviewer of a book or film, this text both describes what happens and offers some value judgments. It often criticizes the flaws, failures, and contradictions inherent in the West. As the story unfolds, it points out the diverse options created during centuries of new ideas and practices by the many peoples that make up the West. Generalizations too often obscure detail and disagreement. Further reading and learning in history should reveal where this version is more or less objective, and what it has omitted or over-interpreted. In a comparatively few pages, though, it offers a starting point to understand the essential people, events, and ideas of the West.

Historians offer the hope that we can learn from history to improve ourselves. They write some things with certainty, much with confidence, and some with caution. The ultimate challenge for each of us is to form an opinion about history. Ask yourself: What can I learn that can give life more meaning? How can I make better decisions today based on the successes and failures of our ancestors? What knowledge of our heritage should I pass on to our descendants? This book offers some perspectives to help you answer those questions.

Review: *How can we evaluate history?*

Response:

PRIMARY SOURCE PROJECT 1: THUCYDIDES VERSUS VON RANKE ABOUT THE AIM OF HISTORY

Modern historians often credit the ancient Greek writer Thucydides with the first work of critical historical writing. His work called The Peloponnesian War *describes a conflict fought during his lifetime. Thucydides thought it the most significant of all wars up until then. In this passage, he describes his approach to writing the book. More than two thousand years later, the young Leopold von Ranke produced his work on other wars, fought four hundred years before his own lifetime. He began his study of people in the Renaissance of Latin and Germanic origin with a preface that called for a new, more methodological and neutral kind of historical writing.*

Source 1: *The Peloponnesian War* by Thucydides (ca. 400 BC)

Having now given the result of my inquiries into early times, I grant that there will be a difficulty in believing every particular detail. The way that most men deal with traditions, even traditions of their own country, is to receive them all alike as they are delivered, without applying any critical test whatever. . . .

So little pains do the vulgar take in the investigation of truth, accepting readily the first story that comes to hand. On the whole, however, the conclusions I have drawn from the proofs quoted may, I believe, safely be relied on. Assuredly they will not be disturbed either by the lays of a poet displaying the exaggeration of his craft, or by the compositions of the chroniclers that are attractive at truth's expense; the subjects they treat of being out of the reach of evidence, and time having robbed most of them of historical value by enthroning them in the region of legend. Turning from these, we can rest satisfied with having proceeded upon the clearest data, and having arrived at conclusions as exact as can be expected in matters of such antiquity. . . .

With reference to the speeches in this history, some were delivered before the war began, others while it was going on; some I heard myself, others I got from various quarters; it was in all cases difficult to carry them word for word in one's memory, so my habit has been to make the speakers say what was in my opinion demanded of them by the various occasions, of course adhering as closely as possible to the general sense of what they really said. And with reference to the narrative of events, far from permitting myself to derive it from the first source that came to hand, I did not even trust my own impressions, but it rests partly on what I saw myself, partly on what others saw for me, the accuracy of the report being always tried by the most severe and detailed tests possible. My conclusions have cost me some labor from the want of coincidence between accounts of the same occurrences by different eye-witnesses, arising sometimes from imperfect memory, sometimes from undue partiality for one side or the other. The absence of romance in my history will, I fear, detract somewhat from its interest; but if it be judged useful by those inquirers who desire an exact knowledge of the past as an aid to the interpretation of the future, which in the course of human things must resemble if it does not reflect it, I shall be content. In fine, I have written my work, not as an essay which is to win the applause of the moment, but as a possession for all time.

Source 2: *History of Roman and German Peoples from 1494 to 1535 by von Ranke (1824)*

Some have claimed for history the aim to judge the past, to instruct us today for the benefit of future years. The present attempt does not dare to reach such high aims: it will merely state, how it actually was [*wie es eigentlich gewesen*].

Yet how could this be newly researched? The foundation of this present text, the origin of its material are memoirs, diaries, letters, diplomatic reports and original testimonies of eyewitnesses; other writings only either when they are directly derived from those sources, or through some original knowledge appear to be equivalent to them. Every page cites the relevant works; the manner of research and the critical results will be presented in a second volume, that will be published with the present one on the same day. . . .

Intention and material give rise to the form. One cannot expect from a history the free expression, which at least, in theory, one seeks in a poetical work. And I do not know whether with fairness one could believe such is found in the works of Greek or Roman masters. Strict description of the facts, as limited and uncomfortable as they may be, is without doubt the highest law. A second, for myself, was the development of unity and the sequence of events. Instead of, as might be expected, beginning with a general description of the political relationships in Europe (which might not have confused the perspective, but certainly would have distracted the focus), I have prioritized, from every people, every power, every particular, as they were, only then to describe them thoroughly, when they enter upon the stage as significantly active or leading. It does not worry me—for how could their existence have forever remained untouched?—that already ahead of time, here and there, they must be mentioned. In this manner at least the course, which they in general held, the path that they followed, the thoughts that moved them, could all the better be delineated.

Finally, what can one say about such treatment in detail, a so essential part of historical works? Will it not appear often hard, fragmented, bland, and tiresome? There exists for this problem noble models, both old—and not to be forgotten—also new; yet I have not attempted to imitate them: their world was another one. There exists an exalted ideal to strive toward: that is the event itself in its human dimension, its unity, its fullness. I know how far I have remained from that. What else is to say? One makes the effort, one strives, in the end one has not reached the goal. If only nobody would be impatient with that! The main thing is always, we are dealing with . . . humanity as it is, explainable or inexplicable: the life of the individual, the kinfolk, the people, at times with the hand of God over them.

Questions:

- *What kind of sources does each historian draw on and what is the difficulty with them?*
- *Against what kind of history does each historian write and toward what goal(s) does each historian aspire for his own work?*
- *How do these authors' comments illustrate the value of studying history?*

Responses:

Make your own timeline! Here is an example of information you could add to the blank timelines at the end of each chapter. Just write down terms, names, dates, whatever you think important, in chronological order. Do not worry about spacing or neatness—just get it down.

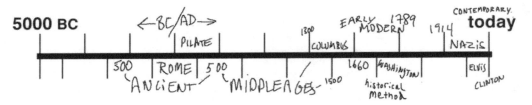

Citations

Thucydides. *History of the Peloponnesian War*. Translated by Richard Crawley. New York: E. P. Dutton, 1910, pp. 13–15.

von Ranke, Leopold. *Geschichten der romanischen und germanischen Völker von 1494 bis 1535*. Vol. 1. Leipzig and Berlin: G. Reimer, 1824, pp. v–viii. (Translated by Brian A. Pavlac.)

For more on these sources, go to http://www.concisewesternciv.com/sources/psc1a .html.

CHAPTER 2

Wanderers and Settlers

The Ancient Middle East to 400 BC

Every human society tells stories that explain the dawn of the universe, the world, and human beings. In our society, the beginnings of human history have become controversial. Some people today agree with ancient peoples who calculated that the age of the world was only a few thousand years. Most people agree with the scientific and historical methods explained in the first chapter that the origins of both the earth and humanity stretch much further back into time. The scientific-historical viewpoint of this textbook accepts scientific evidence that the first human beings wandered out of our ancestral home in Africa tens of thousands of years ago. Several thousand years ago, some humans settled on the civilized way of life. Still later, the ancient civilizations in Egypt and Mesopotamia produced knowledge to teach the early Europeans.

THE APES' COUSINS

What we know about our oldest ancestors comes from the archeological record of their physical remains, in their bones and creations, as well as comparisons to primates and hunter-gatherer groups that have survived until today (whose contact with or avoidance of civilization may have altered their behavior). Thus our knowledge is fragmentary and tentative, subject to revision with new discoveries and studies. The first humanlike creatures, called **hominins**, appeared on the earth millions of years ago. One of our earliest direct ancestors, *Australopithecus* (southern ape), lived about four million years before us. These hominins shared much of their genetic structure and basic anatomy with their closest great ape relatives, hominids, whose descendants would eventually evolve into modern primates of orangutans, bonobos, chimpanzees, and gorillas. Various differences gave hominins and their descendants advantages in the life-and-death struggles in a dangerous world of predators.

First, physical differences made up for their inferiority of sight and smell, strength, and speed. The erect stance on two legs first distinguished hominins from most other creatures. About two million years ago, the hominins came down from

19

the trees of the jungle and began to walk on two legs across the African savanna. Because they could see and travel farther than other apes, they gained access to wider varieties of food. An opposable thumb allowed hominins to make a fist and grasp **tools**.

Second, this ability to manipulate material objects into complex tools gave hominins another advantage. Although an ape might be able to make a primitive tool from a rock or a stick, hominin hands began to craft much more efficient and useful devices. **Weapons** made up for their lack of claw, fang, and muscle. Knives, needles, hooks, and hatchets fashioned from stone and bone were the sources left behind by the first humans. Using these, our ancestors fashioned protective **clothing** and carrying bags that made them still more mobile. They learned to control fire to provide warmth and to make more varieties of food edible by cooking. Tools became one of the great driving forces of human history.

Third, a larger and more complex brain enabled more advanced thought and speech. Gorillas and chimpanzees can be taught some simple ways to form basic words and phrases. As far as science can detect, though, they lack anything approaching our sophistication of narrative language. The language of human words and sentences allowed more extensive communication than did the squeaks, yelps, and buzzes of other animals. This allowed people to form ideas about how to survive through words, games, and role-playing. Humans with their more flexible and adaptive brains rely less on instinct and more on learning.

Perhaps the most important idea conveyed by speech and human experience is that we die. On their own, children, teenagers, and even often adults have a sense of invulnerability and immortality. Yet stories and experience teach that death is certain. Our consciousness of our own mortality leads to another basic principle:

> **Humans know they are going to die; therefore, most people form supernatural beliefs about what their purpose is in this life and what happens after death.**

Religion, the structure we give to a set of supernatural beliefs, may have been the first human invention. Religion answers that most basic of human questions: "What is the meaning of life?" This very question recognizes that for each of us, life ends in death, at least in the natural world. Yet nearly all religions suppose that a "super"-natural world also exists beyond or above our senses. Most humans rely on beliefs about a supernatural realm to help them cope with everyday troubles in the struggle for survival. Our first ancestors probably practiced some form of simple *animism*: the belief that nature is alive with spirits and ghosts that affect our natural world.

Religion's development depended on another difference between the apes and us, namely our ability for complex verbal and pictorial communication. In human culture, the ideas of religion were conveyed in stories and images. Religious information through symbols was probably the first form of art, in **paintings** and small

sculptures. Cave paintings and artifacts portrayed what people were interested in, primarily beasts being hunted, sexualized figures of men and women, and strange beings mixing the animal and the human, apparently supernatural, since no good evidence of them exists.

Historians call this long period of human evolution, from over two million to ten thousand years ago, the **Paleolithic Age** (from the Greek for "Old Stone Age"), named after the stone tools used then. Instead of being lion food, they ate what lions ate, even if they had to steal carrion from lions rather than kill their food themselves. Then the hominins mastered fire for cooking previously inedible foods and for providing warmth in the coldest places. So our ancestors moved out of the tropical climates in Africa, where they had evolved, to spread over much of Eurasia.

Fourth, hominins moved in social **communities**, since there was strength in numbers. Even the behavior of our ape cousins shows the usefulness of groups for individual survival. Like baboons and gorillas, early peoples formed packs, often called bands or tribes, ranging from probably twenty to a hundred individuals. Observations of bonobos and chimpanzees interestingly reveal two different attitudes toward social structure. Chimpanzees usually live in relative peace with one another under a dominant male who keeps order, but sometimes they break out in murderous violent slaughter. In contrast, bonobos remain peaceful under the guidance of females, with social tensions soothed by all kinds of sexual activity. As for humans, tribes developed more complex social hierarchies involving bonds among men and women, young and old, each mutually dependent and involved with the other. Meanwhile, isolated humans found it much more difficult to survive. And without family and friends, their death, of course, ended their history. Social bonds among people were essential for culture to grow and for history to be remembered.

Within a human tribe, the **family** became the simplest social unit. The smallest grouping called a family was a parent and child (whether born of sexual reproduction or adopted). Larger collections included parents united through marriage, grandparents, aunts and uncles, cousins, friends, helpers, hangers-on, or anyone defined by its members as belonging. One family could not exist by itself for long, given questions of safety and prohibitions against inbreeding. Maybe a half dozen to a dozen families made up the typical human community for many of the millennia during which our ancestors evolved. These tribes then interacted with others for the purposes of exchanging goods, people, and worship. Many different tribes may have come together in large gatherings of thousands during seasons of plenty, living briefly in complex social hierarchies that organized some accumulation of wealth (as attested to by rich burials) and the building of primitive monuments. Then they would go their separate ways, with nomads only able to own what they could carry.

Within these families and communities the interrelationship of men and women and their children varies widely within our historical heritage. Since women bear the children, they have throughout history devoted much of their time and energy to raising the young. Men found it easier to get away from their children, whether on the hunt or (later) in the public square. Yet some men could not hunt to save their lives, and some women can be terrible or murderous mothers. A basic principle expresses a more realistic perspective on family relationships:

> **Only chromosomal women can bear children; everything else about people's social roles is up for argument.**

There are very few ways in which everyone agrees that people are either essentially the same or different from one another. Otherwise societies construct opinions about morality, customs, and expectations, which they then use to force people into categories or compartments. Certainly biological differences between men and women exist, but how significant are they, especially when technology can be an equalizer? Some people argue that because men on average are bigger, stronger, and more aggressive than women, they should naturally have the superior social role. Yet we know that the biggest man can be the gentlest father, while the smallest mother with a weapon can kill the largest man.

Recorded history is dominated by men. One reason is that historical and scientific studies show that men are statistically more aggressive than women, especially because of the hormone testosterone. This quality has both a positive and a negative side for human society. Too much violence and the community is destroyed from within; too little ferocity and it can be destroyed by outsiders. Hence, male aggressiveness is useful when warriors are trained to kill for their community but harmful when men murder their family, friends, or neighbors. Much of our history has been a harsh tale of channeling aggression.

The other side of history is peaceful management of the inevitable squabbles within and quarrels among these communities. Our ancestors' first political arrangements organized where to camp, when to move, how to punish, and even how to protect the young and to raise them with all the knowledge necessary for survival. Hominins developed increasingly complicated rules of behavior of command and obedience, without which communities would fall apart in anger and jealousy. The first political organization meant the choosing of leaders who could interact well with the rest of the group and resolve conflicts. Sought-after qualities were usually wisdom, charisma, and the ability to persuade or intimidate. While women rarely gained leadership, as wives and lovers they could influence their spouses and mates.

Hominins also formed a primitive economic system of **hunting and gathering** that wrung the necessities of life from nature. Hunter-gatherers followed the game and the ripening plants as nomads. Everyone in the community participated in foraging for food and raw materials and in consuming them. Tribes traded and exchanged with other tribes for food, tools, and breeding partners. In these early tribal communities, everyone knew one another.

Superficial differences in appearance and behavior soon emerged in the tribes who multiplied and spread to different parts of the globe. Scholars describe these variations as *ethnicity*. Humans used the idea of ethnicity to create, unify, or separate themselves into communities we often categorize as "peoples." Over time, groups of people who intermarried had inherited certain physical attributes (skin color, eye shape, hair, height, etc.) which set them visually apart from others. While scientific studies have shown no significant genetic impact caused by these attributes, peoples have often found such noticeable distinctions essential in deciding who does or does not belong. More important in determining ethnicity has been learned culture (language, tradition, fashion, cuisine, manners, religion, etc.). People applied imagined ideas behind behavior to divide people into ethnic groups which then influenced political and economic decisions. When this text refers to a "people," such as Greeks, Vikings, or English, it recognizes a society of those who formed a certain cultural (and perhaps political) unity from their own point of view at some time in the past or from the vantage point of the present.

In the course of history, various ethnic communities formed, reformed, or fell apart and vanished as they came into contact with others. Sometimes differing societies settling near one another provoked hostility and conflict; other times it fostered friendship and cooperation. Many ethnic groups define others as inferior or superior to themselves, focusing on socially constructed differences rather than common humanity. Others do not care. Whatever any nominal ethnic divisions, however, all human beings belong to the same biological species categorized by scientists as *Homo sapiens sapiens* (thinking, thinking human), first born in the original human homeland of Africa about two hundred thousand years ago.

In sum, the anatomy of human ancestors, their tools and weapons, their creative minds, and their social, political, and economic cooperation gave them advantages over most other animals. They allowed humans to survive four great ice ages that lasted for tens of thousands of years. The global climate change was catastrophic for many species of plant and animal life. Vast ice sheets covered much of the landmasses. Growing seasons shortened. Those living things that could not cope became extinct. Scientists have not yet established what began or ended those ice ages in the past, and we ourselves might just be living in a brief geologic pause between one ice age and another.

In the midst of those ice ages, humans flourished. Beginning between two hundred thousand and sixty thousand years ago, the first humans, like their hominin ancestors before them, migrated out of Africa and adapted to every climate on the entire planet, from the sweltering jungle to the frigid Arctic. Aside from descendents of the original humans in Africa who remained on that continent, everyone else is an immigrant. Humans reached Asia about one hundred thousand years ago, getting all the way to Australia about forty thousand years ago. After living some time on the Bering Strait land bridge, now underwater because of rising sea levels, humans moved into the Americas about fourteen thousand years ago, and the Pacific shortly afterward (see map 2.1).

Humans immigrated to Europe about forty-five thousand years ago. Along the way, in the Middle East and Africa, our human ancestors encountered the hominin Neanderthals (and in Asia the recently discovered Denisovans). By about 39,000 BC, Neanderthals and Denisovans had become extinct.[1] Did our human relatives

---

1. As new evidence is unearthed, scientists keep rearranging dates and ideas about our ancient ancestors. Neanderthals were named after the German valley where modern archaeolo-

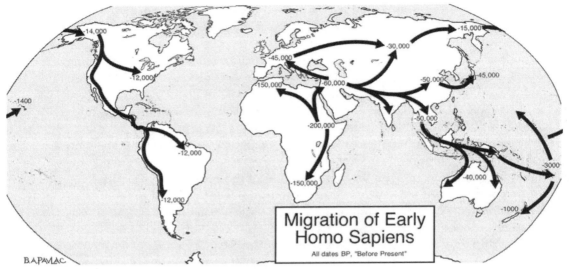

Map 2.1.   Migrations of Early Homo Sapiens.
All routes and dates on this map are based on current educated estimates
and may change with new evidence. Temperatures were colder and sea
levels were lower during many of these dates, increasing the size of most
landmasses and coverage by ice and glaciers. How would that and other
geographic factors have affected migration?

go extinct because we could survive climate change and better seize natural resources? Or did *Homo sapiens sapiens* exterminate these original inhabitants?
About ten thousand years ago, the climate warmed again, the summers lengthened,
and the glaciers retreated. Humans survived in a precarious place within the world's
ecosystem, poised for greater things.

Review: *What important cultural survival techniques did our hunter-gatherer ancestors
use in the Old Stone Age?*

Response:

gists found the first skull attributed to the species; Denisovans were named after a cave in Siberia
where archaeologists found a finger bone. Scientific studies show that Neanderthal and Deniso-
van DNA survives in some modern people.

BOUND TO THE SOIL

The end of the last ice age allowed what could be considered the most fundamental and radical change in human history, the so-called **Neolithic Agricultural Revolution**. For historians, the term *revolution* represents a major transformation of human politics, society, and culture. People lived different lives after revolutions from those they lived before. This first important human revolution occurred during the Neolithic Age (from the Greek for "New Stone Age"), named after the new kinds of tools used, different from those of earlier hunter-gatherers. Archaeological evidence has shown how ten thousand years ago hoes and sickles, the tools for planting and harvesting, began to be made, in addition to the arrowheads and spear points suitable for hunting. Humankind discovered farming, forever changing our way of life. While hunter-gatherers adapted themselves to nature, civilized people began adapting nature to themselves.

The culture of farming, or **agriculture**, the growing of plants and raising of animals, seems so natural to us today that we hardly think of it as a human invention. One can imagine how some person, after gathering grains or fruits, noticed that the seeds dropped on the ground produced those same plants weeks later. The logical next step was to push the seeds into the ground and wait for them to grow instead of wandering around, looking for the plants. If people stored enough to live on during the growing periods, they could simply stay put year round instead of wearing out their feet walking. So rather than living in moveable tents or temporary huts, people built sturdy **houses** from logs, mud, or baked clay bricks. Homes offered better shelter against the elements.

Domestication of animals, or husbandry, was equally important as finding the right plants to grow. Dogs had first begun bonding with humans (or vice versa) during the ice ages. While a few societies have dined on dog, most have viewed them as companions and useful helpers in the hunt. Once people settled down to farm, they surely reasoned that if dogs could be tamed, why not try it with the beasts that they hunted? Sometimes they succeeded in breeding the wildness out. Aurochs became cattle, boars became pigs, and jungle fowl became chickens. With taming of both plants and animals, human communities settled down and became tied to plots of land to raise their food. This revolution might be better called an evolution. The switch to farming moved very slowly, over the course of thousands of years. And some people refused to join in, remaining hunter-gatherers or animal herders (pastoralists), and sometimes failed farmers reverted to foraging and herding.

For those who joined in farming, one cannot exaggerate the vast change for human ways of living. Before agriculture, everyone had been at the mercy of the environment, depending on nature to provide sustenance. Nature was still important, of course, and its awesome force remained dangerous. An extended drought or a brief flood could kill many people. Nevertheless, farming meant that humans began to dominate nature. Soon the people who managed food production even learned to outproduce nature. They selected and bred stronger, hardier crops and animals. They weeded out invasive plants that would steal water and nutrients.

They irrigated, digging trenches that led water from distant streams to feed the roots of their seedlings. They chased away the wild creatures that would devour the stalks. They diversified their crops and animals to provide more resources. From all this hard work and innovation, people produced more food, allowing families to grow as fast as hungry infant mouths could be filled. Since women did not have to worry about long treks as nomads, they could more easily endure pregnancies while looking after their other young children at the same time. Farmers soon grew enough extra foodstuffs so that a few people no longer had to work in agricultural production.

Farming thus led to a whole range of new occupations beyond tilling the soil. **Division of labor** made urban life more efficient. While all hunter-gatherers hunted and gathered, civilized people might focus on work for which they were most suited or that they found most enjoyable. Some people could devote their energy to making garments. Weavers wove the fibers of flax and hemp on a loom to produce cloth. Tailors cut cloth into unusual styles and colored it with dyes in patterns never seen on plant or animal. Some fashions promoted comfort and protection from weather; others emphasized social roles at the expense of comfortable fit. Cooks mixed, roasted, baked, and boiled increasing varieties of plant and animal stuffs into cuisine. Potters baked clay pots that better preserved food, free from spoilage and vermin. Cartwrights built wagons to transport large loads over long distances. Masons stacked bricks and stone into secure buildings, beginning the art of **architecture**.

Especially where land could be put to use for growing crops or raising animals, economic success led to growing communities where larger numbers of families could reside within a limited geographic space. Small **villages** might contain a few families or numbers up to two hundred people. Villages might grow into **towns**, which might hold a few thousand people. Then great **cities** bloomed, ranging from many thousands to today's huge urban areas of millions of people. This complex life of interconnected cities is called **civilization**. Urban living provided a rich, creative, evolving dynamic that expanded and intensified human domination of the planet. The word *civilization* in this sense describes how people can be united by common culture, social and economic interaction, and political organization.

The first civilized political organization, the **city-state**, was literally the smallest viable unit of civilization. It included the city itself (made up of homes, businesses, and public buildings) and the surrounding countryside of farmland from which the people of the city fed and supplied themselves. These larger numbers of people confined in a small area often created new kinds of leaders to organize the increasingly complex human activities.

The first important leaders perhaps made use of religion as a key source of convincing others to obey. Agriculture encouraged new, more complex religions. Most were a form of ***polytheism***, the belief in many gods and goddesses, divine beings connected to the new practices of farming (see table 2.1). Storm gods and earth goddesses tended to have more distinct personalities and defined attributes than the vague spirits of animism. **Priests** (and, less often, priestesses) conducted elaborate rituals and prayers intended to appease the gods. People often shared in communal meals to celebrate the goodness of what the gods had provided in

Table 2.1.   Comparisons of Gods and Goddesses of Ancient Polytheisms

Attribute	Mesopotamian	Egyptian	Greek	Roman	Norse
Ruler of gods	Enlil, Marduk, Asshur	Ra	Zeus	Jupiter	Odin
Sky/storm	Anu	Nut, Horus	Zeus	Jupiter	Thor
Earth	Ninhursag	Geb	Gaia	Terra/Tellus	Erda
Water/sea	Apsu, Enki	Tefnut	Poseidon	Neptune	Aegir
Sun	Shamash	Ra	Apollo	Apollo	Sunna
Moon	Sin	Thoth	Artemis	Diana	Moon
Wisdom	Ea, Nabu	Thoth	Athena	Minerva	Odin
War	Ninurta/Ishtar	Nit, Menhit	Ares	Mars	Tyr
Magic	Enki	Isis	Hermes	Mercury	Odin
Crop fertility	Dumuzi	Ernutet	Demeter	Ceres	Freyr
Alcoholic drink	Ninkasi, Geshtinanna	Osiris	Dionysius	Bacchus	Byggvir
Technology			Hephaestus	Vulcan	
Trickster		Set	Hermes	Mercury	Loki
Love	Ishtar	Hathor	Aphrodite	Venus	Freya
Fire/hearth	Gibil	Bes	Hestia	Vesta	Frigga
Marriage	Innana	Hathor	Hera	Hymen, Juno	Frigga
Death	Ereshkigal	Osiris	Hades	Pluto	Hel

Note: The deities of ancient religions performed similar functions for agricultural peoples in early civilizations.

nature. Ironically, priests and priestesses who managed the temples as centers of worship actually drew much of their alleged power not from their communication with supernatural beings but from their practical, more systematic knowledge of nature.

This brings up one of the most important basic principles:

Knowledge is power.

As these ancient religious leaders studied the natural world, looking for evidence of the gods, they found data about seasons, climate, and soil conditions. Priests observed the heavens and calculated the **calendar**; they measured, added, and divided to plan and build their temples and irrigation canals; they quantified trade and agricultural production; they told stories (usually in the form of epic poems about heroes) that defined for their culture the connections of humans to gods; they invented **writing** to keep track of it all. Thus, the fields of astronomy, mathematics, and literature became basic to the civilized way of life.

The priests passed on their knowledge in **schools**, one of the essential institutions of civilization. Instead of having education provided by parents and community leaders, as in hunter-gatherer societies, children of different families more efficiently learned from professional teachers. Usually, though, privileged elites allowed only boys from prosperous families access to a formal education, excluding girls and the poor from higher knowledge.

Priests had to share leadership of society with **kings**, who became the dominant political figures. **Monarchy**, the rule of kings, has been the most frequent form of government throughout civilized history. The first kings probably came to power either by election or usurpation. People chose a king or he claimed authority for himself, probably in the name of the gods, and people went along with it. The essential political questions then became (first) how many decisions affecting other people's lives could the king make and (second) who might influence or share in making those decisions. Some kings possessed only minimal power to command obedience, enjoying tightly limited roles as figureheads or mere symbols of authority. Members of the royal family, favorites, and court officials or the upper classes might actually run the kingdom behind the scenes. Kings typically strove to rule according to ***absolutism***, the practice that one person should dominate as much as possible in authority and decision making.[2] The acceptance of absolute monarchy allowed a ruler to exercise as much power as human limitations allowed. Attempts by rulers to establish absolute monarchies and resistance to such efforts have driven many political changes in history.

Whether weak or strong, kings held three essential roles. First, they represented the unity of the people. Each was symbolically the father of his country, the head of the most important family of families. The importance of family often eased the creation of a **dynasty**, where political power passed from parent to child. Dynasts often justified their monopoly on power by claiming connections to the gods. The gods were their relatives or specially chose them to be rulers. Even today, powerful political leaders endowed with charisma are often seen as superior to normal citizens. The preference for male, paternal authority often meant that power went from father to son. While this limited the ability of females to rule, women did sometimes come to hold formal power. Otherwise, their power worked like those of many women throughout history, influencing the family members of their dynasties behind the scenes. The people worshipped these "Oriental despots" almost as elaborately as the gods they represented. Despite such divine connections, however, accident, disease, and infertility might end dynasties. Lack of a proper successor sparked political violence, even civil war, about who should then rule.

A king's second role was to preserve peace among his own people. In this role, a king usually acted as supreme judge (which was also a divine attribute). People petitioned the ruler for righting of wrongs. To settle the increasing number of cases brought about by the rising populations of cities, kings began to establish **laws**. The most famous early law code was that which King Hammurabi of Babylon commanded to be carved onto a black stone pillar around 1700 BC. A picture above the **Law Code of Hammurabi** shows a god himself handing the laws to the king. Here the king was not going through the priests but interacted directly with the gods, becoming the lawgiver within the cosmic order. Such divine connections inspired legal systems for many early peoples. They believed that keeping the law pleased the gods.

---

2. Historians and political theorists most often apply the term *absolutism* to European monarchs of the seventeenth and eighteenth centuries AD. While queens and kings during those years clearly argued for unlimited authority, the concept does apply to all ages.

The laws, of course, laid out right and wrong in practical ways, dealing with social conflict. Culture is encoded in a society's laws, which reflect what matters and what does not. One of the most essential rights in societies throughout recorded history has been protecting **property**, whether land for farming or other possessions accumulated by civilized people. Hunter-gatherers could possess only as much property as they could carry. Civilized people could claim as much property as they could defend or get others to defend for them.

At the foundation of all private property is the government's protection of that right to such possessions. That is a social contract which began when our ancestors turned from hunter-gatherers into agriculturalists. Laws guaranteed that land could not be easily taken away from owners and ensured that after the owner's death it went to the correct heirs. Laws defined which property belonged to whom and prescribed punishments for those who damaged, destroyed, or tried to take it. Courts, police forces, and armies paid through taxes enforced those laws. Without the social contract, each one of us as individuals would be responsible for protecting and defending our private property always. Without the rule of law maintained by governments, any ruthless person's force would decide who has what.

Another universal legal issue for rulers has been regulating violence among people. While hunter-gatherers often punished crimes with isolation or exile, civilized regimes punished by confiscating wealth or inflicting physical pain. A fundamental question for all societies has been to categorize the killing of one human by another. Was it the defense of the nation by a soldier or of his family by a parent? Was it capital punishment inflicted by the state for justice? Was it a vicious crime by a murderer? Was it manslaughter by accident? Or did it matter at all? Many ancient laws, like Hammurabi's, punished a wide variety of crimes with death, crimes that today we might consider unworthy of such a high price. Laws also began to regulate drunkenness, after ancient farmers discovered how to manage the fermentation processes for turning grapes into wine and grains into beer. For example, a wine seller not reporting bad characters in his establishment to the authorities might be executed for that oversight. Many other punishments involved mutilation. In Hammurabi's Code, for example, a son who hit his father deserved having his hand cut off. Fines and banishment also were common, but not prison, because of the high cost of keeping a person confined.

The third role of a king was as a war leader against foreign foes. Brute force and the ability to kill is an obvious form of power. Yet no king could fight on his own, except in legend, such as the superhuman hero Gilgamesh of Sumerian literature (see below). A king needed warriors. One of the basic questions through history is, "Whom do the soldiers obey?" Whoever can convince others to kill for them has real power.

By his nature, the king's command over life and death in peace and war gave him supreme authority within a society. The earliest kings ruled over city-states, the smallest and most cohesive political units. Because city-states were vulnerable, owing to their small size and because wealth and power tempted kings, they soon desired to dominate other societies. If a king gained power over similar people in a number of cities, he would rule a **kingdom**. As kingdoms grew larger and more powerful, kings often were tempted to conquer their foreign neighbors. Thus arose the practice of *imperialism*, taking over other peoples in order to build an **empire**. A king who came to govern other peoples who may have differed in ethnicity, religion, language, history, or any number of other ways became an **emperor**. Empires became the largest political structures of all, although they were inherently unstable because of the diversity of the emperor's subjects. Many successful empire builders united their imperial subjects through acculturation. When voluntary cooperation failed, forced obedience often followed.

Whether organized in an empire, kingdom, or city-state, the new culture of civilization derived from farming became the way of life for the majority of human beings in Africa, Asia, and Europe by about 3000 BC. At first, civilized agriculturalists and their uncivilized neighbors lived side by side. Many peoples stopped just short of civilization and did not live in a society with cities, even until a few centuries ago. Some made their livings as nomadic pastoral herders of animals on the plains and steppes of the Americas, Asia, and Africa. A few groups of hunter-gatherers also continued to flourish.

The economic and political expansion of people living in civilizations, however, progressively destroyed nonagricultural societies. The civilized people often insulted the noncivilized by calling them *barbarian*. They set up a dichotomy of themselves as generous, refined citizens (what the word *civilized* also means to many people) and the others as selfish, uneducated savages. Of course, virtue does not live only in cities and wickedness among the nomads. Instead, civilizations embraced their power, created by highly structured social hierarchies supported by agriculture. Relentlessly, powerful, organized agricultural societies grabbed whatever good land could be found for farming, mining, or building. The dwindling pastoralists and hunter-gatherers retreated to isolated jungles or deserts where farming remained impossible or unprofitable. This trend continues even today, where modern encroaching civilizations require the last few "barbarians" either to convert to civilization or be killed off.

Review: What did agriculture cultivate as the key components of civilization?

Response:

THE PRICE OF CIVILIZATION

The new way of life of cities became habits based on ideas about how these new societies should be managed. Evidence shows that most civilizations invented or adopted from neighbors similar social, political, and economic roles of priests, schoolteachers, kings, private property, and laws. While the vast wealth of civilization produced numerous comforts, life in cities clearly had some serious drawbacks. We live with these problems as long as we lead civilized lives. Our lifestyle complicates our relation to the environment and to one another. Whether and how we recognize and address these problems is up to us.

First, serious health issues arose with life in cities. Famine could easily strike, since despite the best planning, a drought or flood could destroy all the food available in a particular region. The limited abilities of transportation often meant that little food could be imported. In contrast, hunter-gatherers faced with natural disaster could move on to other hunting grounds. Agricultural people, though, felt compelled to stay, for two main reasons. First, they believed that one day the land would be productive again, and so they stayed to prevent anyone else from taking it over. Second, most other nearby land suitable for farming was already taken. Good farmland is a precious and limited commodity. To find new land, farmers might have had to journey a long distance. Lacking the skills to hunt and gather along the way, many would have perished on the move. Farming peoples stuck out the hard times and, consequently, many died where they stood.

Surprisingly, another health problem was poor nutrition. The hunter-gatherer almost naturally ate a balanced diet out of what nature provides. In contrast, civilized people chose what they wanted to eat rather than what nature offered to them. They often wanted to go heavier on the meats, avoided certain roots and vegetables, and devoured sweets. Our "sweet tooth" derives from our body's requirements for carbohydrates and fats. For hunter-gatherers, concentrated sugars were limited and rare in the wild. Agricultural people, however, could produce and consume sugars in large qualities, unaware of how obesity risked health and sugar rotted teeth.

Contagious diseases also threatened civilized society. Hunter-gatherers lived in small groups that wandered regularly. Their contact with other groups of people was brief. In contrast, cities opened themselves up for illness, encouraging close and regular contact with travelers and traders from other communities. Widespread outbreaks of disease, called epidemics or **plagues**, regularly devastated urban populations. Some epidemics spread by water (dysentery, cholera, typhoid), some by human contact (measles, smallpox), some through fleas and lice (typhus, bubonic plague), and some through the air (influenza, pneumonia). We know now that the causes of all these (as explained in chapter 11) are microscopic bacteria and viruses, which live all around and on us. Harmful germs flourished as civilized people lived in increasingly large groups that dumped their waste all around them. Up until a few hundred years ago, few people knew this enough to care much about cleanliness. For instance, until recently, more soldiers died of infections than enemy attacks during wars. Ignorant of the real causes for disease, civilized people could often do little more than suffer through them.

Another negative consequence of civilization, for half the human species, was an increase in *sexism*. Sexism is the belief that one sex (usually the male) is better than the other (usually the female). From birth, we usually separate humans into these two groups, male and female, with that common first question, "Is it a boy or a girl?" Sometimes physical or genetic irregularities complicate the answer to that question.[3] Regardless of the biology of chromosomes and anatomy, all societies set expectations about gender behaviors. They use both custom and law to shape how individuals should perform gender attitudes of masculinity or femininity, as well as romantic feelings and physical desire. Studies by modern social scientists and historians suggest that differences of sexual attraction and gender identity are much more complicated than we usually like to think.

In hunter-gatherer families and tribes, sex roles seem to have been much more undifferentiated and fluid than in civilized societies. In a community on the move, where everyone bore his or her own share, men and women were more equal in status. Also, in such small communities, everyone knew one another. In civilization, however, sexism began to grant more advantages to males. The acquisition of property changed everything. Ownership of farmland led to yet another, and simple, basic principle:

> **Land is wealth; wealth is power.**

Of course, land is not the only means to wealth—later commerce, industry, and finance would provide much more efficient ways to become wealthy. Nor is wealth the only route to power—charisma, military force, ruthless violence, and other methods all can be useful in seizing dominion. When agriculture has dominated the economy, though, land has meant power.

Once civilized through owning land, men effectively excluded women from power by their near-exclusive control of property within the family. This control by men had nothing to do with our Western, traditional idea that the men are out sweating in the fields while the women are keeping house. Indeed, in many farming societies women work in the fields as much as or more than men, especially during planting and harvest. The first governments and their laws institutionalized family habits and structures with the full weight of law. Formal laws regulated property transferred through inheritances, or in gifts at the time of betrothal or marriage; laws turned those agreements into legal contracts; laws monitored sexual fidelity (usually allowing husbands more leeway than wives). How spouses treated one another, and how parents raised their children, even with the power of life and death, were matters of community, not just private, concern. Informal reputation based on known behavior impacted family members' social status, which in turn could affect their political and economic success.

Another reason for women's exclusion from public roles may be that once people settled down, women had more young children to care for (since only women bear children). With increased food production, more children could be fed. In

---

3. People who say humans are born either biologically male or female are ignorant of conditions that modern physicians label as intersex or disorders of sexual development, once known as hermaphroditism after a figure in Greek mythology. One might say, God not only made Adam and Eve, but also Stevie.

turn, more children provided cheap labor for farmwork. Women undoubtedly worked behind the scenes, in the kitchens and bedrooms, at mealtimes and in the fields, influencing the decisions of fathers and brothers, husbands and sons. Nevertheless, men largely monopolized the formal and accepted social roles of status and power that developed in civilization. Women's domestic work freed the men from chores so that they could take the lead in public life. Since mothers usually did most of the child rearing, they may have crucially formed the character of their children (leading to the later cliché, "The hand that rocks the cradle rules the world"). Mothers' influence on grown children and wives' on their husbands certainly affected decisions made by men that changed history.

It remains difficult, though, to illuminate their role within families, since comparatively few sources survive (but examples for some that do are the Sources on Family in this and each following chapter). Therefore, women's roles in driving decisive changes in history were once rarely examined. Only in the twentieth century did numbers of Western women gain rights comparable with or the same as those that men have long had (see chapter 14). The dominance of men over subservient women became traditional in civilizations.

In most societies, many social divisions have gone unquestioned, whether applied to gender or labor. Most civilizations produced **social classes**, groups of people defined around intersecting cultural and economic status. These developed out of a division of labor or specialization in economic production typical of urban civilizations. As mentioned already, weavers, tailors, potters, cartwrights, smiths, bakers, and masons carried out their crafts with greater efficiency than if each individual personally wove and sewed cloth, molded pots, built carts, forged tools, baked bread, or laid bricks. Instead of treating all kinds of labor as equal, some people earned a greater portion of wealth from theirs than others. Urban cultures usually separated people into at least three groups, traditionally reflecting a hierarchy of political power, wealth, and social influence. First, the **upper class** lorded their status over the other classes. A tiny minority of people took charge, controlling the knowledge, possessing most of the land, and taking the best goods that society had to offer. They became **royalty** at the top, followed by **aristocrats**, with the **nobles** just below, who declared themselves destined to pass on dominance from generation to generation. These elites organized society. Second, a tiny **middle class** formed around **artisans** (who made pots, shoes, and furniture) and **merchants** (who bought and sold goods). Third, the vast majority of others, the **lower class** or commoners, did the heavy labor of farmwork. Through most of civilized history they were simple farmers called **peasants**. They worked the land and produced the food so that the aristocrats and artisans did not have to. The hard work of peasants raising food from the land was at first, and often still is, the foundation of civilization. Although they created much wealth, peasants often saw few of its benefits. Ranked even below them, however, were the jobless poor, who hardly even counted as a class. Poverty did not exist among hunter-gatherers, since those who belonged shared in the group's resources, while those who did not belong died in the wilderness. In cities, though, people who had lost most social connections and the ability to work could still survive on the margins and with the scraps of urban wealth. Some took up what has been called "the oldest profession," or prostitution, selling their sexuality.

Throughout most of civilized history, the majority of people remained in the class they had been born into. Response to pressure for change sometimes led to adding new classes or subdividing old ones, with each new group placed in the established pecking order. Usually, though, one's parents determined one's status. Born to upper-class parents, one could easily stay upper class. Born to poor parents, one could hardly ever rise in status. So a few families sat at the top of society and decreed economic, political, and religious decisions. The large numbers of people without power usually obeyed these decisions and reinforced the authority of the elites in the marketplace, on the battlefield, and within sacred spaces. The masses had little choice.

Class conflict, or attempts by the masses to achieve power alongside the elites, did drive some historical change. Now and then the thought crossed common people's minds, "Why should we suffer just because we were born to lowborn parents?" Resentful of their imposed inferiority, the lower classes every so often rebelled against their superiors. Mostly they failed.

Two changes explain how a few aristocratic families exercised supremacy over the multitude of peasants for so long. One was the aristocratic role in warfare at the beginning of civilization. In hunter-gatherer groups, most adult males fought. Hunting even provided training in tactics similar to battle, with its organization of killing. Farming techniques, however, did not resemble warfare. Civilized warfare thus became the work of specialists: warriors were freed from the daily grind of farming so that they could dedicate themselves to training for combat. The king as war leader shared with a few associated warriors some of his aura of power. The best weapons became more expensive.

Another change to explain the rise of the aristocracy was stability. In a hunter-gatherer group, the nomadic wandering imposed equality. Any one person could possess only as much property as he or she could carry. Most everyone, from chief to child, did the same kind of work: hunting and gathering. In civilization, however, any one person had as much property as could be accumulated, stored, and defended, by oneself or with the support of others. Leadership soon became held by the few, while followers were many. Through most of civilized history, in most places, a few powerful families have run large human communities.

The elites kept their superiority through law and custom. Clothing reveals and conceals, sometimes both at the same time. With civilization, higher-status people imposed sumptuary laws about fashion, making it obvious to any passersby on the street to which class one belonged. Where one lived, in how elaborate a residence, also reflected status. Most important, laws regulated this more complicated social order. The earliest laws of Hammurabi and all laws until the eighteenth century AD recognized different classes of people, divided at least into aristocrats and commoners. Even crime and punishment usually depended on one's social status. If an aristocrat stole something, he paid compensation thirtyfold; a commoner paid only tenfold. If a person had no money, however, he paid with his life.

With these divisions of labor and class arrived the first **taxes**. Governments can tax anything at any rate they can get away with. Two and a half centuries ago,

Benjamin Franklin famously quipped that death and taxes were the only sure things in life. More accurate is the following basic principle:

The only certainty in civilization is death and taxes. The only essential questions are these: Who pays, and how much?

Not everyone pays taxes. In some civilizations, the privileged are tax exempt. Uncivilized barbarians do not pay taxes either: in their small, self-sufficient groups, hunter-gatherer peoples do not divide up their labor and leadership. Yet civilized society cannot exist without the taxes that pay for the rule keepers, warriors, and infrastructure that have kept human interchanges functioning smoothly. Most of the time, the poorer classes, hardworking peasants, have paid for the privileges of the richer classes, landowning aristocrats.

The lowest of all people in a society were slaves. This bondage denied any social status to certain humans who became mere property. Some persons became slaves to pay off debt (for example, fathers could sell their daughters for such purposes). Others were enslaved as punishment for crime. Many people defeated in conquest endured servitude rather than suffer death. The harshness of the slave system—how well the enslaved peoples were cared for or how hard they were worked—varied according to the customs of a civilization and either the beneficence or intelligence of the masters.

Despite being inhumane, slavery has been a key component of almost every civilization. Slavery among hunter-gatherers was much more difficult to manage. If a hunter-gatherer was enslaved but managed to escape, she could live off the land until she managed to find some friendly people of her own. In contrast, a civilized slave who escaped did not know how to survive in the woods, which plants to eat, or how to make shelter. Thus, the civilized form of slavery was much more hopeless for those trapped in its system.

The slave economy was supported by a final negative consequence of the rise of civilization: the perfection of **war**. Some romantics have suggested that human conflict did not exist among hunter-gatherers, who reputedly lived in some idyllic paradise. It seems, however, that humans have always organized to fight with one another, over pride, power, or possessions. When hunter-gatherers came under attack, though, they could run away—they knew how to live in the wild and thus could give up a hunting ground rather than be exterminated. Further, the world was less crowded when more people were nomads. Hunter-gatherers also possessed comparatively little of value to plunder.

Agriculture and cities, in contrast, added a more lethal intensity to human conflict. Once people settled down as farmers, the available space became much more restricted: good farmland was limited to well-watered plains. Farmers would not leave their land when threatened by invaders any more than when threatened by flood or famine. Thus, people stayed and fought with more determination and more destruction. The wealth of cities provided more temptation for invaders to take quickly and easily (they hoped) what others had wrung from the soil by long, hard labor. Agriculture also enabled the recruiting and supplying of larger and more complex armies, which in turn could more readily devastate a region.

Besides destruction, war also promoted cooperation. First, war was expensive, requiring the material support of many who were not warriors. Many noncombatants, mostly old men, all women and children, and those dedicated to religions, provided weapons, equipment, food, and emotional and ideological support. Warriors defended ideals such as the protection of noncombatants, the companionship of fighters, and the trust of allies. Second, any army must have a system of obedience and command in order to coordinate individual soldiers into a killing unit. Third, the nature of battle encouraged people to limit participants to only two opposing sides. The best way to defeat an army was to attack it on its flank (or in the rear) instead of head on. Any more than two participants in a battle exposed the flanks too easily. This battlefield reality led to alliances, where different political units either stood together or would be defeated separately. Thus, kings and emperors started a pattern that has endured throughout the history of civilization: conquest and subjugation.

History is not merely the record of wars and battles. Yet no history can ignore these events, for they often determined the rise or fall of civilizations. Most successful civilizations in history defended their supremacy through warfare. Many failed civilizations have dissolved by losing wars. A war won or lost, though, is usually not the only reason for a civilization's expansion or disappearance. Effective cultural, social, economic, and political developments at all levels contribute to victory or defeat.

Wars have melded or destroyed groups of peoples who become part of one civilization or another. Imperialists, those who support building empires, bring diverse peoples into one state. On the one hand, imperialists usually have confidence in the rightness of their efforts. Imperialists have often believed that their dominance in power proves their superior virtues. On the other hand, the fate and attitudes of the conquered could vary quite a bit. While conquests might destroy a people outright, usually conquerors have preserved large numbers of the conquered, if only to use them for labor. Because most rulers encourage uniformity, it could be hard to keep an ethnic identity. Once conquered, people have sometimes assimilated, or merged, into the ethnicity of their masters. Sometimes, if the conquered people were numerous enough, they have blended with the conquerors, both creating a new identity. Or conquerors have even been absorbed into the conquered. On occasion, people have broken free again, either through their own power or through allies. Empires have frequently been so large or lasted so briefly that diversity of peoples has survived. Civilization and war have been close companions throughout history.

Review: *What often-ignored problems did civilization create?*

Response:

SOURCES ON FAMILIES: LAW CODE OF HAMMURABI (CA. 1750 BC)

Hammurabi's law code shows how family has been a focus of government since the beginning of civilization. A number of his laws relate to family issues such as marital fidelity, male authority, women's roles, rights of children, and procreation. While the Babylonian concepts of marriage and family differed in significant ways from our own, we share with them the desire to regulate personal behavior.

110. If a consecrated woman, who is not living in the convent, has opened a wine shop or has entered a wine shop for drink, one shall burn that woman.

117. If a man has fallen into debt, and he has given his wife, his son, his daughter for the money, or has handed over to work off the debt, for three years they shall work in the house of their buyer or exploiter, who in the fourth year shall give them their liberty.

129. If the wife of a man has been caught in lying with another male, one shall bind them and throw them into the waters. If the owner of the wife would save his wife or the king would save his servant (he may).

130. If a man has forced the wife of a man who has not known the male and is dwelling in the house of her father, and has lain in her bosom and one has caught him, that man shall be killed, the woman herself shall go free.

131. If a husband has accused his wife, and she has not been caught in lying with another male, she shall swear by God and shall return to her house.

134. If a man has been taken captive, and his house is not being maintained, and his wife has entered into the house of another, that woman has no blame.

138. If a man has put away his bride who has not borne him children, he shall give her money as much as her dowry, and shall pay her the marriage portion which she brought from her father's house, and shall put her aside.

142. If a woman hates her husband and has said "Thou shalt not possess me," one shall enquire into her past what is her lack, and if she has been economical and has no vice, and her husband has gone out and greatly belittled her, that woman has no blame, she shall take her marriage portion and go off to her father's house.

143. If she has not been economical, a goer about, has wasted her house, has belittled her husband, one shall throw that woman into the waters.

148. If a man has married a wife and a sickness has seized her, he has set his face to marry a second wife, he may marry her, his wife whom the sickness has seized he shall not put her away, in the home she shall dwell, and as long as she lives he shall sustain her.

152. If from the time that that woman entered into the house of the man a debt has come upon them, both together they shall answer the merchant.

162. If a man has married a wife and she has borne him children, and that woman has gone to her fate, her father shall have no claim on her marriage portion, her marriage portion is her children's forsooth.

165. If a man has apportioned to his son, the first in his eyes, field, garden, and house, has written him a sealed deed, after the father has gone to his fate, when the brothers divide, the present his father gave him he shall take, and over and above he shall share equally in the goods of the father's house.

194. If a man has given his son to a wet nurse, that son has died in the hand of the wet nurse, the wet nurse without consent of his father and his mother has procured another child, one shall put her to account, and because, without consent of his father and his mother, she has procured another child, one shall cut off her breasts.

195. If a man has struck his father, one shall cut off his hands.

209. If a man has struck a gentleman's daughter and caused her to drop what is in her womb, he shall pay ten shekels of silver for what was in her womb.

210. If that woman has died, one shall put to death his daughter.

211. If the daughter of a poor man through his blows he has caused to drop that which is in her womb, he shall pay five shekels of silver.

212. If that woman has died, he shall pay half a mina of silver.

213. If he has struck a gentleman's maidservant and caused her to drop that which is in her womb, he shall pay two shekels of silver.

214. If that maidservant has died, he shall pay one-third of a mina of silver.

Questions:

- *What role does wealth and property play?*
- *What opportunities for agency do women have?*
- *How does social status intersect with sex roles?*

Responses:

THE RISE AND FALL OF PRACTICALLY ALL MIDDLE EASTERN EMPIRES

Historians still argue about which civilization was the first. Evidence is too fragmentary to fully determine which people get boasting rights for being number one.

Between seven and six thousand years ago, the first civilizations lay along great river systems that provided enough water for agriculture. In South Asia the Indus River nurtured Indian civilization, in East Asia the Hwang Ho (Yellow River) gave rise to Chinese civilization, and the valleys of the Nile and those of the Tigris and Euphrates fertilized Middle Eastern civilizations. China and India were too far away to have much influence on the formative West, at least at first.

The Middle East, however, laid the foundations for the later rise of the West (see map 2.2). Westerners coined the name *Middle East* about a hundred years ago as they were defining this region as different from both the Far East of India and China and their own West. Europeans often call it the Near East; some geographers prefer labeling the regions North Africa and Southwest Asia. Whatever the name, the Middle East today includes countries stretching from northeast Africa through the Arabian Peninsula; northward through the Levant (the eastern coast of the Mediterranean), Asia Minor, and Mesopotamia; and eastward to Iran. Today, Islam substantially defines the culture (see chapter 6). But long before Islam, the Middle East was rich, cultured, and powerful.

Today we often think of the Middle East as desert. Indeed, thousands of years of human overpopulation, soil exhaustion, deforestation, and water overuse, as well as climatic change, have left much of the area arid. In ancient times, however,

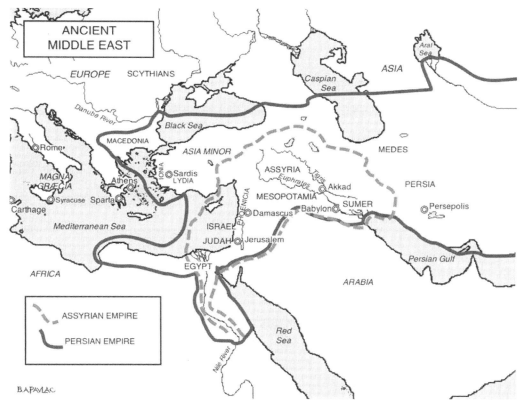

Map 2.2. Ancient Middle East.
What geographic factors shaped the Middle Eastern empires?

ten thousand years ago, the core of the region deserved the name Fertile Crescent. An arc of agriculturally productive land from the Nile River valley up through Palestine and down across the Tigris and Euphrates to the Persian Gulf soon fed peoples far more advanced than their neighbors in Europe, Africa, and Asia.

Helping these new agricultural civilizations succeed was their discovery of how to make **metal** tools. Humans had been using wood, bone, and stone for millions of years. Embedded in many stones were ores that, when heated or smelted, could be purified into an elemental metal, such as copper or tin. Thus, the Neolithic or New Stone Age of technology began to end around 4000 BC as humans began to mine copper for tools. They soon learned how to make an even better alloy, blending copper and tin into bronze. Technology of the **Bronze Age** prevailed from about 3000 to 800 BC. Based on these technologies, two civilizations arose in the Middle East, in **Mesopotamia** and **Egypt**. Each was relatively isolated from the other at first, but both were soon joined in commerce and conquest.

Mesopotamian civilization began around 3500 BC, when the Sumerians migrated into the land of the two rivers of the Tigris and Euphrates (mostly in modern-day Iraq). They founded the earliest significant political units in the form of city-states. The Sumerians were the first of many Mesopotamian peoples who shared a similar culture. As their most important public buildings they built ziggurats: huge step pyramids of baked brick that served as temples for worship of the gods and storehouses for grain. Priests and priestesses celebrated **fertility rituals**. In doing so, they imitated the imagined sexual couplings of the gods, believing that such activity sustained the annual cycle of seasons (in other words, sex made the world go round). By studying and learning about the skies, the priests divided the stars into the twelve constellations of the zodiac (creating twelve months), set twenty-four hours to the day, and set seven days to the week. They wrote such knowledge in cuneiform, block symbols formed by a wedge-shaped stylus pressed into clay (see figure 2.1).

On such tablets they composed epic poetry, the most enduring form of literature, popular for thousands of years. Epics are long poems (using verse, rhythm, and often rhyme) composed to tell stories of heroes and gods. The first great epic poem told of the king **Gilgamesh**, transformed by the poem written six hundred years after his reign from a human ruler into a two-thirds divine hero. The poem recounts how after the death of his friend, Enkidu, with whom he had shared many adventures and hardships, the sorrowful Gilgamesh sought the meaning of life. He learned that although the gods failed at wiping out all humankind by a great flood, they still doomed men to death, by wild animals, famine, and plague. Such a gloomy view of existence seemed common in Mesopotamia, despite the riches of the civilization.

The second great Middle Eastern civilization, Egypt, arose in the Nile River valley of northeastern Africa. Powerful kings called pharaohs united Egypt by around 3100 BC. These men and a few women, such as the now-famous Hatshepsut, not only held the power of kings but were also believed to have been actual gods incarnate on earth.[4] They often intensified their bloodline connection to the gods by marrying

---

4. History forgot about Hatshepsut (r. ca. 1479–1458 BC) for millennia because her son and heir tried to erase every single mention of her after he came to power. Historians rediscovered

Figure 2.1.   The wedge-shaped lines of cuneiform, the writing of ancient Mesopotamia, scrawl over the sculpture of an Assyrian.

their royal brothers or sisters. As divine beings, pharaohs were exempt from the usual social prohibition against incest. The pharaohs, their officials, and priests wielded power through their abilities to calculate and to write (in pictographs called hieroglyphics) (see figure 2.2). With these skills, they controlled agriculture: they accurately predicted the regular annual rise and fall of the Nile floods that nourished the fields. The Egyptian kingdom offered comparative stability and prosperity.

Hence, Egyptians seemed more optimistic about the afterlife than their Mesopotamian neighbors. The Egyptians hoped that, after death, their souls would be judged worthy by the gods, and thus they could spend a luxurious afterlife full of pleasure. According to *The Book of the Dead*, a dead person appeared before the god Osiris, where their spirit was weighed on scales against a feather. The deceased recited a long list of sins not committed and good deeds done. Based on the truth of the declaration and the weight, souls lighter than a feather went to heaven; souls heavier suffered from the Devouress; those equally balanced were servants in the afterlife.

Their belief in some sort of bodily resurrection after death led the ancient Egyptians to mummify their loved ones' dead bodies. So many hundreds of thousands of mummified people (and cats) survived to the nineteenth century that they were ground up for fertilizer or medicine (although Mark Twain joked that mummies were also used to stoke fires for locomotives). For the ancient Egyptians, the most wealth and effort was spent on the bodies of the pharaohs. Several pharaohs commanded tens of thousands of people over decades to build giant pyramids as funereal monuments to house their own mummies and treasure. Sadly for them and for

her impressive and peaceful reign only about a hundred years ago. To reinforce her status as ruler, she often wore the same artificial long, thin beards that male pharaohs wore. Perhaps to compensate for his "mommy issues," her son started a number of wars.

Figure 2.2.   The hieroglyphics (pictogram writing) of the ancient Egyptians decorate the walls of this tomb. The centerpiece is the god Anubis preparing for the afterlife a sarcophagus in which lies a mummy. (iStock/zanskar)

our ability to appreciate the past, most tombs were looted over the centuries, even when they were buried in the isolated Valley of the Kings. At the height of the Egyptian civilization, though, the regular pattern of life and death, the flood and fall of the Nile, and the rising and setting of the sun offered Egyptians a comforting cycle of expectation in this world while they also hoped for a better life in the next.

One brief exception in Egypt's cyclical history was the Amarna period, created by the rule of Pharaoh Ahkenaton (r. ca. 1352–1335 BC). He came to power with the traditional name Amenhotep IV but was inspired to transform Egyptian religion and, thus, his status as pharaoh. Instead of the many gods of traditional Egyptian polytheism, he encouraged worship of one god, Aton, the sun, with whom Ahkenaton had a special, divine connection, of course. Some historians think this focus on Aton established the first *monotheism*, or belief in only one god. Ahkenaton's ideas, though, did not long outlive him. Whether the priests saw him as a creative individualistic innovator or an ugly slothful fanatic, they and most Egyptians soon went back to worshipping according to the traditional patterns. Later pharaohs erased Ahkenaton's very name from their dynastic records. A brief artistic revolution, though, created lively and fascinating art of the Amarna period that differed from the static, unchanging forms of most Egyptian painting and sculpture. This art has come down to us in the treasures from the rare unplundered tomb of his successor, the boy pharaoh Tutankhamen (r. ca. 1335–1325 BC), or King Tut. Archaeologists discovered Tut's tomb in AD 1922. Stories of a mummy's curse that afflicted the tomb's excavators exaggerate the mundane circumstances surrounding the deaths of a few of them.

The curse of warfare, though, nearly killed off these early Middle Eastern civilizations in Mesopotamia and Egypt. Mesopotamia was particularly vulnerable to attack. Again and again, warriors from the surrounding hills stormed into the fertile valleys to plunder and conquer. Similarly, neighboring kings fought to dominate one another. Mesopotamia, never united for long, offered a dismal and depressing chronicle of slaughter.

After 2500 BC, various peoples, called Semites by modern scholars, entered Mesopotamia from the Arabian Peninsula. Their name is based upon the similar languages they spoke, supposedly linked to a biblical character, Shem, son of Noah. Modern Semitic languages include Aramaic, Hebrew, and Arabic. Soon, the Semitic speakers began to dominate the region's politics even as they adopted Sumerian culture. By 2300 BC, Sargon of Akkad had formed one of the first great empires by conquering Sumer and many of his Mesopotamian neighbors and then installing his relatives as sub-rulers. His descendants lost their grip on power, and several city-states restored their independence or built new, fragile kingdoms and empires. In the chaos, the Sumerian civilization died out. King Hammurabi of Babylon (r. ca. 1790–1750 BC) expanded the power of his Semitic people, the Amorites, to replace the Sumerians. Within a century after Hammurabi's reign, various peoples such as Kassites and Hittites had in turn destroyed his Babylonian Empire.

Meanwhile, the Egyptians managed a little more stability, unified by their pharaoh and protected by the desert. Even they, however, eventually suffered invasion. Their impressive Old Kingdom (a long line of dynastic stability) endured for nearly a thousand years, from 3100 to 2200 BC, until it collapsed in civil disorder. By 2050 BC, a new dynasty consolidated the Middle Kingdom, which lasted a mere 250 years until foreign invaders brought it down. Finally, the New Kingdom flourished from 1600 to about 1200 BC.

Another people, the **Phoenicians**, built a different kind of empire, based on trade, beginning around 1500 BC. They were a Semitic people originally based along the Levantine or eastern coast of the Mediterranean Sea that runs from Asia Minor to Egypt. Unlike the imperialism of Mesopotamians and Egyptians, who marched to conquer their neighbors, the Phoenicians sailed across the Mediterranean for *colonialism*. Peoples founded colonies by having portions from their population occupy foreign territory at a distance from their homeland. Through this piecemeal migration, the Phoenicians gained footholds in new lands through trade in dyed cloth, dogs, and wine. Soon Phoenician cities predominated along the western African Mediterranean coast and all the way to the Atlantic shores of the Iberian Peninsula. Some Phoenicians sailed as far as Great Britain, around the coast of Africa, and perhaps even to the Americas.

The Phoenicians gained an advantage with their invention of the first **alphabet**. All previous and contemporary civilizations, Sumer with its cuneiform and Egypt with its hieroglyphics (or, for that matter, China and India), used written systems composed of thousands of symbols, many of which represented only one word. Instead, the Phoenicians chose about two dozen symbols to represent sounds. With these few symbols to signify consonants and vowels, they could spell out phonetically (from *Phoenicians*!) any word that could be pronounced.[5] Most neighboring cultures, including the Hebrews, the Hellenes, and even the Egyptians, soon adapted the Phoenician alphabet idea to their own use. Indeed, soon people forgot how to read cuneiform or hieroglyphics, and much of the rich culture of Middle Eastern civilizations remained unknown until Western scholars relearned those writing systems in the nineteenth century (using, for example, the famous Rosetta Stone to translate ancient Egyptian) (see figure 2.3).

The Phoenicians with their colonies managed to survive massive invasions that overwhelmed much of the Middle East beginning around 1200 BC. Two technological innovations about this time made war even more destructive. First, around 1500 BC, the Hittites were the first to figure out how to smelt iron ore and forge iron tools. Iron, except for the problem of rust, was stronger and could hold an edge far better than bronze. Iron swords, spear points, and arrowheads became more lethally efficient. Heavy iron helmets, breastplates, and shields likewise offered better protection, although only to those who could afford them or bear their heavy weight. As other peoples adopted this metal as their key material, the **Iron Age** (1200 BC–AD 1870) began and endured until just over a century ago. Second, the Hittites domesticated horses from the steppes of Asia, either as military transportation for individual riders or harnessed to chariots. Both of these new warfare techniques enabled ambitious kings to dominate others and build a "universal" empire, a term that means the political unification of most of the peoples of the early Middle East (not the whole world, but the part of the world important to them). While these invaders by land and sea did not construct any enduring states for themselves, their destruction of dominant powers left room for others to develop.

The **Assyrian Empire** (ca. 750–600 BC) was the first new state to make a mark in the region. Historians call it the first "universal empire," as it stretched from the Persian Gulf to the Nile, uniting both Egypt and Mesopotamia. The Assyrians, with their swift cavalry, iron swords, and utter ruthlessness, were among the early wholehearted believers in *militarism*: the idea that virtues such as discipline, obedience, courage, and willingness to kill for the state are the highest values a civilized society can hold. Assyrians loved the hunt and the exercise of their power. Their brutality, however, inspired little affection among the dozens of conquered peoples. If any people dared to resist conquest, the Assyrians punished the defeated populations either by burning alive many men, women, and children or beheading them and flaying off their skins to drape over city walls; they mutilated many survivors by hacking off hands, arms, noses, ears, or genitals and enslaved survivors. These practices swiftly destroyed many ethnic groups. Many others surrendered rather than resist.

Those survivors, though, organized against their Assyrian conquerors. The Assyrian Empire lasted only about 150 years. Two allied peoples destroyed the Assyrians in 600 BC: the Chaldeans (or Neo-Babylonians, since they had occupied

---

5. English is not a very phonetic language. For example, the phrase "write the right way" could be misspelled as "wright the rite weigh." Languages such as Latin and Greek or German, on the other hand, are spelled pretty much the way they sound when pronounced.

Figure 2.3. In 1799, a soldier in Napoleon's army found the Rosetta Stone at the place it is named after. It described a royal dedication in three kinds of writing, Egyptian hieroglyphics, Egyptian common writing (Demotic), and Greek (at the bottom). Historians used the stone to finally unlock the lost reading of hieroglyphics, enabling them to study Egyptian history more thoroughly. (iStock/gyro)

Babylon) and the Medes from the hills north of Persia (as it was called by the Greeks, although the Medes named their own country Iran, as it is called today). The Neo-Babylonian–Median alliance completely wiped out the Assyrians, as they themselves had done to so many others. Of the Assyrian civilization only the ruins of their grand monuments to hunting and war survived.

After ridding themselves of the Assyrians, the Neo-Babylonians and Medes lived in an uneasy relationship. Both competed for dominion over weaker societies. During one of the wars, there occurred the first scientifically verifiable date in history: 28 May 585 BC—when a battle between the Medes and the Lydians in Asia Minor was broken off because of a solar eclipse (whose exact date modern astronomers can confirm).

Following a few decades of intermittent warfare, both Neo-Babylonians and Medes were surprised by the sudden rise of Cyrus "the Great" of Persia. In 550 BC, Cyrus defeated the Medes and eleven years later took Babylon. Cyrus established the **Persian Empire** (550–330 BC), the second, even larger universal empire, comprising Egypt, the Fertile Crescent, the Medes' lands, and his own Persia. As the shah, the "king of kings," Cyrus ruled over all, venerated like a god on earth. Yet his rule was benevolent compared with that of the Assyrians. He set up satraps (provincial governors) as his eyes and ears throughout the empire. With broad authority, they kept his various subjects in order. The native Persian religion of *Zoroastrianism*, founded by a prophet named Zarathustra, spread through the empire. Its belief system is called *dualism*, recognizing two powerful divine forces at war with each other in the universe: the good of spirit and ideas against the evil of matter and flesh. Humanity had to choose between the two. While Cyrus and his dynasty favored their own dualistic faith, they did not force conversions. Instead, Cyrus allowed many of his subject peoples to keep their unique customs and religions. The Persians even encouraged the foreign (to them) Semitic language of Aramaic as a common means for most people to communicate with one another, rather than their own Farsi.[6] Most of the diverse peoples found the Persian shah's rule beneficial (see Primary Source Project 2).

The Persians encouraged trade, helped by the invention of **money** in their recently conquered province of Lydia in Asia Minor. Money appeared surprisingly late as a means of economic exchange, or at least it might seem so to us who take it for granted. For thousands of years of civilization, though, no one could trust it. Before money, people bartered for goods and services, trading their labor or goods such as pots, cows, or women. Using money meant that specially made lumps of precious metals (usually copper, silver, or gold) could be used instead, creating a more stable and consistent pricing system. One problem, though, with any precious metal was determining its purity. Money will circulate only when people trust its value. Copper, silver, and gold could be easily degraded with baser metals such as tin or nickel into alloys and thus be worth less than the expected value. Gold could be tested somewhat because of its softness—and thus the custom arose of people biting gold coins to see whether they dented. Silver was a much more common and useful metal for making money, especially after the Lydians figured out how to use a touchstone (a rock on which metals left a specific color streak) to prove the purity of silver coins. The power of government also contributed to the use of money. Rulers put their own faces on the coins and ensured their value by setting purity standards and punishing forgers who debased coins. Hence, out of the Persian Empire came the long-standing practice that the government is responsible for money and therefore always intimately involved in the economy.

The Persians were great and powerful, yet even their empire survived little more than two centuries before another people conquered it. Nevertheless, the Persian Empire represented the high point of Middle Eastern civilization. The diverse peoples of the Fertile Crescent and Nile River basin had developed much of agriculture

---

6. Aramaic became so accepted that even Jews such as Jesus of Nazareth spoke it rather than Hebrew. A few people in modern-day Lebanon, Syria, and Iraq still speak it.

and architecture, metallurgy and mathematics, literature and law. Their influence on Western civilization was to set an example of these basic practices for other peoples who lived on the fringes of the great empires.

While Bronze Age Egypt and Sumer first reached their high points, various peoples lived without the benefits of civilization in what we now call Europe. The cultures of the earliest hunter-gatherers and agriculturalists who moved into Europe from the Middle East and the steppes of northern Siberia over seven thousand years ago have not survived. The oldest Europeans surviving today as an ethnic group were probably the Basques. Their settlements on both sides of the Pyrenees Mountains in modern France and Spain probably sheltered them from later invasions. The 1991 discovery in the Alps of a mummy, since nicknamed Ötzi, provided a few insights into the hunter-gatherers of five thousand years ago.[7] About four thousand years ago, farming peoples who had originated in the Caucasus Mountains migrated into Europe. Scholars call them Indo-Europeans because of their related languages spoken now across Eurasia.

The European peninsula in the far western corner of Eurasia was off the beaten track of the major civilizations of India, China, and the Middle East. Nonetheless, early Europeans found an area well suited for human habitation. Flooding was less devastating than along the great rivers of Africa, the Middle East, or Asia, since the major waterways were not nearly so vast. Europe suffered few earthquakes. The temperate climate prevented many insects that bore lethal tropical diseases. The hills contained rich deposits of mineral ores. As people cleared dense forests to create farmland, the plentiful wood provided excellent building material and fuel. Their domesticated animals and plants easily adapted to the new environment. We know little of these prehistorical cultures. The huge ring of stones at Stonehenge in present-day England is impressive, but it tells us little of the people who began it around 3000 BC (see figure 2.4). And even they were replaced shortly after by new immigrants, the Beaker people, named after their pots.

Along with these benefits, the Europeans were enriched by migrations of civilized people and ideas from the Middle East, Asia, and Africa. They readily borrowed or stole political practices, economic systems, social customs, art and literature, religion, and schools. Drawing on the wisdom of ancient Mesopotamia and Egypt, the two peoples of the Greeks and Romans who had settled on the southern edge of Europe along the Mediterranean Sea would build their own civilizations. First, however, the obscure Middle Eastern Jews, who barely survived the rise and fall of empires, became essential to the West.

---

7. One of the lessons taught by Ötzi and other mummies is the legacy of human violence. Several years after his discovery, scientists discovered that he had been shot and killed by an arrow in the back. Bog bodies, such as the twenty-four-hundred-year-old Tollund man from Denmark, seem to have been executed by strangling and then tossed into a swamp, which preserved them.

Figure 2.4. The mysterious, massive blocks of Stonehenge rise from a meadow in the south of England. The monument is clearly connected to astronomy, with various stones aligned with heavenly bodies. Beyond that, the reasons why people built it remain a mystery.

Review: What did various Ancient Middle Eastern civilizations offer to the early peoples of the West?

Response:

PRIMARY SOURCE PROJECT 2: XENOPHON VERSUS HERODOTUS ABOUT REPUTATION

Two Greek historians offer perspectives on the death of Cyrus "the Great" of Persia. Xenophon in his Cyropaedia *tells of Cyrus speaking from his deathbed to his two heirs, Cambyses (who inherits most of the realm) and Tanaoxares. The shah gives them counsel about good rule based on kindness toward all and support for one another. After his death, the brothers did not follow his advice. Herodotus in his* History *presents Cyrus as more of a villain, dishonest and dishonorable. He suffers a brutal death at the hands of the Massagetai, whose kingdom lay between the Black and Caspian Seas. Where does the truth lie?*

Source 1: *The Death of Cyrus* by Xenophon (ca. 380 BC)

My sons, and friends of mine, the end of my life is at hand. . . . And as the years passed, I seemed to find my powers grow with them, so that I never felt my old age weaker than my youth, nor can I think of anything I attempted or desired wherein I failed. Moreover, I have seen my friends made happy by my means, and my enemies crushed beneath my hand. This my fatherland, which was once of no account in Asia, I leave at the height of power, and of all that I won I think I have lost nothing. . . .

These are the principles that I leave with you, sanctioned by time, ingrained in our customs, embodied in our laws. . . . Cambyses, you know of yourself, without words from me, that your kingdom is not guarded by this golden scepter, but by faithful friends; their loyalty is your true staff, a scepter which shall not fail. But never think that loyal hearts grow up by nature as the grass grows in the field; if that were so, the same men would be loyal to all alike, even as all natural objects are the same to all mankind. No, every leader must win his own followers for himself, and the way to win them is not by violence but by loving-kindness.

Let no one, Tanaoxares, be more eager than yourself to obey your brother and support him: to no one can his triumph or his danger come so near. Ask yourself from whom you could win a richer reward for any kindness? Who could give you stouter help in return for your own support? And where is coldness so ugly as between brothers? Or where is reverence so beautiful? And remember, Cambyses, only the brother who holds pre-eminence in a brother's heart can be safe from the jealousy of the world. . . .

And after the gods, I would have you reverence the whole race of man, as it renews itself for ever; for the gods have not hidden you in the darkness, but your deeds will be manifest in the eyes of all mankind. And if they be righteous deeds and pure from iniquity, they will blazon forth your power. But if you meditate evil against each other, you will forfeit the confidence of every man. For no man can trust you, even though he should desire it, if he sees you wrong him whom above all you are bound to love.

Therefore, if my words are strong enough to teach you your duty to one another, it is well. But, if not, let history teach you, and there is no better teacher. For the most part, parents have shown kindness to their children and brothers to their brothers, but it has been otherwise with some. Look, then, and see which conduct has brought success, choose to follow that, and your choice will be wise. . . .

Remember my last saying: show kindness to your friends, and then shall you have it in your power to chastise your enemies. Good-bye, my dear sons, bid your mother good-bye for me. And all my friends, who are here or far away, good-bye.

Source 2: *Death of Cyrus* by Herodotus (ca. 420 BC)

At this time the Massagetai were ruled by a queen, named Tomyris. . . . To her Cyrus sent ambassadors, with instructions to court her on his part, pretending that he wished to take her to wife. Tomyris, however, aware that it was her kingdom, and not herself, that he courted, forbade the men to approach. Cyrus, therefore, finding that he did not advance his designs by this deceit, marched . . . openly displaying his hostile intentions. . . .

Tomyris sent a herald to him, who said, "King of the Medes, cease to press this enterprise. . . . Be content to rule in peace your own kingdom, and bear to see us reign over the countries that are ours to govern. . . ."

But Croesus the Lydian [said] . . . "[W]ere it not disgrace intolerable for Cyrus the son of Cambyses to retire before and yield ground to a woman? . . . My counsel, therefore, is that we . . . get the better of them by stratagem. I am told they are unacquainted with the good things on which the Persians live, and have never tasted the great delights of life. Let us then prepare a feast for them in our camp; let sheep be slaughtered without stint, and the wine cups be filled full of noble liquor, and let all manner of dishes be prepared. . . . Unless I very much mistake, when they see the good fare set out, they will forget all else and fall to. Then it will remain for us to do our parts manfully." . . .

Cyrus, having advanced a day's march from the river, did as Croesus had advised him. . . . Soon afterwards, a detachment of the Massagetai, one-third of their entire army, led by Spargapises, son of the queen Tomyris, . . . seeing the banquet prepared, they sat down and began to feast. When they had eaten and drunk their fill, and were now sunk in sleep, the Persians under Cyrus arrived, slaughtered a great multitude, and made even a larger number prisoners. Among these last was Spargapises himself.

When Tomyris heard what had befallen her son and her army, she sent a herald to Cyrus, who thus addressed the conqueror: "You bloodthirsty Cyrus, pride not yourself on this poor success; . . . it was this poison by which you ensnared my child, and so overcame him, not in fair open fight. . . . Restore my son to me and get you from the land unharmed. . . . Refuse, and I swear by the sun, the sovereign lord of the Massagetai, bloodthirsty as you are, I will give you your fill of blood."

To the words of this message Cyrus paid no manner of regard. As for Spargapises, . . . he killed himself.

Tomyris, when she found that Cyrus paid no heed to her advice, collected all the forces of her kingdom, and gave him battle. . . . The greater part of the army of the Persians was destroyed and Cyrus himself fell, after reigning nine and twenty years. Search was made among the slain by order of the queen for the body of Cyrus. And when it was found she took a skin, and, filling it full of human blood, she dipped the head of Cyrus in the gore, saying, as she thus insulted the corpse: "I live and have conquered you in battle, and yet by you am I ruined, for you took my son with guile. But thus I make good my threat, and give you your fill of blood."

Of the many different accounts which are given of the death of Cyrus, this which I have followed appears to me most worthy of credit.

Questions:

- *How do the two sources differ in their method of conveying information?*
- *What specific words or deeds show how Cyrus respected law and justice, or not?*
- *What do the authors seek to have readers understand about Cyrus's legacy?*

Responses:

Make your own timeline.

8000 BC   **400 BC**

Citations

Xenophon. *The Education of Cyrus*. Translated by Henry Graham Dakyns. Revised by F. M. Stawell. New York: E. P. Dutton, 1914, book 8, chap. 7, pp. 291–95.

Herodotus. *The History of Herodotus*. 4 vols. New York: D. Appleton, 1859, book 1, chaps. 205–14, pp. 1:268–72.

For more on these sources, go to http://www.concisewesternciv.com/sources/psc2.html.

CHAPTER 3

The Chosen People

Hebrews and Jews, 2000 BC to AD 135

At first, the **Hebrews** seemed insignificant compared with the peoples of ancient North Africa, Mesopotamia, Persia, and Asia Minor who developed essential practices of civilization upon which the West would build. The Hebrews lived in a tiny territory near the Dead Sea and along the Levantine coast of the Eastern Mediterranean. Their petty kingdoms barely budged the course of history, while numerous vast empires rose and fell around and over them. Amazingly, they survived these cataclysms. They came to be called **Jews** during their domination by the Persian Empire. Then and after, many Jews moved into cities of the Middle East and Europe, where they participated in ancient and modern civilization. They and their religion of *Judaism*, which asserted that they were the special people of an omnipotent God, became a key component of the West.

BETWEEN AND UNDER EMPIRES

The Hebrews were similar to many other pastoral peoples who lived in the Middle East several millennia ago. Looking back into the past, the Hebrews came together into a coherent nation as they crafted a meaningful history for themselves. A century ago, modern professional historians enthusiastically accepted and endorsed the Hebrews' version of their own past, since those accounts reinforced the historians' own cultural view of a heroic religious legacy. More recently, however, archaeologists and historians have doubted the accuracy and legitimacy of much of what the ancient Hebrews wrote about their foundations and origins. Because this history is intimately interwoven with the Hebrew faith of Judaism, determining the truth has been all the more complicated. As so often happens, myths that describe a people's character and purpose seem to outweigh the verifiable facts.

The ancient Hebrews collected their histories into their own sacred scriptures called the Tanakh, an acronym for the Torah (first five books), the writings of prophets, and other writings. Later, Christians included Hebrew scripture as the **Old Testament** of their **Bible**. In the beginning, according to biblical scripture, God created the heavens and the earth. The Hebrews saw their God not only as the creator, but also as the only true deity. The other gods and goddesses of Mesopotamia, Egypt, or any other people were petty demons or fakes in comparison. Since this Hebrew God also would later be revered by most of Western civilization, his name in English is conventionally spelled with a capital *G* to distinguish "Him" from all other (false) gods.

According to their Bible stories, God's influence on humanity started with the beginning of all history, in their story about creation.[1] The Hebrews believed that God created two human beings, a man and a woman (although there are two versions of the story offering two contradictory accounts of their formation). They believed that all the rest of humanity descended from these first two people, Adam and Hawwah (Eve in English).

The creation myth not only narrated how God created the universe but also described how things went wrong for humans because of bad choices. The Archangel Michael threw Adam and Hawwah (or Eve) out of paradise as punishment for eating the fruit of the tree of knowledge of good and evil. As generation begot generation, sins multiplied. At one point, God became fed up with humanity and killed almost everyone with a great flood. Only Noah and his family survived in a large ship, the ark, which also harbored pairs of all living creatures.

Many cultures have similar myths of original couples falling from perfection and of devastating floods covering the earth. No valid scientific or historical evidence exists to prove such creation or flood myths. No physical location for paradise has been found; its existence is improbable in this world. A ship built according to the biblical design could not possibly hold all species of animals and sustenance for them. Although stories of origins cannot be literally true, they resonate with miraculous mythic power in our culture.

The first founding figure of Judaism, the biblical Noah's descendant Abram (later Abraham), has little better evidence for his existence: archaeologists have difficulty connecting many biblical people and timelines with evidence from their digs. According to the story, though, Abram and his family followed his God's call to leave Mesopotamia. Abram and his people allegedly settled in the land of the Canaanites, where Hivites, Perizzites, Girgashites, and Jebusites, among others, also lived. The early Hebrews prospered as pastoral herders of livestock. The biblical Abraham's grandson, Jacob, also called Israel, had ten sons and two grandsons who formed the twelve "tribes" of Israel, who both fought and lived peaceably with their neighbors, as peoples have done before and since. Then, the Bible story goes, in the sixteenth century BC, during a time of famine, the Hebrews fell under Egyptian domination and moved there.

Historians have yet to find Egyptian sources that mention this captivity of the tribes of Israel, but the oppression by Egyptians provided a pivotal historical moment for the Hebrews.[2] According to Hebrew scripture, a leader named Moses

---

1. Most Jewish authorities calculate their calendar from the year AM 1 (from the Latin *anno mundi*—the beginning of the world), equivalent to 3761 BC. The Jewish calendar is lunar based (thus changing the number of days in the year), and so the New Year holiday moves, usually taking place in the Gregorian month of September. Thus, most of the year AD 2020 is AM 5780.

2. In any case, they did not help build the pyramids, which had been finished centuries earlier.

led his people out of Egypt in the mid-1200s BC. This event, called the Exodus, is the defining moment of Hebrew history, celebrated ever since in the religious festival of the Passover. The Hebrews wandered in the wilderness (the time length of forty years is probably a mythologized number). Then the Hebrews invaded the land of Canaan (although the region was actually ruled by Egypt) and began to replace the natives by conquest, slaughter, and assimilation. The story about their leader Joshua blowing horns to bring down the walls of the ancient city of Jericho is popular in children's Bible stories. Usually children do not hear how the Hebrews completely destroyed the city and put to the sword all the men and women, whether young or old, and even slaughtered the livestock, sparing only the family of Rahab the harlot, who had helped Joshua's spies. Archaeologists have not yet found evidence for this military conquest. All that they can confirm is that identifiable Hebrews lived among the Canaanites by about 1200 BC. About 1150 BC, a new "sea people," the Philistines, landed on the Levantine coast. The Philistines began their own migration and conquest, armed with superior iron weapons, and soon dominated enough for the region later to be named after them as **Palestine**.

Meanwhile, the Hebrews held a precarious place in a dangerous land, living among foreigners whom their scriptures instructed them to treat well. Their political organization remained fragile, with a loose confederation led by figures called judges (such as Gideon, Samson, and even a woman, Deborah). The judges' leadership derived both from their military ability and apparent divine sanction. Still, many Hebrews began to insist on having a king, just as their neighboring peoples had. The failures of the first king, Saul, prompted a rebellion by David, son of the shepherd Jesse. Even after Saul's death in battle against the Philistines, the new King David needed to fight for the loyalty of all Hebrews. He eventually succeeded and established a dynasty, passing the crown to his son Solomon. Under Solomon, the Hebrew kingdom reached its peak during a weak period for Egypt and Mesopotamia. The Bible describes these kings as important and wealthy, yet historical evidence so far suggests that they were insignificant and poor.

The fragile unity achieved by these three kings broke down after Solomon's death, shortly after 1000 BC. The Northern Kingdom, including ten of the tribes, took the name of **Israel**. The Southern Kingdom of the other two tribes became **Judaea** (or **Judah**), named after one of Israel/Jacob's sons. The uneasy rivalry of these kingdoms made them an even more tempting target for neighboring empires. The militaristic Assyrians attacked in 722 BC. Within two years they had annihilated the Northern Kingdom: its people disappeared, either killed or enslaved and assimilated, becoming known as the "lost tribes of Israel." The people known as Samaritans repopulated the northern lands. The Samaritans adopted a version of the Hebrews' faith, but their worship at shrines on mountaintops offended the temple priests of Jerusalem.

The Southern Kingdom narrowly escaped Assyrian conquest in 701 BC (see the Primary Source Project). Nevertheless, Judaea's time was limited. In 598/597 BC, the Babylonians, who had recently destroyed the Assyrians, picked up where the latter had left off. The Babylonian Empire conquered the Southern Kingdom and dragged off many thousands to Mesopotamia as slaves.

The following years between 598 and 538 BC became known as the **Baby-lonian Captivity**, another important turning point for the Hebrew people. Instead of disappearing into the large category of lost peoples of history, the Hebrews endured. They kept their religion; they held their social integrity; they survived despite oppression. After only a few generations of suffering, a rescuer appeared in the person of Cyrus "the Great," the same who destroyed Babylon and founded the new Persian Empire. The magnanimous Cyrus took pity on the Jews and allowed them to return to Judaea once again. Many did return, and they rebuilt their temple in Jerusalem, resuming life under the benevolent protection of the shahs of Persia.

The Hebrews' history to that point was indeed remarkable in that they had managed to survive as a people. Many cultures and nations had already become extinct over the millennia, including the Sumerians, Hyksos, Hittites, and Assyrians. All these peoples had been far more powerful than the Hebrews. Yet the Hebrews persevered despite their stories of multiple migrations: into Palestine, out of Palestine, into Palestine, out, again and again. Nevertheless, this achievement of surviving between and under the power of various empires would still not have rated the Hebrews much of a mention in ancient history were it not for their religion.

Review: *How did the history of the Hebrews/Jews contrast with that of other ancient peoples?*

Response:

PRIMARY SOURCE PROJECT 3: SENNACHERIB'S ANNALIST VERSUS CHRONICLES WRITER ABOUT DIVINE FAVOR

Although the Assyrians overran the Kingdom of Israel, they did not conquer the Kingdom of Judah with its capital of Jerusalem. These two sources offer two different versions about why. On a prism-shaped clay object, an unknown writer provides the Assyrian point of view. The Assyrian ruler Sennacherib's actions against the Hebrew king Hezekiah are recorded here, as well as his other successful conquests. In contrast, the Book of Chronicles *from the Hebrew sacred scriptures (or Christian Old Testament of the Bible) offers another explanation for Judah's survival.*

Source 1: *Sennacherib Prism Inscription* by Anonymous (ca. AD 121)

In my Third Campaign to the land of Syria I went. Luliah, King of Sidon (for the fearful splendor of my Majesty had overwhelmed him), to a distant spot in the midst of the sea fled. His land I entered. [Many provinces], his cities and castles, walled and fenced, and his finest towns (for the flash of the weapons of Ashur my Lord had overcome them) made submission at my feet. Tubal, upon the throne over them I seated. A fixed tribute to my Majesty, paid yearly without fail, I imposed upon him. . . .

The chief priests, noblemen, and people of Ekron whom Pariah their King (holding the faith and worship of Assyria) had placed in chains of iron, and unto Hezekiah King of Judah had delivered him and had acted towards the deity with hostility: these men were now terrified in their hearts. The Kings of Egypt and the soldiers, archers, chariots, and horses of Ethiopia, forces innumerable, gathered together and came to their assistance. In the plains of Altaku in front of me they placed their battle array: they discharged their arrows: with the weapons of Ashur my Lord, with them I fought, and I defeated them. . . .

Then I drew nigh the city of Ekron. The chief priests and noblemen who had committed these crimes, I put to death; on stakes all round the city I hung their bodies: the people of the city who had committed sins and crimes to slavery I gave. The rest of them who had not been guilty of faults and crimes, and who sinful things against the deity had not done, to spare them I gave command. Pariah their King from the midst of Jerusalem I brought out, and on a throne of royalty over them I seated. Tribute payable to my Majesty I fixed upon him.

And Hezekiah, King of Judah, who had not bowed down at my feet, 46 of his strong cities, forts, and the smaller towns in their neighborhood beyond number, with warlike engines. . . . I attacked and captured. 200,150 people small and great, male and female, horses, mares, asses, camels, oxen, and sheep beyond number, for the midst of them I carried off and distributed as spoil. He himself, like a bird in a cage, inside Jerusalem his royal city, I shut him up: siege-towers against him I constructed, (for he had given command to renew the bulwarks of the great gate of his city). His cities which I plundered, from his kingdom I cut off. . . . I diminished his kingdom. Beyond the former scale of their yearly gifts their tribute and gifts to my Majesty I augmented and imposed upon them. He himself Hezekiah the fearful splendor of my Majesty had overwhelmed him. The workmen, soldiers, and build-ers whom for the fortification of Jerusalem his royal city he had collected within it, now carried tribute and with 30 talents of gold, 800 talents of silver; woven cloth, scarlet, embroidered; precious stones of large size, couches of ivory, moveable thrones of ivory, skins of buffaloes, teeth of buffaloes, dan wood, ku wood, a great treasure of every kind, and his daughters, and the male and female inmates of his palace, male slaves and female slaves, unto Nineveh my royal city after me he sent; to pay tribute and do homage he sent his envoy.

Source 2: 2 Chronicles 32:1–30 (ca. 350 BC)

After these things, and the establishment thereof, Sennacherib king of Assyria came, and entered into Judah, and encamped against the fenced cities, and thought to win them for himself. And when Hezekiah saw that Sennacherib was come, and that he was purposed to fight against Jerusalem, he took counsel with his princes and his mighty men to stop the waters of the fountains which were without the city: and they did help him.

So there was gathered much people together, who stopped all the fountains, and the brook that ran through the midst of the land, saying, Why should the kings of Assyria come, and find much water?

Also he strengthened himself, and built up all the wall that was broken, and raised it up to the towers, and another wall without, and repaired Millo in the city of David, and made darts and shields in abundance. And he set captains of war over the people, and gathered them together to him in the street of the gate of the city, and spake comfortably to them, saying,

"Be strong and courageous, be not afraid nor dismayed for the king of Assyria, nor for all the multitude that is with him: for there be more with us than with him. With him is an arm of flesh; but with us is the Lord our God to help us, and to fight our battles." And the people rested themselves upon the words of Hezekiah king of Judah.

After this did Sennacherib king of Assyria send his servants to Jerusalem, (but he himself laid siege against Lachish, and all his power with him,) unto Hezekiah king of Judah, and unto all Judah that were at Jerusalem, saying,

"Thus saith Sennacherib king of Assyria, Whereon do ye trust, that ye abide in the siege in Jerusalem? Doth not Hezekiah persuade you to give over yourselves to die by famine and by thirst, saying, 'The Lord our God shall deliver us out of the hand of the king of Assyria?' Hath not the same Hezekiah taken away his high places and his altars, and commanded Judah and Jerusalem, saying, 'Ye shall worship before one altar, and burn incense upon it.' Know ye not what I and my fathers have done unto all the people of other lands? Were the gods of the nations of those lands any ways able to deliver their lands out of mine hand? Who was there among all the gods of those nations that my fathers utterly destroyed, that could deliver his people out of mine hand, that your God should be able to deliver you out of mine hand? Now therefore let not Hezekiah deceive you, nor persuade you on this manner, neither yet believe him: for no god of any nation or kingdom was able to deliver his people out of mine hand, and out of the hand of my fathers: how much less shall your God deliver you out of mine hand?"

And his servants spake yet more against the Lord God, and against his servant Hezekiah.

He wrote also letters to rail on the Lord God of Israel, and to speak against him, saying, "As the gods of the nations of other lands have not delivered their people out of mine hand, so shall not the God of Hezekiah deliver his people out of mine hand."

Then they cried with a loud voice in the Jews' speech unto the people of Jerusalem that were on the wall, to affright them, and to trouble them; that they might take the city. And they spake against the God of Jerusalem, as against the gods of the people of the earth, which were the work of the hands of man.

And for this cause Hezekiah the king, and the prophet Isaiah the son of Amoz, prayed and cried to heaven. And the Lord sent an angel, which cut off all the mighty men of valor, and the leaders and captains in the camp of the king of Assyria. So he returned with shame of face to his own land. And when he was come into the house of his god, they that came forth of his own bowels slew him there with the sword.

Thus the Lord saved Hezekiah and the inhabitants of Jerusalem from the hand of Sennacherib the king of Assyria, and from the hand of all other, and guided them on every side.

And many brought gifts unto the Lord to Jerusalem, and presents to Hezekiah king of Judah: so that he was magnified in the sight of all nations from thenceforth. . . .

And Hezekiah had exceeding much riches and honor: and he made himself treasuries for silver, and for gold, and for precious stones, and for spices, and for shields, and for all manner of pleasant jewels; storehouses also for the increase of corn, and wine, and oil; and stalls for all manner of beasts, and cotes for flocks. Moreover he provided him cities, and possessions of flocks and herds in abundance: for God had given him substance very much. . . . And Hezekiah prospered in all his works.

Questions:

- *What qualities does each source give its ruler and his rival?*
- *What specific actions prevent Judah from being conquered, according to each source?*
- *What roles do supernatural beings play in each source?*

Responses:

Citations

"Annals of Sennacherib." *The Library of Original Sources: Ideas that have Influenced Civilization, in the Original Documents, Translated*. Vol. 1, *The Ancient World*, edited by Oliver J. Thatcher, translated by H. F. Talbot. Edition de Luxe. Milwaukee: University Research Extension Co., 1915, pp. 416–18.

2 Chronicles. The King James Bible (Authorized Version). 1611.

For more on these sources, go to http://www.concisewesternciv.com/sources/psc3a.html.

BOUND BY LAW

During the course of their mythic history, the Hebrews continued claiming that they could see the hand of God regularly revealed. History permeated their religion of Judaism and vice versa. Other Middle Eastern religions emphasized the cyclical nature of creation and destruction, where nothing really changed. The rulers ruled, the people worked, year after year, century after century, millennium after millennium. In contrast, the Hebrews saw a direction to their experiences. From the Hebrews' point of view, the whole purpose of history was to illuminate their relationship with their God, who, for unknown reasons, had selected the people of Israel as his special favorites. The Hebrew people sinned and failed as much as any other group of people. Nonetheless, they claimed that a special relationship grew out of their obedience to God.

One main component of this obedience to God was resisting syncretism. The other great Mesopotamian and Egyptian civilizations provided not only knowledge of agriculture, architecture, mathematics, astronomy, metallurgy, and political organization. Along with these other ideas came religion. Many peoples of the ancient world readily absorbed and adapted one another's spiritual beliefs and the rites of their neighbors. The Hebrews tried not to.

The Hebrews repeatedly insisted that their religion was different. They developed monotheism, devotion to one divine being. God was transcendent, beyond nature, not of this world; rather, "He" had made it himself. They did not even utter their God's name: "He" was YHWH, perhaps meaning "I am who I am" (sometimes rendered in English as Jehovah). Judaism's almost unique conception of the divine (remember Pharaoh Akhenaton) required that the Hebrews reject polytheistic practices, as tempting as fertility cults might be. Their God was jealous and allowed no other gods. In many ways, such as the sacrificial rituals in the temple, the Hebrews' religion resembled those of their neighbors. Nevertheless, they insisted on their own exclusive relationship with God.

At the core of Judaism was the **covenant** that God had concluded with the Hebrews alone. Covenants were political treaties and contracts between greater and lesser peoples. God's contract was laid out not only in the famous **Ten Commandments** (see table 3.1) but also in more than six hundred other laws and regulations for everything from murder and debt to food and sex. The Hebrews believed that if they kept his laws, God would make of the Hebrews a great nation, multiplying them, giving them a promised land of milk and honey, and cursing their enemies.

The exact nature of this promised land of milk and honey was a matter of dispute. Some Hebrews held that it was the land of Canaan/Palestine/Israel/Judaea—a land physically in this world. Others believed that it was a metaphysical land in the next world, a heaven after death. Judaism's position on the afterlife was varied. Some Hebrews believed that since God acted in this world, then his promised paradise would happen here—there was no life after death. Others believed that some sort of paradise was attainable after death, with or without a bodily resurrection such as the kind the Egyptians believed in. Judaism has always mainly emphasized

Table 3.1.   Which Ten Commandments?

Jewish	Orthodox	Most Protestant	Roman Catholic	Exodus 20: 2–17
1				2 I am the LORD thy God, which have brought thee out of the land of Egypt, out of the house of bondage.
		1		3 Thou shalt have no other gods before me.
2			1	4 Thou shalt not make unto thee any graven image, or any likeness of any thing that is in heaven above, or that is in the earth beneath, or that is in the water under the earth: 5 Thou shalt not bow down thyself to them, nor serve them: for I the LORD thy God am a jealous God, visiting the iniquity of the fathers upon the children unto the third and fourth generation of them that hate me; 6 And shewing mercy unto thousands of them that love me, and keep my commandments.
3			2	7 Thou shalt not take the name of the LORD thy God in vain; for the LORD will not hold him guiltless that taketh his name in vain.
4			3	8 Remember the sabbath day, to keep it holy. 9 Six days shalt thou labor, and do all thy work: 10 But the seventh day is the sabbath of the LORD thy God: in it thou shalt not do any work, thou, nor thy son, nor thy daughter, thy servant, nor thy maidservant, nor thy cattle, nor thy stranger that is within thy gates: 11 For in six days the LORD made heaven and earth, the sea, and all that in them is, and rested the seventh day: wherefore the LORD blessed the sabbath day, and hallowed it.
5			4	12 Honour thy father and thy mother: that thy days may be long upon the land which the LORD thy God giveth thee.
6			5	13 Thou shalt not kill.
7			6	14 Thou shalt not commit adultery.
8			7	15 Thou shalt not steal.
9			8	16 Thou shalt not bear false witness against thy neighbour.
10			9	17 Thou shalt not covet thy neighbour's house, thou shalt not covet thy neighbour's wife,
			10	nor his manservant, nor his maidservant, nor his ox, nor his ass, nor any thing that is thy neighbour's.

Note: While people often refer to the Ten Commandments as the foundational laws of our culture, the exact rules are difficult to pin down. Two slightly different versions exist, one, as here, and the other, as in Deuteronomy 5:6–21. Translation challenges lead to different word choices ("kill" or "murder") or archaic phrasing, such as in this, the King James Version. In the original Hebrew, there was no numbering—verse numbers appeared only as late as the twelfth century AD. Jews, Roman Catholics, Orthodox, and Protestants numbered the commandments in different ways, so where some commandments ended and others began was open to interpretation.

living a moral life for God in this world, not the afterlife. Religion and morality are indivisible for Judaism. The Jewish emphasis on morality later influenced its successor faiths of Christianity and Islam.

Besides monotheism, another remarkable feature of Judaism was its organization. God made the covenant with the people without the intervening mediation of kings or priests. A caste of priests maintained the single temple in Jerusalem, but at first the most important religious figures were the **prophets**, who had a direct relationship with God. They proved their worth through miracles and the validity of their prophecy (although historians would argue that few of the prophecies in the Bible came true in the lifetime of their predictors—they were realized only by reading history backward). During their lifetimes, prophets often suffered rejection. Both powerful rulers and substantial numbers of the population frequently ignored and punished the prophets. For example, when the prophet Samuel anointed David to replace Saul as king, the multitudes did not listen and rally to his cause. Yet the moral voices of the prophets like Samuel, Ezekiel, Jeremiah, and Isaiah have resonated through the centuries. Their proclamation of God's word, religion, and his people survived. The prophets called the Hebrews to the path of righteousness and away from worshipping the gods of their neighbors, which many Israelites often did nevertheless.

The Hebrews were likewise unusual in the secular nature of their kings. Unlike monarchs of the Middle East, few Hebrew rulers had a serious devotion to the divine. The early history of the Hebrews from before Abraham to Moses included no kings. The judges who reconquered Canaan were not kings. And what happened according to their scriptures once God granted the Hebrews a king? Saul, their first king and allegedly chosen by God, suffered civil war and committed suicide after defeat by the Philistines. The next two, David and Solomon, did much good and lived into old age, but they also sinned mightily. David committed adultery with Bathsheba, the wife of his general, whom he arranged to have killed. Solomon built shrines to the gods of his many foreign wives. Subsequent kings quarreled; the tribes broke apart and were destroyed. What use were kings for the chosen people of God? They did just as much harm as good. Judaism absorbed the lesson that political states were not essential for faith. God made a covenant with the people of Israel, not the kings of Israel.

Thus originated the Western principle of the separation of church and state. This ideal certainly did not mean that the populace lacked religion. On the contrary, the Hebrew people were religious (or not) independent of the status of their government. The emphasis on God's rule did incline them toward *theocracy*, the idea that religion ruled a society through its officials and ministers. Such tendencies, though, never lasted for long. While Hebrew priests played an essential role in ritual and the maintenance of religious laws, the Hebrews insisted on having secular rulers. This practice differed from Mesopotamian kings who claimed divine powers or Egyptian pharaohs who asserted themselves as gods incarnate. When those states fell, so did their religions. No one today reveres Ishtar or Osiris. For most of history, however, the Hebrews, the Jews, have done without any state at all. They and their religion survived. God does not care about what constitution a kingdom has, they believed, but how faithful his people are.

Even with God and the prophets to follow, it was difficult for the Hebrews to maintain their distinctive faith with so many nature-worshipping polytheists around and among them. They had little tolerance for the ways of their neighbors, whom the Hebrews feared would seduce them into idolatry and demon worship. The polytheist fertility rituals and sex imitation of the gods were tempting. Kings like David or Solomon built up huge treasuries and married many wives. The queens from foreign peoples often lured their royal spouses into allowing the worship of other deities in Israel. The scriptures paint Jezebel as one of the worst queens, since she talked her husband, King Ahab of Israel, into promoting her Canaanite fertility god, Baal. The scriptures say that she died a miserable death, tossed out a window by her own eunuchs, trampled by horses, and most of her corpse eaten by dogs. These stories warned political leaders of the dangers of sin despite their royal power.

The Hebrews' failure to have a powerful kingdom like other peoples did not doom them. Their life under the Persian Empire was tolerable. The local governor often gave way to the leadership of priests in local affairs. When the Persian Empire fell in 330 BC to Alexander (see the next chapter), Greek kings based in Egypt or Syria ruled the Jews for several centuries, often allowing them substantial autonomy.

That conquest by the Greeks began the last great turning point of Jewish history: the **Diaspora** (dispersion or scattering). Some Jews were dragged out of Palestine as soldiers or slaves. Others, encouraged by cosmopolitan freedom under other Greek rulers, left their chosen home for distant lands to live among other peoples. Within an international cultural and political system dominated by Greeks, many Jews found it easy to emigrate from Palestine and settle in enclaves in distant cosmopolitan cities throughout the Mediterranean and Middle East, even as far as India.

Jews who remained in Judaea found one more brief moment to claim their own worldly kingdom. In 165 BC, a Hellenistic king desecrated the temple in Jerusalem in honor of his own Greek gods. In reaction, the Maccabee (or Hammer) family led a revolt, winning about a century of independence again for the Jews. Then, in the first century BC, Roman armies marched into the Middle East (see chapter 5). By 63 BC, the Romans had easily conquered the weak Jewish kingdom, although keeping order among the Jews proved much more difficult. A Jewish civil war became a rebellion against the empire, which led the Romans to destroy the temple in AD 70 (see figure 3.1) and intensify the Diaspora by forcefully ejecting most Jews from Palestine after AD 135. From that time until the twentieth century, most Jews lived outside of their ancient homeland and had no political autonomy of their own. They lived in small enclaves in the cities of the kingdoms and empires of other peoples.

The Jews lost their kings, their temple and its priests, and their agricultural base as they moved into foreign cities. Out of necessity, the Jews no longer were peasant farmers and instead became urban traders and merchants. Teachers trained in their scriptures, called **rabbis**, came to lead Jewish communities instead of priests or kings. Commentaries by thousands of rabbis were collected into the Talmud (both in Jerusalem and in Babylonia toward the end of the western Roman Empire), which helped Jews interpret their sacred scripture. The Diaspora and lack of central authority meant that Jews were often diverse in their interpretation of scripture and manner of living. Jews may have been monotheists, but they were not monolithic. And enough

Figure 3.1.   The Romans take plunder from the Jerusalem Temple (most notably the menorah) and commemorate their success in crushing the Jewish Rebellion, on the Arch of Titus in the forum in Rome.

tolerance in the Hellenistic and Roman cosmopolitan cities allowed the fragmented Jews to keep practicing their religion across the Mediterranean world.

Toleration went only so far, however. Most states have justified their existence through a divine connection; thus a different faith implied a lack of allegiance. Jews also remained a perpetual irritant for authorities who preferred conformity, because the Jews were so often capable of maintaining their distinct religion. Outsiders often resented the Jews' view of themselves as the universe's specially chosen people. That perspective could be interpreted as excluding all others from divine favor. As the Jews came under Roman rule, they annoyed their new overlords by refusing to make religious sacrifices to the Roman gods, especially the emperor. Fortunately, the Romans concluded, in their usual tolerant manner toward religion, that Judaism predated their own rituals. Abraham, Moses, and David had lived centuries before the founding of Rome. So the Romans exempted the Jews from worship of the gods by special license.

Despite this sympathy for differences, Jewish cultural identity has continually provoked hostility in their neighbors. Our modern word for this hatred toward Jews is ***antisemitism***.[3] Through the centuries, the results of that hatred have ranged

---

3. The word *antisemitism* is highly contested. It was coined during the growing of racist ideology of the nineteenth century. It obscures the difference between Jews from other Semitic

from mere dislike for Jews as "different," to discrimination in jobs and housing, to violent persecution, and even to extermination. Had the Jews assimilated, given up any unique clothing, religious practices, and ways of speech or life, then antisemitism might have disappeared. But then Jews would have ceased to be Jews. Since many Jews have remained faithful to their concept of how to obey God, they have often faced difficulties with majorities who wanted them to conform or convert.

The Jews survived as a small but significant minority in the ancient world of the Middle East, Europe, and even deeper into South and East Asia. Compared with the rise of the other ancient empires, the political history of the Hebrew kingdoms mattered little. Ancient peoples likewise expressed little interest in the religion of Judaism compared with the other prevalent currents of faith and superstition in the ancient world. Nonetheless, the Jewish people have endured without a homeland as only a few peoples in world history have done. Also, out of their religion arose other beliefs that would shake the West and the world to their foundations. As residents in the cities of Europe, they would contribute from their culture to the growth of Western—or by another name, Judeo-Christian—civilization. Before those moments, however, two other Mediterranean peoples added their own groundwork to Western civilization.

Review: *How did the Jews maintain their cultural identity?*

Response:

SOURCES ON FAMILIES: DEUTERONOMY (CA. 625 BC)

The book of Deuteronomy (or Second Law) in the Torah (or Christian Old Testament in the Bible) presents directions for ritual practices along with rules for behavior. These rules for the Hebrews resembled those of other Middle Eastern civilizations, as presented in Hammurabi's Law Code. These particular selections from chapters 20–25 mostly focus on the relations of men and women, both within

people; it may also obscure the causes among hostility toward Judaism as a religion and Jews as an ethnic group. While some spell the word using a hyphen and a capital first *S*, the all-lowercase version seems now preferred. Scholars also question whether it is appropriate to apply the concept of antisemitism to the ancient world, or even medieval or early modern European history.

a marriage and without, in violence and in peace. Today's Jews and Christians have to choose how many of these laws to follow or ignore.

When thou goest forth to war against thine enemies, and the Lord thy God hath delivered them into thine hands, and thou hast taken them captive, And seest among the captives a beautiful woman, and hast a desire unto her, that thou wouldest have her to thy wife;

Then thou shalt bring her home to thine house, and she shall shave her head, and pare her nails; And she shall put the raiment of her captivity from off her, and shall remain in thine house, and bewail her father and her mother a full month: and after that thou shalt go in unto her, and be her husband, and she shall be thy wife. And it shall be, if thou have no delight in her, then thou shalt let her go whither she will; but thou shalt not sell her at all for money, thou shalt not make merchandise of her, because thou hast humbled her.

If a man have two wives, one beloved, and another hated, and they have born him children, both the beloved and the hated; and if the firstborn son be hers that was hated: Then it shall be, when he maketh his sons to inherit that which he hath, that he may not make the son of the beloved firstborn before the son of the hated, which is indeed the firstborn: But he shall acknowledge the son of the hated for the firstborn, by giving him a double portion of all that he hath: for he is the beginning of his strength; the right of the firstborn is his.

If a man have a stubborn and rebellious son, which will not obey the voice of his father, or the voice of his mother, and that, when they have chastened him, will not hearken unto them: Then shall his father and his mother lay hold on him, and bring him out unto the elders of his city, and unto the gate of his place; And they shall say unto the elders of his city, This our son is stubborn and rebellious, he will not obey our voice; he is a glutton, and a drunkard. And all the men of his city shall stone him with stones, that he die: so shalt thou put evil away from among you; and all Israel shall hear, and fear.

The woman shall not wear that which pertaineth unto a man, neither shall a man put on a woman's garment: for all that do so are abomination unto the Lord thy God.

If a man be found lying with a woman married to an husband, then they shall both of them die, both the man that lay with the woman, and the woman: so shalt thou put away evil from Israel.

If a damsel that is a virgin be betrothed unto an husband, and a man find her in the city, and lie with her; Then ye shall bring them both out unto the gate of that city, and ye shall stone them with stones that they die; the damsel, because she cried not, being in the city; and the man, because he hath humbled his neighbor's wife: so thou shalt put away evil from among you.

But if a man find a betrothed damsel in the field, and the man force her, and lie with her: then the man only that lay with her shall die. But unto the damsel thou shalt do nothing; there is in the damsel no sin worthy of death: for as when a man riseth against his neighbor, and slayeth him, even so is this matter: For he found her in the field, and the betrothed damsel cried, and there was none to save her.

If a man find a damsel that is a virgin, which is not betrothed, and lay hold on her, and lie with her, and they be found; Then the man that lay with her shall give unto the damsel's father fifty shekels of silver, and she shall be his wife; because he hath humbled her, he may not put her away all his days.

He that is wounded in the stones, or hath his privy member cut off, shall not enter into the congregation of the Lord.

A bastard shall not enter into the congregation of the Lord; even to his tenth generation shall he not enter into the congregation of the Lord.

When a man hath taken a wife, and married her, and it come to pass that she find no favor in his eyes, because he hath found some uncleanness in her: then let him write her a bill of divorcement, and give it in her hand, and send her out of his house. And when she is departed out of his house, she may go and be another man's wife. . . . Her former husband, which sent her away, may not take her again to be his wife, after that she is defiled; for that is abomination before the Lord: and thou shalt not cause the land to sin, which the Lord thy God giveth thee for an inheritance.

When a man hath taken a new wife, he shall not go out to war, neither shall he be charged with any business: but he shall be free at home one year, and shall cheer up his wife which he hath taken.

When men strive together one with another, and the wife of the one draweth near for to deliver her husband out of the hand of him that smiteth him, and putteth forth her hand, and taketh him by the secrets: Then thou shalt cut off her hand, thine eye shall not pity her.

Questions:

- *What euphemisms does the source use (such as for love, desire, sexual intercourse, genitals)?*
- *What opportunities for agency do women have?*
- *What role does "the Lord thy God" play in maintaining these laws?*

Responses:

Make your own timeline.

2000 BC   **AD 135**

Citation

Deuteronomy. The King James Bible (Authorized Version). 1611.

For more on this source, go to http://www.concisewesternciv.com/sources/sof3
.html.

CHAPTER 4

Trial of the Hellenes

The Ancient Greeks, 1200 BC to AD 146

While the ancient Hebrew kingdoms were oppressed on all sides by conquerors, another people, the **Greeks**, were able to prosper far away from the dangerous Middle East, at least at first. Then shortly after the Persian Empire restored the Jews to Palestine, it turned its wrath on the Greeks. The Greeks could have been utterly destroyed like the "lost tribes" of Israel or beaten into political impotence like the last Kingdom of Judaea. Instead, for a brief moment in history, the Greeks triumphed to dominate the Eastern Mediterranean and much of the Middle East. Yet a tragic flaw in their success drove the Greeks into political irrelevance. Nevertheless, the Greeks' cultural achievements made them the second founding people of Western civilization.

TO THE SEA

The Greeks called themselves Hellenes, the descendants of a legendary founder named Hellas. They first came together as a people sometime at the dawn of the Iron Age around 1200 BC, when so many other civilizations suffered crises. Two of those civilized peoples, the Mycenaeans (who had lived at the southern tip of the Balkan Peninsula) and the Minoans (who had been centered on the nearby island of Crete) rose and fell, surviving only through myths and stories of the Trojan War (for the former) and the Minotaur of the labyrinth (for the latter). These were the Greek "Dark Ages," so called because we know so little about what happened then, since records are sparse. Yet from about 1200 to 800 BC the first Hellenes invaded and took over the southern Balkans, displacing, intermarrying, and blending with the surviving indigenous people to become the Greeks. They themselves distinguished three main ethnicities: Dorians, Ionians, and Aeolians.

Although the Greeks remained loosely connected through their language and culture, geography inclined them toward political fractiousness. Greece's sparse landscape seemed inadequate for civilized agriculture compared with the vast fertile plains of the Nile and Mesopotamian river valleys. The southern end of the Balkan Peninsula and the neighboring islands in the Aegean Sea were mountainous and rugged, with only a few regions suitable for grain farming. Grapevines and olive trees, though, grew well there and provided useful produce of wine and oil for export. Also, numerous inlets and bays where the mountains slouched into the sea provided excellent harbors. Therefore, the Greeks became seafarers, prospering less by farming and more by commerce, buying and selling, as they exchanged what they had for what they needed. And if a little piracy was necessary now and then, they did not mind that either.

The Greeks were so successful that by 800 BC the southern Balkan Peninsula and the Aegean islands had become too crowded. In the Greek homeland, the Greeks lived without a king, divided into separate, independent city-states, each one called a *polis* (in the singular; *poleis* in the plural). Elsewhere, though, good farmland lay available for those who could take it. So the Greeks seized upon the form of conquest called colonialism, just as the Phoenicians had done before them. Greek colonization differed from the imperialism imposed by Assyria or Persia, both in scale and purpose. Greek colonies followed from small invasions, which did not bring in royal or imperial domination. In forming colonies, a crowded city-state would encourage groups of families, as many as two hundred men and their dependents, to emigrate. The Hellenes sailed across seas rather than crossing plains or rivers to conquer neighboring lands. There, on some other island or distant shore with a good harbor and a hill to build a fort, the emigrants would found a new city-state. Many indigenous peoples were killed, assimilated, enslaved, or driven away to live in the areas between Greek territories. The Hellenes lacked a common king or emperor as most other peoples had. Instead, the Greeks fostered political diversity. The new colonies remained only loosely connected to their founding state. They became free *poleis*, responsible to no higher political authority.

Most of these independent new colonies succeeded. The Greeks occupied all the islands of the Aegean Sea, where they still live today. More Greek populations migrated to western Asia Minor (called Ionia), along the shores of the Black Sea, and all around the Mediterranean, often near Phoenician colonies. Greek settlements survived for many centuries, although people of Greek ethnicity no longer live in those places today (see chapter 14). By 500 BC, more Greeks were actually living in the region of southern Italy and Sicily called Magna Græcia (or Greater Greece) than in the old Greek homeland. The colonies promoted trade networks and encouraged innovation and invention as the Greeks built new homes and thrived in strange lands.

The Greeks, in fact, succeeded beyond anyone's imagining except, perhaps, their own. The Hellenes had a supreme confidence in their own superiority. They called all non-Greeks *barbarians*, a word derived from what the Greeks thought these foreigners were speaking, namely babbled nonsense. In the Western Mediterranean, the Greeks were often more technologically advanced and sophisticated than natives who lived to their north, such as the Celts. The Greeks also labeled as barbarians peoples like the Egyptians or Babylonians, who had brought forth great civilizations millennia before the Greeks existed and were still wealthy and mighty compared with the few and scattered Hellenes. Such distinctions were of no importance to the Greeks. They felt themselves to be the only truly civilized people.

Some Greek attitudes seemed rather strange to their neighbors at the time. For one, romantic and sexual relationships between men were more common and accepted in Greece than elsewhere. With limited evidence from pottery, philosophical writings, poetry, and some court cases, historians do not fully understand these relationships. On the one hand, it seems that often a male prepubescent was initiated into adulthood through a liaison with an older man. These relationships were not like modern homosexuality and might not necessarily have had a physical sexual dimension—Plato wanted them to follow his ideal of sexless "Platonic love." Warriors of the Sacred Band of Thebes or the Spartans seemed to have strong same-sex customs. On the other hand, some Greeks (even Plato in one dialogue) condemn same-sex relationships. Idealization of male beauty is reflected in the practice of Greek men exercising in gymnasia or competing in sports in the nude. The athletes in the famous **Olympic Games** ran, hurled, boxed, and wrestled bare naked for male spectators (although some young virgin girls were allowed to attend, partly to check out prospective husband material). Not only women, but also non-Greek men were excluded from competing in the Olympics. The Hellenes played out our modern Olympic ideal of bringing together all nations of the world in sports on a more restricted scale. Although famous through the ancient world, the Olympic Games expressed ***pan-hellenism***, the idea that Greeks were a special community. They used the competitions to bind together the different *poleis* (who were forbidden to make war while the games were in session). Barbarians (by which they meant all non-Greeks) were not welcome on the playing field.

The Greeks were also different from the non-Greeks they considered barbarians because for a time they resisted the trend toward empire that had become so characteristic of the Middle East. Instead, they mostly organized themselves into smaller, independent units. Each Greek held allegiance to his own *polis* before and above any allegiance to the Hellenes as a whole. This political particularism further intensified into the idea of personhood called ***individualism***. The heroic individual mattered more than the family, more than the city or its people. The great epic poem, Homer's *Iliad*, shows how Achilles and his many virtues, called *arête*, were hard to balance against the needs of the larger community. As the hero sulked in his tent, the Greeks were stalemated in their war against the Trojans. Because of the pride of Achilles, many died, including his best friend. Should readers admire Achilles or admonish him? In either case, Achilles earned praise for being the best warrior. In everything, from war to theater, the Greeks competed with one another. How the Greeks would deal with this feeling of superiority, exclusiveness, and individuality became their greatest trial.

Review: *How did the Greeks begin as a people and expand through the Mediterranean?*

Response:

THE POLITICAL ANIMAL

As the Greeks built their civilization, they entered a remarkable period of political experimentation. The word *polis* gives us our word *politics*. The Mesopotamian kings and emperors, Egyptian pharaohs, and Persian shahs lacked politics in our modern, Western sense. Their commands were to go unquestioned, endorsed by divine mandate. Only a few select elites, the aristocrats, had any part in the decision-making process that affected tens of thousands of subjects. In contrast, the Greeks originated ***democracy*** as a form of government. The Hellenic innovation of true politics broadened the decision making to include many people, which is what *democracy* literally means: rule by the people. More people participated in deciding who paid taxes and how much, whether to make war or preserve peace. Despite the difficulties and failures of the Greeks, their politics have continued to inspire us to this day.

The first step toward power for the people came in rejecting the most common political institution of the ancient world: monarchy. Instead of allowing their kings to become gods like most other ancient peoples, the Greeks got rid of most of them. The Greeks did not, of course, cast off the gods themselves. They still believed their societies depended upon the favor of deities. At the heart of every city was an acropolis, "the high citadel," in which the people built their temples, held their most important religious ceremonies, and kept their treasures. Yet kings were no longer needed to play mediator, and neither were priests, at least as a special social group. When the Greeks got rid of royal dynasties, they also eliminated the ruling priestly caste. Instead, members of the community shared and alternated in the role of mediators and officiators in religious ceremonies.

Although the Greeks eliminated the political roles of the royal dynasties and priestly castes, the next step, of breaking the power of the wealthy and well-born families, was much more difficult. ***Aristocracy***, rule of the better born, replaced monarchy at first. Recall that a few well-connected families usually run things. Such happened also in ancient Hellas. The aristocrats supported their power through their wealth in land, control of commerce, and monopoly of leadership in war. The expensive bronze armor and weaponry of the aristocratic warrior, such as Achilles had wielded in myth, made the aristocrats dominant on the battlefield, which in turn secured their monopoly in political counsels.

In the seventh century BC, politics changed when new military technology and tactics created new kinds of warriors. The rough terrain of the southern Balkans was unsuitable for cavalry, and so foot soldiers became the most important warriors. Then the growing use of iron allowed for new weapons, as it had for the Assyrians. As trade increased and iron metals became more accessible, a new type of Greek warrior appeared: the **hoplite**. The hoplite was lightly protected by a helmet and a large round shield and armed with a long spear and a short sword.

The key to the hoplite's success on the battlefield was fighting in coordination with other hoplites in a **phalanx**. Each phalanx consisted of about four hundred men standing in lines eight ranks deep; each man defended himself with his helmet and large shield that covered both part of himself and his neighbor. To attack, soldiers wielded nine-foot-long spears as they ran together to smash the enemy. The battle often turned into a shoving match, each side pushing until the other started to give way from exhaustion, fear, or the loss of hoplites to wounds. If spears were useless in close combat, then soldiers swung short chopping swords.

At the same time, they perfected a new warship for the all-important battles at sea: the trireme. While triremes did have sails, banks of rowers called *thetes* provided the essential means of propulsion. A large ram on the prow could crash into an enemy ship, aiming to sink it. If that was unsuccessful, armed *thetes* would board the enemy ship and fight hand to hand to seize it. Navies organized ships to fight in groups, like a phalanx at sea.

These two innovations, hoplite and trireme, broke the dominance of the aristocracy in combat and lost them their political monopoly. Repeatedly in history, innovations in military methods have forced changes in political structures. In ancient Greece, a simple peasant could afford the few weapons of a hoplite and then spend several weeks training to march in formation and kill. Anyone with a strong back and limbs could be a *thete*. Once the peasants and merchants realized that they were putting their lives on the line for their "country," they demanded a share of the power and wealth controlled by the aristocrats. Many peasants called for **land reform**, taking away some land from those who had inherited a great deal and giving it to those who had little. Peasants have called for this redistribution regularly throughout the history of our civilization. Getting the great landowners to surrender power, however, has been more difficult.

The struggle for dominance in Greek city-states reflected the eternal tension between politics and violence. Ideally, politics should mean that people peacefully make a decision after civil discussion. The Greek aristocrats personified warriors of privilege, who believed that their dominance had been granted by the gods. They resisted any land reform, correctly perceiving it as not in their own best interest. The Greek peasants, in turn, were equally determined to gain their version of justice and fought back. Thus, rebellion and strife have been political tools just as often as laws and votes. The Greeks labeled a situation when all political discourse had broken down into riot as anarchy (from the Greek word for a society without the archons, the appointed administrators). After a struggle, a winning group reasserted the rule of law and order as the winners interpreted it.

A few members of the aristocracy who sympathized with the plight of the peasants assisted the commoners in the seventh and sixth centuries BC. These leaders seized power from their fellows and won the favor of the masses by pushing through reforms. These popular rulers have been given the name of **tyrants**. To accuse someone of *tyranny* nowadays implies ruthless rule for one's own gain, and indeed that did happen in Greece. More often, though, the tyrants ruled with harshness in order to break the power of their fellow aristocrats and grant rights to the peasants. Greek tyrants were rarely able to establish a dynasty and pass power to their descendants. Instead, the same people who had helped the tyrants subsequently overthrew them, believing, correctly, that they no longer needed the tyrants once the power of the aristocrats was broken. The mechanisms of political power had shifted.

After all this bloodshed and suffering, most Greeks settled on some form of democracy by 500 BC. Politically eligible citizens were expected to live up to their obligations. The ancient Athenians literally called someone who did not serve in public office or deliberate in civic affairs an "idiot." The Greek democracy nevertheless excluded many people from political decisions. The city-state restricted the political rights of **citizenship**, the concept that certain members of the polity have defined rights and responsibilities. First, resident "foreigners" could not participate. A foreigner was defined as anyone not descended from the founders of the particular *polis*, ethnic Greek or not. Second, adult women had no legitimate political role (as would continue to be true in the West until the twentieth century). Third, children were excluded, as they are today. Fourth, the large numbers of enslaved persons were, of course, excluded. Fifth, property requirements still kept many of the poor from participation. In sum, Greeks usually limited democracy to adult male citizens who held a defined amount of wealth, which varied from city to city. So the percentage of people actually engaged in democracy ranged from 30 percent down to only 3 percent of any city-state's population. Nevertheless, this percentage was a substantial improvement on the less than 1 percent of people involved in early Greek states or most Middle Eastern civilizations at the time. It also compares well with modern democracies, where sometimes only one-third of the population votes in elections. The Greek philosopher Aristotle may have called man "a political animal," but even he did not expect all people to participate.

These restrictions on voting in Greek *poleis* created the first tension within democracy, which leads to another basic principle:

Democracy is difficult.

Throughout the history of democracy, people not only argued but also killed one another over political principle. Most people cannot easily give up power. Most people cannot peacefully accept that others with whom they disagree should have power over them. Most people cannot resist the temptation to enrich themselves through political office rather than work to improve the community as a whole. Despite these sad realities, sometimes people have accepted the rules of democracy and created real and just democratic governments. A truly functional democracy requires the rule of law and at least two different ideological positions that can both legitimately disagree and compromise with the other. Rules require that political process, not violent power, should guide change.

The Hellenes developed two basic political directions that are still with us today, what they called democracy and *oligarchy*. The word *democracy* had a double meaning. First, it meant the general political principle of the direct rule by the people, under laws, and through argument and compromise as well as the factions. Second, factions of citizens in Greek *poleis* that included the adult males of the lower classes called their policy democracy. In contrast, oligarchy limited rule to a few, usually the old aristocrats and the newly wealthy. Also, oligarchs leaned toward the past tradition (often mythologized), while democrats inclined toward the unknown future (always idealized). While oligarchs and democrats competed for political support in most city-states, two *poleis* exemplified each political ideal: **Sparta** and **Athens**. Both were more democratic in a general way than other empires and kingdoms of the ancient world. Both also adopted different political structures.

The oligarchic Spartans called themselves Laconians, which has given us the expression "speaking laconically"—using few words to convey great meaning. Their city-state was unique among the Greeks because it founded almost no overseas colonies. Instead, the Spartans conquered their neighboring Greeks in the Peloponnesus, the hand-shaped peninsula at the southern tip of the Balkans. Most of those conquered Greeks became helots, subjects who held no political rights and had to surrender half of their agricultural produce annually. The free citizens of Sparta themselves made up only a small subset, perhaps 3 percent of the total population, who ruled over all. Since the unfree helots retained their Greek inclination for fierce independence, the Spartan citizens always feared revolt.

To prevent a successful slave rebellion, the Spartans therefore organized their entire state around militarism and ***egalitarianism***, claiming that these values were an ancient tradition. Egalitarian values meant that all citizens were considered rigorously equal. For example, the government divided up the agricultural plantations into relatively equal portions for each family. Money was made of large iron weights, which were too difficult to store, spend, or steal. Trade and artisanship in luxury goods was discouraged, since it would have increased the display of wealth. The common good (for the elite minority) was seen as better than the individual good.

More famous has been the Spartan commitment to militarism. The first priority of all male citizens was military service. Male children were taken away from their parents at the age of seven, and from then on they were raised in military barracks to train for the army. As part of their training, they were supposed to sneak and steal food from the local population. If an adult caught a boy stealing, he could beat the young one, sometimes so harshly that the boy died. At eighteen, a man who survived was allowed to marry. Even then, a husband ate meals in the warriors' mess until he was sixty. Even on the wedding night, the husband had to return to the barracks after consummation of the marriage. Women were esteemed if they produced male children. Spartan parents often exposed female babies to the elements to die because, as was common in the ancient world, they valued girls less than boys. Likewise, the Spartans also tossed into a chasm any male infant whom a group of elders deemed unlikely to mature into a proper warrior. The public interest in strong children overrode any parental rights or affections.

Sparta's oligarchic government nevertheless functioned democratically, at least for those few considered full-fledged citizens. No one person could be all powerful. At age thirty, men became citizens with full political rights. Two traditional kings ruled Sparta as a pair, but they were really figureheads—real power rested with appointed magistrates and a council of elders (about thirty of the leading citizens over age sixty). Generations of Spartans tried to maintain this system with as little change as possible because for them it embodied the virtues of the past and their founding father, Lykurgus. When a political crisis arose, those who promoted a policy always tried to claim, "It's what Lykurgus would have wanted!"

The democratic Athenians contrasted with the Spartans in many ways. Our concept of the civilization of ancient Greece is usually their direct democracy and classical culture. The Athenians emphasized individualism rather than Sparta's egalitarianism and militarism. Athenian society encouraged its citizens to excel in politics, business, art, literature, and philosophy, according to their talents. Athens's location on a broad fertile plain with easy access to the sea allowed its inhabitants a prosperous economy and a large population. From early on, Athens needed to resolve differences among three different constituencies: those of the city, those of the plain, and those of the hills. Each had different priorities and loyalties.

These divisions hindered the formation of a more democratic form of government until a series of tyrants began reforming the system. Draco, one of the first tyrants, became infamous for his set of laws issued in 621 BC. Many of the laws mandated the death penalty, even for minor crimes. Consequently, his name has become a byword for excessive harshness: *draconian*. A few years after 600 BC, the tyrant Solon solved so many problems that his name became a byword for political wisdom. To stop unrest, Solon divided the people into classes based on property, canceled farmers' debts outright, and expanded citizenship to the poor. Finally, by about 500 BC, Cleisthenes left Athens with a substantially democratic structure.

Cleisthenes's balanced constitutional system served Athens for most of the fifth century BC. First, Cleisthenes brought all citizens together into a political body called the Assembly. As the supreme legislative body, it included all male citizens over eighteen, about 10 percent of the population. Anyone was allowed to speak and vote, and a simple majority decided most issues. The Assembly declared war, made peace, spent tax money, chose magistrates, and judged capital crimes. Thus, every citizen was involved in making the most important state decisions. How was the citizen to make up his mind how to vote in the Assembly? Politicians became orators, speech makers striving to sway the crowd. If a politician became too powerful, the citizens could impose **ostracism**. Each citizen "voted" by writing a politician's name on a piece of broken pottery (*ostracon*), and the winner was sent into exile. To prevent such votes and hold on to power, politicians built up factions, groups of followers on whom they could rely. In Athens, as in most city-states, one faction tended toward democracy, the other toward oligarchy.

The Assembly met only periodically. Select citizens carried out the day-to-day administration of the city. Interestingly, the Athenians filled most administrative positions by lot: a chance name drawn from a barrel. They reserved actual voting within each tribe (*ethnos*, the word from which we get our *ethnicity*) for elections of generals (*strategoi*, the word from which we get our *strategy*). An advantage was that election ensured the generals had the support of their troops. They could hardly disobey someone they themselves had elected. A disadvantage was that soldiers did not always elect the best strategists or tacticians. Popular charisma is not always the best quality in battle. From the point of view of the city's leaders, though, dividing power among ten commanders prevented any one general from possessing too much military power.

Cleisthenes's second innovation aimed to end old feuds between people living in the three different geographic regions. The merchants of the city, the farmers of the plain, and the shepherds of the hills felt they had little in common with one another. Cleisthenes broke up loyalties by imposing new ties that were not based on blood, occupation, or social status. He divided each of the three regions (city, plain, and hills) into ten districts. One district from each of the three regions was then combined into a new "tribe," artificially forcing the divergent people of city, plain, and hills to work and fight together. These tribes determined both a citizen's role in the rotating administration and their units in military service. Finally, the ten tribes sent fifty representatives each to the Council of Five Hundred. This important body prepared bills for the Assembly, supervised the administration and magistrates, and negotiated with foreign powers.

The Athenian democratic idea, as we shall see in later chapters, would endure and continue to inspire change, even violent revolutionary change, up to the present day. Nevertheless, throughout most of Western history, cultural conservatives have attacked democracy and democratic tendencies. Indeed, most Hellenes themselves admired and claimed to prefer the oligarchic Spartans to the democratic Athenians. It seemed less messy to have a more authoritarian system of government. The chaotic debate and passions of the Athenian crowd seemed undignified compared with the stoic calm of Spartan deliberation. Either way, as both city-states entered confidently into Greece's **Classical Age** (ca. 500–338 BC), this whole argument was nearly lost to history (see timeline A). Just as these early experiments in self-government had begun, the most powerful empire of the age nearly wiped them out.

Review: How did the Greeks attain degrees of democratic politics?

Response:

METAMORPHOSIS

The Greeks almost vanished as a people because the shah of the vast and powerful Persian Empire decided to crush them. Instead, the Greeks metamorphosed (their word for transformed) into a political power to be reckoned with. The first stage of this transformation was their defeat of the Persian invasions. After that, however, they nearly defeated themselves. They regrouped under new leadership to invade and conquer the Persian Empire itself, only to become again a conquered people themselves.

As seen in the previous chapter, by 500 BC Persia's power covered most of Asia Minor, where many Greeks lived. Although the supreme rule of the shah satisfied most of his diverse subjects, the independent-minded Greeks chafed under the absolutist Persian yoke. The Greeks put the conflict in simple terms: freedom versus servitude. In 499 BC, many Greeks in Ionia rebelled against their Persian imperial masters and burned the city of Sardis, a provincial capital. The Persians simply saw arson and violent rebellion. In retaliation, Persian troops burned the Greek cities in Ionia and enslaved their residents. Then Emperor Darius found out that the rebels had received help from across the Aegean, from the Athenians and a few of their fellow Greeks. Obviously, these supporters of rebels should be smashed, so Darius invaded Greece. Thus began the **Persian Wars** (494–449 BC).

In 490 BC, the Persian forces landed about twenty-four miles east of Athens, near the village of Marathon. The story of a messenger who ran to the Spartans for aid soon grew into the myth of the heroic marathon runner who delivered his message with his dying breath. The distance from Athens to Marathon has given us the modern Olympic race, although the Greeks themselves never ran such a long distance in sport. Surprisingly, the Athenians did not actually need help from the militaristic Spartans. The Athenians and a few allied forces of hoplites managed to push the Persians back from the beaches into the sea, even though the enemy landing force was twice their number.

Ten years later, Darius's successor, Xerxes, decided to avenge his father's defeat, especially after the Greeks encouraged a revolt by Egyptians against Persian imperial rule. Xerxes amassed the largest army that had ever been assembled in the region, reportedly several hundred thousand troops from all corners of the diverse empire (including Greeks who had submitted to his authority). To avoid the dangers of a sea-to-land invasion, he built a bridge across the narrow straits of the Dardanelles that separated Europe from Asia. As the Persian army marched into Greece, most Greeks surrendered and begged for mercy.

Others, led by Athens and Sparta, resolved to fight. Athens had built a major fleet of triremes, financed by a recently discovered silver mine. The militaristic state of Sparta, of course, had the best hoplites, but a majority of its leaders refused to commit themselves to a common defense of Hellas. So out of a possible army of eight thousand, only a small force of three hundred Spartans, joined by several hundred hoplites from other city-states such as Thebes and Thespia, advanced to hold off the advancing Persian army in the narrow pass at Thermopylae (or Hot Gates). Mountains protected the Spartans' left flank, and the Athenian navy supported their right. After a few days of heroic resistance, some traitorous Greeks led Persian forces along a mountain path behind the Spartan line. The Persian army surrounded and slaughtered the Spartans. The outnumbered Athenian and allied navy, which had also fought well against the Persians, withdrew.

With the road now clear of opposing armies, all of Greece lay open to annihilation. The Persian army marched into Athens only to find it abandoned. Xerxes set fire to the city and waited for his fleet to bring essential support to his troops. Then, as the Persian fleet entered the straits of Salamis, the Athenian and allied Greek navy sprang a surprise attack. In the narrow strait, the Persian captains panicked. One Persian captain, Queen Artemisia of Halicarnassus, even attacked her Persian allies in order to retreat. Xerxes had to withdraw. He invaded again the next year, but the Greek phalanxes defeated his army at Plataea. Against all odds, puny Greeks had beaten the greatest empire in their world.

The Greeks portrayed their victory as liberty and civilized virtue over oppression and barbarian vice. We might, however, be skeptical about their labels. On their own side, Greek prosperity was based on owning slaves (or, in Sparta, helots). And on the other side, the Persians had maintained a relatively tolerant empire. They had allowed the Jews to resettle Palestine. They had created general prosperity and stable rule with which many of their subjects were satisfied. If the Persians had won, some sort of Western civilization still might have developed. Perhaps the Persians could have gone on to conquer the rest of Europe. Or maybe the Romans or Phoenicians could have stopped and reversed the Persian advance. In any case, the Greek triumph did not guarantee success for their versions of liberty and virtue. They would betray those values themselves.

Buoyed by victory for the moment, the Athenians entered their brief Golden Age, which lasted only fifty years, from 480 to 430, less than one lifetime. To commemorate their success, some Greeks invented a new literary genre: history. Two famous books frame that age: one describes the war that enabled the Golden Age, the other the war that ended it. Both are early examples of historical writing since they relate how human choices rather than divine intervention drove events. First, Herodotus of Halicarnassus wrote his *History*, a retelling of the Persian Wars. Herodotus developed the theme of Europeans versus Asians, the Hellenes against the barbarians, but carefully evaluated and balanced his sources. For this achievement he is considered the father of historical writing. Second, Thucydides wrote of the civil war fought by Greeks against Greeks, now known as *The Peloponnesian War*. Thucydides was an even better historian than Herodotus, insightfully examining events and evenhandedly assigning fault or merit to the historical players. He also reimagined dialogues and speeches made by leading and representative participants. Such dramatic invention is not like the methodological writing of modern historians, but it makes for great reading.

To some extent, the **Peloponnesian Wars** (460–404 BC) inevitably followed from Greek particularism. Each *polis* pursued its own aims, usually without regard for the greater good of all Greeks. At the heart of these differences was the contradiction between the ideologies of Athens and Sparta. Democratic Athens looked outward and reveled in culture. Oligarchic Sparta gazed inward and worked at discipline. Could two such different cultures coexist in the same civilization? At first, the necessity of the Persian threat demanded it. After the defeat of the Persians at the Battles of Salamis and Plataea, many Greek *poleis* remained together in an alliance dedicated to the final defeat of Persia and the liberation of the Ionian Greeks. This **Delian League** had its original headquarters and treasury on the Aegean island of Delos. All too soon, however, the Athenians manipulated the Delian League to support their increasing domination. In most of the key battles, the Athenians bore the brunt of the fighting because they had the largest war fleet. For them, this sacrifice fully justified their new supremacy among the Greeks. Athenian culture was enormously expensive and cost far more than what the city-state of Athens produced. Thus, the Athenians extracted tribute from the other *poleis* to pay for the navy and troops. The other states submitted to Athens because they, like most people, were willing to let others fight for them.

Soon Athens was a mere city-state no longer—it had become an empire uniting many Greeks. In 455 BC, the Athenians ceased all pretense about their own imperial ambitions and moved the league's treasury from Delos to Athens. Even after Persia officially made peace with the Greeks in 449 BC, the Athenians maintained their supremacy. When member *poleis* tried to withdraw from the Delian League, Athens took over their cities. If nonmember *poleis* threatened Athenian power and prosperity in any way, Athens attacked them (see Primary Source Project 4). Thus, Athens began to achieve political unity for the Greeks through oppression. In their own eyes, they were deservedly the leaders of the Hellenes. Not for the first time would a people practice democracy at home yet imperialism abroad.

The leader of Athens toward the end of this Golden Age was Perikles (b. ca. 490–d. 429 BC). Perikles rose to power as the head of the democratic faction, based on a reputation for honesty and skill in public speaking. He wanted to use the imperial wealth to subsidize the lower classes of Athens. For example, he arranged to pay jurors, thus enabling simple laborers to take time off from their jobs to hear cases. Those in the oligarchic faction of well-born gentlemen considered that their social inferiors were a worthless mob. The oligarchs even resented the building of the Long Walls to protect the city and its port. The expensive project may have protected the homes of vulgar commoners, but it left the oligarchs' fields outside the walls defenseless. The oligarchic faction tended to see Perikles as heading toward tyranny for himself. Since they could not attack Perikles directly, they tried to discredit him by bringing corruption charges against those close to him, such as his mistress Aspasia (a former *hetaira*, or high-class prostitute/courtesan) or Phidias, whose sculptures decorated the Parthenon. Both factions in Athens, though, generally supported Perikles when he proudly rebuilt the city after the Persian devastation with glorious marble temples paid for with the profits of empire.

Other Greeks opposed the Athenian supremacy. Sparta formed a rival Peloponnesian League, which saw Athenian expansionist policies as a threat to liberty as bad as that of the Persians. Corinth, though, began the First Peloponnesian War when it attacked Athens in 460 to stop its expansion. Spartans soon joined in. Neither side, however, fully committed itself to decisive victory because the Spartans were putting down revolts by helots and the Athenians were still fighting the Persians. The two sides signed a thirty-year truce in 445 BC. It lasted only half that long, as mutual hostility between the Spartan and Athenian alliances continued to grow worse. In 431, when some of the allied states began fighting one another, each side thought the situation serious enough to declare war. Each city-state was confident in the virtue of its vision and its arms.

These Peloponnesian Wars were the greatest tragedy for Greece. At first, neither side could effectively fight the other. The Spartans dominated land with their infantry, but they could not breach the high, long walls enveloping Athens. The Athenians ruled the waves with their navy, but they could not land enough infantry to defeat Sparta. And the defensive strategy of the Athenians backfired, when plague struck the crowded, besieged city in 430 BC. It killed Perikles by the next year, and no successor shared his qualities of statesmanship.

In arrogant bids for supremacy, both Athens and Sparta attacked neutral states, thereby forcing all Hellenes to choose sides. Each side basically told other Greeks, "You can have liberty, but only on our terms." In a famous example, the *polis* of Mytiline tried to secede from the Delian League after Athens had been weakened by the plague. In 427 BC, the recovered Athenians decided to punish the Mytilines by killing every male and selling the women and children into slavery. They had second thoughts, however, and killed only a thousand of Mytiline's men. Such political slaughters by winners on both sides piled upon the casualties from battle and disease. Class conflict also increased as Sparta supported oligarchic factions in various *poleis* and Athens encouraged democratic factions. Rather than solving their disagreements through political dialogue and voting, extremists took to violence, assault, rape, arson, and murder. So Greek political structures were attacked from both without and within.

A truce in 421 BC might have ended the war while the Greeks were still strong enough to recover. The Athenians, however, became addicted to power. Thucydides described the Athenian attack on the neutral island city-state of Melos in 416 BC. The Melians appealed to the Athenians to leave them in peace. The Athenians demanded surrender, excusing their supremacy with the harsh reality that stronger societies always dominated weaker societies. As promised, the Athenians defeated the Melian forces. Showing none of the mercy they had shown the Mytilines, the Athenians killed all the adult males on Melos and enslaved the women and children.

Even worse, the Athenians made a grave mistake by pushing their imperial ambitions too far in a poorly planned and unnecessary attack on Greek city-states in Sicily, part of Magna Græcia. Led by the young politician Alkibiades, a majority in the Assembly agreed to outflank the Spartans at sea by establishing power in Magna Græcia. They used the excuse of helping an allied *polis* that had complained of oppression by the great city-state Syracuse, the key to the Western Mediterranean. In 415 BC, the Athenians landed and found a well-prepared enemy and few allies. Instead of withdrawing or gaining a quick victory by assault, the Athenians tried to build a wall to cut off the Syracusans and starve them out. Meanwhile, the Syracusans built a counterwall to isolate the Athenians, who all too soon used up their supplies. For two years, the Athenians were bogged down in a faraway land until their best warriors were killed and thousands more cruelly enslaved to die digging in quarries. Athens lacked the resources to recover from this defeat. The ostracized Alkibiades fled first to Sparta and finally to Persia. Sparta itself finally counterattacked with its own new navy, built with the help of its old enemy and new ally, Persia. The Spartans cut off supplies to Athens by both sea and land, forcing the city to surrender in 404 BC.

Sadly, neither peace nor prosperity followed. Persia stoked the mutual suspicions of the Greeks against one another. Sparta began to act as imperialistically as Athens had. The city-states of Thebes and Corinth attacked their former ally Sparta. Then the Greek helot-slaves of Sparta successfully revolted. Without slave labor, the once-mighty Sparta declined into an obscure village of no account. Meanwhile,

Corinth and Thebes were each too weak to hold new empires of their own. Everywhere, **demagogues** (partisan public speakers) inflamed emotions and manipulated public opinion toward short-term thinking and *factionalism*, or opposing groups' refusal to cooperate with one another. Class warfare worsened. Thus, the Greek *polis* failed politically. Democracy proved too difficult.

A political solution to this chaos came from the north: old-fashioned kingship. The Kingdom of **Macedon** lay along the mountainous northern reaches of Greek civilization. The southerners had always disregarded the rustic Macedonians as insufficiently civilized compared to true Greeks. The Macedonians did not live in cities, they spoke with poor accents, and they had been weak politically. That changed with King **Philip II** (r. 359–336 BC). As a youth, he had been held hostage in the *polis* of Thebes. While classical Greek culture impressed him, the politics of the *polis* did not. He returned to Macedon, reformed the administration of his kingdom, and strengthened his army along Greek lines. He also added cavalry to defend the sides and rear of a more flexible Macedonian phalanx and improved siege machinery to take city walls. Armed with these advantages, Philip began his conquest of Greece, taking city-state after city-state. At the Battle of Chaeronea in 338 BC, Philip's army crushed the last Greek resistance to his rule on the mainland. He was now *hegemon*, captain-general-ruler of the Greek world (from which we get the word *hegemony* for political supremacy). The **Hellenistic Age** (338–146 BC) supplanted the Classical Age of Greece (see map 4.1).

Philip was assassinated at the height of power.[1] The new twenty-year-old King **Alexander** III (r. 336–323 BC) soon gained the title "the Great" for his conquest of much of the known world. As one of the greatest generals who ever lived, Alexander carried out his father's proposal to attack the age-old enemy, Persia. His Macedonian and Greek armies routed the Persian forces in Asia Minor, liberated Egypt from Persian imperial power to put it under his own, and then swept through Mesopotamia to take Iran itself. So awed were people, and he himself, by his success that *deification* began, the belief that a person became a god. Alexander did not discourage the trend and may have believed in his divinity himself.

Whether Alexander "the Great" was god, emperor, general, or fool, his soldiers followed him farther eastward into the foothills of Afghanistan and into the Indus River valley. Only the fierce resistance by the vast populations of the Indian subcontinent finally allowed his soldiers to convince the not quite thirty-three-year-old Alexander to turn home toward Greece. On the way back, after a night of heavy drinking, Alexander fell into a fever. A few days later, whether from too much alcohol, infection, or poison, the conqueror lay dead.

---

1. It might be argued that he was murdered rather than assassinated for political reasons. His killer, Pausanias, had been a lover of Philip but then had been gang-raped by Philip's allies, a crime about which the king did nothing. Some conspiracy theorists then and today suggest also that Philip's wife Olympia and his son Alexander were participants in the conspiracy since Philip's new wife and son threatened their position. The official excuse given to the public cited Persian and foreign intervention.

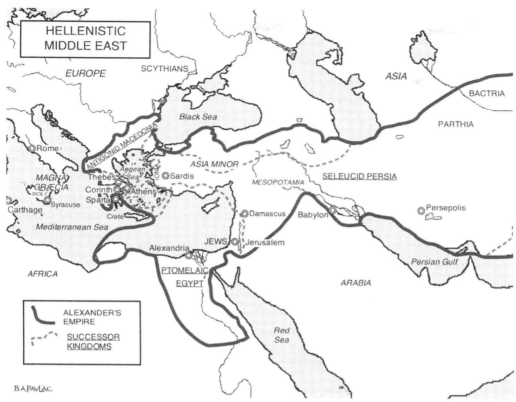

Map 4.1. Hellenistic Middle East.
Why did Alexander expand his empire in only certain directions?

Review: *How did the Greeks enter a brief Golden Age, and how did it collapse?*

Response:

PRIMARY SOURCE PROJECT 4: ATHENIANS VERSUS MELIANS ABOUT THE RULES OF WAR

The Peloponnesian War between Sparta and Athens opposed the idea of liberty against the idea of power. In 416 BC Athenian forces attacked the neutral city-state of Melos, afraid it would ally with Sparta. The historian Thucydides reconstructed the so-called Melian Dialogue between representatives of each side: the

Athenians suggest the city surrender while the Melians ask to be left alone. In the end, the Athenians conquered the city, killed its men, and enslaved its women and children.

Source: *The Peloponnesian War* by Thucydides (ca. 400 BC)

Athenians: And we will now endeavor to show that we have come in the interests of our empire, and that in what we are about to say we are only seeking the preservation of your city. For we want to make you ours with the least trouble to ourselves, and it is for the interests of us both that you should not be destroyed.

Melians: It may be your interest to be our masters, but how can it be ours to be your slaves?

Athenians: To you the gain will be that by submission you will avert the worst; and we shall be all the richer for your preservation.

Melians: But must we be your enemies? Will you not receive us as friends if we are neutral and remain at peace with you?

Athenians: No, your enmity is not half so mischievous to us as your friendship; for the one is in the eyes of our subjects an argument of our power, the other of our weakness.

Melians: But are your subjects really unable to distinguish between states in which you have no concern, and those which are chiefly your own colonies, and in some cases have revolted and been subdued by you?

Athenians: Why, they do not doubt that both of them have a good deal to say for themselves on the score of justice, but they think states like yours are left free because they are able to defend themselves, and that we do not attack them because we dare not. So that your subjection will give us an increase of security, as well as an extension of empire. For we are masters of the sea, and you who are islanders, and insignificant islanders too, must not be allowed to escape us. . . .

Melians: Surely then, if you and your subjects will brave all this risk, you to preserve your empire and [rebellious city-states] to be quit of it, how base and cowardly would it be in us, who retain our freedom, not to do and suffer anything rather than be your slaves?

Athenians: Not so, if you calmly reflect: for you are not fighting against equals to whom you cannot yield without disgrace, but you are deciding whether or not you shall resist an overwhelming force. The question is not one of honor but of prudence.

Melians: But we know that the fortune of war is sometimes impartial, and not always on the side of numbers. If we yield now, all is over; but if we fight, there is yet a hope that we may stand upright.

Athenians: Hope is a good comforter in the hour of danger, and when men have something else to depend upon, although hurtful, she is not ruinous. . . .

Melians: We know only too well how hard the struggle must be against your power, and against fortune, if she does not mean to be impartial. Nevertheless we do not despair of fortune; for we hope to stand as high as you in the favor of heaven, because we are righteous, and you against whom we contend are unrighteous. . . .

Athenians: As for the Gods, we expect to have quite as much of their favor as you: for we are not doing or claiming anything which goes beyond common opinion about divine or men's desires about human things. For of the Gods we believe, and of men we know, that by a law of their nature wherever they can rule they will. This law was not made by us, and we are not the first who have acted upon it; we did but inherit it, and shall bequeath it to all time, and, we know that you and all mankind, if you were as strong as we are, would do as we do. . . .

[Y]ou are showing a great want of sense. For surely you cannot dream of flying to that false sense of honor which has been the ruin of so many when danger and dishonor were staring them in the face. Many men with their eyes still open to the consequences have found the word "honor" too much for them, and have suffered a mere name to lure them on, until it has drawn down upon them real and irretrievable calamities; through their own folly they have incurred a worse dishonor than fortune would have inflicted upon them. If you are wise you will not run this risk.

You ought to see that there can be no disgrace in yielding to a great city which invites you to become her ally on reasonable terms, keeping your own land, and merely paying tribute; and that you will certainly gain no honor if, having to choose between two alternatives, safety and war, you obstinately prefer the worse. To maintain our rights against equals, to be politic with superiors, and to be moderate towards inferiors is the path of safety. Reflect once more when we have withdrawn, and say to yourselves over and over again that you are deliberating about your one and only country, which may be saved or may be destroyed by a single decision.

The Athenians left the conference: the Melians, after consulting among themselves, resolved to persevere in their refusal, and made answer as follows:

"Men of Athens, our resolution is unchanged. We will not in a moment surrender that liberty which our city, founded seven hundred years ago, still enjoys. We will trust to the good fortune which, by the favor of the Gods, has hitherto preserved us, and for human help to the Spartans, and endeavor to save ourselves. We are ready, however, to be your friends, and the enemies neither of you nor of the Spartans, and we ask you to leave our country when you have made such a peace as may appear to be in the interest of both parties."

Questions:

- *What choices are open to each side of the dialogue?*
- *How does each side define its ultimate goal?*
- *What are the principles or beliefs that are common to both sides, even if interpreted differently?*

Response:

Citation

Thucydides. *Thucydides Translated into English*. Translated by B. Jowett. 2 vols. Oxford: Clarendon, 1881, book 5, chaps. 85–113; vol. 2, pp. 398–406.

For more on this source, go to http://www.concisewesternciv.com/sources/psc4 .html.

THE CULTURAL CONQUEST

Opinions about the rise of Macedonian power stir controversy. Critics of Philip and Alexander condemn their use of conquest, destruction of democracy, and overemphasis on the cult of personality. Supporters praise their heroism, reform of government, and unification of Greeks among themselves and with other peoples. Alexander even encouraged his Greek soldiers to marry Persian women. Regardless, Philip and Alexander's brief reigns changed history for the Greeks and all their neighbors. The Hellenistic Age saw Greek power reach diverse peoples across the ancient world. The great cultures of Egypt, Mesopotamia, and Persia briefly collapsed before the armies of Alexander.

Although the political unity of Alexander's empire died with him, the Greeks stayed on as regional rulers. They founded new *poleis* and colonies of Greeks throughout their kingdoms. Greek became the common language, and Greek practices dominated economics, society, and the arts. The conquered peoples adapted to Greek civilization in a process called **hellenization**. Eventually, being Greek became a cultural attitude, not solely a physical descent from their forefather Hellas.

The classic political democracy, though, was not part of this expansion, since democracy lay in ruins. Ending the give-and-take of political debate, Alexander imposed absolutism, like other Middle Eastern semidivine potentates or "Oriental despots." Alexander's successors were generals who seized power and set up royal dynasties. As Hellenistic kings, they likewise employed deification with elaborate rituals emphasizing their similarity to the gods. In the constant tension between independent local control and centralized authority, the city-state vanished under the Hellenistic monarchs.

Alexander's fragile empire fell apart into three great power blocs. One general took Macedon and from there tried to impose Macedonian rule on the Greeks of the south. Another, Ptolemy, seized Egypt, whose rich farmlands and ancient heritage provided the most secure and long-lasting power base. A third, Seleucus, controlled the riches of Asia Minor and ancient Persia. The Macedonian, Ptolemaic, and Seleucid dynasties dominated the Western Mediterranean and Middle East for about two hundred years, until replaced yet again by other rulers (as told in chapter 5).

While the Hellenistic kingdoms failed to establish enduring political unity, they fostered a cultural success that endured for many more centuries. The Greeks lost political choices, but they gained a role in history that would have amazed even the most optimistic Athenian of the Golden Age. Greek culture became the standard for much of the ancient world, as well as the foundation of Western civilization.

Most of that culture reflected Athens and its Golden Age of fifty years after the Persian destruction of 480 BC. The Athenians rebuilt their ruined city in shining marble. The crowning achievement was the temple atop the acropolis, the Parthenon, dedicated to the city's namesake, Athena, the goddess of wisdom (see figure 4.1). It pleases the eye, perfectly proportioned and harmonious, while its design contains nary a perfectly straight line in the Euclidian sense. The Athenians decorated the Parthenon with the most anatomically correct sculptures done by anyone in the West up to that point (although they usually painted the figures in garish colors that would strike us as strange and would horrify later art critics who had learned to admire the shimmering pallid blank white of marble).[2] The ***realism*** and ***naturalism***, mixed with a poised serenity, characterized the art of the Classical Age.

The effort spent on the temple of the Parthenon demonstrated again how religion was the heart of Greek society. The Greek myths and legends showed that the **Olympian gods** were uninspiring from a moral or spiritual sense. The gods followed ***anthropomorphism***; they not only looked like humans but also behaved like them, usually at their worst. For example, the ruler of the gods, Zeus, reigned as a petty tyrant with his thunderbolts. He was notorious for his many affairs with goddesses, mortal women, and even the occasional boy. Likewise, the beauty of Aphrodite, the goddess of love, usually ruined men's lives. The gods' quarrels with one another spilled over into human affairs, and they quickly avenged insults to their divinity. Their divine interference is best recounted in Homer's epic poems,

Figure 4.1. The remains of the Temple of the Olympian Zeus, with the Parthenon on the Acropolis of Athens looming beyond.

2. The Parthenon survived largely intact for almost two thousand years. In AD 1687, during a war between Venice and the Ottoman Empire, the Turks stored ammunition in the temple, and a direct hit blew off the roof. In the early 1800s the British Lord Elgin took to England many of Phidias's sculptures, which had been neglected by Turkish officials. The Greeks and the British continue to argue about returning the originals.

The Iliad and *The Odyssey*. The latter tells of a Greek king trying to return home after the Trojan War. Because he offends the gods while trying to survive, they throw many obstacles in his way: sirens, cyclopes, sorceresses, and even suitors for his faithful wife, Penelope. The legendary Trojan War itself had started because three goddesses fought over who was the most beautiful. Despite, or perhaps because of, this divinely trashy behavior, the Greek myths conveyed a rich and deeply textured heritage. How the human spirit rose above fate and the cruelty of the gods, not the gods themselves, inspires us even today.

The Greeks revered their gods and ancestors by forming restrictive cults that kept those who did not belong out of each *polis*. Indeed, they dedicated each city to a deity, whom they also believed to have sired or borne semidivine heroic founders. **Civic cults** structured the worship of the city's gods in particular and all gods (out of concern to neglect no divine power). The *polis* organized religious ceremonies as a political responsibility. As mentioned before, the Greeks had no priestly caste or class. Instead, every citizen accepted an obligation to ensure that the civic rites of appeasing and worshipping the gods were performed properly. Consulting the gods through **oracles** provided guidance for everyday activities and major political decisions. The city fathers brought the cultic practices into their own homes by tending sacred fires (of which the Olympic torch is an offshoot) and sharing sacred meals.

Some Classical Greeks soon turned away from the austere formality of civic cults and the lack of spirituality in the Greek pantheon. They instead embraced **mystery cults**, which were centered on rituals of fertility, death, and resurrection. We know little about the worship that focused on deities such as Demeter or Dionysius, since their followers kept most of their activities secret. The cults seemed to promise a conquest of death. Although the cults were popular privately, every citizen still upheld the civic rituals in public. All governing was performed in a religious context.

Even the religious cults, however, offered little in the way of a guide for the moral or ethical decisions that always have been at the heart of politics. For answers, the Greeks took one important step beyond religion with their invention of philosophy. The word *philosophy* is from the Greek for "love of wisdom." Philosophy began in the sixth century BC in Ionia, where some men began to wonder about the nature of the universe. Compared with modern scientific investigation (explained in chapter 10), the Greek theories about how the universe was based on air or water seem rather silly. But they were progress. Instead of relying on myth for explanation, these philosophers began to apply the human mind. The concept that the human mind can comprehend the natural world, *rationalism*, became a key component of Western civilization.

The philosophers who examined geometry or the composition of matter were soon joined by others who speculated about humans. By the fifth century, the so-called Sophists (wise men) had started to create ideas about moral behavior that are still with us today. They were itinerant teachers who, for a fee, educated Greeks about the ways of the world. Several distinct schools of thought competed for attention. *Skepticism* doubted knowing anything for certain. *Hedonism* pursued pleasure as the highest good. *Cynicism* abandoned all moral restraints to gain power over other people. Many Sophists seemed to offer methods for becoming wealthy without worrying about moral scruples. Against them, a trinity of Greek philosophers offered alternative views for human action.

First, **Socrates** (b. 469–d. 399 BC) argued against the materialism of the Sophists. As he strolled through the streets and plazas of Athens, Socrates constantly asked questions of his fellow citizens. Moreover, his questioning challenged his fellow men to learn about true values. Such is the Socratic method. Socrates claimed to hold no set of doctrines he wanted to teach; he only desired to seek the truth. Indeed, he said that he knew little at all. When the Delphic Oracle had answered someone's query as to who was the wisest man in Greece with the answer "Socrates," the philosopher was at first puzzled. Then he realized that his self-description ("the only thing I know is that I know nothing") explained the oracle. He concluded that genuine wisdom was self-knowledge. Therefore, Socrates advocated that every person should, according to the Delphic Oracle's motto, "know thyself."

Amid the conflict of the Peloponnesian Wars, the trial of the philosopher Socrates highlights the Greeks' failure to live up to high ideals. In 399 BC, as the Athenians tried to recover from their defeat by Sparta, a new democratic leadership charged the oligarchic Socrates with two crimes: blasphemy and corruption of the young. One day, a jury of five hundred citizens who had been chosen by lot heard the arguments, where plaintiffs and defendants represented themselves. Socrates defended himself of the first charge by openly mocking the nonsense of Greek mythology. How could someone believe in gods who did so many silly and cruel things to humans? He defended himself against the second charge by saying he only encouraged young people to become critical of their elders and society. Socrates gladly saw himself as an annoyance, a gadfly, provoking and reproaching the leaders of Athens. The jury found him guilty. Consequently, when he wryly suggested his own punishment be a state pension, they sentenced him to death. Obedient to the laws of his city, Socrates committed suicide by drinking hemlock, a slow-acting paralytic poison. This political trial illuminated how democracy failed to adapt to changing circumstances.

Second, Socrates's pupil **Plato** (b. 427–d. 347 BC) explored new philosophical directions. Since Plato wrote his philosophy in the form of dialogues conducted by his master Socrates, it is sometimes difficult to decide where Socrates's views end and Plato's begin. Still, Plato offered the doctrine of ideas, or *idealism*, as an answer for the nature of truth. In his famous allegory of the cave, Plato suggested that our reality is like people chained in a cave who can see only strange shadows and hear only odd noises. But if a person were to break free and climb out of the cave, though blinded by sunlight, he would confront the genuine reality. Actual forms in our world only poorly imitate real universal ideas. How could the person who sees truth then describe it to those still inside the cave, who do not share such an experience? Plato argued that the philosophers described ultimate reality.

Third, Plato's student **Aristotle** (b. 384–d. 322 BC) turned away from the more abstract metaphysics of his teacher to refocus on the natural world and people's place in it. Thus, he studied nature and wrote books on subjects from zoology to meteorology that would define scientific views for centuries (even if many were ill informed by our modern standards). Aristotle's rules of logic covered politics, literature, and ethics. He used *syllogisms*, called *dialectic logic*, where two pieces of known information are compared in order to reach a new knowledge. It was the most powerful intellectual tool of its day and indeed for long after. Finally, Aristotle promoted the "golden mean" of living a life of moderation.

Altogether, Socrates, Plato, Aristotle, and many other Greek philosophers helped to establish an idea called *humanism*. As this book will use it, *humanism* means that the world is understood as existing for humans. A phrase by the philosopher Protagoras, that "man is the measure of things," embodies the approach.[3] According to humanism, our experiences, perceptions, and practices are important and useful in dealing with life here and now. This belief has repeatedly offered an alternative to religious ideas emphasizing life after death.

One of the great humanistic triumphs of Greek culture was its literature. Many educated people knew the epic poems of *The Iliad* and *The Odyssey* by heart. Lyric poetry also was quite popular. Then, as today, lyric poems meant shorter, personal poetry about feelings. In Greece, all poetry was literally said, or sung, while someone played the lyre, a stringed instrument, or a flute. Many Greeks declared Sappho as one of the greatest lyric poets. Today, more people now know her name as standing for female same-sex love, *sapphism*; the alternate term *lesbianism* also is connected to Sappho, namely from the island where she had her school, Lesbos. As far as literary historians can tell, though, she loved both men and women. Christians offended by her sensuality later destroyed much of her poetry, so only a few fragments have come down to us.

When the Greeks combined literature and performance, they invented **theater** (see figure 4.2). Like politics, theater had a religious context in Greek culture. Recitation of ritual stories of the gods turned into festivals, where actors dramatized the poetry with voice, movement, music, and even special effects. The most famous of the last is the *deus ex machina* (Latin for "god from the machine"), where a tangled plot could be instantly resolved by divine intervention, an actor playing a god lowered onto the stage from above. The most popular and important plays were tragedies, where the protagonist of the story fails, often due to pride (in Greek, *hybris*). The most famous tragedy is *Oedipus Tyrannos* (*Clubfoot the Tyrant*, usually called *Oedipus Rex*). By trying to do what is right, the title character causes suffering. During the day on which the play takes place, Oedipus reviews his past. He has left his home of Corinth because he heard a prophecy that he would be responsible for the death of his parents. After killing the monstrous sphinx by answering her question, Oedipus has taken over nearby Thebes, whose ruler had recently been killed. In the course of the play Oedipus discovers that he was actually adopted, had killed his own father, and had married his mother. She hangs herself, and he blinds himself and goes into exile. No happy ending there.

Performances of several tragedies would be balanced by a comedy. Some Greek comedies were merely bawdy farces, but others rose to transcendent political satire.

---

3. And the Greeks (especially Aristotle) usually meant specifically "men," since, following the assertions of Aristotle, they considered women to be an inferior version of the idealized male person.

Figure 4.2.   The curved rows of a theater are carved into the hillside of Ephesus, today a ruin in Turkey. In the first century AD, a crowd gathered in the theater to accuse Paul of Tarsus and his Christian companions of blasphemy against the goddess Artemis.

For example, *Lysistrata* by Aristophanes, first performed during the Peloponnesian Wars, struck a blow at both male aggression and ego. The heroine of the title successfully organizes the women of two warring *poleis* to go on a sexual strike until their men stop fighting.

It often happens that enduring culture is produced during brutal war. As rival Greek kings too often fought over their shares of Alexander's empire, the ruling Greek elites fostered a new phase of creativity called Hellenistic civilization (338–146 BC). While critics often characterize Hellenistic culture as less glorious than Athens's Golden Age, elites spread that age's classic works while also fostering their own new products. The cities became cosmopolitan, growing vibrant with peoples from many diverse ethnic groups. Alexander founded several and named them after himself, such as the most successful Hellenistic city, Alexandria, located at the mouth of the Nile. Streets laid out on grids connected places of education and entertainment: schools, theaters, stadiums, and libraries. Commerce in the Eurasian-African trade networks supported luxuries. Sculpture conveyed more emotion and character than the cool calm of the Classical Age. Greek philosophers who studied nature gained enduring knowledge in astronomy, mechanics, and medicine.

The two most popular philosophies to come out of the Hellenistic period reflected pessimism about the future, however. **Epicureanism** sought to find the best way of life to avoid pain in a cruel world. Epicureans taught that the good life lay in withdrawal into a pleasant garden to discuss the meaning of life with friends. In contrast, **stoicism** called for action. Stoics accepted the world's cruelty but called on everyone to dutifully reduce conflict and promote the brotherhood of mankind (women not included, as usual). This duty should be pursued even if one failed, which was likely.

The Greeks ultimately failed in their politics because of fighting among themselves, not because of external enemies. They changed history because a few of their city-states managed to defeat the great empire of Persia. Their civil war allowed them to be taken over by Macedonians, who led them to briefly hold supreme power over masses of Asians and North Africans. The Greeks, however, were too few and too divided to permanently dominate these peoples. Although they contributed many high ideals, they betrayed them just as often. The Greek heritage of art, literature, and philosophy enriched the peoples of the ancient world, as it continues to do for many in the world today. Nevertheless, democracy fell to imperialism, imperial unity fell to particularism, and the intellectual honesty of Socrates fell to fear. The Greeks' cultural arrogance condemned them for a time to become marginalized instead of being the ongoing shapers of history. The next founders of Western civilization, the Romans, would soon conquer most of what Alexander had and add yet more to the foundations of the West.

Review: *What Greek culture expanded through the ancient West?*

Response:

SOURCES ON FAMILIES: PLATO, *THE REPUBLIC* (380 BC)

In The Republic, *the philosopher Plato relates a conversation proposing an ideal kind of society. Plato suggests that the utopian polis should be ruled by philosopher-kings who are aided by an elite group of "guardians." In this selection from Book V, Plato radically proposes that the guardians should have a unique kind of family, removing them from personal loyalties in order to concentrate on the good of the polis.*

Glaucon: What sort of community of women and children is this which is to prevail among our guardians? And how shall we manage the period between birth and education, which seems to require the greatest care? Tell us how these things will be. . . .

Socrates: For men born and educated like our citizens, the only way, in my opinion, of arriving at a right conclusion about the possession and use of women and children is to follow the path on which we originally started, when we said that the men were to be the guardians and watchdogs of the herd. . . . Let us further suppose the birth and education of our women to be subject to similar or nearly similar regulations; then we shall see whether the result accords with our design.

Glaucon: What do you mean?

Socrates: What I mean may be put into the form of a question, I said: Are dogs divided into hes and shes, or do they both share equally in hunting and in keeping watch and in the other duties of dogs? Or do we entrust to the males the entire and exclusive care of the flocks, while we leave the females at home, under the idea that the bearing and suckling their puppies is labor enough for them?

Glaucon: No, they share alike; the only difference between them is that the males are stronger and the females weaker.

Socrates: But can you use different animals for the same purpose, unless they are bred and fed in the same way?

Glaucon: You cannot.

Socrates: Then, if women are to have the same duties as men, they must have the same nurture and education?

Glaucon: Yes.

Socrates: . . . Then women must be taught music and gymnastic and also the art of war, which they must practice like the men?

Glaucon: That is the inference, I suppose.

Socrates: I should rather expect that several of our proposals, if they are carried out, being unusual, may appear ridiculous.

Glaucon: No doubt of it.

Socrates: Yes, and the most ridiculous thing of all will be the sight of women naked in the arena, exercising with the men, especially when they are no longer young; they certainly will not be a vision of beauty, any more than the enthusiastic old men who in spite of wrinkles and ugliness continue to frequent the gymnasia. . . .

[The male and female guardians] must live in common houses and meet at common meals, None of them will have anything specially his or her own; they will be together, and will be brought up together, and will associate at gymnastic exercises. And so they will be drawn by a necessity of their natures to have intercourse with each other—necessity is not too strong a word, I think? . . . And can there be anything better for the interests of the State than that the men and women of a State should be as good as possible? . . . Then let the wives of our guardians strip, for their virtue will be their robe, and let them share in the toils of war and the defense of their country; only in the distribution of labors the lighter are to be assigned to the women, who are the weaker natures, but in other respects their duties are to be the same. And as for the man who laughs at naked women exercising their bodies from the best of motives, in his laughter he is . . . ignorant of what he is laughing at. . . .

. . . The proper officers will take the offspring of the good parents to the pen or fold, and there they will deposit them with certain nurses who dwell in a separate quarter; but the offspring of the inferior, or of the better when they chance to be deformed, will be put away in some mysterious, unknown place, as they should be.

Glaucon: Yes, that must be done if the breed of the guardians is to be kept pure.

Socrates: They will provide for their nurture, and will bring the mothers to the fold when they are full of milk, taking the greatest possible care that no mother recognizes her own child; and other wet-nurses may be engaged if more are required. Care will also be taken that the process of suckling shall not be protracted too long; and the mothers will have no getting up at night or other trouble, but will hand over all this sort of thing to the nurses and attendants.

Both the community of property and the community of families, as I am saying, tend to make them more truly guardians; they will not tear the city in pieces by differing about "mine" and "not mine"; each man dragging any acquisition which he has made into a separate house of his own, where he has a separate wife and children and private pleasures and pains; but all will be affected as far as may be by the same pleasures and pains because they are all of one opinion about what is near and dear to them, and therefore they all tend towards a common end.

Questions:

- *What does Plato see as the differences between men and women?*
- *How are Plato's proposals different from Athenian or modern concepts of family?*
- *How much do Plato's proposals resemble Spartan society?*

Responses:

Make your own timeline.

1200 BC   **AD 146**

Citation

Plato. *The Republic of Plato*. Translated by B. Jowett. 3rd ed. Oxford, UK: Clarendon Press, 1888, pp. 141–59.

For more on this source, go to http://www.concisewesternciv.com/sources/sof4 .html.

CHAPTER 5

Imperium Romanum

The Romans, 753 BC to AD 300

While the Greeks quarreled themselves into fragmentation, another people, the Romans, were proving much more adept at power politics. The Romans forged the most important and enduring empire of the ancient world. This achievement is all the more impressive since Rome started out as just another small city-state. Roman success can perhaps be attributed to the Romans' tendency to be even more vicious and cruel than the Greeks, who, as seen in the preceding chapter, could be fairly nasty themselves. The Romans could be brutal, but nevertheless they were also surprisingly tolerant and inclusive. Their empire rose through military supremacy, cultural diversity, and political innovation (see map 5.1). The glory of the Imperium Romanum, the **Roman Empire**, still appeals to the historical imagination.

WORLD CONQUEST IN SELF-DEFENSE

At first, the city-state of **Rome** was small and surrounded by enemies. According to Rome's own mythological history, refugees from the destroyed city of Troy in Asia Minor had fled westward and eventually immigrated to the province of Latium, which was halfway down the western coast of the Italian Peninsula. It was there, according to the story, that a she-wolf raised two twin brothers, Romulus and Remus. As adults, they argued about the founding of a new city. In one version, in the year 753 BC, Romulus killed his brother Remus and named the new city after himself. Thus Rome was founded on fratricide. The Romans were proud of their violent inheritance; they themselves later became some of the best practitioners of state-sponsored violence in the history of the world.

Whatever truth may lie in the myth of Romulus, Rome's actual founders took advantage of a good location. The Tiber River provided easy navigation to the sea, yet the city was far enough inland to avoid regular raids by pirates. The city also lay along north-south land routes through central Italy. Hence, the founders had ready contact with nearby stronger societies and began to borrow from them liberally. The early Romans cobbled together a hodgepodge culture, learning much from the

Map 5.1.   Roman Europe.
What geographic factors limited the Empire's expansion?

Greeks who lived in the cities of Magna Græcia in southern Italy and Sicily. The Romans borrowed the Greek Olympian gods and goddesses, usually giving the deities new names better suited to the Romans' language of **Latin**. Another important influence on Roman culture were the neighbors to the north, the Etruscans (who have lent their name to Tuscany). For much of Rome's early history, the city itself was so weak that Etruscan kings ruled the Romans.

Roman myth supplied another violent story about winning freedom from the Etruscans. According to the legendary history, Sextus, the son of an Etruscan king, lusted after Lucretia, the wife of a Roman aristocrat. When the husband was away from home one day, Sextus demanded that Lucretia have sex with him. If she did not, he promised to kill both her and a male servant. He promised he would then put them in bed together and report that he had found and rightfully killed them for shameful adultery and violation of class distinctions. So Lucretia gave in to Sextus. When her husband and his companions returned home, Lucretia confessed what had happened before stabbing herself in the heart to remove her shame. The outraged Romans organized a rebellion and threw the Etruscans out of their city. Thus, rape and suicide inspired Roman political freedom.

This charming tale passed down through the generations probably has as little fact behind it as the tale of Romulus and Remus. For the Romans, though, this myth proudly showed once again how violence and honor were woven into their history. Moreover, historical and archaeological evidence indicates that around 500 BC the Romans had indeed won freedom from Etruscan domination.

What the Romans then did with their new freedom was something remarkable: they chose a democratic form of government. Technically, the Romans founded a **republic**, where citizens chose other citizens to represent them. So, like the Greeks, they had no kings. Unlike the Greeks, they did not require all citizens to hold public office. The most important government institution was the **Senate**, a council of elders who protected the unwritten constitution and were involved in all major decisions. Initially, the Senate had three hundred members who served for life and were supposed to embody the collective wisdom of the state. As the head of their city-state, the Romans elected two consuls as administrators. These two ran the city government, commanded the army, spent the money, and exercised judicial power. The two consuls held office at the same time, and each had veto power over the other. The consuls served only a year, with only two terms permitted for any individual in a lifetime. Many other magistrate positions (praetors, quaestors, censors, lictors) were similarly limited. Thus, the Senate and People of Rome (using the initials SPQR) began an elaborate system of **checks and balances**, where, according to their constitutional structure, no single individual or family could gain too much power.

Officially, all male citizens voted and could hold official government offices, while privately, a handful of families actually made the major decisions behind the scenes. Roman society was divided into two main groups: the aristocrats (a few dozen families called **patricians**) and the free-born peasants (called **plebians**). In the early centuries of the Roman Republic, patricians controlled all the political positions. Indeed, someone could hardly hold office without patrician wealth since government service was unpaid.

A key event that pushed these military changes was Rome's near destruction by the **Celts** (or **Gauls**). These peoples were migrating through primitive Europe from the sixth through the fourth centuries BC in search of a new homeland. Many eventually settled in what is now France and the British Isles, retaining their ethnic identity to the present in Brittany, Cornwall, Wales, and Scotland. In the course of their ancient travels, they stormed down the Italian Peninsula, plundering and laying waste. They attacked Rome itself in 390 BC, occupying and destroying much of the city. Only the last fortress on the Capitoline Hill managed to hold out, barely saved from a surprise attack by the honking of disturbed geese. The Romans then regrouped and drove off the Celts. This Celtic invasion wounded the Roman worldview. The Romans decided to make their nation so powerful that it would never be conquered again. For eight hundred years they succeeded in this goal—a good run for any empire.

The key military innovation that enabled such success was the Roman **legion**. The Romans improved upon the Greek phalanx, which they must have encountered in Magna Græcia. The legion used smaller, more maneuverable groups of men who marched in formation but threw their spears at the enemy. Then, in the clash of close combat, the legionaries stabbed their foes with their short swords. Supported by cavalry and siege weapons, the Romans replaced the Greeks as the best warriors of antiquity.

While the city-state used aggression against its neighbors, its own citizens sought more representative government where disagreements could be worked out peacefully. The aristocratic patricians became less essential on the battlefield. Since the plebians supplied most of the troops for the burgeoning empire, they wanted a larger say in government. Unlike the Greeks who went through the phase of violent tyranny, Roman plebians threatened to strike rather than fight. The aristocratic patricians, numerically incapable of defending Rome on their own, began to make concessions. Patricians created the political office of the **tribunes**, who protected the plebian citizens from aristocratic magistrates who unjustly intimidated the plebians. Tribunician authority was one of the broadest and most powerful in the state. Patricians soon allowed the plebians a major political body of their own: the Assembly of Tribes. By 287 BC, the assembly gained the power to make binding laws, declare war and peace, and elect judges. Patricians finally allowed wealthy plebians to become magistrates as well. Thus, more checks and balances perfected the ideal republican government of the Senate and People of Rome (SPQR) (see diagram 5.1).

Although the Romans developed republican government at home, they had to decide how to adapt politics to their subject peoples in what was becoming an

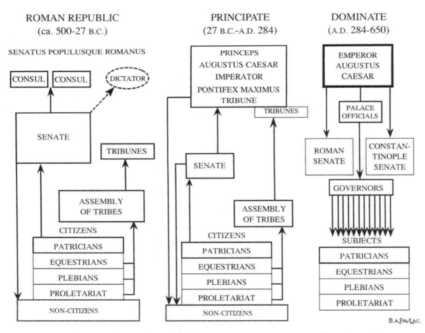

Diagram 5.1.   Three Phases of Roman Government. After throwing out the Etruscan kings, the Romans established the Roman Republic. Representatives of the people worked through various governing institutions, calling on a dictator only in case of emergency. Later, under the Principate, the emperor's power worked through surviving republican institutions. With the Dominate, the overwhelming power of the emperor reduced participatory citizens to obedient subjects.

empire. By 250 BC, the Roman legions took over most of Italy, including "foreign-ers" such as the Samnians, who were actually more native to the peninsula than the Romans were. The secret to Roman success was not pure military force but a good dose of inclusiveness, which had been so foreign to the Greeks. Resistance to Rome might mean annihilation, as happened to the Etruscans and others. Yet the Romans offered a ***romanization*** policy to many of the survivors in their new conquests. The vanquished were allowed to become more like Romans instead of beaten peo-ple. Locals had the option of keeping local government and even their traditional gods and religion. All they had to do was accept Roman control of foreign affairs, contribute taxes, and provide military service. While originally only Roman citizens held the political power of voting and holding important offices, their subject peo-ples slowly gained these privileges as well, especially as they intermarried with Roman families. Slowly, naturally, Roman culture took over as other peoples throughout the Italian Peninsula were romanized. Many diverse peoples gave up their own languages and adopted Latin, accepted the sensible Roman laws, wor-shipped the Roman deities, and even espoused Roman virtues like responsibility and seriousness. From these small beginnings Romans would come to rule most of western Europe.

The city-state of Rome became the model throughout what was its empire (in fact, if not yet in name). The center of Roman society was the city, even though most people lived and worked in the countryside as farmers. Where cities existed, the Romans transformed them; where cities did not exist, the Romans built them. Most of these cities were small, with only a few thousand inhabitants each. The heart of each city was the **forum**, a market surrounded by government buildings and temples. The public bathhouse was the most essential institution of civilized life—the Romans were clean people. Their public latrines fed into sewers and helped with hygiene (named from the Roman goddess Hygia). For entertainment they built theaters for plays, arenas for the brutal slaughter of beasts and gladiators, and, most popular of all, stadiums for the chariot races. Architectural innovations such as the arch and the dome, as well as the use of **concrete** as a construction material, allowed Roman cities to erect taller, more graceful, and more grand build-ings than many other cities in the ancient world. The dome of the Pantheon has inspired architects ever since (see figure 5.1). Aqueducts brought in fresh water from distant hills and springs (see figure 5.2). The Roman roads were so well designed that some, such as the Appian Way from Rome to Naples, are still being driven on today. While the roads were first meant to serve the military, commerce and civil communication naturally followed and flourished. Roman roads were so widespread that "all roads lead to Rome" became a byword for their civilization.

As the Romans marched along these roads, they carried their laws to other peoples. Roman law not only supported one of the most sophisticated governments of the ancient world but also influenced other legal systems for centuries to come. The founding point was around 450 BC, when the plebians insisted on a codifica-tion of laws, the Twelve Tables. Roman magistrates defined law for everyone's bene-fit. Clarity about the laws protected citizens against abusive government. Both the patrician and the plebian (through the tribunes) could appeal arbitrary enforce-ment of rules by a magistrate.

Figure 5.1. Light shining through the oculus of the dome of the Pantheon in Rome. Into this temple the Romans welcomed all the gods worshipped by people in the empire.

Figure 5.2. Roman civilization relied on clean, fresh water, here brought by a tall aqueduct into Segovia, now in modern Spain.

Roman law became a flexible system that recognized political change. Divine law, such as what Hammurabi or Moses received, could not be changed except by the gods. But the Romans began to invent the idea of **natural law**. This theory accepted that deities designed nature and humans to act in a certain way, but it proposed that human understanding of nature could change as we learn more. Through practice and experience, humans could create laws that were in better harmony with the natural order, consequently shaping a more just society. The Romans thought that if a law did not work, then a new one should be fashioned. Legal decisions and judgments were supposed to be founded on facts and rational argumentation, not divine intervention. As such, Roman law became the basis for many European legal systems today.

The Romans also established that all citizens should be treated equally by the law. Expanding rights of citizenship broke down the barriers between upper and lower classes, ethnic Romans, and others. Citizenship granted important status and political participation (although, of course, while women might be citizens and had some rights over property, the political system shut them out). To manage this growing and complicated system, the Romans also invented professional helpers in the law: lawyers. Roman lawyers had as bad a reputation in their own time as many lawyers have today. They were seen as greedy, loud, and annoying. Regardless, lawyers were essential to the smooth functioning of civil society. The Roman legal and political systems allowed people to have more of a voice and choice in politics than in most other societies in the ancient world. This republican government designed for a city-state, however, found itself strained as it expanded ever further. The romanization policy could not resolve increasing tensions within Rome's imperial rule.

Review: How did Rome grow from a small city-state to a vast multicultural empire?

Response:

THE PRICE OF POWER

Despite admirable legal innovation, civil society in Rome nearly collapsed in the third century BC because of the Roman addiction to world domination. Their military success fed the Romans' appetite for conquest. The next hill always hid some possible danger to Rome, and such a threat forever justified another expedition. Soon the Romans decided not to stop at the water's edge of the Italian Peninsula and set their eyes on Sicily. This target, however, led to a life-or-death crisis for Rome.

The Phoenicians had been competitors with the Greeks in forming colonies across the Mediterranean. Their major city of **Carthage**, located on the north coast of Africa across the sea from Sicily, controlled the central Mediterranean sea routes. Greek cities complaining of Phoenician oppression gave the Romans the opportunity to intervene, using the excuse of defending liberty. The Phoenicians opposed the Romans expanding onto the island of Sicily. The determined Romans began the **Punic Wars** (named after the Latin word for the Phoenicians), fought over several generations from 264 to 146 BC.

The most memorable stage of the Punic Wars was the invasion of Italy by the Carthaginian general **Hannibal**. In 218 BC, he marched his armies (including war elephants) from Carthaginian territories in the Iberian Peninsula (Hispania) over the Pyrenees and Alps to enter Italy from the north. This brilliant feat of military command and logistics astonished the Romans. Unfortunately for Carthage, Hannibal failed to seize his most important objective, Rome itself. He did rampage up and down the peninsula, causing great fear and considerable damage, but he was unable to inflict a fatal defeat on Rome. This delay in capturing Rome gave the Romans the chance to learn from Hannibal's strategy and tactics. The Romans also proved their organizational abilities by recovering from defeats in particular battles and raising new troops in a country under constant threat. They then counterattacked by invading Africa in 203. Hannibal returned to defend his own capital city of Carthage. The next year the Phoenicians and Romans fought at Zama. The Romans defeated the fearsome Phoenician elephants by frightening them with trumpets or letting them pass through the lines without opposition. The legions surrounded the rest of the Carthaginian army and forced Hannibal to surrender. Rome wielded undisputed mastery over the Western Mediterranean.

The Phoenicians, severely weakened by this defeat, offered no further threat to Roman expansion. Within only a few years, though, demagogues in Rome began to chant the slogan "*Carthago delenda est*" (Carthage must be destroyed). The Romans finally carried out that final devastation in 146 BC, tearing down the city and sowing the fields with salt with the intention that nothing would grow again. The Romans erased Phoenician civilization, its literature, and its culture from history.

In contrast, the Romans embraced Greek civilization. Also in 146 BC, the Romans destroyed Corinth, the last independent Greek city-state in the Balkans. Since the collapse of Alexander's empire, the Greeks had been fighting among one another. The Macedonian kingdom had continuously tried to dominate the Greeks in the southern tip of the Balkan Peninsula, but supremacy remained elusive. Some Greeks sought help against the Macedonians by inviting the Romans in as mediators, then as protectors. Soon the Romans stayed as rulers. Those Greeks who resisted were conquered and enslaved, of course, but the Romans by and large enjoyed Hellenistic civilization. And many Greeks accepted the Romans, who brought order and peace. With the fall of Corinth, Romans were well on their way to naming the entire Mediterranean as *Mare Nostrum* (Our Sea).

The Romans did not notice at first that their victories came at great cost, as imperialism so often does. How could the political institutions designed for a city-state manage a vast multiethnic empire? The weak spots in Rome's society worsened. One great flaw was the classic economic recipe for social disaster: the cliché of "the rich get richer while the poor get poorer." The vast and productive new provinces fell under the exploitation of the aristocrats of Rome. As these patricians profited from the distant lands, discontent spread abroad while envy arose at home. One of the great new sources of wealth was the enslavement of the defeated peoples, who were forced to work on large plantations (called *latifundia*). The plantation owners began to grow cash crops such as olives and wine, which outsold the produce of simple farmers. Before the Punic Wars, the farmer-plebians had been the backbone of Roman society and the army. Afterward, rich slave owners prospered from slave labor while free peasants lost their farms. These unemployed masses, forming the new social underclass of the **proletariat**, migrated to the cities, especially to Rome itself.

This mass urban migration shredded the social fabric of urban life. To keep the poor occupied, the patricians created an expensive welfare system known as "bread and circuses." They handed out grain (the bread) and provided entertainments (the circuses—meaning chariot races on which people gambled). Many other Romans increasingly complained that traditional values were vanishing. Some Romans blamed imported "Greek customs," such as fashion, legal and political procedures, sexual practices, or alleged hedonism. Meanwhile the Roman noble equestrian class (named after its members' ability to afford horses for cavalry service) had become well-off from the burgeoning trans-Mediterranean trade. They resented the aristocratic patricians who excluded equestrians from the true mechanisms of power.

By the late second century BC, these social tensions sparked civil wars that lasted for the next hundred years. In such times of emergency, Roman constitutional law provided for tough solutions. For example, the Senate might appoint a sole dictator who did not have to worry about another consul second-guessing his decisions during a six-month term. Or the Romans practiced **proscription** to remove overly powerful politicians. When a politician's name was posted on the *rostrum*, the speaking platform of the tribunes in the main forum, he was declared an outlaw. Anyone could kill him without penalty—a fate rather more harsh than the Athenian ostracism and exile. Meanwhile, the patricians divided into two factions. Those called *optimates* united to preserve oligarchy with as few social or economic reforms as possible. Those called *populares* advocated democracy, a broader political base, and land reform.

Two patrician brothers in the *populares* party, **Tiberius** and **Gaius Gracchus**, tried to help the plebians, as the tyrants had once done in Greece for the commoners. In doing so, the Gracchi brothers used extralegal violence to their advantage. In turn, the rival *optimates* led mobs to kill them both in 133 BC. Their deaths meant that the previous system of democratic politics, where checks and balances peacefully compensated for class differences, fell to fights over tyranny.

Violence soon became routine politics. A new permanent standing army only fueled bloodshed. Rome had risen to regional supremacy based on the idea of citizen-soldiers, peasants who would serve for set terms in an emergency. Late in the second century, imperial defense and the danger of slave revolts required an army of recruits who served their whole working lives. Many recruits came from newly conquered peoples who had not been fully converted to republican-style politics. This professionalization led to soldiers becoming more loyal to their commanders than to the idea of Rome. Soon, generals such as Marius and Sulla began to fight one another over the wealth and power of the empire, while soldiers and citizens paid with their lives. Dictators stayed in power for the long term instead of only during a crisis. Proscription became a regular practice to eliminate hundreds of enemies, rather than a rare tool to maintain a constitutional balance. The ability to intimidate and kill mattered more than the talent to persuade. The Roman Republic staggered from bloody crisis to crisis.

Review: How did Rome's conquests end in a long civil war?

Response:

THE ABSOLUTIST SOLUTION

Only the collapse of the democratic-republican government and the establishment of absolutism resolved Rome's political and social crises. One politician and general, **Julius Caesar** (b. 100–d. 44 BC), almost succeeded in restoring order. Caesar rose to prominence and popularity as a leader of the *populares*. In 62 BC he formed the First Triumvirate, a three-man coalition with two other powerful Romans, Pompey and Crassus. They briefly restored peace to the political system.

Caesar's ambition was to surpass his two partners, who had gained reputations as generals. Pompey already had a solid reputation, having conquered Hellenistic kingdoms in Asia Minor and the province of Judaea, thus bringing the homeland of the Jews into the growing Roman Empire. Crassus gained fame by crushing a dangerous slave revolt. Spartacus, a free man who had fought in Rome's army only to be enslaved to fight as a gladiator, led an army of rebel gladiators and other people freed from slavery in 73–71 BC. Yet they could not escape the empire determined to uphold the social order. Crassus defeated the slave army and crucified more than six thousand captured rebels along the Appian Way. Caesar sought to outdo his two colleagues by conquering the Celts in northern Gaul.

Since their near conquest of Rome in 390 BC, the Gauls had done little to harm the Romans. The Celts and Germans who lived in the Gaul of Caesar's time were civilized, were comparably prosperous, and even wore pants (while Roman men still wore skirts). They already interacted with the Græco-Roman Mediterranean culture, supplying agricultural products and slaves from prisoners captured in wars between the tribes. Several tribes had even agreed to defense treaties with Rome. When the Helvetii (ancestors of the modern Swiss) tried to move through a territory of a tribe allied with Rome, those Gauls asked for Roman help.

Caesar seized the opportunity to enhance his reputation by expanding Roman dominion (see map 5.1). For eight years, from 59 to 50 BC, Caesar exploited the fighting among different Celtic tribes to conquer Gaul (and even briefly to invade Britain). Although the integration of the Celtic Gauls into the Roman Empire would take several generations, Caesar wrote a book about his "successful" conquest, *The Gallic War*, to make sure people recognized his good leadership.

With his fame established, Caesar turned to his real aim: leadership in Rome. He declared his intentions of becoming sole dictator by leading his army from Gaul into Italy in 49 BC. His crossing of the river Rubicon (now a metaphor for an irrevocable decision) set him at war with his former allies and the Roman constitution itself. Inevitably, might made right. By 46 BC Caesar had defeated his rivals and become dictator. He built on his success by making an alliance with Egypt. He supported its queen, Cleopatra, who had been quarreling with her brother over sharing power. Caesar's sexual and political association with Cleopatra gave him control over Egypt, the breadbasket of the Mediterranean.

Like the better Greek tyrants, Julius Caesar did not rule solely to satisfy his own lust for power; he also addressed real issues. He carried out land reform, especially by rewarding his army veterans with confiscated property. He extended Roman citizenship to conquered peoples in Gaul and Hispania (the Iberian Peninsula), improved the administration, lowered taxes, and built public works such as aqueducts, baths, and temples. He even made sense out of the seasons through his reform of the calendar. Caesar's **Julian calendar** reform gave us the basic system that we use now.[1]

Caesar's enemies both envied his success and feared that he might make himself king. The Romans had disliked kingship ever since they had rebelled against Etruscan kings at the beginning of their republic. For some, a monarchy struck at the core of Roman identity. So a handful of senators plotted to assassinate Caesar. In 44 BC, during the ides (the middle of a month) of March, as Caesar entered the Senate's meeting place, they stabbed him twenty-three times.

---

1. The twelve months that we use now were set then, with February shortchanged because of a periodic leap day, which better accounted for the fraction of a day longer in an astronomical year than 365 days. They had not fully committed to a clear beginning of each new year, however. September through December were originally their seventh through tenth months, as their Latin translations indicate. And the Romans honored Julius by renaming the "fifth month" July. When they honored Caesar's nephew with August, poor February lost another day.

Yet this political murder still did not resolve the constitutional difficulty of governing Rome. Immediately, another war broke out over Caesar's legacy, about who could inherit his mantle. Rather than being hailed as heroes who liberated Rome from tyranny, Caesar's assassins became outlaws, quickly discredited and killed. Caesar's lieutenant, Marc Antony, first claimed succession.[2] But Marc Antony had fatefully taken up with Caesar's paramour Cleopatra. Many Romans disapproved of the queen of Egypt, who was too Greek and too female. To prevent civil war, he briefly formed the Second Triumvirate with the wealthy patrician Lepidus and with **Octavian**, Caesar's eighteen-year-old grandnephew and posthumously adopted heir. The arrangement did not last long. In the course of several years of warfare, Octavian grew into leadership until he had utterly destroyed all rivals, including Antony and Cleopatra. With this takeover, the last Hellenistic kingdom formed by Alexander's generals ended its independent rule. By 27 BC, Octavian ruled over an empire that came to symbolize Roman greatness. With the civil wars largely ended, the empire entered the period called the Pax Romana—a period of peace and prosperity maintained by Roman power.

Octavian replaced the Roman Republic's form of government with his own version of absolutism, which historians call the **Principate** (27 BC–AD 284) (see diagram 5.1). The new master of Rome was smart enough not to repeat his late uncle's mistakes. He vigorously professed modesty and a reluctance to assume power. Octavian claimed to restore the order and stability of the old republic and refused the title of king. Instead, he merely accepted the rank of "first citizen" or *princeps* (from which we derive our word *prince*, a powerful ruler, not only the son of a king). The republic's name lived on, since officially the Senate and People of Rome (SPQR) retained their traditional government roles.

Despite his humble platitudes, Octavian actually concentrated all power in his own hands. His actions reveal another basic principle:

> **Sometimes politicians do the exact opposite of what they say they are doing.**

He continued to collect titles and offices, such as consul, tribune, and even *pontifex maximus*, the head priest. To make sure he was not assassinated, he assembled a special group of soldiers to protect his person, the **Praetorian Guard**. The key to Octavian's power was the office of *imperator*, or commander of the armed forces (and from which we derive the word *emperor*). For the common people, Octavian continued the reforming trends begun by Julius Caesar and set standards of behavior and efficiency for the imperial ***bureaucracy*** (meaning rule by bureaus, cupboards with drawers to store documents and records). Even the census called by him was to promote efficient and fair taxation.

---

2. Marc Antony and his claim are linked forever with the speech that Shakespeare put in his mouth: "Friends, Romans, Countrymen, lend me your ears. I come to bury Caesar, not to praise him."

Senators authorized the changes that violated the old constitution. Octavian granted to many of them a large share of the empire's wealth, although retaining for himself a large share of the rule and profits of the overseas provinces. The senators called Octavian the father of the country and granted him the title **Augustus** (r. 31 BC–AD 14), or "honored one," by which he is often known today. Indeed, both his family name of Caesar and his honorific Augustus became synonyms for the word "emperor." Even more, he proclaimed the spirit of his "father" Julius Caesar to be elevated to godhood. As his heir, of course, Augustus shared in some of that divinity. Therefore, Augustus began the process of deification in Rome; the emperors became gods, as important for worship as the old mythological civic gods had been. The Romans thus imitated the "Oriental despots" of Persia, as Alexander had, harnessing godhood for political stability. And so Augustus became the first Roman emperor.

Augustus's system functioned well, but it possessed one great weakness: it was based on lies. Rome, of course, had been an empire for centuries, based on its rule of many different peoples. The republican labels survived, but the Principate concentrated government in Augustus's hands (see diagram 5.1). Officially, Augustus pretended not to be as powerful as a king or emperor, but everyone knew he was. Since there was officially and legally no emperor, the Romans lacked a formal process for succession. As a consequence, the emperor's death raised questions of legitimacy.

Members of Augustus's family, called the Julio-Claudian dynasty, used the lack of clarity to assume rule of the empire. Roman historians tell lurid tales of their imperial excesses. Augustus's first heir, Tiberius, almost lost control as he brooded in his sex den on the resort island of Capri while his lieutenant Sejanus gathered power. Just in time, Tiberius had Sejanus, his wife, and their young children bloodily executed. The next emperor, Caligula, was probably insane, believing that he had indeed become a god. Caligula named his horse to be a senator, raped senators' wives, and married his own sister before being murdered by his own Praetorian Guard. Caligula's older uncle Claudius survived to become emperor because until Caligula's death, everyone thought Claudius was a fool. Although Claudius ruled reasonably well, his third wife, Messalina, was a sex maniac, while his fourth, Agrippina, probably poisoned him. Agrippina's son, Nero, followed as emperor and soon had his helpful mother assassinated. He proclaimed himself the world's greatest actor and forced rich and poor to sit through his awful performances of singing and strumming a lyre.[3] He flamboyantly staged public orgies and capriciously executed many of his generals. After revolts in the provinces, the fed-up Senate ordered him to be stripped naked and flogged to death. Instead his servant helped him commit suicide with a knife in the throat. Just before, he lamented, "Thus perishes a great artist."

Since Nero's death in AD 68 meant that all male heirs in Augustus's dynasty had died, the Romans fought a brief civil war in AD 69, the year of four emperors. The

---

3. He is infamous for "fiddling" while a good part of the city of Rome burned, although he was probably innocent of that bad behavior. He certainly did not play a fiddle, since it had not yet been invented.

winner was the new dynasty of the Flavians, who started out well with Vespasian and his elder son Titus. Each ruled briefly, with sense and moderation. Then the younger son Domitian followed. He became increasingly paranoid and violent until his servants murdered him in AD 96. That Rome did not collapse into anarchy under so many cruel and capricious rulers was a testament to its own vitality and the success of the reforms made by Julius and Augustus Caesar.

The leaders who followed Domitian from AD 96 to 180 have become known as the Five Good Emperors. They secured Rome's everlasting glory. The great eighteenth-century historian of Rome, Edward Gibbon, credited the greatness of Rome to the wise and virtuous reigns of Nerva, Trajan, Hadrian, Antoninus Pius, and Marcus Aurelius. Trajan conquered and plundered a final major province for Rome, exterminating the people of Dacia north of the Danube River by the Black Sea (see figure 5.3). The Romans who replaced the Dacians laid the foundation of the modern Romanian language.

While Gibbon certainly exaggerated, this golden age of Rome has always been attractive to readers of history. Rome flourished by providing a structure for political peace while allowing substantial cultural freedom. The empire of this period stood for universalism—"all is Rome"—but the emperors did not crush particularism. People worshipped diverse gods and deities, wore their own ethnic fashions, and ate their exotic cuisine. The Roman urban culture, fostered by planting colonies

Figure 5.3.   Trajan's Column presents the victorious Romans holding up heads of the Dacians for their emperor.

of retired Latin soldiers, helped diverse peoples become romanized to various degrees. Previous cultures gradually and peacefully faded as everyone adopted Roman social ways and the responsibilities and benefits of citizenship. While some local ways of life dwindled away altogether, other regional and ethnic diversity remained. The Romans advocated Latin as a language, yet every educated Roman also spoke Greek. Many Greeks, who predominated in the eastern regions of the empire, barely bothered to learn Latin. The protections of Roman law increasingly covered non-Latins as citizens, until virtually everyone born free within the borders of the empire could claim the privilege of Roman citizenship (although it counted more for men than women). Even many enslaved persons had opportunities to win their freedom.

Outside the Roman Empire's borders, though, lived many peoples who did not share in its riches and looked on in envy. The Romans had tried to conquer the world in self-defense, but they had not succeeded. Their ability to organize resources and raise armies hit a metaphorical wall. Two of the empire's borders seemed secure. In the far north, much of Great Britain had been brought under the Roman yoke in the first century AD. Yet the ferocious Picts in the island's north stopped Roman advancement. Giving up the idea of invading the highlands, Emperor Hadrian built a wall across the island to separate and defend the Roman province from the wild northerners. The Celts on the island of Hibernia (Ireland) were not even considered worth conquering. These two free peoples, though, hardly threatened the empire's interests. Likewise, on the border in the south, the Sahara Desert provided a natural barrier to the rest of Africa. Most of Rome's other borders, however, remained dangerously vulnerable. Slow communications by foot, horseback, or ship meant that responses to emergencies took much too long.

The first major threat to the empire's border loomed in the heartland of Europe. There the **Germans** or **Goths** dwelt in dark forests and resisted subjugation by Rome. The Romans categorized the Germans as barbarians. They were, in the sense that the Germans did not live in organized fashion around cities and empire. Instead, they remained in loose and quarreling pastoral and agricultural tribes along Rome's central European borders. They sometimes traded, and other times raided to gain Rome's luxury goods. They pursued comparatively egalitarian lives, enjoying hunting and warfare.

During the age of Augustus, a German leader called Arminius in Latin (Hermann in German) briefly frustrated Roman ambitions. Hermann learned Roman ways from his life as an imperial soldier who rose through the ranks. Back in his homeland, Hermann led his people to ambush and slaughter three Roman legions in the Teutoburger Forest in Germany in AD 9. This defeat seemed so decisive that Augustus and the later Romans refrained from further expansion in that direction. Instead, the Romans built a line of defensive fortifications, the *limes*, along the Rhine and Danube Rivers, trying to defend against what they could not conquer.

In the east, the Persians presented the second threat to Rome. Since Rome had finished conquering various Hellenistic kingdoms in the first century BC, they had inherited the Greeks' traditional enemy. At the same time, the Parthians, horse-riding archers migrating westward from the Asian steppes, seized the Persian Empire, toppling the last of the Seleucid Hellenistic dynasts. In between lay the rich

Mesopotamian heartland of Middle Eastern civilization, tempting both the Roman and Parthian/Persian Empires. After overcoming some Parthian opposition, the Romans occupied Mesopotamia by early in the second century AD. Yet the Romans failed to defeat Persia, unlike Alexander the Great.

Thus, Rome could no longer expand, limited by the Germans in central Europe and the Parthians/Persians in the Middle East. Failure to defeat the Germans and Persians marked the Romans' doom. Only the internal rivalries among both the German tribes and Parthian elites postponed for a few decades any catastrophic confrontations with Rome.

During this pause, as the second century AD wore on, preservation of the Roman Empire became more necessary than expansion. First foreign threats and then internal weakness brought on crises that threatened to tear the Roman Empire apart, as had almost happened in the civil wars of the first century BC. The office of emperor finally failed to preserve the functioning of the bureaucracy. The Five Good Emperors also did not solve the problem of finding successors. The first four of those five emperors, who had no sons, did implement a policy of adoption and designation, which showed promise. The reigning emperor sought out a good, qualified successor and then adopted that person as his heir. This imitation dynasty borrowed the stability of family rule to ensure talented leadership. Tragically, in AD 180, Marcus Aurelius's son, Commodus, inherited the empire from his father. This end to the successful policy of adoption and designation was bad enough, but Commodus's insanity (combining paranoia with the belief that he was Hercules incarnate) was catastrophic. Conspirators had his wrestling partner strangle him, launching a series of briberies, murders, and war over who would take the imperial office. Without the plunder from new conquests, defending the borders became expensive. Plague also ravaged the empire, further reducing the ability of Rome to recruit and pay for soldiers.

Then, in the late second century, both the Germans and the Persians attacked. Clumsy Roman interventions in Mesopotamia allowed the native Persian Sassanian dynasty to replace the weakened Parthian rulers of the Persian Empire and revive its power. The Sassanian-led Persians aggressively pushed the Romans back toward the Mediterranean. In central Europe, the Germans invaded across the *limes*.

This time when Rome required capable leadership, it had none. Constant violence crippled imperial authority. Just as during the collapsing republic of the second century BC, experienced Roman generals were too busy fighting one another over control of Rome. Unfortunately for political stability, generals have rarely been successful as politicians. In the rough century between AD 180 and 284, thirty-two emperors served an average of about three years each, with many less than a year. Such brief reigns weakened government, as did the manner of their deaths. Only two or three died naturally and peacefully in their beds; the others fell in battle against armies of Roman rivals or were murdered by the Praetorian Guards, other bodyguards, or their own troops. The "barbarian" Germans actually killed in battle one "civilized" emperor, Decius. The Persians captured and enslaved another, Valerian, who became a human footstool for the shah. Such humiliations deeply shocked the proud Romans. Even worse, rampaging Germans sacked Roman cities. Emperors tried to cover expenses by minting too many coins, which fed inflation.

Trade suffered, urban life cracked, and citizens turned to local leaders for organization and defense. Many towns hurriedly built walls, believing the far-off emperor could not help. The Roman Empire almost fell apart in the third century AD.

Then, in AD 284, one more general, **Diocletian** (r. 284–305), seized the imperial throne. As the son of a freedman (a manumitted slave), he had worked his way up through the army ranks and through the rivals for the empire until he stood alone at the top. Fortunately for Rome, Diocletian proved to be a rare man of talent and vision. He created Rome's third system of government, which historians call the **Dominate** (284–ca. 650) because it finally recognized the emperor's domination (see diagram 5.1). Diocletian kept only traces of the republican system of citizen rule. Instead, based on the style of "Oriental despots," he wanted his subjects to exalt him as mysterious and semidivine. He reinforced deification and emperor worship. More importantly, he implemented practical solutions for the challenges of good government. He appointed governors to run his administration across the many and varied provinces, and he made them more professional and well paid. He also planted secret informers to report on government abuses. At the same time, the military abandoned the now-outdated legion system. The emperor created a large field army under his direct command, one that relied more on heavy cavalry. Diocletian also strengthened border defenses with more forts.

All these government expenses, especially armies and war, required a great deal of money, so Diocletian raised taxes. To collect sufficient taxes, he needed a good economy. Since economies require stability, he instituted government controls on wages and prices. Indeed, Diocletian went so far as to make professions hereditary. If a man's father was a soldier, the son soldiered; if the father was a baker, then the son baked. These limitations on economic freedom sparked complaints and did not work as well as hoped, but neither did the economy collapse. By expanding the emperor's authority and reducing people's rights, Diocletian lengthened the life of the Roman Empire for centuries. Diocletian's policies show that sometimes the solution is more government, not less.

Not that Diocletian's regime was entirely successful. His regulation of the wage and price controls did not really work. His creative solution to the ongoing problem of regulating the imperial succession also failed. First, Diocletian recognized that the empire was too difficult for one man to govern, so he divided the empire in half on a north-south line along the western edge of the Balkans. Second, he aimed to revive a form of the adoption and designation policy used in the second century AD. For the two halves of the empire, he designated himself and a co-emperor as leaders, each called "Augustus." Each augustus then designated an assistant, called "Caesar." When the augustus retired or died, the caesar would succeed him as augustus and then designate a new assistant as caesar. Such a complicated system could not last. While Diocletian's successors altered his model of succession, they largely preserved and expanded his other governmental reforms.

In the year 300, Rome still reigned as one of the great empires of the ancient world. From the Roman Republic through the Principate, Rome's greatness once more seemed secure under the Dominate. Having risen from an obscure city-state, Rome had survived internal political conflict, invasions by external enemies, and success itself. The Romans of course thanked their gods for these triumphs. The new god-emperor Diocletian, however, particularly hated one religious sect, the Christians. These "criminals" refused to recognize his divinity or that of any of the gods of Greece and Rome. Diocletian stepped up persecuting Christians but could not wipe them out. These survivors of Diocletian's religious intolerance would, surprisingly, be running the empire within only a few years.

Review: *How did key rulers establish order within the Roman Empire?*

Response:

PRIMARY SOURCE PROJECT 5: GALGACUS VERSUS AGRICOLA ABOUT MOTIVATIONS FOR BATTLE

The Roman historian Tacitus reconstructs two speeches offering opposing views of Roman conquest just before the Battle of Mons Graupius (AD 83 or 84) in the north of the island of Great Britain. First, Galgacus, the chief of the Caledonians or Picts, gives his troops reasons to fight. Second, Tacitus's hero, the Roman commander Agricola, encourages his legions. At the end of the day, the Romans won a decisive victory, briefly securing most of the island of Great Britain for the empire.

Source: *The Life of Agricola* by Tacitus (ca. AD 100)

Galgacus

Every time that I look at the reasons we have for fighting, and the fact that we have no choice but to fight, my heart beats high at the thought that this morn, which sees your united hosts assembled, is the dawn of liberty for all Britain. . . .

During the struggles waged in the past by the Britons against the Romans, struggles sometimes lost and sometimes won, we were always in the background as a last hope and resource. . . . No other tribe stands behind us; naught is yonder but the rocks and waves, and the Romans more cruel yet. . . . The plunderers of the world, they have laid waste the land till there is no more left, and now they scour the sea.

If a people are rich they are worth robbing, if poor they are worth enslaving; and not the East and not the West can content their greedy maw. They are the only men in all the world whose lust of conquest makes them find in wealth and in poverty equally tempting baits. To robbery, murder, and outrage they give the lying name of government, and where they make a desert they call it peace.

. . . Cast away, then, all hope of finding mercy, and summon up your courage like men who fight for dear life as well as for love of honor. . . . Do you really imagine that the courage of the Romans in war is equal to their licentiousness in peace? It is our quarrels and our discords that give them their fame, for they turn the faults of their enemies to the glory of their own army, that mongrel army of a mixed multitude of peoples which is only kept together by prosperity, and must assuredly dissolve under defeat. Or can you believe that the Gaul, the German, and the Briton—yes, shame that I must say it! of Britons not a few—are following the standards of Rome from loyalty and love? . . . Fear and dread are the bonds that bind them, bonds all too weak in the place of love.

Break their bonds, and, as their fears vanish, hatred will spring to life. On our side is everything that can spur men on to victory. The Romans have no wives to fire their hearts, no kinsfolk to brand them as cowards if they fly. Most of them are men without a country, or if they have one it is some other than Rome. Few in number, bewildered and lost, they turn their eyes to sky, and sea, and forest, and all alike are strange to them. Verily they are as men fettered and taken in the snare, and thus the gods have delivered them into our hands.

. . . Here before you stand their general and their army; behind them come the tribute, the penal labor in the mines, and all the anguish of slavery, which you must endure for ever and ever; or else strike home upon this field today. Remember your fathers, remember your children, and let your last thoughts be of them ere you rush upon the foe.

Agricola

It is now eight years, comrades, that I have shared in your conquests in Britain; conquests due to your loyalty and your devotion, inspired by the valor and the majesty of imperial Rome. Side by side in many a march and many a fight, whether the call was for courage against the foe, or for patient effort to overcome the obstacles offered by nature herself, we have been well content with each other, you and I. We have pushed our way far beyond any point that other generals and other armies have ever reached, and are masters of this extremity of the land, thanks not to our prestige or our reputation, but to our camps and our good swords. You have been the explorers of Britain, you have been its conquerors as well.

. . . In our triumphant advance we have travelled a long, long road, we have threaded forests, and we have forded estuaries, all of which are so many additions to our glory. If we flee now, all these things do but multiply our perils. We have no knowledge of the country, such as our enemies have; we have no means of getting supplies like them; what we have are our swords and our strong arms, and having them we have all things. . . . Death on the field of honor is better than a life of shame; but in our position life and honor go hand in hand, while to fall at the point where the natural world itself comes to an end would be to find a glorious tomb.

. . . As it is, I say count over your own victories and ask your own eyes. . . . Thus, the stoutest-hearted of the Britons have long since bitten the dust; the remainder are but a pack of panic-stricken poltroons.

The reason that at last you find them here in front of you is not that they have turned to bay, but that they are caught in a trap. Their desperate case and their paralyzing fears have nailed them to the spot where they stand, and on that spot you shall show the world the spectacle of a brilliant and memorable victory.

Here make an end to these campaigns. Let fifty years of conquest have their crowning day. Prove to Rome that her army never falters with its work, nor leaves behind it the seeds of fresh rebellions.

Questions:

- *How does each speaker criticize his opponents?*
- *What virtues does each speaker claim for his own side?*
- *What will be the final result of the battle, according to each speaker?*

Responses:

Citations

Tacitus. *The Agricola and Germania*. Translated by K. B. Townshend. London: Methuen, 1894, chap. 30–34, pp. 32–38.

For more on this source, go to http://www.concisewesternciv.com/sources/psc5 .html.

THE ROADS TO KNOWLEDGE

If Rome's greatness had been based only on its ability to conquer, it would have faded as quickly as had the Assyrian Empire. The Romans, though, believed they were civilizers. Their efforts at romanization succeeded in making diverse peoples loyal to the empire. Likewise, they absorbed much from those they ruled over, laying a foundation of culture that has inspired us ever since. Through the Middle Ages, into the Renaissance of the fifteenth century, through the Enlightenment, and even into the twenty-first century, the culture of classical antiquity fostered by Rome has taught us about ourselves.

Three hundred years ago, some Italians digging a well struck upon a treasure trove of lost history, the buried Roman city of Herculaneum. A few decades later, others found Pompeii. Both cities had been buried in the year AD 79 by the sudden eruption of the nearby volcano Vesuvius. As the earth shook and a dark mushroom cloud filled the sky, many people started to flee toward the sea; others took refuge where they could. Poisonous overheated gas killed many people (see figure 5.4). Hot mud then drowned Herculaneum, while fiery ash, cinder, and stone smothered Pompeii. Archeologists have restored a semblance of the bodies of the dead with gray, rough castings. Their silence still speaks to us of human mortality. Nevertheless, much of the cities themselves and their evidence of the everyday life of Romans survived. Their art of frescoes, mosaics, and sculptures depicting gods, heroes, and friends; their taverns, villas, and brothels; their gardens, stadia, and baths; and their utensils, furniture, and jewelry all offer invaluable artifacts to help us appreciate the civilized, urban culture fostered by the Roman Empire at its height.

One of the most important cultural attitudes of the Romans was their appreciation of Hellenistic civilization. From their earliest history, the Romans accepted Greek influences, beginning with the stories of their gods. Roman polytheism simply renamed and rewrote the Olympian gods and their myths (see table 2.1). Ovid's *Metamorphoses* retold many of the amusing, tragic, and bawdy stories about gods

Figure 5.4.   The casts of Romans who died in the eruption of the volcano Vesuvius near Pompeii show their huddled attempt to survive.

and people changing forms. From the Eastern Mediterranean the Romans also imported various mystery cults, as long as their followers did not disturb the peace. *Mithraism* was particularly popular among the soldiers of the legions. This religion believed that the son of the sun god born from a rock on 25 December grew up to slaughter a magical bull to provide fertility for the world, died, was reborn, and served as a mediator between heaven and earth. Mithras's followers (men only) were baptized in blood, celebrated with a common meal of bread and wine, and believed they would attain eternal life. These elements of belief may sound familiar.

The Romans also loved Greek art. Most of the white marble statues of Hercules or Venus we have today are copies made for eager Roman collectors from Greek originals depicting Herakles or Aphrodite. Roman architecture drew directly on Greek orders of columns: Doric, Ionic, and Corinthian (the last especially favored by Roman architects). In their own right, Roman artists developed a particular talent for portraiture. Paintings and busts not only capture unique features but underlying feelings of their subjects. The Romans pushed much of their artistic effort into propaganda. The impressive temples of the forums, lofty triumphal arches, and noble statues of emperors reminded people in the cities of their rulers.

Not only art, but also Greek literature flourished under Roman rule. As mentioned earlier, every educated Roman learned Greek and often spoke it in everyday life. Most of the populations in the Eastern Mediterranean who spoke Greek as a common language before Roman rule continued to do so. The Romans read Herodotus about the Persian Wars and Thucydides about the Peloponnesian Wars. Newer Greek writers found patrons in Rome to support them as they wrote their poetry, history, and science. Plutarch's popular collection of biographies, *Parallel Lives*, compared Greek and Roman heroes and villains. Ptolemy's views on astronomy and Galen's on medicine, translated into Latin, would have a long-lasting influence on the West for more than a thousand years after they wrote.

The Romans also produced their own literature in Latin. They especially differed from the Greeks in their plays for the theater. Rather than the tragedies preferred by the Greeks, where the violence usually happened offstage, Romans most enjoyed bawdy comedies or violent melodramas, where murder and mayhem were reenacted onstage. Actual killing, of course, happened in the amphitheaters, such as the Colosseum. In rhetoric, or the art of communication, the greatest orator or speech maker was Cicero, who during the fall of the republic opposed Caesar and was killed by Antony's proscription. His writings provide us with models of rhetorical discourse on the duties of citizens. In the next generation, Vergil's epic poem, *The Aeneid*, about the founding of Rome by refugees from the Trojan War, celebrated the virtues of Augustus's Principate. Later historians, such as Suetonius and Tacitus, however, insightfully analyzed both the virtues and the vices of emperors.

The Romans appreciated Greek philosophy, although their favorites were Epicureanism and stoicism. Romans particularly found in stoicism a reflection of their traditional values of following rules, performing one's duty, and doing hard work. The stoic philosopher Seneca's failure to satisfy the emperor Nero led to his dutiful suicide. Emperor Marcus Aurelius himself penned a collection of stoic sayings called the *Meditations*.

Late in the empire's history, some scholars organized the Roman educational curriculum, a "running path" to follow toward knowledge. They chose seven subjects, called the **seven liberal arts**, which they split into two parts. The first part was the "three roads," or *trivium* (from which we unfairly derive the word *trivial*). These included grammar, rhetoric, and logic. Second was the "four roads," or *quadrivium*, of arithmetic, geometry, music, and astronomy. All seven of these subjects taught the skills (arts) that would enable people to be free (the "liberal" in liberal arts equated to liberty). Later generations in the West would draw on this heritage of Rome to emphasize freedom from the slavery of ignorance.

Actual freedom in Rome, despite the rhetoric, could be quite limited. The economy relied on millions of enslaved persons drawn from diverse peoples both within and without the empire's borders. Female citizens did not enjoy the same status as their male counterparts. Many nations were forced into the empire by conquest, not by choice. The Romans purposefully destroyed the cultures of the Etruscans, Phoenicians, Celts, Dacians, and others; ignored the Germans as barbarians; and opposed the Persians as traditional enemies of Europe. At the height of its creative power, though, the mixed pagan culture of Greece and Rome gained a new, unexpected enemy in Christianity. This religion would claim to offer classical antiquity a new kind of freedom.

Review: *How did the Romans bring together the cultural heritage of classical antiquity?*

Response:

SOURCES ON FAMILIES: SUETONIUS, *THE TWELVE CAESARS*, AUGUSTUS

Proper marriages and family were an important part of Roman cultural values. The first Roman emperor Augustus does not represent a typical Roman, but his biographer, the historian Suetonius, appropriately covers issues of marriage and family. In the first section (XXXIV), Suetonius tells how Augustus tried to improve marriage through government regulation. In the second section (LXII–LXV), the story of Augustus's own family problems illustrates how actual lives failed to live up to ideals.

XXXIV. He revised existing laws and enacted some new ones, for example, on extravagance, on adultery and chastity, on bribery, and on the encouragement of marriage among the various classes of citizens. Having made somewhat more stringent changes in the last of these than in the others, he was unable to carry it out because of an open revolt against its provisions, until he had abolished or mitigated a part of the penalties, besides increasing the rewards and allowing a three years' exemption from the obligation to marry after the death of a husband or wife. When the equestrians even then persistently called for its repeal at a public show, he sent for the children of Germanicus [possibly Nero and Caligula] and exhibited them, some in his own lap and some in their father's, intimating by his gestures and expression that they should not refuse to follow that young man's example. And on finding that the spirit of the law was being evaded by betrothal with immature girls and by frequent changes of wives, he shortened the duration of betrothals and set a limit on divorce.

LXII. In his youth he was betrothed to the daughter of Publius Servilius Isauricus, but when he became reconciled with Antonius after their first quarrel, and their troops begged that the rivals be further united by some tie of kinship, he took to wife Antonius' stepdaughter Claudia, daughter of Fulvia . . . although she was barely of marriageable age; but because of a falling out with his mother-in-law Fulvia, he divorced her before they had begun to live together. Shortly after that he married Scribonia, who had been wedded before to two ex-consuls, and was a mother by one of them. He divorced her also, "unable to put up with her shrewish disposition," as he himself writes, and at once took Livia Drusilla from her husband Tiberius Nero, although she was with child at the time; and he loved and esteemed her to the end without a rival.

LXIII. By Scribonia he had a daughter Julia, by Livia no children at all, although he earnestly desired issue. One baby was conceived, but was prematurely born. . . . Augustus, after considering various alliances for a long time, even in the equestrian order, finally chose his stepson Tiberius, obliging him to divorce his wife, who was with child and by whom he was already a father. . . .

LXIV. . . . In bringing up his daughter and his granddaughters he even had them taught spinning and weaving, and he forbade them to say or do anything except openly and such as might be recorded in the household diary [a record of the imperial household, which apparently dated from the time of Augustus]. He was most strict in keeping them from meeting strangers. . . . He taught his grandsons [Gaius and Lucius] reading, swimming, and the other elements of education, for the most part himself, taking special pains to train them to imitate his own handwriting; and he never dined in their company unless they sat beside him on the lowest couch, or made a journey unless they preceded his carriage or rode close by it on either side.

LXV. But at the height of his happiness and his confidence in his family and its training, Fortune proved fickle. He found the two Julias, his daughter and granddaughter, guilty of every form of vice, and banished them. He lost Gaius and Lucius within the span of eighteen months. . . . He then publicly adopted his third grandson Agrippa and at the same time his stepson Tiberius by a bill passed in the assembly of the curiae; but he soon disowned Agrippa because of his low tastes and violent temper. . . . He bore the death of his kin with far more resignation than their misconduct . . . and for very shame would meet no one for a long time, and even thought of putting [the elder Julia] to death. At all events, when one of her confidantes, a freedwoman called Phoebe, hanged herself at about that same time, he said: "I would rather have been Phoebe's father." After Julia was banished, he denied her the use of wine and every form of luxury, and would not allow any man, bond or free, to come near her without his permission, and then not without being informed of his stature, complexion, and even of any marks or scars upon his body. . . . But he could not by any means be prevailed on to recall her altogether, and when the Roman people several times interceded for her and urgently pressed their suit, he in open assembly called upon the gods to curse them with like daughters and like wives. He would not allow the child born to his granddaughter Julia after her sentence to be recognized or reared. . . . [A]t every mention of [Agrippa] and of the Julias he would sigh deeply and even cry out: "Would that I ne'er had wedded and would I had died without offspring" [a quote from *The Iliad* III.40]; and he never alluded to them except as his three boils and his three ulcers.

Questions:

- *What policies does Augustus institute to promote families and children?*
- *How does Augustus's own family history compare to his official policies?*
- *What do Augustus's problems with his own family indicate about how families are challenging?*

Responses:

Make your own timeline.

753 BC   AD 300

Citation

Suetonius. [*Lives of the Caesars*.] Translated by J. C. Rolfe. The Loeb Classical Library. 2 vols. Cambridge, MA: Harvard University Press, 1913, vol. 1, pp. 177–79, 217–25.

For more on this source, go to http://www.concisewesternciv.com/sources/sof5 .html.

CHAPTER 6

The Revolutionary Rabbi

Christianity, the Roman Empire, and Islam,
4 BC to AD 1453

While Augustus was sorting out his new imperial government, in one small part of his empire called Palestine many Jews resented Roman rule. A handful of them soon began an obscure cult that later grew into the major religion called **Christianity**. From its insignificant beginnings among a few believers in Judaea, this new faith triumphed over the whole Roman Empire, becoming an essential part of Western civilization.

THE SON OF MAN

Christianity started with Yeshua (or Joshua, meaning "Yahweh is salvation") benJoseph of Nazareth. He has since become better known by the Latinized version of his name: **Jesus Christ**. The Yeshua of history became the Jesus of religion. Later myths settled the date of his birth on 25 December, the year 1 of the "Year of the Lord" (AD, or in Latin, *anno Domini*). According to the best modern historians, Jesus was actually born in the springtime in one of the years between 7 and 4 BC.[1] As mentioned in the first chapter, medieval historians considered the appearance of Jesus in this world important enough to create the major dividing point in the calculation of the history of the universe, between BC ("Before Christ") and AD.

Historically, Yeshua lived and died a Jew. The **Gospels** ("Good News") are the only surviving descriptions of his life, written years later. The nominal authors of these stories, Matthew, Mark, Luke, and John, were probably not those named in the Gospels themselves as Yeshua's disciples. His followers (and, later, the leaders of Jewish communities) called him by the title "rabbi," which meant "teacher" or "master." His ministry, which lasted just a few years, consisted of preaching to large

---

1. Roughly five hundred years after Christ's birth, the medieval monk Dennis Exiguus ("the Short" or "the Humble") miscalculated his proposed year 1 AD for Jesus's birth, at least according to modern scholars.

crowds, teaching to a smaller group of disciples, and sending out apostles to convert and heal others in Yeshua's name. These Gospels did not always clearly reveal Yeshua's teachings, complicating all interpretations about him ever since. Yeshua often used challenging parables to illustrate his teachings and did not propose an organized set of principles. Therefore, much of what we know about Jesus Christ has to be taken on faith, not facts.

Still, some general trends are observable. Yeshua criticized the Jewish religious establishment of his day and other diverse Jewish groups such as Pharisees, Sadducees, Zealots, and Essenes. He taught more clearly that people were to repent of their faults or sins to prepare properly for the Kingdom of God. Our life in this world, he taught, determined our place in the next world, after death. The life after death, the Kingdom of God, was far more important than treasures accumulated in this worldly existence. Yeshua constantly emphasized moral action and repentance of sin over strictly following the letter of the Jewish religious laws. He criticized the rich, wanted to help the poor, and preached pacifism and forgiveness. According to the Gospels, he worked miracles (especially healing the sick) to confirm and reinforce his mission.

During his three years of ministry, Yeshua generally avoided trouble with the Roman Empire ("Give to the emperors the things that are the emperors', and to God the things that are God's," Mark 12:17). About the year AD 27, certain Jewish leaders who feared that Yeshua wanted to overthrow their system pressured the local Roman imperial governor, Pontius Pilate. He convicted Jesus of treason on an alleged claim to be the king of the Jews. Instead of resisting, Yeshua surrendered himself to death and ended up more powerful than ever. Pilate had Yeshua executed in the same way as the Romans did many other condemned criminals: crucifixion. The victims of crucifixion were nailed alive to a large cross and hung on it until dehydration, hunger, exhaustion, or suffocation finally killed them in a painful ordeal that could last for days.

After Yeshua's execution by the Romans, his followers claimed that Jesus "the Christ" was resurrected in a new body—that he physically became alive again and walked the earth until he ascended into heaven. Belief in resurrections was not unusual in those times (indeed, Yeshua is recorded as himself raising several people from the dead). Regardless of any debate about the truth of the resurrection, belief in it encouraged his followers. They multiplied from a small, persecuted group of Jews to a force that changed the course of Roman history.

"Who exactly was Jesus?" was the first question faced by his followers after Jesus's departure from this world. During his lifetime, he referred to himself most often as the "Son of Man," but that term's meaning is unclear. A few times he is recorded as using the name "Anointed One" ("**Messiah**" in Hebrew or "Christ" from the Greek). The concept of the Messiah was a recurring theme in Jewish thought at the time. Many Jews in the first century were awaiting a savior who would rescue them from the troubles of this world. Jewish believers disagreed upon the exact manner of salvation, but they most often imagined a warrior-king. While Jesus certainly did not fit that view, Christians soon considered him to be much more than the Messiah. According to two of the Gospels, Jesus had a human as a mother and God as a father—but what does that actually mean? What is Jesus's connection to

God and vice versa? These questions challenged the first Christians and still confuse many Christians today.

His followers' explanation about who Jesus was took four centuries to work itself out. They had to decide what was **orthodoxy**, the genuine position supported by most of tradition, and what was **heresy**, a belief close to, but rejected by, the religious authorities. A large group eventually identified as heretics held to **Gnosticism**. Gnostics believed in secret knowledge that emphasized dualism, considering Jesus's human aspects as bad but his divine as good. Christian leaders eventually concluded that Jesus was not just the Christ, or the Son of God; Jesus was God, incarnate, in the flesh, divine and human at the same time. Christians asserted that the Trinity of God the Father, God the Son, and God the Holy Spirit has ordained a universe where people live and die. After death, humans could end up in either one of two places: righteous Christians who believed in Jesus's resurrection and behaved morally would be saved to spend eternity in blissful unity with God in heaven; sinners would be forever damned to hell, surmised as a place of horrible suffering.

In coming to these conclusions about Jesus, the Christians worked their way through available sources. It took until the fourth century for orthodox Christians to agree that their Bible (which means "book") would include, and only include, the Hebrew scriptures as an Old Testament and a **New Testament** of the four Gospels, the Acts of the Apostles, twenty-one letters (epistles), and an apocalyptic text (about the future end of this world). Some writers who brilliantly expounded on the faith during the first few centuries of Christianity came to be called church fathers. They often took the role of apologists, which meant defending Christian viewpoints against those of Judaism, ancient philosophies, and mystery cults. Other writings, such as the Gospels of Thomas or of Mary Magdalene, were excluded, banned, and destroyed as heretical misinformation.

Another early action of the Christians was to organize themselves into an institution called the church. While all baptized Christians could be considered members of the church, selected people became the church's leaders and administrators. Many Christians accepted the idea of **apostolic succession**, the belief that those whom Jesus had charged with his mission could pass on that authority to others, one to the next, and they, in turn, to still others (see figure 6.1). Thus began a distinction between the laity (normal Christians) and the **secular clergy** (church officials). Overseers (later evolving into **bishops**) began to manage elders (priests) and servers (deacons). Soon each bishop had a special church called a cathedral (from the Latin for the "bishop's chair") from which he administered a territory called a diocese (or a see, or a bishopric). Church **councils**, starting with the first major one described in the Acts of the Apostles, brought the Christian leaders together to debate and resolve important controversies (guided, they believed, by the Holy Spirit).

Through these discussions and interpretations of the scriptures, the church leaders established several methods to help people in their earthly pilgrimage toward heaven. The church taught that grace (God's gift of salvation) could be obtained through the beliefs, sacraments, and ceremonies of Christian worship. Centuries later, the western church eventually settled on seven sacraments or holy

Figure 6.1.   A graffito in Rome of an early priest shows him standing behind an altar, his arms raised in prayer (and perhaps the presence of the Holy Spirit in the form of a bird).

acts important on the earthly path. First, ***baptism***, performed on all infants, initiated involvement in church life. In the sacrament of reconciliation, one was supposed to confess one's sins and be absolved before the most important regular sacrament, the **Eucharist**, also called Communion or the mass. Like many religious services in a variety of cultures, the mass involved a performance with processions, prayers, readings, songs, and a sermon, which culminated in a sacred meal. For most people it became the custom to attend mass on Sunday morning, which the Christians turned into their Lord's Day, replacing as their day of worship the Jewish Sabbath (sundown Friday to sundown Saturday). Young people underwent confirmation, recommitting themselves to vows made in their name as babies. As an adult, one might be married or be ordained into holy orders of priests or monastics. Last, extreme unction, a final blessing at the time of death, were last rites that carried one into the afterlife (nowadays it has become merely anointing of the sick).

The sacraments became so important that the church could threaten anyone who strayed from the proper orthodox path with ***excommunication***. That punishment excluded a sinner from the sacraments until he or she asked for forgiveness. The average person rarely worried about excommunication, though. The beliefs and rituals of Christianity did relieve some of the daily grind of life and the fear of death. The Christian calendar of the seven-day week, ending with a day of worship and rest, combined with various holidays (holy days) such as Easter (the day of Christ's resurrection) or Pentecost (fifty days later, when the Holy Spirit entered Christ's followers), increasingly shaped the living patterns of Christian society for the next few centuries.

In these early formative centuries, Christianity did not appear fully formed and obvious. It rose from discussions and controversy among believers. The early Christians disagreed with one another over what Jesus actually taught, either about morality and behavior or about authority and obedience. These same questions confront Christians today, who have splintered into many different denominations over these same issues. The solution to these questions was even more difficult in antiquity because the early Christians lived within a culture that was hostile to them.

Review: *How did the new religion of Christianity begin and define itself?*

Response:

SOURCES ON FAMILIES: PAUL, FIRST EPISTLE TO TIMOTHY (AD 65–150)

Early Christians called for family values that were different from those of contemporary pagans. The First Epistle to Timothy touches on issues of morality and marriage, especially for the new leaders of bishops and deacons. Although attributed to Paul of Tarsus, many scholars argue that the I Timothy letter was written by a follower using his name, decades after the apostle's death. Either way, many modern Christians use these verses to assign roles and determine policies toward men and women (leaving aside the whole problematic of translating arsenokoitai*).*

. . . But we know that the law is good, if a man use it lawfully;

Knowing this, that the law is not made for a righteous man, but for the lawless and disobedient, for the ungodly and for sinners, for unholy and profane, parricides and matricides, for manslayers, for whoremongers, for them that defile themselves with mankind [*arsenokoitai*], for menstealers, for liars, for perjured persons, and if there be any other thing that is contrary to sound doctrine; according to the glorious gospel of the blessed God, which was committed to my trust. . . .

I want, therefore, that men pray every where, lifting up holy hands, without wrath and doubting.

In like manner also, that women adorn themselves in modest apparel, with shamefacedness and sobriety; not with braided hair, or gold, or pearls, or costly array; but (which becomes women professing godliness) with good works.

Let the woman learn in silence with all subjection. But I suffer not a woman to teach, nor to usurp authority over the man, but to be in silence. For Adam was first formed, then Eve. And Adam was not deceived, but the woman being deceived was in the transgression. Notwithstanding she shall be saved in childbearing, if they continue in faith and charity and holiness with sobriety.

This is a true saying, if a man desire the office of a bishop, he desires a good work. A bishop then must be blameless, the husband of one wife, vigilant, sober, of good behavior, given to hospitality, apt to teach; not given to wine, no striker, not greedy; but patient, not a brawler, not covetous; one that rules well his own house, having his children in subjection with all gravity. (For if a man know not how to rule his own house, how shall he take care of the church of God?) Not a novice, lest being lifted up with pride he fall into the condemnation of the devil. . . .

Likewise must the deacons be grave, not doubletongued, not given to much wine, not greedy; holding the mystery of the faith in a pure conscience. And let these also first be proved; then let them use the office of a deacon, being found blameless. Even so must their wives be grave, not slanderers, sober, faithful in all things. Let the deacons be the husbands of one wife, ruling their children and their own houses well. . . .

Now the Spirit speaks expressly, that in the latter times some shall depart from the faith, giving heed to seducing spirits, and doctrines of devils; speaking lies in hypocrisy; having their conscience seared with a hot iron; forbidding to marry, and commanding to abstain from meats, which God hath created to be received with thanksgiving of them which believe and know the truth. For every creature of God is good, and nothing to be refused, if it be received with thanksgiving: For it is sanctified by the word of God and prayer. . . .

Rebuke not an elder, but treat him as a father; and the younger men as brethren. The elder women as mothers; the younger as sisters, with all purity.

Honor widows that are widows indeed. But if any widow have children or nephews, let them learn first to show piety at home, and to support their parents: for that is good and acceptable before God. Now she that is a widow indeed, and desolate, trusts in God and continues in supplications and prayers night and day. But she that lives in pleasure is dead while she lives. . . .

But if any provide not for his own, and specially for those of his own house, he has denied the faith, and is worse than an unbeliever. Let not a widow be taken into the membership under sixty years old, having been the wife of only one man, well reported of for good works; if she have brought up children, if she have lodged strangers, if she have washed the saints' feet, if she have relieved the afflicted, if she have diligently followed every good work.

But the younger widows refuse: for when they have begun to wax wanton against Christ, they will marry, earning damnation, because they have cast off their first faith. And at the same time they learn to be idle, wandering about from house to house; and not only idle, but tattlers also and busybodies, speaking things which they ought not.

I intend, therefore, that the younger women marry, bear children, guide the house, give no occasion for opponents to speak reproachfully. For some are already turned aside toward Satan.

If any man or woman who is a believer has widowed relatives, let them care for them, and let not the church be obligated, so that it can care for those who are really widows. . . .

Questions:

- *What specific restrictions are suggested for women as opposed to men?*
- *What standards in marriage are outlined for bishops and deacons?*
- *Why should the early church have been so concerned about who was a deserving widow?*

Responses:

Citation

I Timothy. The King James Bible (Authorized Version). 1611.

For more on this source, go to http://www.concisewesternciv.com/sources/sof6 .html.

THE CULTURAL WAR

Not surprisingly, the Jews were the first to attack the Christians, who had themselves all originally been Jewish. From Judaism the Christians had adapted the key belief system regarding Jesus as Messiah and God. For the Jews, however, Christianity was heresy. Many hostile Jews had Christians arrested or stoned to death. Foremost among the persecutors was Saul of Tarsus. Then, on the road from Jerusalem to Damascus one day, Saul claimed to have had a vision of Jesus and converted to Christianity. He changed his name to **Paul of Tarsus** and became one of the leading apostles.

Encouraged by Paul's missionary work among the Gentiles (non-Jews) of Asia Minor and Greece, Christians took a decisive step away from Judaism when they opened up Christianity as a universal religion. While theoretically anyone could convert to Judaism, Jews tended to emphasize ethnic inheritance. In contrast, Christians abandoned obligations to many of the Jewish dietary rules and other restrictive laws to make their faith more hospitable to Gentiles. Unlike the Jews, Christians regularly used syncretism, adapting foreign customs to Christian practices, such as replacing pagan holidays with Christian ones. For example, church authorities chose 25 December as the date for Christmas because it could replace pagan festivals of the winter solstice. Indeed, almost anyone could easily become a Christian, even among socially disadvantaged groups such as women, the poor, outcasts, and slaves. Women even took on leadership roles as patrons, deacons, and apostles in the early church. The Christian message of love and the example of charity attracted many who found little caring within other ancient religions and philosophies.

Christianity quickly spread outward from Palestine, whether to Jewish communities of the Diaspora or directly into the hellenized and Roman towns and cities of antiquity. At first, Christianity was an urban religion, as opposed to ancient polytheism, which became known as either *paganism* (after the word for farmers) or *heathenism* (after those who live on uncultivated land). As a belief system, Christianity offered something different from other civic religions, mystery cults, and schools of philosophy, which were all sanctioned and supported by the state. The official myth-based religions were too empty of fervor, the mystery cults were too exclusive and secretive, and philosophy was too intellectually challenging. In comparison, Christianity offered a religion of passion, open to all, Greek or Roman, rich or poor, male or female, slave or free.

The Roman Empire, however, did not make life easy for Christians. By the first century AD, the Romans had unified their empire through a state religion based on sacrifices to the gods of Rome, including their deified emperors. Romans insisted that only diligent sacrifices prevented the gods from punishing the state with destruction. The government labeled as a traitor anyone who refused to support the state through ritual civic sacrifice. Thus, all citizens and subjects were obligated to acknowledge the Græco-Roman gods through a simple act, usually burning incense or sacrificing a bird on an altar. Christians, however, refused to perform even such superficial rites.

In the view of the imperial authorities, Christianity was therefore illegal. As explained in chapter 3, the Jews, who regarded such actions as idolatry, were exempted from performing this sacrifice. In contrast, the Romans considered that since Christianity had been founded within living memory, it deserved no special exemption. Many emperors and magistrates therefore persecuted the Christians by arresting and punishing them in various creative ways. Christians were sold for use as enslaved miners, forced to become temple prostitutes, beheaded, or even ripped apart at gladiatorial games by wild animals. Christians who suffered death for the sake of faith were believed to become **martyrs** and immediately enter heaven.[2]

Fortunately for the Christians, these persecutions failed to destroy the faith, because the Roman emperors could neither apply enough pressure nor maintain the scope of hunting down Christians for very long. The Christians were able to outlast the attention span and strength of the most powerful rulers in the ancient world. Also, the noble death of so many Christians inspired many Romans to consider Christianity more seriously. Still, Christians had not convinced a large number of Romans to convert. By AD 300, Christians probably made up only 10 percent of the empire's population.

In the fourth century AD, Christians suddenly attained safety and security, largely because of one man: Emperor **Constantine** (r. 306–337). His father had

---

2. In case you wondered, no one can choose martyrdom; it has to be forced on a person. Thus Christians were not allowed to simply walk up to Romans and announce their faith, hoping to be executed and thus become martyrs.

become an augustus in Diocletian's system of imperial succession (see figure 6.2). But the system of four emperors did not work. They just made war on each other, fighting to come out on top. The troops proclaimed Constantine an imperial successor upon his father's death in AD 306 (see figure 6.3). Over the next few years, Constantine successfully defeated other claimants, seizing the imperial supremacy for himself.

As the sole Roman emperor, Constantine continued the strong imperial government revitalized by Diocletian, adding three improvements of his own. First, he solved the question of succession by creating an old-fashioned dynasty. A son (or sons in the divided empire) would inherit from the father. While this system had the usual flaw of dynasties (sons and cousins might and did fight over the throne), it limited the claimants to within the imperial family rather than ambitious generals proclaimed by legions. Second, Constantine built a new capital for the eastern half

Figure 6.2. Statues of four Roman emperors, two *augusti* and two *caesares*, cling to one another as they try to hold the empire together.

Figure 6.3. The colossal face of Emperor Constantine stares into the future.

of the administratively divided empire. He chose the location of the Greek city of Byzantion, situated on the Bosphorus, the entrance from the Aegean to the Black Sea. Strategically, it was an excellent choice: close to key trade routes, in the heart of the vital Greek population, and easily defensible. He modestly named the new capital after himself, **Constantinople**.

His third improvement reversed Diocletian's religious policy of exterminating all Christians. Instead, Constantine decided to help them. As the story went, Constantine was fighting against a rival who was a great persecutor of Christians. Constantine had a vision and a dream of the Christian symbol of the *labarum* (similar to the letter *P* with a crossbar) in the sun (which held a special connection to his family as a patron deity). He won victory over the imperial rival under this sign in a battle at the Milvian Bridge, just to the north of Rome. Although Constantine himself probably remained a pagan until his death, the victorious emperor ordered all of the empire to tolerate Christians by issuing the **Edict of Milan** in 313. This law reinforced a previous Edict of Toleration of two years earlier. In this edict, the Christians were exempted from making sacrifices to the emperors. After 313, Christians in the Roman Empire were no longer criminals because of their faith.

Beyond simply tolerating the Christians, Constantine showered his imperial largesse upon them. He favored them with land and buildings. The design of the new public Christian churches, basilicas, was based on that of imperial meeting halls. Constantine bestowed special privileges on Christians, such as rights of self-government and exemptions from imperial services. He probably thought Christianity, which had proved so resistant to persecution, could help the empire through its prayers and zeal. Overnight, Christianity had moved from being the counterculture to being the establishment.

Saints served as new role models for Christian society, since martyrs became a rarity without persecutions (although many martyrs did become saints). Originally, a saint referred to any faithful Christian. Over time, the term *saint* became restricted to those who both lived the virtuous life in this world and proved their divine connection by working miracles after their death. Saints' lives became meaningful not only in stories but also in their physical remains. The faithful believed that parts of saints' bodies or objects associated with them channeled divine power to work miracles long after the saint's death. The relics of specific saints preserved in and around altars often gave churches their names. For example, the grill on which St. Lawrence was roasted and the headless body of St. Agnes reside at their respective churches located outside the walls of ancient Rome. New churches were being built openly in great numbers to hold all the recent converts.

In one of those amazing ironies of history, just when they reached social acceptance, Christians began to attack one another. Uncertainty raised by Gnostics about the combined humanity and divinity of Jesus burst out into the open. These conflicts threatened Constantine's aim for Christianity to provide stability, so he called the **Council of Nicaea** in 325 to help the church settle the matter. The majority of church leaders decided on the formula that Jesus was simultaneously fully God and fully human, embedding this idea and other basic beliefs into the Nicene Creed that is still professed in many Christian churches today. That creed became catholic orthodoxy (the universally held, genuine beliefs). The large majority believed along catholic (universal) orthodox (genuine) lines. Orthodox catholics labeled those who disagreed with them as heretics, no longer Christian.

A large group of heretics, the Arians, remained unconvinced about Jesus's complete combination of divinity and humanity.[3] They continued to spread their version of the faith and tried to convince the majority to change its mind. Over the next

---

3. Arians take their name from one of their important theologians, Arius. They are not to be confused with "Aryans." That term is a racist-tinged and outdated concept describing European ancestors who originated in India (see chapter 13).

few decades they even convinced emperors to switch sides. They also succeeded in converting many Germans along and outside the borders of the Roman Empire to their version of the Christian faith. For a long time, heretical *Arianism* looked as if it would become the orthodox faith. The Christian leadership, convinced that the Holy Spirit worked through them, persecuted, exiled, or even executed the heretics. By the sixth century, only a few Arian Christians survived in the empire, but many, called Nestorians, spread their version of Christ throughout Asia.

Christians also adopted a new relationship with the Jews, whose religion was the undoubted foundation for Christianity. Through the centuries, many Christians have respected the Jews, recognizing their position as God's chosen people. Such Christians tolerated Jews who continued to live as a religious minority within Christian cities and society. Jews maintained their distinct religion and avoided completely assimilating into the dominant Christian culture of the West.

Too many Christians, however, turned toward antisemitism or hating Jews. Nominal excuses for this hatred ranged from blaming Jews for killing Christ, through disliking Jewish refusal to recognize their truth of Jesus as the Messiah, to resenting Jewish religious obligations that the Christians had rejected. Nonsensical reasons included blaming the Jews for plague or for committing ritual murders. Whatever the excuses, many Christians persecuted Jews once Christianity gained supremacy. Increasingly over the centuries, and particularly in the West, Christians restricted Jewish civil rights. Christians limited Jews to certain occupations, had them confined in ghettoes, forced Jews to convert or emigrate, or simply killed them. Christians were, and remain, burdened by these uncomfortable relations with their Jewish brethren.

Besides deciding on orthodox beliefs and how to relate to the Jews, Christians needed to decide their attitude toward Græco-Roman culture, which dominated the Roman Empire during the centuries after Christ. With the famous question, "What has Athens to do with Jerusalem?" some Christians attacked and wanted to reject the classical heritage. Indeed, Christianity threatened to wipe out much of Græco-Roman civilization, even through violence. Christians thought that pagans like Socrates, Plato, or Aristotle had little to say to the followers of Jesus Christ. What could the histories of Herodotus or Thucydides teach those who followed the greater history of the Hebrew people, the apostles, and the saints? When Christianity became the sole legal religion of the Roman Empire in 380, the government banned paganism and many of its works. The Christians toppled temples, destroyed shrines, burned sacred groves, shredded classical literature, shut philosophical schools that had been started by Plato and Aristotle, silenced oracles, halted gladiatorial contests, and abolished the Olympic Games. A Christian mob murdered the mathematician and polytheist philosopher Hypatia by cutting her down with shards of pottery in the middle of a public street. The murderers and instigators (who may have included the bishop) went unpunished.

Eventually, however, the Christian church embraced much from classical antiquity. This attitude was an important milestone in the West's cultural development, perhaps the most important. If narrow-minded zealots had won this culture war, church leaders might have only gazed inward at the Gospels and focused on the

Kingdom of Heaven alone. Such **anti-intellectualism**, or rejecting human rationalism and empiricism by educated people, would have stagnated civilization. To this day, some Christians still condemn knowledge that does not fit in with their view of what is godly. Instead, the church usually embraced **intellectualism**, requiring advanced education in its leaders. Christianity partly succeeded because it compromised with the secular world and opened itself up to the voices of others. In doing so, Christianity adapted and prospered in unexpected ways over the centuries and eventually spread around the world. Before that could happen, however, barbarians almost wiped out this newly Christian civilization.

Review: *How did conflicts among the Jews, Christians, and pagans lead to the Romans creating a new cultural landscape?*

Response:

PRIMARY SOURCE PROJECT 6: PAUL VERSUS PLINY AND TRAJAN ABOUT THE VALUE OF CHRISTIANITY

Christianity offered new ways of believing in and experiencing the supernatural divine. The first source witnesses the apostle Paul of Tarsus preaching at the Areopagus (Mars' Hill), where the Athenians held their trials. The second source is an exchange of letters between Pliny the Younger (Gaius Plinius Caecilius Secundus) and the Roman emperor Trajan. As governor of Bithnya-Pontus (in northern Asia Minor, along the Black Sea), Pliny often sought the advice of his superior. This particular exchange provides some of the earliest evidence of Roman interactions with the new Christian faith.

Source 1: Sermon at the Areopagus from the Acts of the Apostles (ca. AD 90)

Now while Paul waited for them at Athens, his spirit was stirred in him, when he saw the city wholly given to idolatry. Therefore he disputed in the synagogue with the Jews, and with the devout persons, and in the market daily with them that were there. Then certain philosophers of the Epicureans, and of the Stoics, encountered him. And some said, "What will this babbler say?" Others said, "He seems to be a setter forth of strange gods," because he preached to them Jesus and the resurrection.

And they took him, and brought him to the Areopagus, saying, "May we know what is this new doctrine of which you speak? For you bring certain strange things to our ears: we would know therefore what these things mean." (For all the Athenians and foreigners which were there spent their time in nothing else, but telling or hearing about new things.)

Then Paul stood in the midst of Mars' hill, and said, "You men of Athens, I perceive that in all things you are too superstitious. For as I walked around and beheld your devotions, I found an altar with this inscription: 'TO THE UNKNOWN GOD.' Whom you ignorantly worship there, Him I declare unto you. God that made the world and all things therein, seeing that He is Lord of heaven and earth, He dwells not in temples made with hands. Neither is He worshipped with men's hands, as though he needed anything, seeing as He gives to all life and breath and all things. And He has made from one ancestor all nations of men to dwell on the face of the earth, and has determined the times of their lives, and the bounds of their habitation. Thus they should seek the Lord, so that perhaps they might seek after Him, and find Him, though He is not far from every one of us: 'For in Him we live, and move, and have our being'; as certain also of your own poets have said, 'For we are also His offspring.'

"Forasmuch as we are the offspring of God, we ought not to think that the Godhead is like gold, or silver, or stone, graven by art and man's device. And God winked at such times of ignorance; but now commands all men every where to repent: Because He has appointed a day, in the which He will judge the world in righteousness by that man whom He had ordained; whereof He has given assurance to all men, in that He has raised him from the dead."

And when they heard of the resurrection of the dead, some mocked: and others said, "We will hear you again on this matter." So Paul departed from among them. Yet certain men clung to him, and believed, including Dionysius the Areopagite, a woman named Damaris, and others with them.

Source 2: Letters by Pliny the Younger and Trajan (ca. AD 112)

Pliny the Younger to Emperor Trajan

It is my custom, lord, to refer to you all things concerning which I am in doubt. For who can better guide my indecision or enlighten my ignorance?

I have never taken part in the trials of Christians: hence I do not know for what crime or to what extent it is customary to punish or investigate. . . . Meanwhile I have followed this procedure in the case of those who have been brought before me as Christians. I asked them whether they were Christians a second and a third time with threats of punishment; I questioned those who confessed; I ordered those who were obstinate to be executed. For I did not doubt that, whatever it was that they confessed, their stubbornness and inflexible obstinacy ought certainly to be punished. There were others of similar madness, who because they were Roman citizens, I have noted for sending to Rome.

Soon, . . . more cases arose. Those who denied that they were or had been Christians, ought, I thought, to be dismissed since they repeated after me a prayer to the gods and made supplication with incense and wine to your image . . . and since besides they cursed Christ, not one of which things, they say, those who are really Christians can be compelled to do. . . .

[Christians] continued to maintain that . . . on a fixed day, they used to come together before daylight and sing by turns a hymn to Christ as a god; and that they bound themselves by oath, not for some crime, but that they would not commit robbery, theft, or adultery, that they would not betray a trust or refuse to repay a debt when called upon. After this it was their custom to disperse and to come together again to partake of food, of an ordinary and harmless kind; however, even this they ceased to do after the publication of my edict, in which according to your command, I had forbidden secret associations. Hence I believed it necessary to examine two female slaves, who were called ministers, in order to find out what was true, and to do it by torture. I found nothing but a vicious, extravagant superstition.

Consequently I postponed the examination and make haste to consult you. . . . For many of all ages, of every rank, and even of both sexes are and will be called into danger. The infection of superstition has not only spread to the cities, but even to the villages and country districts. It seems possible to stop it and bring about a reform. It is clear that the temples, which had been almost deserted, have begun to be frequented again, that the sacred rites, which had been neglected for a long time, have begun to be restored, and that sacrificial animals, for which until now there was scarcely a purchaser, are being sold. From this, one may readily imagine that a great many people can be reclaimed if penitence is permitted.

Trajan's Reply

You have followed the correct procedure, my Secundus, in conducting the cases of those who were accused before you as Christians, for no general rule can be laid down as a set form. They ought not to be sought out; if they are brought before you and convicted they ought to be punished; with the exception that he who denies that he is a Christian, and proves this by making supplication to our gods . . . shall secure pardon through penitence. No attention should be paid to anonymous charges, for they afford a bad precedent and are not worthy of our age.

Questions:

- *How does the structure of each source serve to carry its message?*
- *How does Paul use Græco-Roman culture to make his point?*
- *What is most important for the Roman government officials?*

Responses:

Citations

Acts of the Apostles. The King James Bible (Authorized Version). 1611.

"Attitude of Pliny and Hadrian." In *The Library of Original Sources*, edited by Oliver J. Thatcher. Milwaukee: University Research Extension, 1907, vol. 4, pp. 7–9.

For more on these sources, go to http://www.concisewesternciv.com/sources/psc6 .html.

ROMA DELENDA EST

In another of those amazing ironies of history, just after Christians overthrew the Romans' religion, various Germans triumphed over the Romans' armies. In AD 410, the army of the Visigoths (western Germans) sacked Rome, the first time since the Celts had done so eight centuries before, in 390 BC. The Visigoth armies then marched on to plunder other regions while more Germanic peoples crossed the open borders and took what they wanted. It seemed the Roman curse "*Carthago delenda est*" (Carthage must be destroyed) had come back against Rome itself. Many Romans who had not been thoroughly Christianized, still believing in the old gods, naturally blamed the Christians for this catastrophe. They connected Christianity as the state religion with the barbarians' plundering of the city of Rome for the first time in eight hundred years. Some interpreted that the pagan gods were showing their anger at the rise of Christians by removing their protection from Rome. Calamities seemed a sure sign of divine wrath, as people often still believe in our own time.

To answer this charge against the Christians, Bishop **Augustine** of Hippo (d. AD 430) wrote the book *The City of God*. This book defended Christianity by presenting Augustine's view of God's working in history. Augustine said that people were divided into two groups who dwelt in metaphysical cities: those who lived for God and were bound for heaven and those who resided in this world and were doomed to hell. Every political state, such as the Roman Empire, contained both kinds of people. While Rome had been useful to help Christianity flourish, whether it fell or not was probably in the end irrelevant to God's plan. This argument emphasized the separation of church and state. God sanctioned no state, not even a Christian Roman Empire. Instead, individuals ought to live as faithful Christians, even while the so-called barbarians attacked. Indeed, shortly after Augustine's death, Germanic armies destroyed the city over which he was bishop, Hippo, near ancient Carthage.

How did the Germanic tribes and their allies come to conquer Hippo and so many other cities of the Roman Empire? Historians have proposed a number of explanations, some better than others. Reasons such as the poisoning of the Roman elites by lead water pipes are silly. It is likewise absurd, as some cultural critics do, to blame the fall of Rome on sinful moral corruption. When it fell, Rome was as Christian and moral a state as there ever could be. The Christians, such as Bishop Augustine, were in control. Many Romans may have been imperfect sinners, but a closer cooperation of church and state could hardly be imagined. Despite this, the great historian of the fall of Rome, Edward Gibbon, blamed much of the Roman collapse on this rise of Christianity, saying that its values of *pacifism* undermined Rome's warrior spirit. Pacifists protested war, taking seriously Jesus's criticism of people who "live by the sword" and his title as Prince of Peace. According to Gibbon, the conflicts among orthodox Christians, heretic Arians, and lingering pagans also weakened the empire. Modern historians embrace neither Augustine's nor Gibbon's explanations.

The better explanations of Rome's fall focus on its economic troubles, which remained unsolved by imperial mandates. First, plagues had reduced the numbers of Roman citizens. Rome was no longer strong enough to conquer and exploit new provinces. No expansion meant taxes at home burdened the smaller population.

Second, the shortage of revenues also meant smaller armies. Therefore, the Romans began to recruit the unconquered Germanic peoples living on their borders. Troop levels still fell short despite the German reinforcements. Transfers of warriors from one part of the border to the other left gaps in the defenses. The Roman superiority in organization could not make up for the lack of manpower.

Imperial armies soon depended on these inexpensive barbarians to defend Rome from other barbarians. Germanic immigrants never became as integrated or romanized into Roman society as had other earlier-conquered peoples. As the Goths increased their power and influence, they tended rather to barbarize the Romans, at least in their systems of politics based on personal relationships rather than written laws. Here, as with the Greeks, changes in military structures affected politics and society. Given the wealth of its civilization, though, the Romans still stood a good chance of defending the empire against the majority of Germanic tribes and peoples, who had no serious reason to launch major assaults.

The military situation changed, however, when the **Huns**, a horse-riding people from the steppes of Asia, swept into Europe. The Huns reputedly slaughtered most people in their path, drank blood and ate babies, and enslaved the few survivors. The terrified Germanic peoples in eastern and northern Europe fled from the Huns in the only direction possible: into the Roman Empire. Most historians think they entered not just as an invading army but as entire peoples with the elderly, the women, and the young. Thus, these movements are sometimes called the **Germanic barbarian migrations**. Far from being uncountable hordes, the newcomers were comparatively few, each tribe numbering only in the tens of thousands. Even after they had moved into the Roman Empire, the Germanic tribes and nations themselves remained in flux. Under inspired warrior kings, the tribes absorbed and re-formed as different groups melded together or fell apart. Some tribes remained a force for decades or even centuries, while others broke up and rapidly re-formed with different tribes and nations. What changed history was the German migrants taking over the rule of Rome in the western half of the Roman Empire.

The transfer of power began when the group called Visigoths by later historians crossed imperial boundaries, with permission, in AD 376. Two years later, their quarrels with imperial authorities culminated in the Battle of Adrianople. The Germans crushed the Roman army and killed the eastern emperor. Afterward, the inexperienced Roman emperors and commanders were unwilling to risk another battle, so the Visigoths briefly settled along the Danube. But pressure from plundering raids by the Huns continued to push new Goths against the borders, threatening both Romans and the Visigoths. A new Visigothic leader, Alaric, led his people across the empire looking for a permanent place to settle. As mentioned before, the Visigothic army carried out the sack of Rome in 410 after the Romans refused to negotiate about a homeland for them. Alaric died shortly after, but within a few years, the Visigoths had settled down into a kingdom that straddled the Pyrenees from the south of Gaul into the Iberian Peninsula.

Worse was to come. More barbarians poured across Rome's once well-defended borders. A frozen Rhine River allowed large numbers of Alans (mostly Asians), Alemanni, Suebi, and Vandals simply to walk into Roman Gaul on the last night of December AD 406. The Vandals fought their way through the Franks, who were already setting up a claim in eastern and northern Gaul, then passed through the Visigothic kingdom, crossed the Mediterranean, and finally conquered North Africa (including Carthage and Augustine's Hippo) for a kingdom of their own. From there, the Vandals carried out one of the worst sacks of Rome in 455, lending their name to the word *vandalism*.

By then Rome had left Britain defenseless by withdrawing troops to the mainland. Angles, Saxons, and Jutes who sailed across the North Sea in the mid-fifth century conquered the island, despite a defense by a leader who later became known as the legendary King Arthur. Finally, the long-feared Huns moved into the empire. Actually, they turned out not quite as monstrous as the tales spread about them. They were just one more collection of peoples seeking a place to live and grabbing as much power as they could. The Romans even negotiated with the Huns, surrendering territory along the Danube and paying tribute to them rather than fighting.

For a time, the leader of the Huns, Attila, thought he could conquer the remnants of the Roman Empire. When he moved west into Gaul in 451 and south into Italy in 452, Roman legions resisted Hunnic forces by joining with armies drawn from the Germanic tribes now living there. The allied Romans and Germans held off Hunnic conquest (although one story says that the bishop of Rome, called Pope Leo, singlehandedly convinced Attila to turn back from another sack of his city). The next year, Attila died of a nosebleed on his wedding night to his (perhaps) seventh bride. After Attila's unexpected death, no competent ruler followed. The Hunnic Empire dissolved, and the Huns disappeared as a people, retreating back to Asia or blending in among the diverse new Europeans.

Instead of a Roman recovery, the so-called **Germanic barbarian kingdoms** became supreme throughout western Europe. German chieftains and kings soon finished off the Roman imperial administration in the West. In AD 476, the Gothic king and commander of Roman armies Odavacar (or Odoaker) seized power by toppling the last emperor in the western half of the Roman Empire.[4] This unwarranted deposition annoyed the current Roman emperor in the east, so he commissioned the Ostrogoths (eastern Germans) under their king Theodoric to invade

---

4. The last emperor had the myth-rich name of Romulus Augustus, which evoked the founder of Rome and the founder of the Principate government. Critical contemporaries added as an insult the suffix *-ulus* (meaning small) for the teenager who was a puppet of his father, Orestes. Roman leadership had become so weak that Orestes had been the commander of Roman

Italy on his behalf. After several years of warfare, Odavacar surrendered. The victorious Theodoric assassinated Odavacar at dinner and then proclaimed himself ruler, backed up by his Ostrogothic warriors. Theodoric ruled without restriction over an Ostrogothic kingdom in the Italian Peninsula. Although he remained a heretical Arian Christian, he tried to forge a society that tolerated religious and ethnic differences among Romans and Germans.

The western half of the Roman Empire fell because its armies could not defend it. It must not be forgotten, however, that the Roman Empire continued for another thousand years. The barbarians' feet had trampled only the western portion of the empire. The eastern half continued to fight on and to preserve Roman civilization. For centuries the new capital of Constantinople was one of the greatest cities in the world. Later historians have designated that part of the Roman Empire as **Byzantium** or the **Byzantine Empire**, named after the Greek city Byzantion that Constantine had made his capital. The emperors maintained their roles as protector and promoter of the Christian church, in the tradition of Constantine. Historians call this cooperation between imperial and ecclesiastical leaders *caesaro-papism*. A "sacred" emperor appointed the bishops who worked with the unified Christian state. After the fall of the western half of the Roman Empire, the eastern half increasingly took on a Greek flavor, since ethnic Greeks filled all the leadership positions. Once more the Greeks ruled a powerful political state.

The reign of **Emperor Justinian** (r. 527–565) marked the transition from the ancient Roman Empire to the medieval Byzantine Empire. Justinian has been considered both the last emperor of Rome and the first Byzantine emperor. He had several notable achievements. First, he ordered built one of the greatest churches of the world in Constantinople, the Hagia Sophia (Holy Wisdom) (see figure 6.4). Second, he had the old Roman laws reorganized into the Book of Civil Laws, often called the **Justinian Code**. This legal handbook not only secured the authority of Byzantine emperors for centuries to come; it also helped the West rebuild its governments after the twelfth century (see chapter 8).

Justinian's attempt to restore the Imperium Romanum in the west was less successful. His armies, led by brilliant generals such as Belisarius and Narses, managed some reconquests, including the Vandal kingdom in North Africa and much of the Ostrogothic kingdom in the Italian Peninsula. These victories notwithstanding, Byzantine intrigues at the court undermined the generals. In the long run, the eastern empire also lacked the resources and power to hold on to the old western provinces of Rome. Shortly after Emperor Justinian's death, most of Italy fell back under the control of squabbling German kings. From then on, the German kings ignored Constantinople, and Byzantium ignored them right back.

---

armies in Gaul, despite being a German (Pannonian) who had worked with Attila. Orestes and his troops had toppled the previous Roman emperor in Ravenna only one year before Romulus Augustulus's own fall.

Figure 6.4. Justinian's Hagia Sophia, the Church of Holy Wisdom, rose over Constantinople at the emperor's command. The minarets were added later, when it was converted into a mosque after the fall of the Byzantine Empire in 1453. Today it is secularized as a museum.

Review: How did the Roman Empire fall in the west, yet not in the east?

Response:

STRUGGLE FOR THE REALM OF SUBMISSION

The sudden rise of the Islamic civilization in the seventh century surprised everyone. The new religion of *Islam* (which means "submission" in Arabic) worshipped the same omnipotent God as Judaism and Christianity. All three are called the Abrahamic religions, since Abraham and his God figured in the scriptures of each. Islam originated in Arabia, an arid peninsula that had so far largely remained outside the political domination of major civilizations. Muhammad (b. ca. 570–d. 632), an Arab merchant from Mecca, became Islam's founder and final prophet. At about the age of forty, he claimed that the angel Gabriel revealed to him the message of God (called Allah in Arabic).

He recorded these in the Qur'an (meaning "Recitation"), the book containing the essentials of Islam. These are usually summed up as five "pillars." The first is *shahadah*, the simple proclamation of faith that there is no God except Allah and that Muhammad is his last prophet. Second is *salat*, praying five times a day, at the beginning of day, noon, afternoon, sunset, and before bed, always on one's knees and facing toward Mecca, whether in a mosque or not. Third is *zakat*, the obligation to pay alms to care for the poor. Fourth is *sawm*, to fast from sunrise to sunset every day during the lunar month of Ramadan. Last is a pilgrimage (*hajj*) to Mecca that should be undertaken once in one's lifetime. Everyone who keeps these pillars is a Muslim and is promised eternal life after death.

Other issues such as polygamy or restrictions on food or alcohol were less important but added to the discipline of submission to divine commands. Islam was syncretic: it combined the Arab's polytheistic religion centered on the moon (hence the crescent symbol), the Persian dualism of Zoroastrianism, a connection with Judaism via Abraham as a common ancestor, and even a recognition of Jesus as a prophet (although not God incarnate). Scholars over the next decades developed rules of behavior or sets of laws called *shari'a*, based on their interpretation of Muhammad and the Qur'an.

Most in Mecca refused to believe in Muhammad's calls for submission to God's commands. In AD 622 he fled Mecca to a nearby city. The residents of his hometown had refused to listen to him. That flight (*Hegira* or *Hijra*) marks the founding year of the calendar still used today in Islam, namely 1 AH, from the Latin *anno Hegirae* (in the year of the emigration). The place of his refuge became known as "the City of the Prophet," or Medina. There he successfully won converts called **Muslims**. His followers soon launched a series of conquests, starting with Mecca, to force their neighbors' submission to the commands of God's prophet.

The meaning of the term applied to these assaults, *jihad*, ranges from a "struggle" to a Muslim version of holy war. Clearly, his followers interpreted Muhammad's message to mean that Islamic submission to Allah should reign everywhere. When peaceful, voluntary conversions failed, the alternative was war to establish political supremacy over non-Muslims. By the time of his death, Muhammad ruled over much of Arabia. His successors went on to conquer a third of what had been the Roman Empire (from the Iberian Peninsula, across North Africa, and over Palestine and Mesopotamia), as well as the Persian Empire. Within a hundred years of Muhammad's death, Muslim armies had won territories from the Atlantic Ocean to southern Asia, into the Indian subcontinent.

The Muslim conquest succeeded for several reasons. First, the fanaticism and skill of the nomadic Arab warriors from the desert overwhelmed many armies fighting for uninspiring emperors and kings. Second, the Eastern Roman/Byzantine Empire and Persia had both exhausted themselves from their long and inconclusive wars over Mesopotamia. Third, many Muslim rulers were tolerant of the religious diversity among their new subjects. So long as Muslims ruled, they did not force those who believed in the same God to fully convert. Muslim rulers usually allowed Jews and Christians to keep their lives and their religions, burdening them only with paying extra taxes. So although individuals may have converted to Islam, the Christian, Jewish, and even Zoroastrian or polytheistic communities endured for centuries within Muslim states.

Through their conquests, Arabs became a new cultural contender. Islam's domination of the Iberian Peninsula, North Africa, and Mesopotamia prevented those former areas of the Roman Empire from participating in developments in the rest of the West. Instead, the Muslims took the shared Græco-Roman heritage in another direction. Within their territories, the new Arab rulers carried out their own *islamization*, encouraging the faith and practices of Islam, as well as *arabization*, promoting Arabic culture and language among their new subjects. Since the faithful were supposed to read the Qur'an in the original language in which it was written, namely Arabic, most educated Muslims learned to read that language. In much of Mesopotamia and North Africa, Arabic became the dominant language, replacing the Greek, Latin, Coptic, Aramaic, and other languages of the conquered peoples. Only in Persia did the natives resist linguistic conversion, although the Persians shared their own rich civilized heritage with their fellow Muslims.

Islamic civilization drew on what the Greeks and Romans had united, adding in Persian and other cultures. While Roman cities in western Europe crumbled under barbarian neglect, Muslim cities blossomed with learning and sophistication. They had paved streets and plumbing. Although their religion prohibited pictures and sculptures of people, Islamic civilization created impressive public buildings, especially mosques with lofty domes and towering minarets, decorated with elaborate calligraphy, patterns, and designs. Communities of scholars studied in libraries both the Qur'an and other facets of knowledge. Some Muslims became Sufis, exploring the religious experience through mysticism, the idea that people can attain a direct experience with God. Philosophers expanded the fields of metaphysics, medicine, mathematics, and science. Al-Khawarizmi, for example, popularized "Arabic" numbers, which had been invented in non-Muslim India. His name is remembered today through the words *algebra* and *algorithm*. In commerce, merchants with their luxury goods of silks, ceramics, and spices ventured far into Asia and Africa, by land and by sea, to bargain and trade. Muslim pilgrims traveled hundreds of miles within the Muslim-Arabic Empire in safety.

This Arabic Empire surpassed Alexander's in size and civilization. Unfortunately for Islam, it did not last much longer. Muhammad and the Qur'an left little guidance about who should lead the Muslim community after Muhammad's death. Muslims split over who should be Muhammad's successor, called the caliph (meaning "deputy"), the ultimate judge in all matters political or religious. The majority of Muslims, or the Sunni (meaning "traditional"), were willing to accept any respectable dynasty, whether established in Medina, Damascus, Baghdad, or Istanbul (as they would be over the centuries). Hence, Sunnis were open to competing rulers and did not worry much about political divisions. A minority, the Shia or Shi'i (meaning "sect"), thought the heirs of Muhammad's family should unite all Muslims in Dar al-Islam (the realm of Submission to God). But the caliphs descended from Muhammad all had died natural deaths or had been assassinated or killed in battle by AD

680 (or 61 AH). Although no physical descendants remained to unite Islam, Shiites then believed that a holy figure, the imam, would miraculously unite Muslims again someday. Besides these ongoing disagreements between Shiites and Sunnis, ethnic differences among Arabs, Berbers, Egyptians, Mesopotamians, and Persians also weakened solidarity and loyalty toward any one empire. Islam thus lost its political unity and has been unable to regain it ever since.

In addition to internal fighting, Islam faced hostile borders with Christians in western Europe and in the Byzantine Empire. In particular, the Byzantine Empire successfully fended off multiple Muslim attacks, helped by "Greek fire," a liquid spray that burned sailors and ships, even on water. Although the Byzantine emperors lost substantial territory south of Asia Minor to Muslims, they managed a few compensatory gains in the Balkan Peninsula. Slavic invaders had settled in that region after the Hunnic Empire vanished.[5] By the eighth century, missionaries from the Byzantine Empire had converted most of the **Slavs** in the Balkans to Christianity. The Cyrillic alphabet, modeled on Greek letters, became the written script of many southern Slavs. But the Byzantine Empire still had to fight to gain direct rule over these Balkan Christians. For example, Emperor Basil II, the "Bulgar Slayer" (r. 976–1025), expanded dominion over the Albanians, Serbs, and Bulgars (an Asiatic people who had blended with the Slavs). Basil earned his harsh nickname not only by killing many Bulgarians in battle but also by allegedly blinding thousands of Bulgarian prisoners before sending them home.

For a time, the multicultural Byzantine Empire of Greeks, southern Slavs, and other ethnic minorities straddling the Balkans and Asia Minor seemed secure. Then the **Turks** seized power in Persia (AD 1040; 431 AH). The Turks were horse-riding warriors who swept off the Asiatic steppes toward Europe, as the Huns had done before and as the Mongols would do later. The Turkish Seljuk dynasty converted to Islam, allowing it to win support among Muslims of other ethnicities. With surprising swiftness, the Seljuks conquered Mesopotamia and moved into the Byzantine Empire. They defeated, captured, and humiliated the Byzantine emperor of the Romans at the Battle of Manzikert (AD 1071; 453 AH). This decisive Turkish victory gained them Asia Minor, which became their new Turkish homeland, the basis of the country of Turkey early in the twentieth century.

The lands of Asia Minor had been some of the most important and prosperous areas of the Byzantine Empire. Their loss further weakened the empire, leaving it less able to resist attack by the Turks or anyone. As a result, the Byzantines sought reinforcements from the west even though a religious schism had soured relations. That request unleashed the Crusades against the Muslims in the Holy Land (see chapter 8). Instead of strengthening Byzantium, the Crusades weakened the empire, as western forces seized lands for themselves, increased Islamic fanaticism, and even briefly conquered much of the Byzantine Empire itself. A revived Bulgarian Empire, then a new Serbian Empire, and finally the Ottoman Empire of Turks in the mid-fourteenth century sucked away Byzantine power (see chapter 9).

---

5. Because so many slaves were taken from those peoples during the Middle Ages, often to be sold in the markets of Constantinople, the word for *slave* in several languages was adapted from the name of the Slavs.

Finally, in AD 1453 (or 857 AH), the last "Roman" emperor died on Constantinople's walls, fighting alongside his handful of imperial troops and volunteers. The Ottoman Turks made Constantinople the capital of their own Muslim empire, renamed as Istanbul (probably from the Greek phrase "to the city"). The Greeks were a conquered people once more.

If the Roman Empire had survived intact or if the attempted Muslim conquest of Europe had succeeded, the West as we know it would never have existed. Civilization would have had a very different geographic foundation, centered, like the Roman Empire, on the Mediterranean. Byzantium or Islam could have bound western Europe together with the Balkans, North Africa, and the Middle East.

Instead, the collapse of Roman power in western Europe, combined with the rise and fall of the Byzantine and various Muslim empires, meant that eastern Europe, Africa, and Asia remained outside the main development of Western civilization for the next thousand years or more. In their portions of the former united Roman Empire, the Orthodox Christian Byzantine Empire and the various Muslim realms directly inherited a rich Græco-Roman culture of classical antiquity. Yet Byzantines and Muslims flourished on the other side of a cultural divide that arose after the Germanic conquest of the western portion of the Roman Empire. Only in western Europe did various elements of Græco-Roman, Judeo-Christian, and Germanic cultures meld through many difficult centuries to become Western civilization.

Review: *How did Islam rise as a rival civilization?*

Response:

Make your own timeline.

4 BC   AD 1453

CHAPTER 7

From Old Rome to the New West

The Early Middle Ages, AD 500 to 1000

The collapse of the western half of the Roman Empire during the fifth century AD marked the end of "ancient" history and the beginning of "medieval" history (see timeline B). The intellectuals after the fifteenth century who coined the term **Middle Ages** (whose Latin form provides *medieval*) saw the thousand years of history between classical antiquity and their own (early modern) day as one horrible detour for civilization. For the intellectuals of the so-called Renaissance (see chapter 9), the previous thousand years seemed simply barbaric when compared to the glories of Greece and Rome. Even today, "medieval" describes something backward, vicious, or stupid. These meanings do not actually reflect the historical truth. Rather, much improved over the course of the Middle Ages. Modern historians divide the thousand years between AD 500 and 1500 into three periods (early, high or central, and later), hence the use of the plural "ages." First came the **early Middle Ages** (about 450–1050), during which Europe rebuilt after the collapse of Rome (see map 7.1).[1] During these centuries, three cultures (Græco-Roman, Christian, and Germanic) wove together to give birth to and nurture the childhood of Western civilization.

GOTHS IN THE GARDEN

The Germans or Goths destroyed the western half of the Roman Empire by settling amid the remnants of its Christianized Græco-Roman civilization. As the new political masters, they oversaw the formation of a new culture. At the end of the Middle Ages, humanist admirers of classical antiquity applied the term *Gothic* as an insult describing the medieval period. Likewise, art historians denigrated the art and architecture of the High and later Middle Ages with the term *Gothic*. They preferred the svelte Corinthian columns and bleached-white calm nudes of antiquity to

---

1. If you noticed that the dates differ between the chapter headline and this sentence, good for you! Historians disagree about when exactly these time periods began or ended—there is no easily identifiable big event (like a war or a leader's death) to mark them.

Map 7.1.   Dark Ages Europe.
How was the former Roman cultural area divided up?

pointed arches and the polychrome tortured crucifixions of late medieval art. Those educated medieval people who saw the difference between their own times and the ancient world often saw themselves much as we refer to ourselves: "we moderns."

Many people view the Middle Ages as unmodern, as lacking in sophistication and enlightenment, because "barbarians" ruined Roman civilization. The illiterate Germanic leaders of the so-called barbarian kingdoms who replaced the officials of imperial Rome left few written records. Thus, the first few centuries after the fall of Rome might justifiably be called the **Dark Ages**, for we are indeed in the dark about much that happened. Sadly, the term *Dark Ages* too often insults the entire Middle Ages as being full of ignorance, cruelty, and superstition.

Although the Germans were uncivilized, they had not intended to destroy all the benefits of civilization. Rome's wealth and comforts were attractive. German regimes clumsily tried to continue the Roman system, but barbarians simply did not know how to manage urban life. They feared and avoided cities. Thus, towns lost populations, sports stadiums sat empty, libraries crumbled, and forums gave way to farmland. Much was lost, unintentionally, from neglect. Ancient technology, such as water mills and glassmaking, went forgotten. Until the new ruling elites learned the ways of civilization, the West lapsed into primitive rural conditions.

The barbarian conquest ended with two large groups living side by side, the ruling Germans and the former Romans. The German kings took the best land for themselves. They preferred woodland and field, as they enjoyed hunting, and agriculture became the mainstay of the new economy and shaped society. Germanic lords lived in manor halls (large structures that housed warriors and dependents) and small villages throughout the countryside. The conquered Roman population often became servile dependents, working for the German warriors in charge. Actual slavery slowly declined, since the uncivilized Germans neither appreciated nor knew how to manage that system of oppression.

The Germans themselves were diverse, as shown by the numerous names of the tribes: Visigoths, Ostrogoths, Alans, Alemanni, Vandals, Suebi, Franks, Angles, Saxons, Jutes, Gepids, Lombards, Frisians, Rugians, Burgundians, Bavarians, and Thuringians. Some were not even Germans, as other peoples entering Europe from Asia attached themselves to successful leaders. Constant warfare left some groups so weak that they either quickly joined a new ethnic conglomeration or disappeared altogether. The various tribes spoke in many different dialects and accents, each almost incomprehensible to the other. In western Europe they separated into many petty realms, regularly trying to conquer one another.

Within the borders of the old empire (except in Britain and near the Rhine and Danube Rivers), the Germans were actually an ethnic minority. Gradually, they stopped speaking their German language and adopted the ever-evolving language of the Romans. Thus, Latin slowly turned into vernacular "Romance" languages: Spanish and Italian (named after Roman geography) and French (named after the Germanic Franks). Over centuries, the distinctive German character of the ruling class also disappeared as they intermarried with the Roman peoples.

The Germans did not comprehend the Roman government with its ideas of laws, citizenship, and the concept that only the government could use violence. Instead Germanic rule was based on blood and oath. They thought of justice as personal rather than state controlled. Instead of loyalty to some distant ruler, impersonal regime, or abstract deity (whether the gods of Rome or the person of the emperor), Germans saw themselves connected to one another through ties of kinship. These bonds ranged from the nuclear family of parents and children to extended families, clans, tribes, "folk," and, finally, to the king as father of all. Kings as war leaders bound their warriors with oaths to dedicate their lives to fight for him. A government built on an impersonal system of laws fell to kinship of blood relations and personal oaths. Families, meanwhile, preferred to take justice into their own hands, avenging wrongs by punishing wrongdoers themselves. So if one family member was robbed, other family members hunted down the robber and exacted punishment (usually death, of course).

Thus, the tendency to use personal punishment soon escalated into larger confrontations. For example, a robber killed in vengeance probably had a family of his own who did not take kindly to his death, perhaps seeing it as murder rather than justice. His family members might then go on to kill one of the killers, and soon reciprocal vengeance might bring on vendettas or **feuds**. Families became trapped in escalating cycles of violence against one another. The German kings and lords tried to prevent feuds through *wergild* (having guilty parties pay families money in compensation for injuries or robberies). When guilt or innocence was still in doubt, the barbarians resorted to **trials by ordeal** instead of Roman criminal court procedures. Trial by combat pitted accuser and accused, or their champions, against one another. A more typical ordeal, that of hot iron, required the accused to carry a red hot metal bar for nine paces without dropping it. The burned hands would then be wrapped. If after three days the wounds were healing, the accused was innocent; if they festered with infection, the accused was guilty and subsequently hanged. The Germans believed that their Christian God guaranteed a just outcome.

Indeed, the Christian church itself was the greatest survivor of Rome's collapse in western Europe. Its institutions and beliefs helped to sustain whatever civilization survived. By the time the Germans invaded Rome, many of them had already been converted to Christianity by missionaries. The invaders were usually respectful of holy places. The network of Christian bishops in the dioceses that had coexisted with Roman imperial provinces continued uninterrupted in many places. The Christian order, however, was somewhat complicated by the heretical Arian form of Christianity held by many of the ruling Germans. The church managed only slowly to bring many Germans back into catholic orthodoxy.

This new society built on the ruins of the Roman Empire often defined itself as the universal realm of Christians, or **Christendom**. Serious divisions throughout the Middle Ages, however, prevented Christendom from ever becoming more than an idea. Secular rivalries remained more powerful than cooperation toward a Christian commonwealth. Religious unity also suffered as a rift grew between western, or Latin-speaking, Christians in western Europe and Eastern, or Greek-speaking, Christians in the Byzantine Empire. The concept of Christendom soon excluded the orthodox Christians in Byzantium. In addition, kings would soon be fighting with their own bishops and with the bishop of Rome over leadership. The idea of Christendom during the Middle Ages remained attractive but unrealized.

The political problems clashed with the importance of faith and led some Christians to withdraw from worldly cares so that they could better concentrate on God. This new way of life, called *monasticism*, organized a few people to devote themselves to strict Christianity. The monastic movement had already begun in the late Roman Empire, as some Christians in the East imitated Jesus's wanderings in the wilderness and isolated themselves to live as hermits. As this isolationist ideology migrated to the West, religious leaders promoted instead cenobitic, or group, monasticism. Its participants, communities of monks led by an abbot (or, for females, nuns under an abbess), gathered together apart from the bustling world to dedicate their life to prayer and meditation.

In the 520s, Benedict of Nursia became the most influential abbot when he set up the monastery of Monte Cassino in southern Italy. To guide his flock of monks, Benedict wrote down a set of rules or regulations for this special lifestyle. While life under the **Benedictine Rule** was not unduly harsh, it was not particularly comfortable, either. The abbot (or abbess) exercised parental authority in leading monks (or nuns) in a life of work and prayer. Their basic principle was *asceticism*, choosing to avoid material comforts and sensual pleasures. Monks or nuns were to have few changes of clothing. Unless they fell ill, they ate as vegetarians. The brothers slept together in common dormitories, chastely, in separate beds. They spent their days farming the land and came together to sing psalms eight times from before dawn to long after sunset. Perhaps most important for the future of civilization, they read books. Under the Benedictine Rule, monks and nuns read the pagan classics of Greece and Rome in addition to the Bible and spiritual writings of the church fathers. They laboriously copied these texts by hand onto parchment bound into books, thus preserving much of the literature of the ancients in their small libraries. For a while, monasteries were isolated islands of learning in a sea of barbaric illiteracy. In time, these islands would provide fertilizer and seed for the later regrowth of civilization.

The rise of monasticism divided the ministers of the church into two groups: first, the monks, known as **"regular" clergy** (abbots and monks guided by regulations and separated from lay communities), and second, the "secular" clergy (bishops and priests involved in the world). Of the two, the monks were the role models of the early Middle Ages for the laity as well as the rest of the population of lords and peasants. Cloisters seemed to create a heavenly community here on earth. The lay magnates and lords who wanted to support monastic work donated land to them or sent their extra children (whose inheritance or dowry might weaken the family landholdings) to join the monastic communities. Even the roughest sinner, when he felt death's hand upon his neck, might join a monastery, renounce the world, and partake in a blessed community that seemed a sure path toward paradise.

The Christian monks and bishops did much to educate the uncivilized Germans, but they could not easily reduce their warrior habits. Some bishops even retained their customs from the noble families from which they came. Kingdoms also remained fragile and temporary because of rivalry among the fluctuating Germanic tribes and the desire to attain political supremacy in western Europe. The Ostrogoths seized the Italian Peninsula; the Lombards soon replaced them. The Visigoths grabbed the Iberian Peninsula only to fall to the Muslims, as did the Vandals who took North Africa. Most German kingdoms briefly rose in power, only to soon vanish into history.

Ethnic differences, though, left traces in the *regionalism* that still flourishes in many provinces of Europe today. European regions inherited their diversity both from the peoples, such as Gauls and Celts, romanized to varying degrees after Roman conquest, and from *germanization* following the new German conquerors. The Jews remained a barely tolerated minority. They lived scattered through the decaying cities, keeping their culture relatively segregated and intact, as usual. The integration and assimilation of former Roman citizens and enslaved workers with the new German warriors progressed slowly over a few centuries. The unified regime of Rome with its culture of Christian and Græco-Roman citizens under an emperor had been replaced by numerous kings who saw themselves and their peoples more divided than united by their German ancestries.

Despite this diversity of kingdoms, only two large groups of Germans survived these early medieval centuries to dominate and provide the political and social framework for Western civilization: the Anglo-Saxons and the Franks. Interestingly, both of these German peoples had entered the Roman Empire as pagans (not as heretics, like many other Germans).

The name of the **Anglo-Saxons** reflects members of several different tribes, mostly Angles, Saxons, and Jutes, who invaded the island of Great Britain from across the North Sea, beginning around 450. Since the Roman military had largely withdrawn decades earlier, the Romano-Britons were easily overrun (although some trace of native resistance may be seen in the myths of King Arthur). By the sixth century, the Germans ruled most of the formerly Roman areas of Britain, except for the fringes of Cornwall and Wales. The Picts who dwelt in the northern third of the island, beyond Hadrian's Wall, fought off the Anglo-Saxons, just as they had the Romans. These people soon became the Scots of Scotland, closely tied to the Irish of Ireland (who had likewise never been conquered by Rome, although they had been converted to Christianity by Saint Patrick and others). In the southern two-thirds of Great Britain, though, the Anglo-Saxons soon so outnumbered the Romano-Britons that the latter's Celtic and Latin languages disappeared. These Germanic conquerors established numerous small kingdoms, such as those of the Angles (Anglia), the West Saxons (Wessex), the East Saxons (Essex), Mercia (people of the marshes), and the lands in the north around the Humber River (Northumbria).

Christian missionaries from Ireland soon targeted the pagan Anglo-Saxons for conversion. Irish monk-missionaries arrived to preach throughout the northern realms. Meanwhile, other missionaries from the bishop of Rome succeeded in converting the king of Kent in the south by 600. Forced to choose between the Irish and Roman versions of Christianity, the majority of Anglo-Saxon kingdoms accepted unity with Rome at the **Council of Whitby** in 663. Energized with faith, Anglo-Saxon missionaries were soon both enforcing church discipline and evangelizing other Germans on the Continent. The Irish joined them and slowly accepted obedience to Rome.

While the Anglo-Saxons gained religious unity, political divisiveness almost led to their downfall. Beginning in 835, the **Vikings** began raiding the British Isles. The Vikings, Norsemen, or Northmen were a new wave of Germanic peoples who had settled in Scandinavia (modern Denmark, Norway, and Sweden) outside the orbit of ancient Rome or the moderating influence of Christianity. At first, the Vikings plundered ruthlessly. Soon, however, they conquered in order to settle down and farm. Viking emigrants succeed in occupying most of the Anglo-Saxon kingdoms (as well as key portions of what would become Ireland, northern France, Russia, and southern Italy). In all those places they soon assimilated into the culture of the local populations.

Only the Kingdom of Wessex barely survived and came back to defy the invaders under **King Alfred "the Great"** (r. 871–901). As a younger son of a king, Alfred originally wanted to take the vows of a monk. After the deaths of his brothers made him king, Alfred instead found himself at war. He led his armies to fight the Vikings to a standstill, restricting them to a portion of the kingdom called the Danelaw. Secure from conquest, Alfred then tried to promote culture and literacy, especially with his translation of part of the Bible into Old English. Alfred's success established the unified Kingdom of **England** (taking its name from the Angles). Descendants of ancient Celtic conquerors, Roman victors, Anglo-Saxon invaders, and now Viking colonizers all blended together to become the English. In the 990s, another wave of Viking invasions again almost destroyed the kingdom. The Danish king Canute, who had converted to Christianity, managed to seize the English crown. As King Canute of England (r. 1016–1035), he preserved the realm, briefly uniting it with his other possessions around the North Sea. After his death, England once more gained a dynasty separate from Denmark. Despite this shaky, vulnerable start, the English melded together from this diverse Celtic/Roman/Anglo-Saxon/Viking heritage. Another invasion and ethnic clash shortly after Canute's death would force England into the High Middle Ages and to a central role in the development of Western civilization.

Meanwhile, on the Continent, the **Franks** had asserted themselves as the second enduring group of Germans. They started out more united than the English by having a royal dynasty called the **Merovingians**, named after a legendary founder, Merovech. By the end of the fifth century, the Franks had expanded from their base across the northern Rhine into northern Gaul. **King Clovis** (r. 481–511) won the support of the local Roman population and elites when he (and therefore his people) converted directly to orthodox catholic Christianity. He then used his blessing from the clergy to conquer many of his neighboring Germans, such as the Aquitainians, the Burgundians, and the Suebi, heretical Arian Christians who rejected the Nicene Creed. The kingdom that Clovis established was ethnically diverse. It combined the various German tribes with the large population of Roman Gauls. Although Clovis and his successors committed murders, betrayals, and various atrocities, the clerics who wrote histories thought that God specially blessed the Merovingian kings because they championed orthodox catholic Christianity and political unity. In such uncertain times, it seemed possible to honor God through the brutality of warfare.

Like the Anglo-Saxons, the Franks came close to vanishing into history: in 710 they were nearly conquered by Muslims. A combined Arab and Berber army invaded Europe by landing near the southern tip of the Iberian Peninsula, which then became known as Gibraltar (or "Rock of Tarik," named after the Muslim commander). The Muslim army quickly crushed most of the Visigothic kingdom. Then it crossed the Pyrenees Mountains and attacked the Franks. In October 732, at the **Battle of Tours** or **Poitiers** (there has been some dispute about the location), a Frankish army led by Charles Martel ("the Hammer") stopped and turned back the Muslim invaders. The Muslims (who soon were called the Moors or the **Saracens** by the western Europeans) retreated into the Iberian Peninsula, most of which they continued to control for several centuries. The Franks had halted the Muslim advance into Europe, at least for the moment.

The Franks had been able to stand strong only by dispensing with their other political danger: dividing up kingdoms among numerous heirs. Since the time of Clovis, if the king died with more than one son as heir, his realm was split up among the male survivors. Before long, royal brothers and cousins, aided by some of their queens, were fighting against one another over the divisions of the fractured Frankish kingdoms. These kings grew weaker as they handed out lands and authorities to the aristocrats and nobles who did their fighting for them. Within a few decades, the Merovingian dynasts gained the nickname of "do-nothing kings." They gloried in their semidivine royal authority, but did little to govern for the benefit of the people.

Fortunately for the future of the Franks, ambitious royal servants kept Frankish power intact. Managers of the king's household soon seized the important reins of rulership. These mayors (from the Latin word *major*, meaning "greater") of the various royal palaces soon became the powers behind the thrones. One of them, the above-mentioned Charles Martel, managed by 720 to reunify the splintered kingdoms in the name of his Merovingian king. The successes of Mayor Charles Martel helped Western civilization to develop in western Europe.

Review: How did German rule combine with the Roman heritage in the West?

Response:

PRIMARY SOURCE PROJECT 7: BAD BISHOPS VERSUS BENEDICT ABOUT MORAL RULES

Some people in the Dark Ages could choose between religious and secular life-styles. The first source, written by a bishop, illustrates the corrupt condition of some leaders of the church who were supposed to be role models of Christian behavior. Instead, these bad bishops imitated the worst of the aristocracy. In contrast, Benedict of Nursia offered another way of life suitable for Christians. His rule for his monastic community in Monte Cassino provided structure for monks and nuns from then until today.

Source 1: *The History of the Franks* by Gregory of Tours (ca. 590)

An uproar arose against the bishops Salunius and Sagittarius. They . . . became their own masters and in a mad way began to seize property, wound, kill, commit adultery, and various other crimes. . . . When king Gunthram [r. 561–592] learned of it he ordered a synod to meet in Lyons. The bishops assembled . . . and after examining the case found that they were absolutely convicted of the crimes charged to them, and they ordered that men guilty of such acts should be removed from the office of bishop.

But since Salunius and Sagittarius knew that the king was still favorable to them, they went to him complaining that they were unjustly removed and asking for permission to go to the pope of the city of Rome. . . . And [the pope] sent letters to the king in which he directed that they should be restored to their places. This the king did without delay, first rebuking them at length. But, what is worse, no improvement followed. . . . [T]hese men daily engaged in greater crimes and, as we have stated before, they armed themselves like laymen, and killed many with their own hands in the battles which Mummolus [Count of Auxerre] fought with the Lombards. And among their fellow citizens they were carried away by animosity and beat a number with clubs and let their fury carry them as far as the shedding of blood. Because of this the outcry of the people again reached the king. . . .

[T]he king was greatly aroused and took away from them horses, slaves, and whatever they had, and ordered them to be taken and shut up in distant monasteries to do penance there. . . .

Now the king's sons were living at this time, and the older of them began to be sick. And the king's friends went to him and said: . . . "Beware lest perhaps these bishops be condemned to exile though innocent, and the king's sin be increased somewhat, and because of it the son of our master perish." . . . [T]he bishops were released and . . . were so penitent that they apparently never ceased from psalm singing, fasting, almsgiving, reading the book of the songs of David through the day, and spending the night in singing hymns and meditating on the readings.

But this absolute piety did not last long, and they fell a second time and generally spent the nights in feasting and drinking, so that when the clergy were singing the matins in the church these were calling for cups and drinking wine. There was no mention at all of God, no services were observed. When morning came, they arose from dinner and covered themselves with soft coverings; and buried in drunken sleep they would lie till the third hour of the day. And there were women with whom they polluted themselves. And then they would rise and bathe and lie down to eat; in the evening they arose and later they devoted themselves greedily to dinner until the dawn. . . .

Source 2: *Benedictine Rule* by Benedict of Nursia (ca. 530)

33. Whether the Monks Should Have Anything of Their Own

More than anything else is this special vice to be cut off root and branch from the monastery, that one should presume to give or receive anything without the order of the abbot, or should have anything of his own. He should have absolutely nothing: neither a book, nor tablets, nor a pen—nothing at all. For indeed it is not allowed to the monks to have their own bodies or wills in their own power. But all things necessary they must expect from the abbot of the monastery; nor may they have anything which the abbot did not give or permit. . . .

39. Concerning the Amount of Food

We believe, moreover, that . . . two cooked dishes . . . are enough for all tables: so that whoever, perchance, can not eat of one may partake of the other. . . . [I]f it is possible to obtain apples or growing vegetables, a third may be added. One full pound of bread shall suffice for a day. . . . But the eating of the flesh of quadrupeds shall be abstained from altogether by everyone, excepting alone the weak and the sick. . . .

40. Concerning the Amount of Drink

Each one has his own gift from God, the one in this way, the other in that. Therefore it is with some hesitation that we assign the amount of daily sustenance for others. Nevertheless, in view of the weakness of the infirm we believe that [about sixteen ounces] of wine a day is enough for each one. Those moreover to whom God gives the ability of bearing abstinence shall know that they will have their own reward. But the prior shall judge if either the needs of the place, or labor, or the heat of summer, requires more; considering in all things, lest satiety or drunkenness creep in. Indeed, we read that wine is not suitable for monks at all. But because, in our day, it is impossible to persuade the monks of this, let us at least agree that we should not drink until we are sated, but sparingly. For wine can make even the wise to go astray. . . .

48. Concerning the Daily Manual Labor

Idleness is the enemy of the soul. And therefore, at fixed times, the brothers ought to be occupied in manual labor; and again, at fixed times, in sacred reading. . . .

55. Concerning Clothes and Shoes

Vestments shall be given to the brothers according to the nature of the places where they dwell, or the temperature of the air. For in cold regions more is required; but in warm, less. This is for the abbot to decide. We nevertheless consider that for ordinary places there suffices for the monks a cowl and a gown apiece—the cowl, in winter hairy, in summer plain or old—and a working garment, on account of their labor.

Questions:

- *How does the structure of each source serve to carry its message?*
- *How did the bishops fail to meet expectations of Christian leaders?*
- *What rules did Benedict fashion to better regulate virtuous behavior?*

Responses:

Citations

Gregory of Tours. *History of the Franks (extended selections)*. Translated by Ernest Brehaut. Records of Civilization. Vol. 2. New York: Columbia University Press, 1916, pp. 125–27.

"The Rule of St. Benedict." *Select Historical Documents of the Middle Ages*, edited and translated by Ernest F. Henderson. London: George Bell and Sons, 1905, pp. 289–301.

For more on these sources, go to http://www.concisewesternciv.com/sources/psc7 .html.

SOURCES ON FAMILIES: TACITUS, *GERMANIA* (AD 98)

Although the historian Tacitus wrote his Germania *during the height of the Roman Empire, many scholars consider it to be a reasonable view of Goths or early Germans. Others note that Tacitus may have been writing more to comment on Roman* mores *rather than Germanic customs. Either way, this selection portrays Gothic marriage and family as Tacitus admired it.*

XVII . . . The women have the same dress as the men, except that they generally wrap themselves in linen garments, which they embroider with purple, and do not lengthen out the upper part of their clothing into sleeves. The upper and lower arm is thus bare, and the nearest part of the bosom is also exposed.

XVIII Their marriage code, however, is strict, and indeed no part of their manners is more praiseworthy. Almost alone among barbarians they are content with one wife, except a very few among them, and these not from sensuality, but because their noble birth procures for them many offers of alliance. The wife does not bring a dower to the husband but the husband to the wife. The parents and relatives are present, and pass judgment on the marriage-gifts, gifts not meant to suit a woman's taste, nor such as a bride would deck herself with, but oxen, a caparisoned steed, a shield, a lance, and a sword. With these presents the wife is espoused, and she herself in her turn brings her husband a gift of arms. This they count their strongest bond of union, these their sacred mysteries, these their gods of marriage. Lest the woman should think herself to stand apart from aspirations after noble deeds and from the perils of war, she is reminded by the ceremony which inaugurates marriage that she is her husband's partner in toil and danger, destined to suffer and to dare with him alike both in peace and in war. The yoked oxen, the harnessed steed, the gift of arms, proclaim this fact. She must live and die with the feeling that she is receiving what she must hand down to her children neither tarnished nor depreciated, what future daughters-in-law may receive, and may be so passed on to her grand-children.

XIX Thus with their virtue protected they live uncorrupted by the allurements of public shows or the stimulant of feastings. Clandestine correspondence is equally unknown to men and women. Very rare for so numerous a population is adultery, the punishment for which is prompt, and in the husband's power. Having cut off the hair of the adulteress and stripped her naked, he expels her from the house in the presence of her kinsfolk, and then flogs her through the whole village. The loss of chastity meets with no indulgence; neither beauty, youth, nor wealth will procure the culprit a husband. No one in Germany laughs at this vice, nor do they call it the fashion to corrupt and to be corrupted. Still better is the condition of those states in which only maidens are given in marriage, and where the hopes and expectations of a bride are then finally terminated. They receive one husband, as having one body and one life, that they may have no thoughts beyond, no further-reaching desires, that they may love not so much the husband as the married state. To limit the number of their children or to destroy any of their subsequent offspring is accounted infamous, and good habits are here more effectual than good laws elsewhere.

XX In every household the children, naked and filthy, grow up with those stout frames and limbs which we so much admire. Every mother suckles her own offspring, and never entrusts it to servants and nurses. The master is not distinguished from the slave by being brought up with greater delicacy. Both live amid the same flocks and lie on the same ground till the freeborn are distinguished by age and recognized by merit. The young men marry late, and their vigor is thus unimpaired. Nor are the maidens hurried into marriage; the same age and a similar stature is required; well-matched and vigorous they wed, and the offspring reproduce the strength of the parents. Sister's sons are held in as much esteem by their uncles as by their fathers; indeed, some regard the relation as even more sacred and binding, and prefer it in receiving hostages, thinking thus to secure a stronger hold on the affections and a wider bond for the family. But every man's own children are his heirs and successors, and there are no wills. Should there be no issue, the next in succession to the property are his brothers and his uncles on either side. The more relatives he has, the more numerous his connections, the more honored is his old age; nor are there any advantages in childlessness.

Questions:

- *What is the role of property in these German marriages and families?*
- *Compared to the problems of marriage in the Augustan Age (the previous chapter), how does Tacitus contrast those with German marriages?*
- *What specific characteristics do German wives have?*

Responses:

Citation

Tacitus. "Translation of The Germany." *The Agricola and Germany of Tacitus*, translated by Alfred John Church and William Jackson Brodribb. London: Macmillan, 1868, pp. 13–15.

For more on this source, go to http://www.concisewesternciv.com/sources/sof# .html.

CHARLES IN CHARGE

Charles Martel, who won at Tours/Poitiers, belonged to one of the most important families in Western history. Historians call that dynasty the Carolingians, from Carolus, the Latin version of the name Charles. Members of this family rescued the Franks from infighting and made them a powerful force again. Having beaten back the Moors, Charles handed his power to his two sons (although one quickly gave up and retired to a monastery). The remaining sole heir, Pepin or **Pippin "the Short"** (r. 741–768), soon grew dissatisfied with ruling as mayor in the name of the officially crowned King Childeric III of the Merovingian dynasty. Pippin appealed to the person whom he considered to have the best connection to the divine, the bishop of Rome, better known as the **pope**.

The institution of the popes, called the **papacy**, played a key role in the rise of the Carolingians and Western civilization. The name *pope* comes from *papa*, or "father," a title also often used for bishops. A number of bishops called either popes or patriarchs had risen to preeminence by the fifth century in Rome, Alexandria, Antioch, Jerusalem, and Constantinople. Together, in church councils, bishops and other Christians had declared doctrine and settled controversies. With the division of the Roman Empire into two halves and the collapse of Roman authority in the West, four patriarchs remained under the growing authority of the Byzantine emperors in the east. Meanwhile, the bishops of Rome adopted the title of pope for themselves alone and claimed a superior place (primacy) among the other bishops and patriarchs. These other patriarchs might have granted the bishops of Rome a primacy of honor, but not actual authority over them and their churches. In any case, the popes lived too far away to change developments in the Byzantine Empire. In western Europe, though, religious and political circumstances favored a unique role for the bishops of Rome.

The figure who first embodied the early papacy was **Gregory I "the Great"** (r. 590–604). The growing importance of the monastic movement is reflected in his being the first pope who had previously been a monk. Much more important, though, were Gregory's three areas of activity, which defined what later popes did. First, the pope provided spiritual leadership for the West. Since the West lacked a literate population in comparison to the East, Gregory's manuals (models of sermons for preachers and advice on being a good pastor) filled a practical need. His theological writings were so significant that he was later counted as one of the four great church fathers, alongside Ambrose, Jerome, and Augustine, even though Gregory lived nearly two centuries after them. Second, Gregory acted to secure orthodox catholic Christianity all over the West, far outside his diocese in central Italy. Gregory sent missionaries to the Visigoths in the Iberian Peninsula, to Germany, and, most famously, to the British Isles. Third, the pope was a political leader. He helped organize and defend the lands around Rome from the invading Lombard

Germans, helping to found the political power of the popes, which endures to this day in the Vatican City.

The necessity for papal political leadership increased when later popes disagreed with some Byzantine emperors in the eighth century. The eastern Christians were caught up in the **Iconoclastic Controversy**, which interpreted literally the Old Testament commandment against having graven images. Iconoclasts were those who physically sought to shatter religious pictures and sculptures. (Today the word figuratively refers to those seeking to overturn traditional ways). Eastern patriarchs and bishops increasingly began to support iconoclasm and actually destroyed art in churches. When the western popes refused to go along, the Byzantine emperor confiscated lands in southern Italy that had been used to support the papal troops. At the same time, the Germanic Lombard invaders from the north threatened Rome.

At this pivotal moment, when the pope needed a new ally in the West, a letter came from the Frankish mayor of the palace, Pippin "the Short," son and heir of Charles Martel. In the letter, Pippin coolly inquired of the pope whether the one who had the power of a king should actually be the king. Needing Pippin's army, the pope agreed. So the last Merovingian king was shaved of his regal long hair and bundled off to a monastery in 751. Then Pippin became the first Carolingian king. In return for the papal favor, Pippin marched to Italy and defeated the Lombards in 754 and 756. His victories gave him control of the northern half of the Italian Peninsula (while the southern part remained under nominal Byzantine authority for the next few centuries). In his gratitude, Pippin donated a large chunk of territory in central Italy to the pope. This **Donation of Pippin** eventually became known as the **Papal States**. These lands provided the basis for a papal principality that lasted for more than a thousand years. The arrangement also began a mutually supportive relationship, profitable to both the pope and Pippin, which historians call the **Frankish-Papal Alliance**.

The cooperation between the papacy and the Carolingians culminated under Pippin's son, Charles. He is known to history as **Charlemagne** (r. 768–814), which means "Charles the Great." As his father had before him, Charlemagne at first inherited the throne jointly with his brother, but the latter soon found himself deposited in a monastery. As sole ruler, Charles continued to support the popes. First, he invaded Italy, utterly breaking the power of the Lombards. A few years later, after political rivals had roughed up the pope, Charlemagne marched to Rome to restore papal dignity.

On Christmas Day AD 800, the grateful pope crowned Charlemagne as emperor of the Romans. The circumstances surrounding this act have remained unclear. People then and historians since have argued about the coronation's significance. Did it merely recognize Charlemagne's actual authority or give it a new dimension? Was the pope, by placing the crown on Charlemagne's brow, trying to control the ceremony and the office? Did it insult the Byzantine emperor, who was, after all, the real Roman emperor (even if some alleged at the time that the eastern throne was vacant, since a mere woman, Empress Irene, ruled after deposing and blinding her son)? In any case, the coronation resulted in a brief enthusiasm for imitating ancient Rome. An emperor once again ruled the West in the name of Rome's civilization (see map 7.2).

In most ways, though, Charlemagne resembled his barbaric German ancestors more than a Roman Caesar Augustus. He dressed in Frankish clothing and enjoyed beer and beef (instead of wine and fish as the Romans had). A man of action, he led a military campaign almost every year to one portion of his empire or another. Thus, he expanded his rulership and conquered the heartland of Europe, which became the core of the European Community more than a millennium afterward. He deposed the Bavarian duke and took over his duchy. He smashed rebellious Lombards as his father had. He also fought the Saxons in northern Germany (cousins of long-since-Christianized Anglo-Saxons in Britain). The Christian king tried for thirty years to convert the pagan Saxons to both religious and political obedience. These Saxons faced two choices: either be washed in the water of holy baptism or be slaughtered in their own blood. Many died; survivors converted, then were forcibly migrated to other parts of the empire, where they assimilated. Charlemagne wiped out the Avars (Asian raiders who had settled along the Danube). The emperor successfully defended his empire's borders against Danes in the north and Moors in the south. Charlemagne's empire became bigger than any other political structure in the West since Emperor Romulus Augustulus lost his throne in AD 476.

Map 7.2.   Europe, 800.
What were the strengths and limits of Charlemagne's empire?

Charlemagne was more than a bloodthirsty barbarian king. He consciously tried to revive the Roman Empire and its civilization. The government still heavily depended on his person, but he continued the efforts of his predecessors to expand governance into an institution centered on the palace. He had administrators, such as a chamberlain to help manage finances. He collected and wrote down laws for his various peoples. He set up powerful counts and bishops as *missi dominici* (messengers from his household) to check up on local government and enforce those laws. In the law that inaugurated their mission in 802, Charlemagne called on everyone (bishops, abbots, nuns, priests, counts, officials, men, widows, orphans, and more) to follow the right path of law and justice in this world so that everyone could gain eternal life in the next. Charlemagne's government was the most ambitious one that western Europe had experienced in three hundred years.

To improve upon his government, Charlemagne and his international advisors, like Paul the Deacon from Lombardy and Alcuin Albinus from Northumbria, consciously sought to revive civilization. Aachen, or Aix-la-Chapelle (today located in northwestern Germany near Belgium), was built as a new capital city, as another Rome, the first western city built in stone since the barbarians had trampled through the forums. Aachen's centerpiece was an octagonal church, small but splendid and harmonious with its high walls capped by a dome. Aachen soon became an intellectual center. Scribes fashioned a new, legible script called Carolingian minuscule, which standardized the use of lowercase letters, like the ones you are reading right now.[2] Every work of history and literature that scholars could find was recopied in this new style, helping to preserve much of the legacy of Greece and Rome.

Charlemagne's selected scholars also revived the Roman educational curriculum of the fifth century: the **seven liberal arts**. The *trivium* of grammar, rhetoric, and logic with the *quadrivium* of arithmetic, geometry, music, and astronomy were taught once more, this time in schools attached to monasteries and cathedrals. This so-called **Carolingian Renaissance** (780–850) hoped to use education to revitalize a way of life that had disappeared in western Europe since the Germans had swept away Roman rule. The Frankish/German Charlemagne used the liberal learning of Greece and Rome to consolidate the new culture of Western civilization.

Regrettably for the cause of civilization, Charlemagne's revitalization attempt failed. The empire was too large and primitive for the weak institutions of government he was able to cobble together. First, he faced the difficulty of paying for art, literature, architecture, and schools with a poor agricultural economy that offered no functional taxation. Second, Frankish aristocrats saw little value in book learning. Third, Charlemagne's own codifications of laws, written for the Alemanni, Burgundians, or Saxons, preserved ethnic differences rather than binding together a new common imperial unity. A final difficulty for Charlemagne was his own mortality. He drove the system along by force of will and sword, but death was certain. His successors lacked his abilities.

---

2. Everything before had mostly been written ONLY IN CAPITAL LETTERS. People who write that way nowadays are interpreted as shouting. When the printing presses started in the fifteenth century, they used Carolingian minuscule, as rediscovered by the humanists of the Renaissance, as the model for new typefaces or fonts.

Fortunately for imperial unity, Charlemagne's vast empire managed to hold together for a few years after his death because only one son survived him to inherit it all. Under Emperor Louis "the Pious" (r. 814–840), the Carolingian Renaissance peaked. Then Louis prematurely divided up his empire among his own three sons and invested them with authority during his own lifetime. Not surprisingly, they soon bickered with him and with one another. When Louis tried to carve out a share for a fourth son by another wife, civil war broke out. The ensuing hard-fought peace agreement shattered the political unity of western Europe for more than a thousand years.

The **Treaty of Verdun** in 843 broke apart Charlemagne's empire into three sections, each under its own Carolingian dynasty. The actual treaty was written in both early French and German, showing that a linguistic division matched the political one. The treaty established a kingdom of the West Franks, out of which grew **France**; a kingdom of the East Franks, out of which rose **Germany**; and a middle realm, Lotharingia (named after Louis's grandson, Lothar). At the time, Lotharingia was the heart of the empire, including not only today's small province of **Lorraine** on the border of France and Germany but also the Lowlands (modern Belgium, the Netherlands, and Luxembourg), south through Switzerland and over the Alps into northern Italy. This mixed ethnic and linguistic middle realm had no cohesion except its prosperity and its dynasty. Both the West Franks and the East Franks targeted Lorraine after its Carolingian dynasty died out. For the next eleven hundred years, the French and the Germans fought over possession of this middle territory.

As if all of these political divisions were not bad enough, foreign invaders killed any hope for a reunified and coherent empire. From the north, the Vikings or Norsemen sailed in on longships; from the east, the pagan/polytheist **Magyars** or Hungarians swept out of the steppes of Asia on swift ponies; and from the south, from North Africa and the Iberian Peninsula, Muslim Moors or Saracens raided by land and by sea. None of these invaders was Christian. Only the Saracens were civilized. They all plundered, raped, and burned at will. The feuding Carolingian kings could do little to stop these marauders. The fragile and young western Christendom nearly ended under these attacks.

Thus, Charlemagne's brief success at reviving civilization crashed. His quarreling descendents, resentful aristocrats, invading barbarians, and hostile non-Christians almost destroyed everything the Germanic kingdoms had achieved. Few empires could have survived such an assault from both within and without. The popes were of little help, either, as petty Roman nobles fought over the papal throne. In 897, a vengeful pope, Stephen VI, even put on trial the corpse of his predecessor Pope Formosus. Such postmortem vengeance did little good, since Stephen was himself soon deposed and strangled.

Even as the Carolingian Empire died, its corpse became the fertilizer for the future. The empire left a dream of reunification, reinforcing the longing for the onetime unity and cultural greatness of the Roman Empire. The political reality that followed did divide West Franks and East Franks into France and Germany. These two realms, together with England, formed the core of the West. Despite limited resources, these westerners fought off the assaults from without and established a new order and hierarchy from within. The result was the blossoming of medieval Western civilization.

Review: *How did the Carolingian family rise and fall?*

Response:

THE CAVALRY TO THE RESCUE

Without a central government, the peoples of the collapsing Carolingian Empire needed to defend themselves. New leaders inspired others to follow them, whether through their own achievements or claims of dynastic succession. To defend against the Viking attacks, they built military fortresses called **castles** (see figure 7.1). These fortifications were not simply army bases with walls; they were family homes. The quaint saying "A man's home is his castle" quite literally came from this period. Castles were originally primitive stockades or wooden forts on hills. A castle became the home of a local leader who convinced others to build it and help defend it.

Figure 7.1. The square block of an early castle dominates the town of Loches in France.

These castles became new centers of authority from which lords ruled over small areas, usually no larger than a day's ride.

Hiding out in castles was not a long-term solution, however. "The best defense is a good offense" is another saying appropriate to the time period. Fortunately for Western civilization, **knights** rode to the rescue before all could be lost in the onslaughts of Vikings, Magyars, and Saracens. The new stirrups imported from Asia fixed these warriors firmly in the saddles of their warhorses. Their armor for defense and lance and sword for offense made knights effective heavy cavalry when riding together in a charge. A large group of knights and horses, made up of several tons of flesh and iron, overpowered all opponents.

Already by 1050, knights had won Europe a respite from foreign invasions. The three external enemies of Christendom ceased to be threats. The Norsemen stopped raiding, converted to Christianity, and set up the Scandinavian kingdoms of Denmark, Norway, and Sweden, along with the Icelandic Commonwealth. The adventurous spirit of the Norse was redirected to carry some of them across the Atlantic Ocean to settle in Greenland and even, briefly, North America. The Magyars, meanwhile, became Hungarians. Their successful migration settled them in the Pannonian Basin, a great plain along the middle Danube. Their King Stephen consolidated both his rule and the structure of the Kingdom of Hungary with his conversion and that of his people to Christianity in 1000. Only the Saracens remained hostile and unconverted. Rather than continuing to conquer their Christian neighbors, they concentrated their efforts on developing their own civilization in the Iberian Peninsula, called Andalusia. There the descendents of Phoenicians, Celts, Romans, Jews, Visigoths, Arabs, and Berbers lived in relative peace.

Knights won in their own part of Europe because they were the best military technology of the age. Armored heavy cavalry dominated battlefields for the next five hundred years, long after the threats of Vikings, Magyars, and Saracens had dissipated. As we have seen before, a group with a monopoly on the military can rule the rest of society. In the Middle Ages, knights began to claim authority in the name of the public good and elevated themselves above the masses as a closed social caste of nobles. Their ethos of nobility meant that they lived the good life because they risked their lives to defend the women, children, clerics, and peasants of Christendom. They lived in the nicest homes, ate the most delicious food, and wore the most fashionable clothing. Meanwhile, the peasants paid for these comforts.

During the political chaos of the invasions, whoever commanded the loyalty of others became noble. Over time, though, nobles closed their ranks and limited the status of nobility to those who inherited it. After 1100, usually only those who could prove noble ancestry were allowed access to knighthood (with the rare exceptions of kings ennobling talented warriors). This closed social group of the nobility reinforced itself through **chivalry**, the code of the knights. The ceremonies for initiation to knighthood were surrounded with elaborate rituals. In their castles and courts, knights practiced courtesy and refined manners with one another and courtly ladies, such as using "please," "thank you," and napkins. At **tournaments**, they practiced fighting as a form of sport, entertaining crowds and winning prizes. On the battlefield, they applied rules to fight one another fairly, not attacking an unarmed knight, for example.

While there were many regional variations, the organization of these knights required new structures, or *feudal politics*.[3] A vassal (a subordinate knight) promised fealty (loyalty) and homage (personal service on the battlefield or in the political courts) to a lord (a superior knight) in return for a fief (usually agricultural land sufficiently productive for the knight to live from). A lord was as powerful as the number of vassals he could call on. Lords began to take on new titles that reflected the number of vassals each could bind to himself with fiefs. Above the simple knight at the bottom of the hierarchy were, in ascending order, barons, counts (or earls in England), dukes, and, ultimately, the king. Rather than the kingdoms, however, the most important political units in the eleventh and twelfth centuries were baronies, counties, and duchies.

A network of mutual promises of fidelity provided the glue for feudal politics. While governments are ultimately based on whether or not people uphold the rules, feudal politics was about keeping personal promises to one's lord rather than about obeying public authority. Originally, a fief, being a lord's gift, was supposed to revert to the feudal lord upon a vassal's death. The powerful drive of family, however, where parents provided for their children, soon compelled fiefs to become virtually hereditary. Sometimes, lords and vassals broke their pledges of service and loyalty, probably as often as many modern married people break their vows. When vassals defied their lords, only fights among the knights could conclusively settle the dispute. Thus, the feudal age has been renowned for its constant warfare. Yet enough lords and vassals did maintain oaths so that medieval society largely remained stable. The web of mutual promises of loyalty, the gathering at court to give advice and pronounce judgments, the socializing at tournaments, and the shared risks of battle all forged a ruling class that held on to power for centuries.

Even the church could not avoid being drawn into the feudal network, since dioceses and abbeys possessed a great deal of land. Various lords demanded that the church contribute to the common defense. Rather than share their wealth or have knights seize control and turn church-owned farms into fiefs, bishops and abbots became feudal lords themselves. Thus, clerics became responsible for building castles, commanding knights in battle, and presiding over courts. Some bishops and abbots became prince-bishops and prince-abbots who ruled in the same way as feudal dukes and counts. These political obligations recognized the church's real power but often clashed with its spiritual aims.

To compensate somewhat for its involvement in feudal politics, the church tried to suggest that divinely inspired morality was part of the code of chivalry and the rules of war (see figure 7.2). In some regions, bishops and princes proclaimed the **Peace of God**, which both classified clergy, women, and children as noncombatants and limited the reasons for going to war. Church leaders also tried to assert the

---

3. The term *feudalism* carries too many different meanings to be useful as a historical concept anymore; it is best avoided. Likewise, the phrase *feudal system* makes these arrangements sound more organized than they were. Finally, do not confuse "feudal" politics with feuds or vendettas.

Figure 7.2.   This sculpture in Magdeburg Cathedral of the ancient martyr and saint Maurice portrays him as a black African in twelfth-century armor. Thus Christian values identify with knighthood, regardless of ethnicity.

Truce of God, which was supposed to limit how often warfare could be conducted, especially banning it on Sundays, holidays, and during planting and harvesting. Too often, though, fighting went unchecked.

Those who worked the fields—namely, the vast majority of the population—did not share in the same political relationships as the knights. Instead, the peasants participated in similar yet separate, private, sociopolitical arrangements called **manorial** or **seigneurial economics**. The term comes from *manor*, which referred to the medieval economic unit of a village and its fields, or the French word *seigneur* for the lord of that manor. The harsh conditions of the early Middle Ages had forced many manors into self-sufficiency. Trade had nearly vanished since the roads were too dangerous to travel. The peasants cooperated in their local communities to produce much of what everyone needed to survive, such as food, clothing, and tools.

Most of these peasants who worked on medieval manors for manorial lords were **serfs**. Medieval serfs had servile status, but not as low as that of slaves. They were legally connected or bound to the land of their lords. Serfs had few rights to make decisions about their own lives (such as choice of marriage partners or where to live). They owed obedience, some work (on the lord's land or on roads or castles), and dues (usually payments in the form of portions of their crops) to the seigneurs who legally possessed the land. Peasants thus paid for knights' expensive armor, horses, and castles. These burdens kept them poor from generation to generation. Nevertheless, serfs did benefit from having use of the land. Parents and their children lived in the same villages and farmed the same lands, season after season, according to law and custom. These arrangements provided livelihoods, some security, and continuity, since the seigneurs could not throw serfs off the land as long as they fulfilled their customary obligations. Serfs depended on their lords for justice and defense and relied on the parish church for salvation.

The practices of feudal politics and manorial economics intersected where the manorial seigneurs were likewise feudal lords and vassals. Knights as lords of fiefs also acted as lords of manors. The political oaths they made with their noble and free equals as fief holders were distinct from their rule of the inferior serfs as manorial workers.

Soon a simple agricultural innovation on these manors helped Europe prosper as never before. Beginning in the dark times after the fall of the Carolingian Empire, someone came up with the idea of **three-field planting**. Previously, the custom in European farming had been a two-field system, which left half the farmland fallow (without crops) every year to recover its fertility. The new method involved planting one-third with one kind of crop in the spring (such as beans or oats), another third with another crop in the fall (such as wheat or rye), and letting only a third lie fallow. The following year they rotated which crop they planted in each part of the field. This crop rotation resulted in larger harvests for less work and an improved diet for everyone.

New technology, much of which had spread to Europe after being invented in Asia, further enlarged what the manorial peasants could accomplish. The horse collar enabled horses to pull plows without strangling. Windmills ground grain into flour more easily than human or animal labor. These and other agricultural and technological advancements added to the wealth of Europe. The craft and farmwork of the peasants continued to produce wealth at the lord's behest. The rule of the knights defended the fragile kingdoms of France, England, Germany, and the rest. The prayers and labors of the clergy made Christianity the supreme religion of the West. Western civilization appeared secure.

The fall of Rome in the West in the fifth century had initiated a troubled time about which much remains in the dark for historians. In those difficult times, little energy was spent on learning and intellectual endeavors. As most people struggled to survive, only a few could create culture that survived long term, such as the rituals of the church or the epic songs of the Germans. Over the next few centuries after the chaos of the invasions, powerful rulers such as Alfred in England or Charles Martel among the Franks consolidated numerous small barbarian kingdoms into great realms. For a while, it looked as if the Carolingian Empire might unify the West as a revived Roman Empire. Its failure nonetheless left the kingdoms of France and Germany strong enough to hold out against new invasions. A thousand years after Christ's birth, Western civilization was strong and stable. The successful, ordered medieval society of catholic clergy, feudal knights, and manorial peasants (with some of the Jews still living among them) seemed settled forever as God's plan for humanity. The success of Christendom soon led to change, however. More sophisticated political and social structures, together with new ideas, shook up accepted assumptions. As a result, the West passed from the early Middle Ages into the High or Central Middle Ages in the eleventh century between 1000 and 1100.

Review: How did feudal politics and manorial economics help the West recover?

Response:

Make your own timeline.

AD 500   1000

CHAPTER 8

The Medieval Mêlée

The High and Later Middle Ages, 1000 to 1500

Christendom had grown up among the ruins of the western part of the ancient Roman Empire during the early Middle Ages. Thus began a distinct Western civilization, combining the surviving remnants of Græco-Roman culture and Christianity (inspired by Judaism) with the rule of the German conquerors. Medieval politics, economics, ideology, and culture culminated in the **High** or **Central Middle Ages** (1000–1350). The improved manorial agriculture raised the amount of wealth, while the stable feudal governments provided more security. The medieval kingdoms became civilized, as towns and cities provided new avenues to riches. At the same time, though, fighting took place everywhere, from the hand-to-hand mêlée of medieval knightly combat to vast wars about faith. Institutions and ideas fought with one another over which would master the minds, bodies, and souls of Christendom. Afterward, new environmental pressures would shape these conflicts in the **later Middle Ages** (1300–1500). Medieval methods continued to adapt to changing times, reflecting the growing success and power of Europe (see map 8.1).

RETURN OF THE KINGS

After the danger of Vikings, Saracens, and Magyars had passed, the knights of Christendom waged war more and more against one another. These feudal lords would often ignore kings who failed to maintain order. The politics of knights and vassals made their private interests more important than the general public welfare. Violence increased as private wars determined public policy. Kings clung precariously to their thrones, while sometimes able to pass dynastic power on from father to son. They could access fewer resources than the greater lords in their realms. War frequently followed when a dynasty failed to produce an heir. The old Germanic tradition that believed kings were semidivine, combined with the Christian church's desire for a stable sociopolitical order, necessitated a new ruler. Often an aristocrat placed the crown on his own head—someone had to be king.

Map 8.1. Europe, 1200.
How fractured were the states of Christendom?

Despite this weakening of real royal power, kings were still the focus for building a state. The traditional roles of the king (warrior, lawgiver, symbol) and the new feudal structure offered certain advantages to kings. Some kings took measures to reassert their authority by combining the fragmented feudal fiefs into a unified hierarchical structure and moving from the personal oaths of fidelity to the rule of law. Most kings had attained the position of a *suzerain* (supreme lord), at the top of the hierarchy of feudal relationships. Kings pulled their unruly dukes, counts, barons, and knights together with their fiefs into a political system based on royal, not local, authority. Their key difficulty became how to delegate authority without losing control to feudal competitors. The conflicts between kings and their rival aristocrats and nobles over obedience to the throne shaped the various states of Europe.

The first kingdom to experience a reinvigorated royal power was that of the East Franks, which was soon renamed the Kingdom of the Germans. When the Carolingian dynasty began to fail, dukes became more powerful. Dukes promoted feelings of regional unity under their own rule and soon gained greater authority than the nominal kings. As military commanders, dukes also defended their various provinces against the Magyars and Vikings better than did the distant kings. In 911, the last of the Carolingian dynasty, Louis "the Child," died and passed the kingship to the Duke of Franconia—ruler of the heartland of the East Franks. After a troubled reign, that duke in turn handed the kingship over to his strongest rival, the Duke of Saxony. The new king of the Germans was able to found a royal dynasty for Germany, passing power from father to son for several generations. The continuity of these Saxon kings helped to rebuild royal authority.

The most important king of this Saxon dynasty, **Otto I "the Great"** (r. 935–973), originally faced both rebellions and invasions. He managed to quell the revolts begun by his relatives by using both successful military campaigns and the support of the prince-bishops, to whom he granted lands and authority. Since bishops were supposed to be celibate, they had no heirs to whom they could pass on their power. Further, the king usually had the most important voice in selecting a successor bishop. This arrangement bound together many bishops with the German kings.

King Otto I defeated the Magyars at the Battle of Lechfeld in 955, allegedly helped by the Holy Lance that had pierced Christ's side. Afterward, the Magyars ceased to invade, settled down to establish the Kingdom of Hungary, and converted to Christianity. Otto further extended his own rule over much of the Italian Peninsula. His pretext for invading the Kingdom of Italy was the rescue of the young Queen Adelaide, widow of King Lothair II, whom a usurper had locked up in a castle. Otto drove out the usurper, set free Adelaide, and made her his queen (which, of course, then supported his own claims as "king" of Italy).

Otto confirmed his rulership in Italy eleven years later in 962, when he had the pope crown him emperor of the Romans in the tradition of Charlemagne. This act once again employed the name of the ancient Roman Empire, reviving what had first been lost to the West five centuries earlier, what had failed with the Carolingians just a century previously, and what technically still continued in Byzantium. The political state ruled by Emperor Otto I and his successors eventually came to be called the **Holy Roman Empire** (962–1806) both by its rulers and by later historians. At its height, this empire included all the lands of the Germans, Italy from the Papal States northward, much of the Lotharingian middle-realm territories of Burgundy and the Lowlands, Bohemia, and some Slavic lands on the northern plains of central Europe. The Holy Roman Empire dominated European politics for 150 years after Otto "the Great."

While the Germans were building the Holy Roman Empire, the Kingdom of England had just managed to survive another onslaught of Vikings in the tenth century. The short rule of King Canute's dynasty from Denmark settled matters briefly. When this dynasty died out at the beginning of the year 1066, civil war broke out. First, the native English earl Harold Godwinson claimed the English throne. Next, Harold fought off a Scandinavian invasion in the north led by his own brother and the king of Norway. Finally, Harold had to rush to the south to fight an invasion from Normandy. There he fell at the Battle of Hastings (14 October 1066), defeated by the army of the Norman duke, **William "the Conqueror"** (or "the Bastard" from another point of view). The **Norman Conquest** of England changed the course of history.

The Normans were Vikings (Norsemen) who had seized and settled a province of France along the English Channel in the tenth century, calling it Normandy after themselves. They recognized the French king as *suzerain* and soon spoke only French. This combination of Viking immigrants and Frankish locals created an ethnic group that had an extraordinary influence on European history. Other Normans later seized southern Italy and Sicily from the slackening grip of the Byzantine Empire and created a powerful and dynamic state there. In that kingdom, unique in Christendom, the Norman-French rulers fostered prosperity and peace among diverse populations of Italians, Greeks, and Arabs. The Normans also played a leading role in the Crusades (see below).

The victorious Duke William crowned himself King William I of England (r. 1066–1087) on Christmas Day. William replaced virtually all the local magnates with his own loyal vassals after he crushed several rebellions by English nobles (see figure 8.1). England therefore became less and less involved in the Scandinavian affairs of northern Europe and more tied to France and western Europe. The French-speaking Normans only slowly adopted the English language of the conquered subjects. As a result, a French/Viking influence of the Normans added to the previous Viking, Anglo-Saxon, Roman, Celtic, and prehistoric cultures to create England.

William's military victories enabled him to assert a strong monarchical rule and to bind his new land under his law. One example was his command to have the **Domesday Book** written in 1086. It assessed the wealth of most of his new kingdom by counting the possessions of his subjects, from castles and plow land down to cattle and pigs. William used the knowledge of this book to tax everything more effectively. This assessment was the first such official catalog in the West since the time of ancient Rome.

William's dynasty ran into trouble, though, when his son Henry I died from eating too many lampreys in 1135. Henry had sired over twenty bastards, but his only legitimate male heir had drowned in a shipwreck. The result was, of course, civil war. On one side was Henry's daughter, the "Empress" Matilda, the widow of German Holy Roman emperor Henry V and current wife of the powerful Geoffrey, Count of Anjou, a territory just south of Normandy. On the other side, most barons of England supported her cousin, Stephen of Blois, from northern France. Yet Matilda and her husband's forces won Normandy in battle and negotiated a truce, stipulating that after Stephen's death the English throne would go to Geoffrey and Matilda's son, Henry. The young **King Henry II** (r. 1154–1189) thus founded the English royal dynasty of the **Angevins** (the adjective for Anjou), or **Plantagenets** (after a flower adopted as a symbol). The Plantagenets ruled England for the rest of the Middle Ages, from 1154 to 1485. In addition to England, Henry inherited Normandy and Anjou from his mother and father. Moreover, he gained Aquitaine through marriage to its duchess, Eleanor, whose marriage with King Louis VII of France had recently been annulled. Thus, Henry II reigned over an empire that stretched from the Scottish border to the Mediterranean Sea.

Being crowned king and exercising real power were two different things, however, especially since many lords in Henry's vast territories had usurped royal prerogatives during the chaos of civil war. Henry used the widespread desire of many to return to the peace and prosperity of the "good ol' days" as a way to promote innovations in government, especially in England. In a campaign similar to that of

Figure 8.1.   William "the Conqueror" started building a castle, the White Tower of the Tower of London, immediately after his conquest of England. Most of the windows were cut into the walls much later, once fear of invasion or rebellion had waned.

Augustus Caesar to "restore" the republic, Henry claimed he wanted to revive the ways of his grandfather, the last Norman king, Henry I. By doing so, he really concentrated rule in his own hands. Henry II pursued this through four means. First, he needed military domination, so he attacked and demolished all castles that did not have an explicit license from him. He built others in key locations, using the latest technology imported from the Crusades in Palestine (see the next section). He also preferred hired mercenaries to feudal levies. He asked his knights to pay "shield money" instead of providing their required feudal military service in person.

Second, he began a revision of royal finances to pay for this military might. His own treasurer had written that the power of rulers rose and fell according to how much wealth they had: rulers with few funds were vulnerable to foes, while rulers with cash preyed upon those without. Henry obtained good money through currency reform, creating the pound sterling: 120 pennies equaled a pound's worth of silver. If his minters made bad money, with less pure silver than as regulated, he had their hands chopped off. Circulating coins improved his people's ability to pay taxes. Further, he reinforced old sources of taxation, including the Danegeld tax imposed on the descendants of Viking invaders, who had long since become assimilated with the English. He raised crusading taxes to pay for a crusade he never took part in. All these funds were accounted for by the Office of the Exchequer, which took its name from the checkerboard with which officials tracked credits and debits.

Third, in his role as law preserver and keeper, Henry improved the court system. He offered impartial judges as alternatives to the wide variety of local baronial courts. His judges also acquired a solid education at new universities in Oxford and Cambridge, where they trained in a revived study of Roman law based on the Justinian Code. These judges traveled around the country (literally on a circuit), hearing cases that grand juries determined were worthy of trial. The judges often called on a **jury** of peers to examine evidence and decide guilt and innocence rather than relying only on the allegedly divinely guided trial by ordeal. Henry's subjects could also purchase writs, standardized forms where one had only to fill in the blanks of name, date, and so forth in order to bring complaints before the sheriff and thus the king. These innovations increased the jurisdiction of the king's law, making it relatively quick and available to many. At the same time, people became involved on the local level, holding themselves mutually responsible for justice. This system is still used today in many Western countries.

Fourth, Henry II needed a sound administration to organize all this activity, of which the Exchequer was a part. Since he spent two-thirds of his time across the English Channel in his French provinces, Henry needed loyal officials who would exercise authority in his name but without his constant attention. The result revived government by bureaucracy. Officials began to keep and store royal writs and records in bureaus and boxes, and perhaps even consulted them. Some permanent bureaucrats, such as the treasurer or the chancellor, stood in for the king. London started to become a capital city, as it offered a permanent place for people to track down government officials. New personnel were hired from the literate people of the towns rather than from the traditional ruling classes of clergy and nobles. The king held these officials accountable and hired or fired them at will, unlike nobles, who inherited offices almost as easily as they had fiefs. Henry paid the lower grades of officials with food, money, or even the leftover ends of candles, while he compensated higher-ranked ministers with church lands and feudal titles. These civil servants made government more responsive both to change and to the will of the governed, or at least the crown in the early days.

The challenge any king faced in controlling appointed officials came to life in Henry's infamous quarrel with **Thomas Becket** (d. 1172). Becket had risen in Henry's service to the highest office of chancellor, all the while fighting for extended royal rights and prerogatives. Then Henry had Thomas Becket made archbishop of

Canterbury, the highest-ranking church official in England, believing that Becket would serve the royal will in both positions. Unfortunately for Henry, Archbishop Thomas experienced an unexpected religious conversion after his consecration. He became one of the reformers who resisted royal intervention in church affairs (see the next section). Years of dispute ended when four knights bashed Thomas's brains out in his own cathedral. Thomas Becket's martyrdom allowed the English clergy to appeal to Rome in church affairs and to keep the benefit of clergy (that clerics be judged by church courts, not secular ones). Still, many clerics remained royal servants.

Despite bureaucratic innovations, government remained tied to the personality of the ruler. Rebellions by his sons marked the last years of Henry II's reign. His wife and their mother, Eleanor of Aquitaine, helped to organize the revolts. Henry had committed adulterous affairs and kept Eleanor under house arrest after she showed too much independence and resentment. In return, she and her sons found support among barons who resented the king's supremacy. Nevertheless, the dynastic unity of Henry's lands survived for a few years after his demise, largely due to the solidity of his reforms. His immediate heir, King Richard I "the Lionheart" (r. 1189–1199), was away from England for all except ten months of his ten years of rule, yet the system functioned without him.[1] In contrast, Richard's heir, his younger brother King John (r. 1199–1216), pushed the royal power to its limit as he quarreled with King Philip II of France, Pope Innocent III, and his own barons, only to lose most of the Angevin territories in France.

In 1215, John's unhappy subjects forced him to agree to the famous **Magna Carta** (Latin for "great charter"). This treaty between the king, the clergy, the barons, and the townspeople of England accepted royal authority but limited its abuses. In principle, it made the king subject to law, not above it. This policy of requiring the king to consult with representatives of the people became permanent, mostly because John died soon after signing it, leaving a child to inherit power. The clergy, barons, and townspeople grew accustomed to meeting with the king and his representatives. In 1295, King Edward I summoned a model assembly of those who would speak with the king, called **Parliament** (from *parlez* in the French spoken by the elites). This body of representatives of the realm effectively realigned the rights of English kings and their subjects.

Meanwhile, the kings of France, who had started out in the tenth century weaker than those of England, became stronger by the thirteenth century. A French duke seized the throne from the last Carolingian king and founded a new Capetian dynasty that ruled from 987 to 1328. At first, the Capetians held only nominal power, effective only over an area around Paris called the Île de France. With the rise of feudal politics, royal power had almost vanished. Only the king's position as *suzerain*, or keystone of the feudal hierarchy, barely preserved respect for the crown. More powerful than these early kings were the dynastic nobles, especially the Count of Flanders, the Duke of Normandy, the Count of Anjou, and the Duke of Aquitaine.

---

1. Many modern versions of tales about Robin Hood are set during this time. The myth of the hero who robs from the rich and gives to the poor does date back to the Middle Ages, but historians have been unable to connect legend to a historical time or person.

Two particular medieval French kings built France's strong monarchy. **Philip II "Augustus"** (r. 1180–1223) gained a significant advantage over the Angevins. At the beginning of Philip's reign, Henry II's Angevin Empire seemed to doom the French monarchy, since Henry's territories in France of Normandy, Anjou, and Aquitaine overwhelmed the French king's lands. Fortunately for France, Henry's French possessions collapsed under his son John. Philip fought a war against John, sparked by feudal complaints of the vassals. The Battle of Bouvines in 1214 sealed Philip's victory with the conquest of most of the continental possessions of the Plantagenets except for a sliver of Aquitaine called Guyenne. As conqueror (like William of Normandy in his conquest of England), Philip accumulated overwhelming authority. He then carried out reforms modeled on those of Henry II. His new administrative bureaucratic offices were settled in his chosen capital city, Paris. His only mistake was to break his first marriage to Ingeborg of Denmark and marry Agnes of Meran without the permission of the church. The papal interdict on France lasted four years.

By the reign of his descendant **Philip IV "the Fair"** (r. 1285–1314), the king's power in France was supreme. Philip IV further strengthened royal authority with his own representative body, the **Estates-General**. Similar to the English Parliament, the Estates-General included representatives from the clergy, landed nobility, and commons or burghers from towns. These members gave their consent to and participated in enacting new royal taxes and laws. Philip IV also secured royal authority against even the papacy (see the next section).

Thus, the kings in Germany, France, and England had managed to restore authority and create the first three core states of Western civilization. Nevertheless, this fragile Christendom might still have been crushed by yet another invasion, that of Mongols or Tartars, polytheist pony-riding warriors who had come to dominate Asia in the early twelfth century under their leader Chengiz or Genghis Khan. In 1241, the Mongol invaders under Genghis Khan's grandson Batu smashed multinational armies of Christians in both Poland and Hungary. These defeats paved the way for a Mongol invasion, if not conquest, of western Europe, which might have destroyed the young Western civilization. The next year, though, a fight over the Mongol dynasty ended their interest in invading the little western corner of Eurasia. They retreated and only kept control of the Russians on Europe's eastern fringe. The Mongols then turned their attention to the southwestern corner of Eurasia, the Middle East. In 1255 the Mongols began a series of invasions that lasted for the next fifty years. The Abbasid Caliphate in Baghdad fell, giving leadership to the Mamluks, former enslaved Turks and Circassians who had taken over Egypt. The Mamluk Caliphate pushed both the Mongols and Christian crusaders out of the Middle East by the early 1300s. Soon the polytheistic Mongols converted to Islam and the empire fell apart under rival khans. As for Arab/Muslim civilization, many historians cite these devastating invasions as a turning point that ended a centuries-long "golden age."

Meanwhile, Christendom flourished, led by kings who worked closely with the wealth and influence of the church, defeated powerful enemies, and promoted the rule of law. These kings had taken primitive feudal authority and brought their nobles into order and structure, if not full obedience and subjugation. Their rivalries with one another also provided a dynamic of competition, both economic and military. Out of the diversity of these states and others to follow, Western civilization lurched forward in war and peace.

Review: *How did more centralized governments form in western Europe?*

Response:

DISCIPLINE AND DOMINATION

The feudal lords of Christendom struggled to bind people together politically, while the prelates of the church attempted to unify the faithful religiously. The Christian church had survived both the fall of the Roman Empire in the West and the fall of the Carolingian Empire. Most people, peasant and noble, labored on in their roles of farming and administering, attending church as best they could. Large numbers also retreated from the cares of the world to the haven of monasteries to become monks and nuns. Since many regular clergy lacked sincere religious belief, religious dedication slipped. In numerous monasteries, the regulations of Benedict were either unheard or unheeded.

One group of monks in the wild district of Burgundy decided to resist this neglectful attitude with the foundation of the new monastery of Cluny in the year 910. First, the monks of the **Cluniac Reform** dedicated themselves to a strict observance of the Benedictine Rule, including a disciplined practice of the prayers of the Divine Office. Second, in order to maintain reform in their own cloister and in others that imitated it, they held regular meetings to inspire a proper tone and to correct abuses. Third, they exempted themselves from local supervision of either the nobility or the bishop, because both the nobility and higher officers of the church were too compromised by the rough-and-tumble feudal network to be trusted with faith. Instead, the monks placed themselves under the direct supervision of the distant bishop of Rome, the pope.

These reforms were done without either the knowledge or permission of the pope, but they reinforced a trend with enormous consequences for the Christian church in the West. According to tradition and **canon law** (legal rules that governed the institutional church), a local bishop or the king assumed supervision of a monastery. Local nobles might also intrude, using their power of patronage and family connections among the monks and nuns. Charlemagne had also supported the reorganization of the church into provinces, which united the dioceses of several bishops under the supervision of one who became an "archbishop." To weaken this trend, the supporters of bishops "found" a number of charters that documented an overarching authority by the distant pope in Rome. Later organizers of the canon law accepted these forgeries as genuine. Hence, the pope became increasingly exceptional in the canon law, a unique, superior authority. An appeal to Rome over any issue ranging from ownership of a fishpond to possession of a benefice (a paying church position) might bring a local squabble directly to the pope's unique and supreme jurisdiction in a court of last resort, the Roman Curia.

The Cluniacs, meanwhile, had enormous success building new monastic communities and reforming old ones. Aristocrats and nobles abandoned the pleasures of chivalric pursuits to accept a hard obedience and discipline. Over the years, so many nobles donated land to monasteries and sent their children there that some worried that the increasing wealth and influence might distract the Cluniacs from properly focusing on divine worship.

One of the children dedicated to the religious life was Abbess Hildegard of Bingen (b. 1098–d. 1179). Her life illustrates some of the options open to Benedictine nuns. Her noble family sent Hildegard, their tenth child, to join an anchoress when she was only eight years old. As an adult, she became abbess of the neighboring abbey and collected enough donations to found a new nunnery. Hildegard became famous for writings of her visions (which may have been caused by migraines) as well as treatises on medicine, theology, and music.

By the late eleventh and early twelfth centuries, many male monastics supported a new **Cistercian Reform** that sought to go beyond the dedication of the Cluniacs. In monasteries like Chartreuse, Prémontré, and Cîteaux (which gave its name to the movement), these monks interpreted the Benedictine Rule as strictly as possible. The reformed monks also took only converts older than sixteen years, refusing to accept the unwanted children of aristocrats. They journeyed even farther into uninhabited hills, forests, and wastelands to build churches and farms to avoid secular temptations and concerns (see figure 8.2). This internal colonization increased the amount of farmland in the West and, therefore, its wealth. Chartreusians, Premonstratentians, and Cistercians often labored with their own hands, although some orders opened up opportunities to laymen, called *conversi*, who gained the benefits of communal life without being burdened with the obligations of education and prayer. Thus these monastic reforms opened various options for choosing the religious life, either among regular or secular clergy. Some orders emphasized contemplation and learning, others activity in hospitals and the care of souls, and still others spirituality and mysticism. The true calling of these new monks even inspired some diocesan clergy to reform as **canons regular**. As regular canons, these men lived together in communities of prayer, and at the same time, as secular clergy, they served the world as pastors and teachers.

The institution of the papacy needed to rise out of the depths of petty rivalry and become worthy and capable of leading all Christians. For centuries, the papal office had been the pawn of the rambunctious Roman nobility, as one family or

Figure 8.2. This sculpture of the sin of temptation on Strasbourg Cathedral warns about what lies behind a pretty face: poisonous snakes and toads.

another forced its candidate into St. Peter's Chair. Thus, the popes were too often men merely interested in the power and the wealth of the papal office. Christians inspired by monastic reforms, however, wanted a morally worthy spiritual leader. In 1046, after factional squabbles created three popes at once, Henry III, the king of Germany and Holy Roman emperor, arrived in Rome to restore order. Henry called the Synod of Sutri, which dismissed the three popes and then chose a new, universally recognized pope, Leo IX.

This pope and his successors, inspired by the Cluniac Reform, believed that a strong papacy could bring more religious dedication throughout Christendom. These attitudes initiated what historians call the **Hildebrandine** or **Gregorian Reform** (1050–1150), named after the monk Hildebrand, who became **Pope Gregory VII** (r. 1073–1085).

One tragic consequence of this aggressive papal authority was a *schism*, or "tearing" or "splitting," of the orthodox catholic Christian church into two parts:

the Latin-speaking hierarchy in the West, which took the term *Catholic*, and the Greek-speaking hierarchy in the East, which has come to be called *Orthodox*. Since the fall of the western half of the Roman Empire, the church had slowly been separating on organizational, theological, and liturgical grounds. The eastern patriarchs and bishops had kept a close relationship with Byzantine emperors. Although they had lost some dioceses to the Muslim advance in the Middle East and Africa, they had found new missionary success among the peoples of the Balkans and eastern Europe. The bishops of Rome, however, wanted recognition of papal primacy in authority over all the other patriarchs and bishops. The Eastern primates, meanwhile, refused to recognize the popes as their superiors.

In 1054, arguments over relatively minor issues such as the supervision of churches, the addition to the Nicene Creed of the word *filioque* ("and the Son" when mentioning who sent the Holy Spirit), and the use of leavened or unleavened bread in the Eucharist brought on a crisis. Members of a papal commission to Constantinople aggravated the situation by excommunicating the patriarch there, who, of course, excommunicated them right back. Unity between Christians in East and West has never been able to recover from what is called the "Great Schism."[2] The Christian world divided between Eastern **Orthodox Christianity** and Western Catholic Christianity.

For the reforming clerics in the West, though, the increasing papal supremacy justified the split. To help ensure the legitimacy of the pope, a unique election law issued in 1059 revised the election process for the pope. Previously, the pope had been chosen in the same manner as other bishops had been, namely through election by the local clergy and laypersons of the diocese. Practically, though, powerful men, like a king, actually did most of the choosing in the majority of cases. Reformers now entrusted a new role to **cardinals**, who originally had been created as assistants to run the diocese of Rome. Under the new papal election law, only cardinals appointed by popes could elect the next pope. This law removed the pope from being the plaything of the Roman nobility, but it also cut out the influence of the German king who was also Holy Roman emperor.

The reformers in Rome further hoped to encourage a higher quality of cleric by targeting what they considered the two worst problems in the Western Latin church: **simony** and the sexual activity of clerics. First, simony, named after the figure Simon Magus in the New Testament, originally meant the sin of trying to purchase salvation. It had come to mean the crime of bribery, or even using political influence, to acquire a church office or benefice. Reformers wanted to get money out of the election process. The attack on clerical sexual activity was partially related to the opposition to simony. Reformers thought that when clergy had children, the tendency to pass on to their heirs a priestly office (not to mention parish property) compromised the holiness of the priesthood (and the church's possessions).

Additionally, some reformers were squeamish about women and sex. Already in ancient times the church had excluded women from leadership. With this new

---

2. Many historians use the term the "Great Schism" to refer to the popes splitting into separate lines between 1378 and 1417, which this text calls the "Great Western Schism." That minor and brief squabble among Western Christians hardly compares to the ongoing separation since 1054 of East and West.

reform, church authorities in the West tried to restrict married priests from offices or sacraments, insisting on celibacy. They adopted misogynist attitudes from pagan philosophers and culture about female inferiority and corrupt sexuality, cringing at the thought that a priest might handle the holy body and blood of Christ in the mass after having touched the impure flesh of a woman. So reformers began a campaign against the many priests who were married and others who kept concubines or "house companions." Of all the reform efforts, people in the local parishes surely noticed this one the most, whether their priests obeyed or not.

To change clerical attitudes, the papacy began to intervene in local church affairs as never before. Legal scholars collected and commented on old and new canon law in support of the tighter church organization. Popes added lawyers and bureaucrats to their papal court, the Curia. The popes often sent cardinals throughout Christendom as legates, the pope's official representatives who had his full authority. The papal scribes issued bulls (named after the lead seal of authenticity hanging from them) in which the popes, on their own authority, codified law and moral issues. As a result, the pope became less a spiritual leader than the head of a vast bureaucratic machine. While many of the popes over the next centuries were great lawyers and politicians, few had any inclination toward sanctity or sainthood.

Review: How did reforms of monks lead to a reform of the Western Latin Church under the medieval papacy?

Response:

SOURCES ON FAMILIES: JACOBUS DE VORAGINE, "THE LIFE OF SAINT ELIZABETH" (CA. 1260)

Religious life offered a powerful alternative to traditional marriage and family for medieval people. Elizabeth (b. 1207–d. 1231), daughter of the king of Hungary, became a popular saint, although few followed in her footsteps. A princess who married into a powerful family, she rejected the typical marriage and aristocratic lifestyle, devoting herself instead to helping the poor. Her husband supported her activities, which were supervised by her spiritual advisor, Conrad von Marburg (about whom much else could be written). Once widowed, Elizabeth transitioned to a monastic life of serving others.

. . . This holy virgin honored all the solemn feasts of the year with so great reverence that she would not suffer her sleeves to be laced on till the solemnity of the mass was finished, and she heard the office of the mass with so great reverence that when the gospel was read or the sacrament was lifted up, she would take off the brooches of gold and the adornments of her head, as circles or chaplets, and lay them down.

And when she had kept in innocence the degree of virginity, she was compelled to enter into the degree of marriage. . . . And howbeit that she would not have been married, yet she dared not gainsay the commandment of her father. . . . Therefore she consented to conjugal copulation, not in a libidinous fashion, but lest she disobey the command of her father, and to raise children for the service of God. Thus she submitted to the conjugal bed, but avoided sensual gratification. Then was she married to the landgrave of Thuringia, as the divine providence had ordained because she should bring many to the love of our Lord, and teach the ignorant. . . .

On a time when her husband the landgrave was gone to the court of the emperor, which was then at Cremona, she assembled from his granges all the wheat of the year, and administered to the needs of the poor who came from all sides, for at that time was great dearth in the country. And oft when she lacked money she sold off her adornments for to give to the poor people. . . . She did construct a great house under the castle, where she received and nourished a great multitude of poor people, and visited them every day, and she left not to visit them for any sickness or malady that they had, but she washed and wiped them with her own hands. . . . And moreover then she did so nourish in her house poor women's children so sweetly, that they all called her mother. . . .

And the blessed Saint Elizabeth had great desire that her husband should employ his puissance to defend the faith of God, and advised him, by salutary exhortations, that he should go visit the holy land and thither he went, and when he was there, this devout and noble prince, full of faith and of devotion rendered his spirit unto Almighty God, and so died, receiving the glorious fruit of his works. And then she received with devotion the state of widowhood. And when the death of her husband was published and known through all Thuringia, some of the vassals of her husband held her for a fool and wastrels of her goods, and threw her out of her heritage. . . .

And after this, one, her aunt, had great pity of her, and sent her wisely to her uncle, the bishop of Bamberg, who received her respectfully, and intended to marry her off again. [She said,] "and if mine uncle would marry me to any man I shall withstand it to my power and shall gainsay it with words. And if I may not so escape I shall cut off my nose so that every man shall abhor me for my deformity." And then the bishop did send her to a castle against her will, for to abide there until some man should demand to have her in marriage. . . .

She took willful poverty, and her clothing was coarse and vile. She wore a russet mantle, her gown of another foul color, the sleeves of her coat were broken, and amended with pieces of other color.

Her father, king of Hungary, when he heard that his daughter was come to the estate of poverty, he sent a count to her for to bring her to her father; and when the count saw her sit in such a habit and spinning, he cried for sorrow, and said there was never a king's daughter seen that wore such a habit spinning wool. And when he had given his message and desired to have brought her to her father, she in no wise would agree to it. . . . And she prayed our Lord that he would give to her grace to despise all earthly things and take away from her heart the love of her children, and to be firm and constant against the persecutions. And when she had accomplished her prayer she heard our Lord saying: "Thy prayer is heard." . . .

And then this blessed Elizabeth received the habit of religion and put herself diligently to the works of mercy, for she received for her dower two hundred marks, whereof she gave a part to poor people, and of that other she constructed a large hospital in Marburg. Therefore she was called a wasteress and a fool, which all she suffered joyously. And when she had made this hospital she became herself as an humble maid in the service of the poor. And she bore herself humbly in that service, that by night she carried the sick men in her arms for to let them do their necessities, and brought them again, and made clean their clothes and sheets that were foul. . . . And when there were no poor, she would spin wool which was sent to her from an abbey, and from such she gave to the poor people. And when she had been in much poverty she received five hundred marks of her dowry, much of which she gave unto the poor in an orderly fashion. . . .

Questions:

- *What does Elizabeth value most, beyond marriage and family?*
- *What difficulties does she face in living out her calling?*
- *How does Elizabeth build new family relationships through her ministry?*

Responses:

Citation

Adapted from [Jacobus de Voragine]. "The Life of S. Elizabeth." *The Golden Legend of Lives of the Saints as Englished by William Caxton*, edited by F. S. Ellis. Vol. 6. London: J. M. Dent, 1900, pp. 213–30.

For more on this source, go to http://www.concisewesternciv.com/sources/sof8.html.

PLENTY OF PAPAL POWER

As one of their unique prerogatives, the popes asserted the right to call **crusades** (1095–1492), the Christian version of holy war. Before the eleventh century, war was sometimes recognized as a necessity, but it had always been considered sinful. Jesus's clear, explicit commands about nonviolence had even led many Christians in the Roman Empire to become pacifists. Augustine, however, had helped to establish what we call the just war theory, allowing wars to be fought if they were defensive, if they did not involve too much destruction or brutality, and if they aimed at establishing a more just peace. Although this theory could allow Christians to go to war under many circumstances, every act of killing nevertheless remained a sin that required confession, penance, and reconciliation.

But the concept of crusade turned the sin of war into a virtue. Instead of regretting the killing of another human being, the crusader could glory in it. Killing the enemies of God became a holy act, a good deed. No sin was committed—indeed, one got closer to heaven, just as if one were on a pilgrimage. The crusaders, then, were armed pilgrims. Instead of hiking to Santiago de Compostela to pray, they marched to Jerusalem to slay.

Many regions became the target of crusading activity. First, the popes gave their blessing on the crusading movement called the Reconquesta, to reconquer the Iberian Peninsula from the Saracens. Crusaders struck southward from the northern remnants of early medieval Christian kingdoms against the Islamic Moors of Andalusia. Crusading armies expanded the kingdoms of Leon, Castile, and Aragon southward and founded Portugal. These kingdoms would wrangle with one another and the Moors until the end of the Middle Ages.

Second, the most famous crusades were those to liberate the Holy Land, Outremer (French for "across the sea"), or Palestine. These crusades started with a misunderstanding. A Turkish victory at the Battle of Manzikert (1071) allowed many thousands of Turks to migrate into Asia Minor, threatening the core of the Byzantine Empire. Despite the religious schism between the East and West, the Byzantine emperor called on the pope to find mercenaries to help fight the Turkish Muslims. That schism marked a significant turning point for a Christendom divided between West and East. The Byzantine Empire had become too weak to defend itself, while the West under claims of papal leadership had warriors to spare. Pope Urban II used the request for his own purposes. He spread myths of Muslim atrocities and exhorted knights and infantry to drive the Arab Muslims from the lands of Christians, particularly from Jerusalem. The inflamed people shouted, "God wills it!"

Surprisingly, or miraculously (as Western Christians believed), the First Crusade (1095–1099) achieved some success. At first, a ragtag horde of fervent outsiders and peasants marched toward Jerusalem, slaughtering along the way a few European Jews who refused to convert to Christianity. Unfortunately, the Turks massacred or enslaved this rabble in Asia Minor before they ever reached Jerusalem. In 1099, however, a better-organized feudal army under various dukes and counts survived a difficult journey through Europe and Asia Minor. Their zeal overcame many losses brought on by battles, thirst, and hunger (the last sometimes solved by cannibalism). These crusaders then actually conquered the Levantine coast, including Jerusalem itself, allegedly helped by the Holy Lance that had pierced Christ's side, as well as by fasting and processions. As they sacked the "holy city," the Christian crusaders waded up to their ankles in the blood of slaughtered Muslim men, women, and children in a mosque where they had taken refuge. The crusaders also burned Jews alive in their homes and synagogues. Then the rival crusading leaders set up several small principalities.

To survive, as it did for the next two centuries, the Latin Kingdom of Jerusalem and the crusading princedoms needed more than miracles. The new Western princes and knights in Outremer hardly cooperated either with one another or with the Byzantine Empire. They did make some efforts at cooperating with the Muslims who were their subjects and neighbors. They needed and received continued reinforcements from Christendom. These zealous and temporary conquerors disliked the civilizations of Byzantium and Islam as something strange, despite their shared Græco-Roman legacy. Their crusading mentality often prevented the Christians who had settled down in Palestine from working with the pragmatic Muslims or allowing peoples of different heritages to live together in peace.

Also complicating relations was a new clerical ideal inspired by crusading, namely, military monasticism. **Monk-knights** lived Christian lives of chastity, obedience, and prayer like monastic monks but also fought as warriors on the battlefield against the infidels. These militarized religious orders, like the Hospitallers or the Templars, provided much-needed resources of money, social service, and trained warriors.

The Middle East became a complicated jumble of diverse and competing elements. Although the Muslims called all Western Christians "Franks," the crusaders were actually deeply divided. The "Franks" rarely forgot that they came from England, Scotland, France, various provinces of the Holy Roman Empire, Italian merchant city-states, or Norman Sicily, all of whose governments quarreled with one another. Political loyalties, ethnic pride, and religious bickering often weakened their efforts in the Holy Land.

In turn, the "Franks" labeled all their opponents under the blanket term Saracens, which ignored the deep religious divisions of Sunni, Shiite, and even Assassin. This last, a secret sect of alleged hashish smokers, murdered its enemies, giving us the term *assassination*. The Assassin murders of important Muslim leaders helped keep Islamic factions divided, terrorized, and at war with one another. Likewise, ethnic differences among Arabs, Egyptians, Persians, Kurds, and Turks long delayed a united Islamic front. For decades, the divisions among Muslims allowed the crusaders to survive by playing one group off against the other. The Kurdish Saladin (Salah al-Din Yusuf ibn Ayb), who had taken control of the Egyptian caliphate, almost succeeded in defeating the crusaders in the 1180s. But the so-called Third Crusade of Richard "the Lionheart" reestablished a strong Christian foothold, even if Jerusalem remained under Muslim control. Shortly afterward, in the Fourth Crusade of 1204, Latin crusaders attacked the Byzantine Empire itself. They seized and plundered the until-then unconquered Constantinople, briefly making it the center of a Latin Empire that lasted until 1261. Finally, in 1295, unified and zealous Muslims drove the crusaders back beyond the sea and reclaimed Palestine and the Levant.

The Holy Land had been lost, but other crusades continued. The third important region for crusading, after Palestine and the Iberian Peninsula, was in northeastern Europe, along the southern and eastern shores of the Baltic Sea. The **Teutonic Knights**, named after their common German ethnicity, were the most successful crusaders there. They had started as an order of crusading monk-knights in Palestine. Meanwhile, various princes of the Holy Roman Empire were conquering the pagan peoples of eastern Europe and bringing in German immigrants to settle towns and farms in a movement called the *Drang-nach-Osten* (drive to the east). As part of these efforts, the Teutonic Knights gained a papal license to conquer the still-pagan Prussian people and then founded their own state, called **Prussia**. The Teutonic monk-knights henceforth ruled over the Prussian peasants, who were slowly converted to Christianity and assimilated into German culture.

The Crusades sprang from the conviction that Christians held the only answer to the meaning of life, combined with the military power to impose Christian beliefs beyond the heartland of Christendom. The Crusades promoted little cultural exchange. The Muslims who interacted with the Franks considered them uncivilized, even barbaric. With few exceptions, political or intellectual leaders of East and West barely communicated with each other. Many westerners did develop a taste, though, for luxury goods, spices, rugs, porcelain, and silk that came from Muslim merchants, who themselves traded deep into Asia across the Silk Road or the Arabian Sea. And even though the Crusades failed in Palestine, their successes on the borders of Christendom, in the Iberian Peninsula and northeastern Europe, strengthened the supremacy of the Western Latin Church. In the few years since the schism between Eastern and Western Christianity in 1054, the latter had shown itself to be more dynamic and aggressive.

Soon, however, crusading fervor turned even against the Christian kings of the West. Popes began to use their power to call for crusades against foes within western Europe. The Gregorian Reform had created such a powerful papacy that it was even able to challenge royal governments such as the Holy Roman Empire. This was a shift away from the Frankish-Papal Alliance begun under the Carolingians. The papal coronations of Charlemagne in 800 and then Otto "the Great" in 962 as "emperors of the Romans" marked two high points of this bond. Otto I had also expanded the collaboration between church and state by relying on prince-bishops in Germany to help support his royal authority and military might. Furthermore, Otto's descendant, Henry III, reached a high point of royal influence over church affairs when he helped restore the disgraced papacy in 1046.

When Henry III died ten years later, however, the empire faced a crisis because his son and heir, **Henry IV** (r. 1056–1106), was only six years old. Many magnates used the long regency until Henry IV came of age to seize what they could from his royal rights and prerogatives. During this time the papacy also, as mentioned above, regained power and asserted its independence. Further, after a pope attacked the Normans in southern Italy and Sicily and lost, the victorious Normans actually formed an alliance with their former enemy. Thus protected by Sicilian Normans, the popes no longer needed their traditional alliance with the German emperors.

When Henry IV became a ruler in his own right, he wanted to regain the power that his father Henry III had wielded. Henry IV's attempts unleashed a clash between church and state that changed the West. The **Investiture Struggle**, Contest, or Controversy (1075–1122) centered on the appointment of new bishops. It takes its name from the religious ceremony of investiture, which formally installs bishops in their office. The radicals in the papal reform movement had expanded the definition of simony to include any royal involvement in the election of bishops, even when no money changed hands. Their extreme claim for "papal plenitude of power" threatened kings across Europe, who believed that they, by divine right, could install bishops. In the Holy Roman Empire, the Investiture Struggle threatened the royal relations with prince-bishops as both vassals and spiritual leaders. It fueled a civil war.

Disagreements between King Henry IV and Pope Gregory VII over who selected bishops in northern Italy sparked the first open fight over papal versus royal power (see figure 8.3). As King Henry IV's episcopal candidates clashed with papal nominees, Pope Gregory VII threatened Henry with excommunication. In the winter of 1076 Pope Gregory excommunicated Henry IV and declared that he was no longer king.

Although the pope's legal claim to depose Henry was doubtful, Henry's enemies in Germany seized the opportunity to rise up against him. Even many of his bishops abandoned him, although they had supported his denunciation of the pope. In a brilliant move, however, Henry rushed to Italy over frozen Alpine passes. The pope fled to the castle of Canossa, fearing an attack. Yet Henry arrived with only a small retinue. Instead of raging in armor and ferocity, the king stood in sackcloth and repentance before the castle gates for three wintry days. Since the pope was in the job of forgiveness, he lifted Henry's excommunication. Although Henry remained, technically, deposed from his kingship, the confusion about his status gave him the opportunity to regroup his military forces and defeat most of his opponents.

Nonetheless, the war in the empire dragged on, as each side stuck to its interpretation of the role of bishops and their election. Gregory excommunicated Henry a futile second time. In turn, Henry's armies drove Gregory from Rome into exile with the Normans in southern Italy, where he died. Finally, Henry's own son rebelled against him to become Henry V (r. 1105–1125). Henry V was also excommunicated because he needed to choose prince-bishops as his vassals. After two generations of open warfare, the Investiture Struggle between church and state finally ended with the **Concordat of Worms** in 1122. A concordat is an agreement between a state and the church, while Worms, a city on the upper Rhine River, ruled by a bishop, was where the treaty was agreed to by Henry V and the papacy. The treaty was a compromise. The principle that clergy and laypeople of dioceses were to elect their bishops was reasserted (except for Rome's bishop, of course). Still, the king could be present at each election in Germany (and thus exert an influence and even decide deadlocked elections). The German king gave up the right of investiture regarding a bishop's ecclesiastical office, but he could grant feudal possessions before a bishop's full consecration (at least within the German, if not in the Burgundian or Italian, parts of the empire). Similar compromises were eventually worked out in France and England.

Figure 8.3.   A Croatian king of the eleventh century, a contemporary of Emperor Henry IV. If this was King Zvonimir, he may have given obedience of his church to the authority of Pope Gregory VII. Yet the portrait shows someone prostrate at his feet, submitting to royal power.

While the Investiture Struggle was officially over, neither advocates of papal authority nor proponents of royal power were satisfied with this compromise. The Holy Roman Empire especially suffered from ongoing differences between emperors and popes. Emperor Henry V died without an heir in 1125, and not surprisingly a civil war erupted. Two major families took the lead in the competition for support from the magnates: the Welfs and the Staufens. Successive popes, using their influence and their recognized right to crown the German king as Holy Roman emperor, regularly played one side against the other over the next several generations.

By 1256, the Staufen dynasty had been extinguished, while the Welfs had shrunk to mere dukes again. Even worse for German power, the dynastic principle had been broken. Instead, seven powerful magnates (the archbishops of Cologne, Mainz, and Trier, the king of Bohemia, the Duke of Saxony, the Margrave of Brandenburg, and the Count Palatine by the Rhine) asserted themselves as "electoral princes." These seven claimed the sole right to select the next German king. As a result, the office of emperor/king of the Holy Roman Empire declined in power, if not prestige, while the actual rule of the local territorial magnates was magnified. Unfortunately for the popes, their obsession with weakening the Holy Roman emperor led them to ignore two new threats—the kings of England and France.

Review: *How and why did the popes fight against their enemies?*

Response:

PRIMARY SOURCE PROJECT 8: GREGORY VII VERSUS HENRY IV ABOUT CHURCH VERSUS STATE

Two different personalities inflamed the Investiture Struggle, a fight between religious and political leaders in the West. The first source presents a private list presumably drawn up by Pope Gregory VII, wherein he set a high bar for papal plenitude of power. The second source is German king Henry IV's public response to criticisms of his royal authority made by the pope.

Source 1: *Dictatus Papæ* by Pope Gregory VII (ca. 1075)

1. That the Roman Church was founded by God alone.
2. That the Roman bishop alone is properly called universal.
3. That he alone has the power to depose bishops and reinstate them.
4. That his legate, though of inferior rank, takes precedence of all bishops in council, and may give sentence of deposition against them.
5. That the pope has the power to depose [bishops] in their absence.
6. That we should not even stay in the same house with those who are excommunicated by him.
7. That for him alone is it lawful, according to the needs of the time, to make new laws, to assemble together new congregations, to make an abbey of a canonry; and, on the other hand, to divide a rich bishopric and unite the poor ones.
8. That he alone may use the imperial insignia.
9. That the pope is the only person whose feet are kissed by all princes.

10. That his name alone shall be spoken in the churches.

11. That his name is unique in the world.

12. That he has the power to depose emperors.

13. That he may, if necessity require, transfer bishops from one see to another.

14. That he has power to ordain a clerk of any church he may wish.

15. That he who is ordained by him may preside over another church, but may not hold a subordinate position; and that such a one may not receive a higher rank from any bishop.

16. That no general synod may be called without his consent.

17. That no action of a synod, and no book, may be considered canonical without his authority.

18. That his decree may be annulled by no one, and that he alone may annul the decrees of any one.

19. That he may be judged by no one else.

20. That no one shall dare to condemn a person who appeals to the apostolic see.

21. That to this See should be referred the more important cases of every church.

22. That the Roman Church has never erred, nor ever, by the testimony of Scripture, shall err, in perpetuity.

23. That the Roman pontiff, if he shall have been canonically ordained, is undoubtedly made a saint by the merits of blessed Peter, Saint Ennodius, bishop of Pavia, bearing witness, and many holy fathers agreeing with him, and as is contained in the decrees of blessed pope Symmachus.

24. That by his command and consent, it shall be lawful for subordinates to bring accusations.

25. That he may depose and reinstate bishops without assembling a synod.

26. That no one can be considered Catholic who does not agree with the Roman Church.

27. That [the pope] can absolve the subjects of unjust rulers from their oath of fidelity.

Source 2: Letter to Pope Gregory VII by King Henry IV of Germany (27 March 1076)

Henry, king not by usurpation, but by the holy ordination of God, to Hildebrand, not pope, but false monk.

This is the salutation which you deserve, for you have never held any office in the church without making it a source of confusion and a curse to Christian men instead of an honor and a blessing. To mention only the most obvious cases out of many, you have not only dared to touch the Lord's anointed, the archbishops, bishops, and priests; but you have scorned them and abused them, as if they were ignorant servants not fit to know what their master was doing.

This you have done to gain favor with the vulgar crowd. You have declared that the bishops know nothing and that you know everything; but if you have such great wisdom you have used it not to build but to destroy. . . .

All this we have endured because of our respect for the papal office, but you have mistaken our humility for fear, and have dared to make an attack upon the royal and imperial authority which we received from God. You have even threatened to take it away, as if we had received it from you, and as if the empire and kingdom were in your disposal and not in the disposal of God. Our Lord Jesus Christ has called us to the government of the empire, but he never called you to the rule of the church.

This is the way you have gained advancement in the church: through craft you have obtained wealth; through wealth you have obtained favor; through favor, the power of the sword; and through the power of the sword, the papal seat, which is the seat of peace; and then from the seat of peace you have expelled peace. For you have incited subjects to rebel against their prelates by teaching them to despise the bishops, their rightful rulers. You have given to laymen the authority over priests, whereby they condemn and depose those whom the bishops have put over them to teach them. You have attacked me, who, unworthy as I am, have yet been anointed to rule among the anointed of God, and who, according to the teaching of the fathers, can be judged by no one save God alone, and can be deposed for no crime except infidelity. . . .

Come down, then, from that apostolic seat which you have obtained by violence; for you have been declared accursed by St. Paul for your false doctrines and have been condemned by us and our bishops for your evil rule. Let another ascend the throne of St. Peter, one who will not use religion as a cloak of violence, but will teach the life-giving doctrine of that prince of the apostles. I, Henry, king by the grace of God, with all my bishops, say unto you: "Come down, come down, and be accursed through all the ages."

Questions:

- *How does the structure of each source serve to carry its message?*
- *Which statements by Gregory would Henry find most or least objectionable?*
- *How does Henry personalize his argument?*

Responses:

Citations

"45. Gregory VII's Conception of the Papal Authority." In *A Source Book of Medieval History: Documents Illustrative of European Life and Institutions from the*

German Invasions to the Renaissance, edited by Frederick Austin Ogg. New York: American Book Company, 1907, pp. 262–64.

"75. The Deposition of Gregory VII by Henry IV, January 24, 1076." In *A Source Book for Medieval History: Selected Documents Illustrating the History of Europe in the Middle Age*, edited by Oliver J. Thatcher and Edgar H. McNeal. New York: Scribner, 1905, pp. 151–52.

For more on these sources, go to http://www.concisewesternciv.com/sources/psc8 .html.

THE AGE OF FAITH AND REASON

The debates and writings provoked by the protracted conflict over papal authority helped to create a new literature of political theory, where individuals could speculate about the nature and purposes of government. Many of these new ideas came from an unexpected source, the Muslim-dominated Iberian Peninsula called Andalusia. When Christian crusaders liberated the city of Toledo in 1085, they found libraries full of books written in Arabic. Rather than burning them in fanatic zeal, they hired Jews who had long lived peacefully among the Arabs in Toledo to translate the books into Latin. In that city and soon in several more, the writings from the ancient Greeks and Romans as well as more recent Muslims, such as Ibn Sina (Avicenna) and Ibn Rushd (Averroës), became available to medieval scholars. The books revealed the advancements Arab scholars and inventors had made in mathematics, astronomy, geography, medicine, and science. Most important, the westerners rediscovered the writings of Aristotle, whom the Arabs had long appreciated, studied, and interpreted. Aristotle's dialectic logic lit an intellectual fire in the monastic and cathedral schools that had survived the collapse of the Carolingian Empire. Students in the West leapt at the opportunity to learn.

Some of these schools blossomed into **universities**. The seven liberal arts continued as the basic curriculum for education. The new universities in turn provided advanced higher education, where students became "masters" and "doctors" (teachers) by studying canon law, secular law, medicine, theology, or philosophy. A now-familiar kind of person, the scholar, appeared in the West for the first time since the fall of Rome, inspired by the knowledge of antiquity and the scholarship that had continued to be pursued in the Byzantine and Muslim civilizations. The whole point of scholars in universities was to profess new knowledge. They brought the light of education to what had been the darkness of ignorance. Secular rulers likewise recognized the value of these institutions of higher education and encouraged their foundation in places as diverse as Bologna, Salerno, Paris, Oxford, Cambridge, and Heidelberg. Yet academics formed an international guild, taking on themselves the responsibility to maintain quality in research and teaching.

The universities were able to flourish under the protective umbrella of the Western Latin Church, even when secular princes founded them. Members of this system were technically clergy. Therefore, faculty and students fell under the special canon laws of the church or university and not under those of the secular courts. The metaphor of the ivory tower used to describe higher education reflects the legal distinctions that separated universities from the urban communities in which they were located. Conflicts between townspeople and students were considered (and sometimes still are) "town" versus "gown" (although most students these days only wear academic gowns at graduation). Then, as now, youthful enthusiasm for extracurricular activities would sometimes annoy the neighbors. Then, as now, learning was difficult. Then, as now, some students preferred to study varieties of beer and wine rather than versions of Plato and Aristotle.

In the thirteenth century, donors and church officials organized **colleges** as residential and educational spaces to help the young "bachelors" become more disciplined. The collegians might move on to the higher degrees of master or doctor, but many were satisfied with a "bachelor's degree," as they are today. The word *bachelor* also indicates that only men could study at these new, advanced schools. Women might receive some education in monastic schools, either as nuns or students of the nuns. Formal higher education, though, remained closed to women for centuries.

While the Western Latin Church was the cradle for this growing systematic legacy, it almost strangled that baby in the cradle. Some Christians feared that ideas drawn from pagans were dangerous or irrelevant. Sources of knowledge from anything other than divine revelation frightened them. The use of human reason might lead to error, even heresy. The scholar **Peter Abelard** (b. 1080–d. 1142) seemed the perfect example. Through sheer intellectual arrogance, he had become one of the leading academicians of his day. Then his scandalous affair with his pupil Heloïse almost ruined his career. He had arranged for himself to be her private tutor (since the church forbade women to attend schools and universities). After she had his illegitimate child, though, instead of properly marrying her, he seemed to want to put her away in a nunnery.[3] Her angry guardian hired some thugs who castrated Abelard. He recovered to resume his teaching at the university, where his ideas caused more problems for him. His celebrated definition of wisdom asserted that we must first doubt authority and ask questions; questioning will then lead us to the truth. Clearly, however, Abelard's questions led him into trouble, just as Socrates's had in ancient Athens. Their experiences suggest another basic principle:

Questioning authority is dangerous.

Abelard's opponents organized to silence him as a heretic. Those defenders of tradition seized upon his too-subtle explanation of the Trinity to get his ideas condemned at a local church council. They compelled him to stop teaching and even made him throw his own books into the flames.

A century later, though, Aristotle's dialectic method emerged victorious. Other clerics, notably **Thomas Aquinas** (b. 1225–d. 1274), used the tools of Aristotelian

---

3. The influence of Arabic knowledge on these scholars is shown in Abelard's name for his child: Astrolabe, after a device that measures the positions of sun, planets, and stars to help in navigation.

logic, as Abelard had, but were careful to make sure their answers were complete and orthodox. Aquinas thought that human reason, properly used, never conflicted with divine revelation. This **Scholasticism**, or philosophy "of the schools," is clearly expressed in Aquinas's book, *Summa Theologiae* (*Sum of Theology*). Therein he used dialectic arguments to answer everything a Christian could want to know about the universe. Aquinas allayed the fears about Aristotle by harnessing his logic for the Western Latin Church. Eventually Aquinas's logical explications seemed so solid and orthodox that later the Roman Catholic Church declared him its leading philosopher.

Despite Aquinas's success, the intellectual debate did not stop. Philosophers continued to argue about realism. Some drew on Plato's idealism that universal ideas shaped reality; others advocated **nominalism**, which proposed that only particular objects in the observable world existed. Another debate among scholars focused on politics. They developed political theories that were coherent proposals about how best to rule human society. Aquinas argued that the pope was the supreme human authority, but many others fought this idea with words and weapons. Kings sought out scholars and founded universities to argue for the supremacy of kingship and the royal connection to the divine, as had been done since the dawn of ancient civilizations.

Within these debates, the institution of the university further strengthened liberty for everyone by promoting new knowledge. Universities were not intended to convey merely the established dogmas and doctrines of the past or of powerful princes and popes. Instead, professors were, and are, supposed to expand upon inherited wisdom. Once the idea of learning new ideas became acceptable, it inevitably led to change. Nevertheless, popes continued to claim the allegiance of all humanity. Kings still tried to bind their clergy to them as servants to enforce the royal will. Neither of these attempts dominated in the West. By the end of the Middle Ages, no single power, whether the pope, king, one's own connection to God, or the independent human mind itself, would rule both the hearts and minds of mortals. Creative tensions between the demands of faith and the requirements of statehood enriched the choices available to peoples of the West.

During time off from intellectual pursuits, some scholars produced literature, which at the time was not studied at universities. Much of the literature of the Middle Ages was written in the language of scholarship, government, and faith, namely Latin. Student poets called Goliards were famous for their drinking songs, while other clergy produced histories, epic fantasies, mystical tracts, and religious hymns.

Modern universities today usually neglect to teach about this medieval Latin literature. They instead favor studying the literature from vernacular languages, those that people spoke at home and that later evolved into the European languages of today: Romance languages (French, Italian, Portuguese, Spanish, and Romanian), Germanic languages (German, Dutch, Norwegian, Danish, Swedish, and English), Celtic languages (which still survive as Irish Gaelic, Scots, Welsh, and Breton), and even Slavic languages (Polish, Czech, Serbo-Croatian, Bulgarian, Russian, etc.). Vernaculars only slowly drove out Latin from government and universities. These languages that people spoke in their regular lives found validation in literary works that began to be written down after the twelfth century.

Romance became one of the most popular genres of vernacular literature. Works of romance prose or poetry often told of heroic adventures complicated by men and women facing challenges in their love. The most famous work of medieval literature is Dante's *Divine Comedy*, written in the vernacular dialect of Florence, which became the basis of modern Italian. The author had fallen for the ideal girl, Beatrice, but she had died young. In a vision, Dante journeys to hell (*Inferno*), where the Roman poet Vergil (also spelled Virgil) guides him through circles of punishment. Then Beatrice helps him through purgatory and finally to paradise to behold the ultimate love of God. Along the way, Dante sees and converses with many people whose stories and fates illustrate his view of good and evil, right choices and wrong choices.

In religious belief and practice, medieval people did have carefully limited choice. Except for a few Jews and fewer Muslims, everyone who lived in Christendom had to believe in the dogmas of the Western Latin Church and worship in its dioceses and parishes. The structures built for worship, the cathedrals and parish churches, along with abbeys and monastery churches, remain as testimonies to the importance of faith in the Middle Ages. Believers replaced the simple and small churches of the early Middle Ages with such zeal that almost none survive today. Huge amounts of wealth, effort, and design went into constructing the new stone cathedrals, minsters, chapels, and parish churches of the High Middle Ages.

Church floor plans were usually based on the Latin cross or the ancient Roman basilica, which had a long central aisle (or nave, after the Latin word for "ship") with an altar for the Eucharist at the far end. The people gathered in the nave, while clergy carried out the sacrificial ceremonies around the altar. Music increasingly added decorative sound around the spoken word. We still have written copies of medieval music because monks invented a system of musical notation (no texts of Greek or Roman music have survived). Western music began with a simple plainsong, one simple line of notes called Gregorian chant, and evolved into complex polyphony, many notes sung alongside and around each other in harmony.

Two architectural styles of churches can be recognized as medieval. The first style of stone churches we now call Romanesque, because they inherited many of their design elements from ancient Roman buildings, especially the rounded arch (see figures 8.4 and 8.5). These churches, built between 1000 and 1300, tend to have a blocky appearance, with thick walls necessary to hold up the roof. Still, they were built quite large, often airy and full of light. The walls were frequently decorated with frescoes, and the capitals (tops) of columns were carved with sculptures illustrating key ideas of the faith. The second style of churches we now call Gothic (that insulting term mentioned at the beginning of chapter 7), although medieval builders called it the "modern" or the "French" style (see figures 8.6 and 8.7). After Western encounters with Islamic architecture in Andalusia, Sicily, and the Levant, Gothic cathedrals built from about 1150 to 1500 adopted the pointed arches used there. The Gothic or pointed arch allowed architects to build even taller naves and open up the walls to more windows. They filled the windows with colored stained glass, designed in patterns and pictures of faith, pierced by light from heaven.

All these structures required highly skilled builders and a great deal of wealth. Townspeople competed with their neighbors in other communities to have the best

Figure 8.4.   The blocky Romanesque Abbey of Maria Laach sits squarely on the earth, while its towers point to heaven.

possible church or cathedral. Sometimes their efforts to surpass one another led to disaster when improperly designed churches collapsed. Other times, sponsors ran out of resources, and building remained idle for decades, centuries, or forever. Medieval skylines were sometimes defined by castles but always by churches, whose steeples people saw from far away and whose bells they heard throughout the surrounding countryside.

For the people of Christendom of the High Middle Ages, it made sense to devote much time and energy to the religion of Christianity. The worldview that a moral life in this world prepared one for another life after death gave meaning to the troubles people faced as individuals and as a society. Kings might fight with popes, but that did not cast doubt on the meaning of the Gospels. Cluniac monks might live differently from Cistercians, who in turn did not act like Templars, but all observed rules set to conform their lives to the commands of the church.

Review: How did medieval culture reflect both religion and rationalism?

Response:

Figure 8.5.　The bright nave of the Romanesque Abbey of St. Godehard in Hildesheim illuminates the decorated paneled ceiling.

Figure 8.6.   The outside of the Gothic choir of the St. Vitus Cathedral in Prague highlights the flying buttresses holding up the walls, while their pinnacles reach toward heaven.

A NEW ESTATE

While kings and popes quarreled over the leadership of the West, a revived social institution was growing that would overshadow them both: cities. Townspeople did not fit into the usual medieval classifications, typically divided into three estates: priests to pray for all, knights to fight for all, and peasants to work for all. No sooner had this trinitarian social division established itself in the popular imagination than the shock of economic development shattered its reality. By the twelfth century, the growing success and stability of medieval society had brought back civilization. And by definition, towns and cities have been synonymous with civilization.

The growth of these cities sprang directly from improvements in the economy and in political rule. Wealth from three-field farming and from monastic communities now financed those who did not themselves live on and work the land. The peace and order from the kings' feudal suzerainty offered opportunities for cities to organize. The Jews, forbidden from farming, also formed a core community of towns, as they had since Roman times. Some cities sprouted up from those originally founded by the Romans, especially where cathedrals and their clerics had maintained cores of religious communities. Since the time of the ancient Roman Empire, bishops had been obliged to live in their cathedral cities. Although bishops

Figure 8.7. The high Gothic nave of Canterbury Cathedral opens a sacred space.

had been tempted to move away while cities were in decline during the early Middle Ages, boom times in the High Middle Ages made urban life attractive again. New cities also sprang up at the feet of castles, where feudal and manorial lords controlled a ready source of wealth. Some clever ecclesiastical and secular lords who saw the increasing importance of trade even planted new cities at crossroads and river crossings. Thus, cities such as Cambridge or Innsbruck arose, named after the bridges over their rivers.

Cities grew first and fastest in two regions, the Lowlands (modern Belgium, the Netherlands, and Luxembourg) and Lombardy in northern Italy (with nearby coastal cities such as Venice, Genoa, and Pisa). Both regions had dense populations and easy access to seaborne trading routes. By the twelfth century, merchants from those areas gathered at **fairs** in the French province of Champagne (long before the invention of the sparkling wine that has taken the province's name). These fairs were much more than a typical village market, since merchants from many communities competed with one another about price and quality, with products from distant lands. As farmers entered contests for their animals and produce, competition encouraged better and bigger specimens. The festive atmosphere entertained consumers with varieties of new goods to purchase. Today's county fairs across the United States or trade fairs in Europe are descendants of these medieval fairs. Then and now, fairs were engines of economic growth. The triad of the Lowlands, Champagne, and Lombardy became the core of new commerce in the High Middle Ages.

Traders from medieval Europe began to venture even farther abroad. The First Crusade to the Holy Land had founded new Western principalities in the Levant. Traders followed right behind the warriors. The Lombard cities of Genoa, Pisa, and Venice exploited the Mediterranean sea routes, avoiding and soon outselling the Byzantine Empire. As the crusading states failed, the city-state of Venice in particular succeeded in becoming a maritime political power. Venetians continued to oppose Muslim expansion while exploiting every commercial opportunity. They were also behind the brief Western conquest of the Byzantine Empire during the Fourth Crusade in 1204.

Some European merchants even ventured beyond the Eastern Mediterranean. A few traveled along the ancient Silk Road through Central Asia, which had long connected the Middle East with China. The most famous merchant was the Venetian Marco Polo (b. 1254–d. 1324), who with relatives and servants lived for a time in the Chinese Empire and East Asia in the second half of the thirteenth century. He used his free time while a prisoner of war back home in a Genoese jail to write a book about his adventures. Many people scoffed at his tales (and some are scoffworthy), but he did accurately describe much of the wealth and glory of China, which far excelled that of Europe at the time.

Still, the Europeans kept gaining ground. Building on wealth produced from commerce, Europeans were starting to use machines to make products, a process called **industrialization**. Historians disagree about which ideas or technology (such as iron plows, horse collars, drills, gears, and pumps) merchants brought back from the comparatively advanced Chinese, Indian, and Muslim civilizations.

Years ago, history textbooks credited European inventors with technological innovation. Clearly, though, Asians and North Africans used similar machines decades, if not centuries, before the westerners. In the thirteenth century Europeans did invent spectacles or eyeglasses, without which some people today could hardly read this book. Corrective lenses enabled many more people to read or perform fine-detail work. In any case, after the twelfth century, industrialization further increased the availability of goods to Europeans. The word *manufacture*, which originally meant making something by hand, now described people working with machines.

A boom in textiles arose from a **cottage industry**, in which merchants traveled from home to home, door to door, "putting out" goods to be manufactured in individual houses and then picking up the finished products. Family members in one home might spin the raw wool into thread, down the lane they might weave the thread into cloth, and on the other side of the village they might sew the cloth into a tunic. Peasant wives and children had more time to devote to this new work because of labor saved in the farm fields through iron plows, horse collars, and three-field planting. Peasants thus earned extra income that allowed them to purchase still more new goods. An increasing spiral of growth followed. As some people's work became more specialized, they quit being peasants and became artisans and craftspeople who lived in towns, earning their living from the skills of their minds and hands, not from labor on the land.

As mentioned before, these commercial people of towns and cities did not easily fit into the medieval trifold conception of clergy, nobles, and commoners. With no other option, the townspeople became commoners, yet their social status shared little with that of the medieval serf. They gained a new status as burghers, burgesses, or **bourgeoisie** (drawn from the German word for castle). Burghers were free men (bourgeois women, of course, remained less free than their fathers, husbands, and sons). Unlike the subservient serfs, burgesses were not bound to the land but traveled freely. Indeed, the bourgeoisie held the freedom of ownership, buying and selling of property, and possessing it in peace. They were not responsible to the manorial courts. Instead, the townspeople exercised the freedom of self-government, creating laws and representative political institutions such as **mayors** and **town councils**. Many burghers even gained the right to bear arms (at this time, both swords and heraldic crests). Towns might be thought of as huge castles, although with a multitude of families living behind high stone walls instead of only one. Townspeople raised their own troops and defended their castle-like city walls. Many town patricians even gained entrance to the nobility and aristocracy, imitating the lords who dominated society. None imagined that the bourgeois way of life would one day dominate Western civilization.

These freedoms did not come easily. The communal self-government of mayors and town councils slowly revived democratic government in the West. Once again, though, democracy was difficult. The townspeople often had to fight to have their liberties and rights respected by the well-born lords of society. They began to organize **communes**, meaning they sought to have the laws recognize them as a collective group of people who organized their own affairs separately from the rest of nobility-dominated Europe. The kings, dukes, bishops, and magnates often resisted and attacked the communal corporations at first, seeing them as a threat to their authority and social superiority. Eventually, however, the lords largely accepted the townspeople, recognizing the economic advantages of a flourishing urban life that created new wealth. The lords granted charters of liberty to the burghers, defining and affirming their self-government and civil rights.

Having successfully fought the lords, townspeople next fought one another over a share of the authority and wealth. Medieval citizens often mixed politics with violence. The rich and powerful wanted to exclude the poor and the powerless. The elite patricians fought against the middle-class artisans. Both tried to keep down the teeming rabble. If frustrated by loss in an election or by exclusion from any political participation at all, groups of townspeople might assassinate their rivals or riot to overthrow them.

Institutions called **guilds** often provided a peaceful framework for political, social, and economic interaction. These organizations allowed owners (the masters) and workers in a craft or trade (baking, shoemaking, cloth dyeing) to supervise the quality and quantity of production. Even universities (whose product was knowledge) structured themselves as guilds. Master artisans trained the next generations of apprentices and journeymen (day laborers) in the proper skills. Guilds also became the vehicles for social and political cohesion, as they provided social welfare for their members, organized celebrations, and set up candidates for urban elections. Despite some instability that always goes with democracy and economic change, cities and their civilization were a success in the West again. Towns soon began to grow in size and numbers comparable with the contemporary civilized societies of Islam, India, and China.

To minister to these new townspeople, new kinds of monks called **mendicants** began to appear in the thirteenth century. Their name comes from the Latin word for begging, and that is how they were supposed to receive their livelihood. The earlier Benedictine or Cistercian monks drew income from the production of the land. Mendicants were to live from the excess production of town commerce. The townspeople had become wealthy enough to have extra money that they devoted to charity. The mendicants were to preach and teach, living only from alms.

Appropriately, the mendicants preached against the popular values of city life. The new urban elites gloried in wealth and ostentation, imitating the nobility. This attitude was *materialism*, valuing goods and pleasures provided by wealth in this world. The most famous medieval Christian opponent of this materialism was the founder of the Franciscans, **Francis of Assisi** (b. 1181–d. 1226). Francis helped to promote the idea of *apostolic poverty*: that the original apostles were poor, and so modern clergy should be also. He set an example of rejecting the wealth of the patricians and reaching out to the new urban poor.

As seen with previous monastic reforms, the success of mendicant friars led later generations of them to stray from the original ideals. They acquired endowments, properties, and possessions. The Franciscans were soon split between those who sought apostolic poverty and those who observed obedience to the wealthy and politically powerful papacy. Another main group of mendicants, the Dominicans, focused on education and fighting new heresies that were already appearing in the twelfth century. Serious heresies had not been a problem since the German barbarians who were Arian Christians had converted to orthodox catholic Christianity at the beginning of the early Middle Ages. Since then, everyone in the West had to be Christian.

Everyone, that is, with the exception of the Jews. Christian authorities allowed Jews to retain their faith, honoring them as the original "chosen people" of their God. The Christian authorities nevertheless carefully and legally discriminated against the Jews, confining them to living in towns (and usually particular neighborhoods), prohibiting them from owning farmland, and allowing them only certain professions, such as moneylending. Christians periodically stole their wealth, forced Jews to convert, falsely accused them of crimes, and attacked them when things went wrong, such as during a plague. At any time, a king might expel the Jews from the kingdom, as happened in England in 1290 and France in 1306. Even had it been allowed, no Christian would have chosen to convert to Judaism.

The new heresies of the High Middle Ages were different from Judaism, since they offered real alternatives to catholic orthodox Christianity. They probably arose because of the increasing success of the European economy. More trade with the East (eastern Europe, the Middle East, Asia) transported new ideas from those distant places. As some merchants became wealthy, enjoying their own materialism, many decided that the church should not share in their rising economic comforts. Instead, they listened to advocates of apostolic poverty.

One of the first heretics was Pierre Valdès (or Peter Waldo), who lived in the late twelfth century. Like Francis of Assisi a generation later, Waldo called for poverty and simplicity within the church. Bishops uncomfortable with Waldo's call to poverty tried to silence and punish him. Peter Waldo refused and escaped into the Alps, where he set up small groups, the **Waldensians**, some of which survive to this day. A few isolated Waldensian villages survived every effort by the official church to kill or convert them.

The other major heretical movement was that of the **Cathars** (which probably comes from a word meaning "the pure") or **Albigensians** (named after the southern French town of Albi). These heretics were more dangerous to Christianity because they offered a popular alternative belief system, *Catharism*. The Cathars' dualism alleged that God ruled the spirit while the devil claimed material things, a belief similar to the early Christian heresy of Gnosticism. Since in their view even the flesh was evil, Cathars resisted the pleasures of this world in order to gain heaven. They rejected the Western ecclesiastical hierarchy and set up their own counterchurch. As they attracted members from the nobles, townspeople, and peasants, the Cathars broke the monopoly of the official Western Latin Church, especially in southern France.

The western Christians struck back. First, the mendicants preached the Catholic faith, but soon words were not enough. Next, they revived the ancient Roman legal procedure known as the **inquisition**, which comes from the Latin word for inquire or ask. Normally, someone had to submit a complaint before an investigation about a crime could be initiated. To maintain public order, however, the Romans occasionally used the inquisition as an alternative. In this procedure, the government commissioned a tribunal to uncover crimes committed in a certain region, even if no complaints had been officially registered. Traveling judges were empowered to investigate crimes, arrest people, prosecute alleged criminals, and punish them. Thus the modern legal powers that are today divided among police, district attorneys, judges, and juries were combined into one lethally effective instrument.

The Western religious authorities in the thirteenth century thought the situation serious enough to reinstate this method. When the majority of people in a region had converted to heresy, no complaints of the crime would come to authorities. So popes and bishops commissioned investigators, often Dominicans, to ferret out heretics. They could enter a province only with the explicit permission of the local political ruler. After finding heretics guilty, the clerical inquisition then handed them over to the secular arm, namely the local political powers, which burned them to death at the stake. The use of torture during the investigations has disgraced the inquisition in the history of jurisprudence. At times, some historians and critics of religion have exaggerated the inquisition's excesses of brutality and injustice. Unless one believes that any means justifies ending sin, the "Holy Inquisition" and its blessing by lay and religious leaders is a blight on Christianity.

Surprisingly, even the Holy Inquisition did not stamp out heresy. So the Western Latin Church finally resorted to its highest level of violence: a crusade. In 1225, Pope Innocent III sanctioned a Catholic invasion of southern France to destroy the Cathars. The so-called Albigensian Crusade succeeded. One story goes that in a town in the south of France, everyone was massacred. Those who worried that some Catholic Christians might have been caught in the general slaughter were told that "God will know his own," bringing the righteous into heaven and sending the heretics to hell. The success of the Albigensian Crusade strengthened the French king by putting confiscated lands under his direct control. The crusade and subsequent royal rule destroyed a flourishing, distinctly southern French culture, along with the Cathars. In the next centuries, church leaders elsewhere in Christendom likewise called other crusades against several rebellious enemies, since by definition defying the church's authority in any fashion was heretical.

Review: How did the revival of trade and towns change the West?

Response:

NOT THE END OF THE WORLD

The spread of heresy might have threatened people's souls, but the spread of disease surely plagued their bodies. Tragically, trade connections with Asia brought not just spices and silks but also the disaster called the **Black Death**. In 1347, contagions that had swarmed along trade routes from the East entered the crowded and dirty cities of Europe. For the next several years and regularly thereafter, plague sprawled through both urban and rural Christendom. The exact nature of this epidemic, or epidemics, is disputed. The contemporary descriptions that drew on ancient accounts of plagues listed various contradictory symptoms, leading historians to suggest that more than one disease was at work. Regardless, the Black Death swept through the population of western Europe to a degree unseen for centuries, killing probably one out of three people. The impact varied, though, since some regions saw almost no sign of disease while other towns were nearly wiped out. Well into the eighteenth century, less virulent waves of plague returned to strike down tens of thousands of Europeans, over and over.

Aiding the spread of disease was a general cooling of the climate. What historians call a "mini ice age" began about 1300 and lasted until about 1700. The climate in Europe became a few degrees cooler. Winters lasted longer, and summers were shorter. This change shortened growing seasons and increased rainfall where it was not needed. The effects sharply reduced food production, and a hungry European population became even more susceptible to illness.

Historians usually see the period between 1300 and 1350 as the transition from the High Middle Ages (ca. 1000–1350) to the later Middle Ages (ca. 1300–1500). The climatic change and increase in epidemics created what scholars call a demographic catastrophe that sent the gradually rising European population into a sharp decline. The high mortality rates and fear of death led at times to a breakdown of the fragile social order that had been created during the High Middle Ages. As the later Middle Ages followed, everyone had to cope with rougher natural circumstances, the continued political and social dominance of the clergy and knightly nobility, the increasing competition with townspeople, and dissatisfaction among the peasants. The later Middle Ages was a time of increasing unrest and uncertainty.

The reduction in population also caused labor shortages that forced economic changes. Peasant farming shifted from lord-serf to landlord-tenant. Now peasants' uncertain livelihood depended on paying rent instead of long-standing customary obligations such as labor services and portions of crops. Post-plague, if a peasant failed to come up with the rent, he and his family might more easily be thrown off the land and left with nothing. Also, landlords tried to focus more on cash crops like wheat for export instead of vegetables for local consumption. The latter had traditionally been encouraged on the self-sufficient manor, when farmers grew what they needed to eat. While serfdom had limited social and political freedom, being tied to the land allowed serfs a certain economic freedom—they could at least feed their families. Their new change in status left them vulnerable to homelessness, hunger, and poverty.

Peasants began to rebel against both the restrictions of serfdom and, paradoxically, the insecurity caused by its decline. Some even thought of a religious justification, as shown in the rhyme, "When Adam delved and Eve span, who was then the gentleman?"[4] Peasant revolts started to happen with some regularity. The most

---

4. Or, reworded for modern sense: "When the first human beings worked, Adam dug in the ground and Eve spun thread like peasants; no class distinctions existed as they did when nobles ruled and profited from peasant labor."

famous are the Jacquerie, a rebellion in France in 1358, and the Wat Tyler Revolt in England in 1381. In the first stage of rebellions, peasants killed a few landlords, burned some buildings and records, and grabbed property for themselves. Sadly for the peasants, virtually all their revolts ended in defeat. Within weeks, royal or noble armies reorganized and slaughtered hundreds, if not thousands, of peasants. The traditional landholding clergy and nobility, joined by the bourgeoisie, were too well organized, too well armed, and too powerful. That these rebellions increasingly took place at all, though, showed that something was wrong with the order of society.

In France and England, the leadership of the clergy likewise eventually found itself challenged anew by powerful authoritarian kings, which Germany lacked. During the High Middle Ages, when popes had struggled with the Holy Roman emperors over leadership in Christendom, the papacy seemed to have won. The constant change of royal dynasties because of elections made the Holy Roman emperor seem more of an annoyance than a puissant monarch. The German kings of the Holy Roman Empire declined in authority except in their own personal dynastic lands. In contrast, German dukes, counts, prince-bishops, and even barons and some imperial knights ruled as near-sovereign territorial princes.

The kings of France and England, however, became strong monarchs with centralized authority over their realms. The kings of both those countries drew on the power of dynasty, military might, and taxes on towns. They also relied on the advice and support of people through elected representative bodies, the Estates-General in France and the Parliament in England. Both kingdoms were expanding. England almost succeeded in conquering Scotland, held off only by the plucky heroics of William Wallace and Robert the Bruce in the early 1300s. The English did, however, increasingly dominate Ireland and Wales. The French, meanwhile, nibbled away at the Western borders of the Holy Roman Empire. Even more important, France and England offered renewed resistance to papal claims of authority.

A new power conflict appeared during the reign of Pope **Boniface VIII** (r. 1294–1303). Boniface resisted the kings of England and France, who wanted to tax their clergy to finance a war they were preparing to fight against each other. In two papal bulls (from 1296 and 1302), the pope decreed and commanded that papal permission was needed for kings to tax the clergy and church lands. He reminded the monarchs that popes commanded kings, not the other way around. Furthermore, to be saved from hell, every Christian, king and commoner alike, needed to obey the Roman pontiff.

The pope's declarations notwithstanding, the kings of England and France had other ideas. The kings retaliated by shutting down their borders and forbidding all export of precious metals and revenues to Rome. They convened their representative assemblies (Parliament and the Estates-General), many of whose clergy representatives sided with their nations against the pope. The most extreme reaction was from King Philip IV "the Fair" of France. He sent agents to Italy who tried to kidnap the pope while he was enjoying the summer in Anagni, away from the heat of Rome. Although freed by Anagni's townspeople, the shocked Boniface died a month later. If a German emperor had tried to do this fifty years earlier, the next pope would have proclaimed a crusade against him. In this case, the king of France escaped with impunity.

Indeed, Philip IV tried to grab hold of the papacy for himself and his dynasty. He helped to elect a Frenchman as pope, Clement V (r. 1305–1314), a man who not only favored the French king but also packed up and moved the Curia out of Rome to the city of **Avignon** on the southeastern border of France. There the papacy resided throughout the so-called **Babylonian Captivity** (1309–1377), named after the real Hebrew exile 1,800 years earlier. The popes were hardly captives. Actually, they expanded their administration of the Western Latin Church. They paid for their palace and power by collecting tithes and annates (the first year's income from important ecclesiastical offices such as bishop and abbot). Popes even took over provisions or reservations (the right to name men to church offices, especially bishoprics), although these appointments were often done in consultation with, and at the request of, the local princes.

Many Christians were properly aghast at this situation. The pope was, of course, the bishop of Rome, and by canon law a bishop was to reside in his cathedral city. It often seemed, as the number and influence of French-born cardinals increased, that the papacy had become a tool of the French king. Many called for the pope to return to Rome, including the famous inspirational religious figures Catherine of Siena and Bridget of Sweden.

Finally, Pope Gregory XI did return to Rome in 1377, only to die the next year. The cardinals, under pressure from the Roman mob, quickly elected an Italian, Urban VI (r. 1378–1389). To their dismay, the cardinals found him demanding, hot tempered, and cruel. Rather than deal with the situation forthrightly, most of the cardinals left Rome for the cooler temperatures of Anagni. There they declared that their election of Urban was invalid and elected a new pope of French descent, Clement VII (r. 1378–1394). They then blithely returned with their new pope to Avignon. Urban, meanwhile, refused to recognize his deposition and continued to reign in Rome. Thus the Western Latin Church was faced with a unique schism: two popes who had been elected by the same cardinals. Different princes chose allegiance to one pope or the other, often depending on whether they liked the French (and their Avignon puppet) or not.

This "Papal Schism of 1378" or **Great Western Schism** did not turn out as disastrous or long-lasting as the other "Great Schism" that separated Western catholic and Eastern orthodox Christianity back in 1054.[5] Theoretically, this division could have gone on forever, since both popes created cardinals, and each new college of cardinals elected its own papal successor after its pope had died. At one point, the majority of cardinals from both parties decided to end the schism by meeting at Pisa in 1409. In the shadow of the leaning tower, they deposed both the Avignon and Roman pontiffs and elected a new pope. Since the first two refused to recognize their depositions, the Western Latin Church now had three popes!

This Great Western Schism was healed by the old practice of *conciliarism*. The first councils dated back to the days of the church's liberation under Constantine. The ancient church used councils to create hierarchy and to resolve differences.

---

5. A few history books label this schism of multiple popes from 1378 to 1417 as the "Great Schism," without the qualifying terms *papal* or *Western*. That exaggerates its significance compared to the separation of Western and Eastern Christians, which still endures.

Important ecumenical councils of all Christians had then been held for centuries until the Great Schism in 1054 between the catholics and orthodox ended the possibility of truly universal Christian cooperation. As popes revived "universal" councils (for the West only) in the eleventh century, they used them to dominate the Western Latin Church. Now, however, a council saved the papacy. Supported by the Holy Roman emperor, Sigismund of Bohemia, all parties attended the **Council of Constance** (1414–1417). The council first gained the resignation or deposition of the three popes based in Pisa, Avignon, and Rome and then successfully elected a new, universally recognized pope, Martin V.

The representatives to the Council of Constance understood the advantages of representative assemblies such as Parliament in England, the Estates-General in France, the Cortes in Castile, or the Diet in Germany. Therefore, they wrote a constitutional role for councils within the Western Latin Church's governance which required that new councils be called at regularly set intervals. Nevertheless, the recovered papal monarchy stamped out that idea, which diluted their absolute authority. Popes delayed and dissolved later councils until they declared as a heresy any appeal to a future council. The papacy in Rome settled onto its seemingly secure foundations.

Nonetheless, times were changing. The pope's victory faded as the changing structures of civilization ended the Middle Ages and began the early modern period. The Middle Ages had fashioned Western civilization as part of medieval Christendom (see map 8.2). Society was at first divided into three groups: those who prayed (the clergy) and those who both fought (the knights) and ruled over those who worked (the serfs). The successes and struggles within this order transformed the West. Kings struggled to dominate their knights, while nobles strove to keep their independence. Popes strained to rule both their own clergy and the kings, while alternate forms of religious life began to flourish and most kings grew stronger in their kingdoms. These struggles strengthened institutions of various kingdoms and the Western Latin Church overall. Meanwhile, food production by peasants helped revive towns and reestablish civilized life. Faith and wealth fostered cultural creativity and economic growth. The townspeople with their economic power asserted their respectable status among the established medieval nobles and clergy. Before long, old ideas and new practices further fractured Christendom, transforming it into our modern West.

Review: How do the later Middle Ages expose the problems of medieval institutions?

Response:

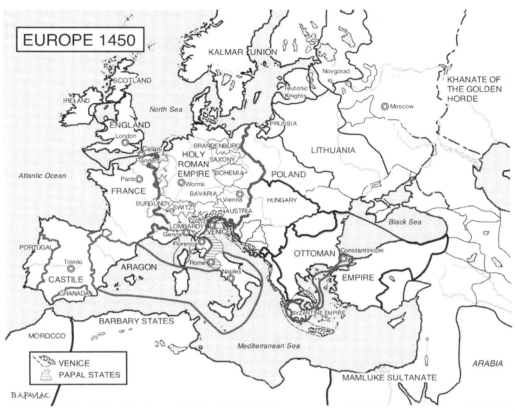

Map 8.2.   Europe, 1450.
How do the fractured states of Western Europe compare to those of the
map of the year 1200 (map 8.1)?

Make your own timeline.

CHAPTER 9

Making the Modern World

The Renaissance and Reformation, 1400 to 1648

Already in the fifteenth century, some intellectuals had begun to claim that centuries of backwardness had given way to a "modern" age. All people, of course, believe they live in modern times, and they do. For historians, this transition to a "modern" time period, or even "early modern," reflects the changing elements of society, state, and culture compared with those of the Middle Ages and before. The key to this transition was a new appreciation for classical antiquity, the culture of ancient Greece and Rome. Historians have named that perception the **Renaissance**, meaning a rebirth of attitudes drawn from Græco-Roman culture. Classical antiquity had, of course, been appreciated to one degree or another since its collapse in the West a thousand years before. Beginning around 1400, however, a renewed interest in ancient history intertwined with economic, political, and religious developments. Reflecting on the past while sailing into the unknown, the Europeans traveled out of the later Middle Ages (ca. 1300–1500) and landed in the early modern period of history (ca. 1400–1815) (see timeline C).

THE PURSE OF PRINCES

As the Europeans recovered from the onslaught of the Black Death, the resurging economics of the towns propelled them into undreamed-of wealth and success. Amid plague and peasant rebellion, a dynamic idea later called *capitalism* began to catch on. Capitalism was a new form of economic practice that went beyond the markets of farmers or fairs. The "capital" of capitalism refers to a substantial amount of wealth that is available, and necessary, for investment. Many businesses require capital to begin operation or maintain themselves. One form of capital is profit, wealth left over after all expenses have been paid. When profits could be obtained, the practice of capitalism dictated what to do with them: reinvest.

In its simplest form, then, capitalism is reinvesting profits gained from invested capital. The usual human inclination is to spend excess wealth on showiness: fine homes, gourmet foods, parties, designer fashions, and grand edifices. One can, of course, give money away or bury it in the ground. Investing profit in one's own operations or in providing start-up and operating funds for another business, however, promoted long-term growth. Successful investments in turn created more profits, which then might be invested still further. Thus, capitalism became an engine for economic progress: wealth bred more wealth. Likewise, capitalism encouraged innovation. Clever investors looked for a new enterprise, a novel endeavor, which, if successful, would bring an even greater profit.

Only much later did historians and theorists use the exact term *capitalism*. Some historians also argue that other civilizations, either Muslim, Indian, or Chinese, practiced capitalism first and that westerners learned its techniques from them. Wherever it came from, more problematic is that people today often misunderstand the term *capitalism*. Many people often confuse capitalism with free markets. While capitalism requires markets (a space for people to exchange goods and services), they do not have to be entirely free (without restrictions imposed by authorities). This leads to another basic principle:

> **There is no such thing as an entirely free market; all markets have rules and costs.**

One of the key arguments among market participants, then and now, is how many regulations or fees there should be. One of the most important rules determines how much honesty is required between buyer and seller. If the market is an actual place, there are expenses for rent, cleaning, and upkeep. Many fees are taken by middlemen. The number of rules and expenses imposed on markets make them more or less free or fair. And breaking the rules meant punishment by law (see figure 9.1).

Another ongoing difficulty with capitalism has been when people lost their capital in financial markets. If a business venture failed, not only was there no profit, but the original capital could also disappear as well. Risk has always existed with capitalism—wealth can simply vanish into thin air. On the one hand, luck, creativity, and business acumen can create huge funds from a small incentive. On the other hand, irrational exuberance, misfortune, stupidity, and economic ignorance can just as easily destroy riches. Poor investors have lost vast assets. For example, a sudden mania for tulips in the Netherlands during the 1630s drove up prices many times their previous worth. At the most extreme, one exotic bulb for a garden cost the equivalent price of a mansion. When the bubble burst, tulip bulbs once again became merely potential flowers, that is, very affordable. Yet since early capitalists succeeded more often than they failed, the European economy grew over the long term. Capitalists may have accumulated most of the new wealth, but they also provided employment and opportunities for others to become wealthier. Indeed, capitalism helped make Western civilization the most powerful culture the world has ever known, during what historians have called the **Commercial Revolution** (1350–1600).

Figure 9.1.   This woodcut from a legal handbook (ca. 1500) shows the various punishments monarchs inflicted on criminals. Top row: cutting off an ear, preparation for dunking, disembowelment, burning alive at the stake, eye gouging, hanging. Bottom row: flaying, beheading, breaking with the wheel, cutting off a hand. (University of Pennsylvania)

The encouragement of innovation and the increase in wealth after the Black Death made medieval economic methods obsolete. The guild's hierarchical, regulated structure stifled progress, as measured by the creation of new forms of business. By definition, the guild promoted one kind of industry and opposed others. The masters who ran guilds increasingly seemed to want only to hold on to their power rather than seek improvements. While guilds had served to help medieval towns thrive, they were too inflexible to adapt to capitalism's drive for change.

The Commercial Revolution put in place more modern economic methods. Replacing the guild as the important structure for business was the partnership or firm. Usually this involved a family or several families pooling their resources to provide capital. As a business evolved, different members or alliances might come and go, which also encouraged creativity.

In the fourteenth century, families began to establish **banks**, the premier capitalist institution. The new banks evolved from benches of money changers into organizations that housed money and earned profits through finance. While bankers paid interest to attract depositors, the collection and safeguarding of deposits was merely a means to accumulate capital. Bankers invested assets as loans. A system of banks also allowed money to flow more easily from one part of Europe to another without actually lugging around boxes of gold bars and bags of silver coins.

Instead, banks issued bills of exchange, the forerunner of the modern check (the idea probably borrowed from Muslim trading partners). Commencing in Italy, bank branches sprang up in cities all over Europe.

This rise of finance as a major economic activity required some religious reform. Up to this time, most moneylending in the medieval West had been carried out by Jews, since Christians interpreted their own scriptures as declaring that making profit from money was sinful usury. But if both the borrower and the lender profited from each other, Christians rationalized that it was no sin. By the close of the Middle Ages, more materialistic church leaders had redefined the sin of usury to allow more lending so that they, too, could borrow to finance palaces and church building.

To keep track of all this wealth, money counters invented double-entry book-keeping. Since ancient times, businesses had simply entered a running tally of incomes and expenses in paragraph form, if they kept records at all. This new method, much like any modern checkbook or bank statement, arranged the moneys into two columns, which could be easily added or subtracted; a third column tracked the running sum of overall credit or debt. Instead of Roman numerals of letters (I, V, X, L, etc.), the math was more easily done with "Arabic" numbers, which Muslims had borrowed from Hindus. Thus a merchant could better account for how much the business had on reserve or owed.

As in most economic revolutions, benefits and costs distributed themselves unevenly among varied social groups. People still earned wealth through agriculture, commerce, and manufacturing, but finance began its rise to predominance. As happens so often, the rich became richer while the poor became poorer. Women were encouraged to work, although in lower-status jobs at lower wages than men were paid for the same work. Women workers' low cost and the ease with which they could be fired helped businesses maintain their profit levels. A growing class of menial laborers piled up at the bottom of the social scale as well-paid family artisans lost out to cheap labor. The wealthiest merchants began to merge with the nobility, becoming indistinguishable from them in their manner of living except for titles and family trees of noble ancestors. As a whole, though, the overall affluence and standard of living in Western society rose.

Princes who took advantage of this economic boom became the monarchs of the late Middle Ages and early modern times. The practice of **public debt**, allowed by the new banking system, financed their expansion of power. Before capitalism, a prince's debts were considered his own—he had to finance them from his dynastic revenues. Although a prince's incomes were often quite substantial, they were limited by agricultural production and a few taxes on trade. The new idea of public debt meant that bankers could finance loans to the princes, and then all of the prince's subjects had to pay the loans off through taxes and customs duties on imports and exports. Throughout history, governments have raised taxes and piled on debt as much as they could get away with. Bankers usually supported this growing debt since they made a profit off the loans. Sometimes, a prince's debts grew too large, and through bankruptcy he defaulted on his debts. Then capital disappeared, followed by business failures and unemployment. More often, however, governments settled up their loans with interest, the bankers got their profits, and the princes became more powerful while the common people paid the price. A prince might also try to raise revenues by plundering a neighboring country, but that was shortsighted. Best was to annex another province, help it prosper, and tax it.

Such control over territories caused the **Hundred Years War** (1338–1453) between France and England. King Edward of England's Plantagenet dynasty wanted to protect some independence for Flanders (for wool) and preserve what few English territories remained in the southwest of France (for wine). The latter region, called Guyenne, was the last remaining French province of Henry II's empire (most of which his son John had lost in the thirteenth century). The kings of France wanted both Guyenne and Flanders for their own. A French dynastic crisis provided King Edward a pretext for war. King Philip IV "the Fair" had died in 1314, leaving three young sons. Within a few years, they had also died without leaving any male heirs in the Capetian dynasty—a situation France had not faced for more than three hundred years. The French aristocracy, without too much fighting, decided on Philip's grandnephew, who succeeded as King Philip VI, the first king of the Valois dynasty (1328–1589). Meanwhile, however, Edward of England claimed the throne of France as a grandson of Philip IV (although through Philip's daughter).

As the name implies, the Hundred Years War took generations to grind its way toward a conclusion. Along the way, war and politics changed decisively from medieval to modern. When the war began, knights still reigned supreme on the battlefield, as they had for centuries. Over time, however, weapon makers had concocted better ways of killing knights and of protecting them. They had also devised new ways to storm castles, while architects planned better ways to defend them. At the time of the Norman Conquest in 1066, knights wore chain mail (heavy coats of linked iron rings). By the middle of the Hundred Years War, jointed plate armor enveloped knights from head to toe. Castles in the eleventh century had been simple wooden forts on hills. By the fourteenth century, they had become elaborate stone fortresses with massive towers and high walls built in concentric circles and surrounded by deep ditches.

England perfected the use of two medieval weapons in its wars with its immediate neighbors. By the fifteenth century, the English had conquered the Welsh but continued to fight off and on in the north against the Scots. These border wars changed English military technology and tactics. The English adopted a unique weapon, the **longbow**. Originally used by the Welsh, the longbow was as tall as a man and required long training and practice to pull. It could pierce armor at four hundred paces and be reloaded more quickly than its only competitor, the crossbow. English skills with the longbow were so important that in 1349 the king banned all sports other than archery. English knights had also learned from fighting the Scottish William Wallace and Robert the Bruce to dismount from vulnerable horses and defend themselves and their archers with **pikes**, long spears of two or three times a man's height. Thus, foot soldiers once more returned as a powerful force on the battlefield, as had been the Greek/Macedonian phalanx.

During the Hundred Years War, the English raided France, devastating the countryside. French knights who tried to stop the raids took a while to realize that they no longer dominated combat. The English archers and dismounted knights wreaked havoc on French armored cavalry in three mighty battles: Crécy (1346), Poitiers (1356), and Agincourt (1415). Each battle turned the tide for the English and nearly led to the destruction of the French monarchy and kingdom. In the Treaty of Troyes (1420), King Henry V of England forced the French king to skip over the legitimate royal heir, holding the title of "Dauphin," and instead grant the succession to the future child of Henry V and his French princess-bride.

Henry's sudden death, however, saved the French. He left an infant heir, Henry VI (r. 1422–1461)—always a precarious situation, as family and others fought over guardianship. The English advantage might still have prevailed over the divided and demoralized French, but then the unique **Joan of Arc** (b. 1412–d. 1431) arrived to save the French kingdom. This lowborn teenager believed that the voices of saints and angels told her to help the uncrowned French prince, the Dauphin Charles. In 1429, Charles put her in shining armor at the head of a French army, which she "miraculously" led to victories over the English. Shortly after the Dauphin gained his crown as King Charles VII (r. 1429–1461), Joan was captured in battle. The French did nothing to rescue Joan, while the English put her on trial as a heretic. The crime of wearing men's clothing doomed her, because it meant she defied the authority of the church to control her. The English burned her alive at the stake and scattered her ashes.

Meanwhile, Charles VII cleverly used the ongoing English occupation of northern France to extort power from the French nobles and townspeople. In 1438, the Estates-General gave him the right to regularly collect taxes, such as those on salt or hearths. Everyone paid the salt tax, while the rich paid more of the hearth tax since their larger homes had more fireplaces. These revenues enabled Charles VII to raise a national, professional army paid by the government rather than one composed of feudal vassals, or hired mercenaries. Such a force had not fought in Europe since the time of the Roman legions. He also invested in the new-to-Europe technology of **gunpowder**, which had found its way from China by the fourteenth century. Charles VII's armies shot guns to punch holes in knights' armor and fired cannons to pound castles to rubble. The French finally drove the English back across the Channel.

The English did not cope well with this defeat. They did become more English, as the elites stopped speaking French, their language of choice since the Norman invasion. Their government, though, briefly spun out of control. When Henry VI turned out to be mentally unbalanced, factions formed to control him. These opposing groups eventually came to blows in civil wars called the **Wars of the Roses** (1455–1487). During these, one aristocratic alliance (Lancaster) lost to another (York), which in turn lost to a third (Tudor) in 1485. King Henry VII (r. 1485–1509) of the new **Tudor dynasty** (1485–1603) provided England with a strong monarchy, exploiting the desire of the English to return to political stability in alliance with the English Parliament. In Parliament's House of Commons, Henry bonded the English monarchy with the English middle class. The Tudor kings working with Parliament gave England a strong and flexible government, able to adapt to changing times.

While English and French kings reaffirmed their ascendance, the Holy Roman emperors slipped even further into impotence. Since the end of the Staufen dynasty in 1256, powerful dynasties had fought over who would succeed as Roman king and emperor, officially chosen by seven electoral princes. The Golden Bull of 1356 established an elective monarchy for the empire. This law strengthened the territorial princes, leaving the Holy Roman emperors more as figureheads than authoritarian rulers. The election of King Frederick III in 1438 offered some stability, although no one realized it at the time. His **Habsburg dynasty** (1438–1918) monopolized the royal and imperial title, with the briefest of interruptions, until the Holy Roman Empire's end in 1806.

Realistically, the Habsburgs' power and interests lay with their own dynastic lands: **Austria** and its neighbors. Effective rule of the rest of the empire remained beyond their grasp. Frederick's son and successor Maximilian (r. 1486–1519) found too little success in wars to expand imperial domination. The spiritual and secular princes, nobility, and free cities even set up a Diet (Reichstag), the German equivalent of Parliament or the Estates-General. Although the imperial office remained weak, marriages arranged for and by Maximilian added numerous territories to the Habsburg dynasty's possessions. His own first marriage brought him parts of Burgundy and the Lowlands after his father-in-law Duke Charles "the Rash" of Burgundy died in battle with the Swiss. Marriages of his children and grandchildren added Bohemia, Hungary, and even Spain. It was said of his dynasty, "Let others wage war for a throne—you, happy Austria, marry."

Looming on Maximilian's Hungarian border, the Ottoman Turkish Empire threatened to unsettle the self-satisfied princes of Christendom. The Seljuk Turks had weakened Byzantium in the eleventh century, leading to the crusades for the Holy Land. By the late thirteenth century, attacks from the Mongols and others had weakened Seljuk rule. The new Ottoman dynasty revived Turkish power. The dynasty (as well as plush, round footstools) was named after its founder, Osman or Othman (d. 1324), who started as one more *bey*, or leader among many Turks in Asia Minor. He and his troops served at first as mercenaries, called into Europe by Byzantine Greeks as they fought with each other and with Serbians, Bulgarians, Genoese, Venetians, and Latin Crusaders in Greece. The Byzantine Empire had ceased to be innovative. Its armies could not defend its shrinking territory, whose tax base was needed to pay for the large imperial bureaucracy.

A decisive moment came in 1354, when the Ottomans seized a permanent base in Gallipoli on the Dardanelles, south of Constantinople, in Europe. From there, Ottoman armies with *ghazi* (religious warriors) expanded in two directions, into southeastern Europe and across Asia Minor. The Ottomans soon took the title of sultans, given to powerful Muslim rulers second in rank only to the caliphs. They aspired to be caliphs themselves.

Southeastern Europe fell under the rule of Turkish Muslims. One conquest was the dual province Bosnia-Herzegovina, where the Bogomils had built up a heretical kingdom united by the dualistic religion of Catharism. Once the Turks had taken Bosnia-Herzegovina, many of the Slavs there converted to Islam. Next the Turks crushed the Serbian kingdom at the Battle of Kosovo Polje (28 June 1389), a site also called the Field of the Blackbirds (after the winged scavengers who fed on the innumerable corpses of Christian warriors). Most of the divided Bulgarian Empire quickly collapsed. A crusading army with troops from western Europe actually tried to confront the Ottoman danger. The Turks slaughtered those crusaders at Nico-polis in Bulgaria (1396), the fleeing Christian knights cutting off the fashionably long tips of their shoes in order to run away more quickly.

The few remaining unconquered Byzantine territories gained a respite when the Ottomans were attacked by the great conqueror Tamerlane, or Timur "the Lame," of Samarkand in central Asia (b. 1336–d. 1405). His reputation for slaughter surpassed that of the Huns or the Mongols. Timur's defeat of the Ottoman armies in 1402 almost ended the dynasty. Three years later, however, Timur was dead, and his empire crumbled.

The Ottoman Empire reconsolidated and expanded. Jews, Orthodox Christians, Muslims, Greeks, Turks, Slavs, Arabs, and Armenians were organized into efficient groups that provided troops and taxes. The Ottomans organized interconnected bureaucracies to manage the diverse peoples and widespread territories. The Otto-man armies also relied on young Christian boys taken from the conquered lands and trained to be expert warriors called janissaries. The Ottoman sultans finally assumed the ancient title of caliph, the religious and political leader of all (Sunni) Muslims. After crushing another crusading army at Varna on the Black Sea in 1444, the Turks besieged Constantinople, the last remnant of the once-mighty Roman Empire. The massive cannons of Mohammed or Mehmet II "the Conqueror" (r. 1451–1481) shelled the city for weeks. Defeat was only a matter of time as the walls became rubble. A Byzantine soldier who forgot to close a door through the walls, though, opened the way to a speedy defeat. The last Byzantine emperor died among his troops, defending the once-impregnable walls. Thus fell the Byzantine or Roman Empire, once and for all, in 1453.

Mehmet II made Constantinople his new imperial capital, which came to be called Istanbul (from the Greek for "to the City"). He rebuilt and repopulated it (although no one told the Turks about the many underground cisterns that had been used to supply the city with water since Roman times). The Ottomans con-quered diverse peoples in the Middle East and North Africa. In 1526, the Turks then seized much of Hungary from the Austrian Habsburgs. The Ottomans were then ready to advance into the Holy Roman Empire itself and perhaps from there con-quer all of Christendom.

By 1600, the Ottomans were equal in power, wealth, and creativity to any of the Europeans (see figure 9.2). Their empire proved its success by conquering huge swathes of territory in the Middle East and North Africa. On the one hand, they allowed people to keep their ethnic identities while welcoming conversions to Islam or becoming more ethnically Turkish. On the other hand, they sometimes exploited ethnic conflicts to maintain their rule, encouraging minorities to dislike one another rather than their masters. Either way, the Ottoman Empire provided a powerful rival to the West.

The victories of the Ottomans ended any medieval dream of a united Chris-tendom. Meager attempts by crusaders to help the Byzantine Empire and other Balkan Christians failed miserably. Western popes and princes worked against one another rather than against the common enemy. The various monarchs were look-ing out for their own narrow dynastic interests first. Western civilization remained in the hands of diverse petty and grand states of Europe.

Figure 9.2.   The Blue Mosque dominating the skyline of Istanbul reflects the glory of the Ottoman Empire around 1600.

Once the notion of a universal Christendom was gone, so was a key component of what had defined the Middle Ages. No one precise moment, event, or battle marks the transition when medieval became modern history. Today, some historians even argue that medieval times lingered into the seventeenth and eighteenth centuries. Transformations in thought and belief, however, further turned the West away from the medieval construct of priests, knights, and peasants. Indeed, Western civilization was becoming the most powerful society in world history.

Review: *How did late medieval monarchs concentrate still more power?*

Response:

MAN AS THE MEASURE

Cities in the Italian Peninsula led the way in ending the Middle Ages. Rich cities in the northern half had been prizes for foreign powers such as German kings and emperors ever since Pippin "the Short" and Otto "the Great." The economic revival of the High Middle Ages allowed cities founded by the Romans, such as Genoa, Pisa, and Venice, to expand and flourish once more. They prospered from trade and finance, persevered through politics and warfare, and won independence from both German emperors and Roman popes. They interacted with Byzantines, Turks, Arabs, and even Mongols.

Self-government was difficult, however. Strained by economic change, citizens easily fought among themselves over control of elections and laws. Class warfare between the wealthy merchants, prosperous artisans, and the poor strained the peace of the towns. In desperation for some order, tyrants known as despots seized power in many Italian towns during the later Middle Ages. These despots started as local nobles, merchants, or even mercenaries (called *condottieri* in Italian). Since these dictators removed at least one source of strife—namely, the struggle for leadership—the citizens often tolerated them, just as had happened in ancient Greece and Rome. Some despots managed to establish dynasties. Thus, these new Italian princes often cut short the towns' initial experiments in democratic, republican government.

A successful despot might provoke war across the Italian Peninsula, seeking for his city-state to dominate others. Ambitious princes began to conquer their neighboring towns, urged on by merchants wanting to eliminate competitors. The Peace of Lodi in 1454, however, granted the entire peninsula a brief respite. For the next four decades, the five great powers upheld a fragile peace. In the south, the Kingdom of Naples was the largest in area, but it was weakened by struggles over the throne between the foreign houses of Anjou (from France) and Aragon (from the Iberian Peninsula). In the center of the Italian Peninsula, the Papal States were bound loosely under the authority of the pope. Just north of Rome, in Tuscany, **Florence** dominated all its immediate neighbors (see figure 9.3). In the northwest,

Figure 9.3.   The Renaissance dome of Florence's medieval cathedral rises above the rest of the city.

Milan ruled the plains of Lombardy. Finally, in the northeast, the maritime power of Venice put down a strong foothold on the mainland, adding to its other possessions stretching along the eastern coast of the Adriatic and into the Aegean Sea. Venice's unique government was an oligarchy of the most powerful merchants, who dominated their elected ruler, called the doge.

This balance of power in the Italian Peninsula ended in 1494, when the French king Charles VIII as heir of Anjou invaded to claim the Kingdom of Naples. Charles's invasion sparked decades of war throughout the peninsula (and spread a new, nasty form of the sexually transmitted disease syphilis, which may have come from the Americas, although it was commonly called the "French" disease). Wars proliferated while French kings, German emperors, Spanish monarchs, and Italian despots fought for supremacy. In the midst of these wars, over several generations, European culture left the Middle Ages and entered the early modern period of history.

The cultural shift called the Renaissance (ca. 1400–1600) also helped push Europe into modernity. The Renaissance started in Florence. While figuring out how best to succeed in their political challenges, the Florentines sought inspiration from the Greeks and Romans of ages past. They could afford spending the time and money to revive humanism from classical antiquity because of the wealth generated from their new capitalist banks. At first, humanism had merely meant an interest in "humane letters" or the reading of classical writers. Inspired by the poet Petrarch (b. 1304–d. 1374), intellectuals had begun to scour old monastic libraries for ancient manuscripts. They edited what they found, creating the intellectual tool of ***textual criticism***—comparing different versions of an author's writings found in manuscripts written by hand at different times in different places in order to recover the best, most accurate text. One famous example is Lorenzo Valla's discourse disproving in 1444 the so-called Donation of Constantine. To the disgruntlement of the church, Valla demonstrated that the document allegedly recording the Roman emperor's gift of secular power to the papacy was a forgery.

Emphasis on the Latin literature of Rome soon led these humanists to appreciate the importance of the Greek language and literature. During the Middle Ages, knowledge of Greek had been virtually lost. The phrase "It's all Greek to me" came about because medieval readers could not decipher passages of Greek quoted by ancient Roman writers. Drawing on help from scholars fleeing the collapsing Byzantine Empire, the Western curriculum expanded to include the literature of ancient Greece. While today literature in the vernacular (that spoken by the common people), like the Italian poetry of Petrarch, is more highly valued, the ancient classics in "dead" Greek and Latin were the focus of Renaissance intellectuals.

Florence's **Medici** family played a key role in supporting this intellectual revival after they took over that city's leadership. They had risen to power in local government financed by their family banking business. Over time, the Medicis survived urban rebellions, assassination plots, invasions, and banishment to found their own aristocratic dynasty. Along the way, they aspired to be patrons of the arts, those who fostered creative interaction with Greece and Rome.

On an intellectual level, Renaissance Neoplatonic philosophers reinterpreted the ideas of Plato. On a visual level, artists drew inspiration from styles of classical art and created the new painting, architecture, and sculpture of Renaissance art.

Artists such as Leonardo da Vinci, Michelangelo, and Raphael pioneered a new naturalism in painting and sculpture that emphasized a realistic view of the world and the human body (see figure 9.4). The one error they made was assuming the ancients left their marble statues unpainted and white. As a result the polychromy so popular in medieval sculpture vanished. On a literary level, intellectuals eagerly sought and read authors from classical antiquity.

One such intellectual was Niccolò **Machiavelli**. At the beginning of the sixteenth century, Machiavelli had himself been tortured and exiled from Florence for

Figure 9.4.   In this selection from the fresco of the School of Athens in the Vatican, Raphael portrays Leonardo da Vinci as Plato in the center left and Michelangelo as the architect leaning on the block in the foreground. The majestic setting and the many other great thinkers from classical antiquity reflect the Renaissance fascination with Greece and Rome. (Art Resource)

supporting the wrong political faction. In those times, suspicion of disloyalty to rulers meant having one's arms jerked out of the sockets on a torture device called the *strappado*, a modified pulley. During his exile from the city, Machiavelli consoled himself every night by reading ancient writers of Greece and Rome. Inspired by them (and to win the favor of the Medici), he wrote ***The Prince*** (1513). This book combined examples of classical antiquity and contemporary politics. It offered advice on how a prince should hold on to power in an occupied territory, suggesting that a ruler's primary goal ought not to be virtue, as political writers had been propounding through the Middle Ages. Instead, a prince was to wield power, using force and fear, lying or largesse, as long as he did not become hated. Many readers claimed to be shocked by this "Machiavellian" advice for amoral political behavior freed from the constraints of Christian morality. In secret, though, most princes and politicians have admired how Machiavelli accurately described brutal power politics. He aimed to end the diversity of Italian principalities by uniting them under one powerful prince. All his practical suggestions were grounded in his humanist scholarship of antiquity.

A major boost to the humanist scholarly enterprise was the invention of the **printing press** in Germany around 1450. Using a few hundred molded pieces of movable type, any sheet of text could be reproduced much more cheaply, easily, and quickly than the laboriously handwritten page of every single book in Europe up to that moment.[1] The multiplication of books further encouraged the expansion of literacy, since more publications gave more people more writing to read.

This flood of printed materials also helped spur a change in education, giving rise to new kinds of schools. The sons of nobles and wealthy townspeople, after getting an education in a primary or "grammar" school, then attended secondary schools. These advanced institutions went beyond the primary education of reading, writing, and arithmetic, but not so far as the serious scholarly study offered by the "higher education" of colleges and universities. In these secondary schools (the forerunners of American high schools), students further refined their knowledge of the classical curriculum of the liberal arts. Through reading ancient Latin and Greek authors, a student was supposed to learn how to be worthy of liberty. The well-rounded gentleman, an individual fit in mind and body, became the Renaissance ideal.

Compared to that of men, the place of women, genteel or not, remained much more restricted. Ladies were to be respected, but few opportunities opened for their advancement. Lack of access to schools and the inability to control property remained the norm. Only a rare individual like **Christine de Pisan** (b. 1363–d. ca. 1430) could make her living from writing. Widowed and with children to support, Christine managed to market her books on history, manners, and poetry to rich male patrons in France and England. She remained an isolated example of the successful woman, unfairly forgotten soon after her death. Society still measured

---

1. Printing with woodblocks, and even movable type made of wood, clay, or bronze, began centuries earlier in China and Korea. The thousands of ideograms necessary for printing limited the usefulness of the technology compared to the flexibility and cost saving offered by Western alphabets, which only had a few dozen letters.

success by a man's achieving his material best, crafting for himself a place of honor in this world. The "Woman Question" began to be asked, although the usual answer was that women remained inferior to men.

Perhaps the greatest writer of the Renaissance, if not of all time, was the English actor, poet, and playwright **William Shakespeare** (b. 1564–d. 1616). The subjects of his plays ranged over histories (such as *Henry IV* and *Henry V*), comedies (such as *Twelfth Night* and *A Midsummer Night's Dream*), and tragedies (such as *Hamlet* and *Macbeth*). His writing captures in poetry and action a sense of universal human drama and character, drawing heavily on the classics. During his lifetime, acting companies built the first public theaters since classical antiquity, including his Globe Theater in London. Theaters soon appeared in European cities, where actors revived plays from ancient writers, adapted to new audiences.

With all this focus on success in the world, the humble path of Christ seemed somehow less attractive. Yet, as Renaissance ideas spread from Italy to northern Europe, many scholars in England, the Lowlands, and Germany did bend humanism to a more Christian view. This **Christian humanism** still emphasized the classics, using one's critical mind, and taking action in the world, but it added an interest in the writings of the Christian faith. Thus, along with Latin and Greek, Christian humanists learned Hebrew in order to read both the Old Testament in its original language and the writings of rabbi commentators.

The most famous Christian humanist was **Erasmus** (b. 1466–d. 1536). He sought to promote the best, most pure form of Christianity as he understood it from his reading in the New Testament and the writings of the early church fathers. His humanist outlook gave him a mocking attitude to authority. In his *Praise of Folly* (1509), Erasmus satirized all the problems of his contemporaries, especially the hypocrisies and failures of the Western Latin Church. Questioning authority became an important intellectual tradition, although authorities have never taken kindly to it.

Although Renaissance humanists encouraged a more critical look at the world, Erasmus and many of his contemporaries credulously accepted and promoted dangerous changes in beliefs about witches and witchcraft (see Primary Source Project 9). Historians have yet to fully understand how and why the fear of witchcraft began during the Renaissance. Prior to 1400, the usual position of the church had been that witches did not exist. The church taught that anyone claiming to be a witch was a dupe of the devil, and any supposed magic spells were meaningless deceptions. After 1400, however, many western church authorities changed their opinions to say that a real conspiracy of witches existed, organized by the devil as a vital threat to Christian society. Actually, no reliable evidence remains that any such organized plot existed or that any magic spells have ever succeeded against anyone.

Regardless, many ecclesiastical and secular leaders began the **witch hunts** (1400–1800), actively seeking out suspected witches, torturing them into confessing impossible crimes, and then executing them. Like the ancient Roman persecution of Christians, the hunts were sporadic, intermittent, and geographically scattered: worst in the Holy Roman Empire; moderate in France, Scotland, and England; and rare in the rest of Europe. Nevertheless, tens of thousands died, with

MAKING THE MODERN WORLD

more untold numbers submitting to false accusations, having loved ones perse-cuted, or suffering from pervasive fear. Authorities most often accused older women living on the margins of society, yet also younger women, men, and even children fell victim to suspicions.

These witch hunts ended once leaders no longer believed in the reality of dia-bolic magic. Fewer bouts of bad weather, the rising power of the state, improving economies, and more rational attitudes promoted by the Renaissance, the Scientific Revolution, and the Enlightenment (see below and chapter 11) all contributed. By the eighteenth century, most leaders, both religious and political, had once more come to the sensible view that witches and witchcraft were imaginary and no threat. The witch hunts reveal a tension between secular and religious values. The Renais-sance encouraged humanist values of questioning settled religious dogma.

While scholars studied the classics and certain magistrates hunted witches, reli-gious leaders began to rethink the accepted tenets of medieval faith. The new, more worldly emphasis of humanism deviated from the basics of medieval Christianity. Humanism prioritized this world; Christianity, the next. Most people in Chris-tendom still found meaning and purpose in their faith. The ongoing need of many people for religious certainty soon broke the unified religious system of the Middle Ages. Just as westerners accepted and fought for separate political states, they embraced and died for divided religious sects.

Review: *How did the Renaissance promote the West's transition into modernity?*

Response:

PRIMARY SOURCE PROJECT 9: WITCH HUNTER VERSUS CONFESSOR ABOUT BELIEF IN WITCHES

The age of the Renaissance and Scientific Revolution was also the time of the witch hunts. In the first source, an ecclesiastical official involved in hunting describes how far persecutions had gone in a German princedom. In contrast, a priest who heard the last confessions of people condemned for witchcraft came to a very different conclusion. In his book titled in Latin Cautio Criminalis *(Warning about Criminal Procedure), Friedrich Spee harshly criticizes the process and belief sys-tem. While he had to publish his book anonymously out of fear of retribution, his arguments soon helped stop the hunts.*

Source 1: "Report on Witch-Hunts" by the Chancellor of the Prince-Bishop of Würzburg (1629)

As to the affair of the witches, which Your Grace thinks brought to an end before this, it has started up afresh, and no words can do justice to it. Ah, the woe and the misery of it—there are still four hundred in the city, high and low, of every rank and sex, nay, even clerics, so strongly accused that they may be arrested at any hour. It is true that, of the people of my Gracious Prince here, some out of all offices and faculties must be executed: clerics, electoral councilors and doctors, city officials, court assessors, several of whom Your Grace knows.

There are law students to be arrested. The Prince-Bishop has over forty students who are soon to be pastors; among them thirteen or fourteen are said to be witches. A few days ago a Dean was arrested; two others who were summoned have fled. The notary of our Church consistory, a very learned man, was yesterday arrested and put to the torture. In a word, a third part of the city is surely involved. The richest, most attractive, most prominent, of the clergy are already executed. A week ago a maiden of nineteen was executed, of whom it is everywhere said that she was the fairest in the whole city, and was held by everybody a girl of singular modesty and purity. She will be followed by seven or eight others of the best and most attractive persons. . . . And thus many are put to death for renouncing God and being at the witch-dances, against whom nobody has ever else spoken a word.

To conclude this wretched matter, there are children of three and four years, to the number of three hundred, who are said to have had intercourse with the Devil. I have seen put to death children of seven, promising students of ten, twelve, fourteen, and fifteen. Of the nobles—but I cannot and must not write more of this misery. There are persons of yet higher rank, whom you know, and would marvel to hear of, nay, would scarcely believe it; let justice be done. . . .

P.S.—Though there are many wonderful and terrible things happening, it is beyond doubt that, at a place called the Fraw-Rengberg, the Devil in person, with eight thousand of his followers, held an assembly and celebrated mass before them all, administering to his audience (that is, the witches) turnip-rinds and parings in place of the Holy Eucharist.

There took place not only foul but most horrible and hideous blasphemies, whereof I shudder to write. It is also true that they all vowed not to be enrolled in the Book of Life, but all agreed to be inscribed by a notary who is well known to me and my colleagues. We hope, too, that the book in which they are enrolled will yet be found, and there is no little search being made for it.

Source 2: Selection from *Cautio Criminalis* by Friedrich Spee (1631)

1. Incredible among us Germans and especially (I blush to say it) among Catholics are the popular superstition, envy, libels, calumnies, insinuations, and the like, which, being neither punished by the magistrates nor refuted by the pulpit, first stir up suspicion of witchcraft. All the divine judgments which God has threatened in Holy Writ are now ascribed to witches. No longer does God or nature do anything, but witches everything.

2. Hence it comes that all at once everybody is clamoring that the magistrates proceed against the witches—those witches whom only their own clamor has made seem so many.

3. Princes, therefore, bid their judges and counselors to begin proceedings against the witches.

4. These at first do not know where to begin, since they have no testimony or proofs, and since their conscience clearly tells them that they ought not to proceed in this rashly. . . .

7. At last, therefore, the Judges yield to their wishes, and in some way contrive at length a starting-point for the trials. . . .

10. And yet, lest it appear that [Gaia, a name for the accused] is indicted on the basis of rumor alone, without other proofs, as the phrase goes, lo a certain presumption is at once obtained against her by posing the following dilemma: Either Gaia has led a bad and improper life, or she has led a good proper one. If a bad one, then, say they, the proof is cogent against her; for from malice to malice the presumption is strong. If, however, she has led a good one, this also is none the less a proof; for thus, they say, are witches wont to cloak themselves and try to seem especially proper.

11. Therefore it is ordered that Gaia be haled away to prison. And lo now a new proof is gained against her by this other dilemma: Either she then shows fear or she does not show it. If she does show it (hearing forsooth of the grievous tortures wont to be used in this matter), this is of itself a proof; for conscience, they say, accuses her. If she does not show it (trusting forsooth in her innocence), this too is a proof; for it is most characteristic of witches, they say, to pretend themselves peculiarly innocent and wear a bold front.

12. Lest, however, further proofs against her should be lacking, the Commissioner has his own creatures, often depraved and notorious, who question into all her past life. This, of course, cannot be done without coming upon some saying or doing of hers which evil-minded men can easily twist or distort into ground for suspicion of witchcraft.

If, too, there are any who have borne her ill will, these, having now a fine opportunity to do her harm, bring against her such charges as it may please them to devise; and on every side there is a clamor that the evidence is heavy against her. . . .

14. And so, as soon as possible, she is hurried to the torture, if indeed she be not subjected to it on the very day of her arrest, as often happens.

15. For in these trials there is granted to nobody an advocate or any means of fair defense, for the cry is that the crime is an exceptional one, and whoever ventures to defend the prisoner is brought into suspicion of the crime—as are all those who dare to utter a protest in these cases and to urge the judges to caution; for they are forthwith dubbed patrons of the witches. Thus all mouths are closed and all pens blunted, lest they speak or write. . . .

19. Before she is tortured, however, she is led aside by the executioner, and, lest she may by magical means have fortified herself against pain, she is searched, her whole body being shaved, although up to this time nothing of the sort was ever found. . . .

21. Then, when Gaia has thus been searched and shaved, she is tortured that she may confess the truth, that is to say, that she may simply declare herself guilty; for whatever else she may say will not be the truth and cannot be. . . .

24. Without any scruples, therefore, after this confession she is executed. Yet she would have been executed, nevertheless, even though she had not confessed; for, when once a beginning has been made with the torture, the die is already cast—she cannot escape, she must die.

25. So, whether she confesses or does not confess, the result is the same. . . .

31. . . . It would be a disgrace to her examiners if when once arrested she should thus go free. Guilty must she be, by fair means or foul, whom they have once but thrown into bonds. . . .

37. Wherefore the judges themselves are obliged at last either to break off the trials and so condemn their own work or else to burn their own folk, aye themselves and everybody. For on all soon or late false accusations fall, and, if only followed by the torture, all are proved guilty.

38. And so at last those are brought into question who at the outset most loudly clamored for the constant feeding of the flames. For the fools rashly failed to foresee that their turn, too, must inevitably come—and by a just verdict of Heaven, since with their poisonous tongues they created us so many witches and sent so many innocents to the flames. . . .

46. From all this there follows this result, worthy to be noted in red ink: that, if only the trials be steadily pushed on with, there is nobody in our day, of whatsoever sex, fortune, rank, or dignity, who is safe, if he have but an enemy and slanderer to bring him into suspicion of witchcraft. . . .

Questions:

- *How does each writer define the problem about witches?*
- *What specific details does each writer use to explain the problem with witches?*
- *How does each writer hope to solve the problem?*

Responses:

Citations

"VII. The Witch-Persecution at Würzburg." In *Translations and Reprints from the Original Sources of European History*, vol. 3, *The Witch Persecutions*, edited by George L. Burr. Philadelphia: University of Pennsylvania Press, 1912, pp. 28–29.

"VIII. The Methods of the Witch-Persecutions." In *Translations and Reprints from the Original Sources of European History*, vol. 3, *The Witch Persecutions*, edited by George L. Burr. Philadelphia: University of Pennsylvania Press, 1912, pp. 30–35.

For more on these sources, go to http://www.concisewesternciv.com/sources/psc9a.html.

HEAVEN KNOWS

A religious revolution called the **Reformation** (1517–1648) fractured the medieval unity of the Christian church in the West beyond recovery. The Reformation first addressed the church's role in the plan of salvation. Yet the Reformation also reflected the ongoing political, economic, and social changes created by Europe's growing wealth and power. The calls for reform in the Western Latin Church had been long and loud since the Great Western Schism had divided the papacy between 1378 and 1417. With the concept of conciliarism crushed, calls for reform went unheeded. The papacy's long avoidance of reform made the Reformation more divisive than it might have been.

Some believers still found comfort and hope in many of the rituals and practices of the medieval church: sacraments (from baptism through the mass to final unction), pilgrimages and shrines, saints' days, the daily office, hospices, and hospitals. An increasingly popular mysticism (the idea that people could attain their own direct experience of God) led some to question the value of a priestly hierarchy. Religious women such as the recluse Julian of Norwich (d. 1416) or the wandering housewife Margery Kempe (d. 1438) continued the practice of Hildegard of Bingen by sharing vivid and novel visions of their interactions with God.

But the church's worldly interventions also alienated many. Popes had not lived down the scandals of the Avignon exile and the Great Western Schism. Even worse, the Renaissance wars in Italy led many to consider the pope to be a typical petty prince rather than a potent moral force and spiritual leader. Christendom watched scandalized as the popes deepened their political rule over the Papal States in central Italy. Papal armies were commanded first by Cesare Borgia for his father, Pope Alexander VI (r. 1492–1503), and later by a pope himself, Julius II (r. 1503–1513). Popes played power politics and lived in pomp as princes. Thus, many Christians gradually grew disillusioned with a papal monarchy. Rome seemed to represent the obstacle to reform.

A successful call for reform rose in an obscure and unexpected place: the small town of Wittenberg in the Holy Roman Empire. There, **Martin Luther** (b. 1483–d. 1546), the simple son of prosperous Saxon peasants, had risen to be a professor at the university. Additionally, Luther dedicated himself to monastic discipline in a house of Augustinian canons regular (sometimes called Austin Friars). Finally, Luther served as the pastor of a local parish church.

As a pastor, Luther became increasingly disturbed when his poor parishioners bought **indulgences** from traveling salesmen. Indulgences had originally developed out of the Western Latin Church's sacramental system of penance. When one committed sin, the church taught, one had to do penance, such as some good deed, prayers, or a pilgrimage. Toward the later Middle Ages, some clever clerics suggested that instead of having a penitent take the time and trouble for a complicated and expensive pilgrimage to Rome, why not just have that person pay the comparable amount of cash instead? Consequently, the Western Latin Church gained money, which it could use for anything it wished. Granted, the church did officially insist that indulgences could not forgive sin unless the purchaser was truly contrite. Nevertheless, the sales pitch by indulgence sellers often overlooked that quibble. Encouraged to buy these fill-in-the-blank forms, people believed that their sins (or those of their dead friends or relatives) were instantly pardoned: a popular saying went, "When the coin in the coffer rings, the soul from purgatory springs."

In Luther's home province of Saxony, the local prince-archbishop of Magdeburg had authorized a vigorous sale of indulgences. The archbishop's share of the profits paid off his debts to the pope, who had suspended canon law so that the archbishop could take possession of more than one prince-bishopric. The pope needed these funds to help build the new Renaissance-style St. Peter's Basilica on the Vatican Hill. This new edifice, the largest church building the world had yet seen, designed by the great artist Michelangelo, replaced the crumbling twelve-hundred-year-old structure built under Constantine.

Ignorant of these back-door financial deals, Martin Luther nevertheless developed his own objections to indulgences. In his own studies of the faith, he began to question the entire concept of indulgences within the plan of salvation. For Luther, sin seemed so pervasive and powerful that he felt any normal means of penance could not erase its stain on the soul. No matter how many good works he undertook or how much he attended church, Luther worried that sin made him unworthy to enter the perfection of heaven. In comparison, he felt like a lump of manure. Luther broke through his dilemma with a revelation upon reading Romans 1:17: "The just shall live by faith." He proposed that a person is assuredly saved, or justified, simply by the belief in the death and resurrection of Jesus Christ. For Luther, worship was to be a moment of faith, not a process of rituals and ceremonies. And if faith alone justified sinners, then the sacraments provided by the ordained priestly hierarchy of the church were unnecessary. Hence, Luther's declaration of "justification by faith alone" undermined the dominant position of the chief priest, the pope, as an arbiter of salvation.

Luther offered his **Ninety-Five Theses**, or arguments, about his developing theological point of view. According to tradition, he posted them on the door of the Wittenberg church on 31 October 1517. Publishers printed these theses and spread them with amazing rapidity across Christendom. Luther became the hero and voice for those who wanted to reform the Western Latin Church.

The church hierarchy largely dismissed his ideas and sought to shut him up. When the pope finally excommunicated Luther in June 1520, the defiant reformer publicly burned the papal bull along with the books of the canon law, thus dismissing the entire structure of the church. The newly elected Holy Roman emperor **Charles V** Habsburg (r. 1519–1556) then convened a Diet in the city of Worms to consider the situation. At the 1521 **Diet of Worms**, Luther refused to recant, asserting his own understanding of scripture and reason and his own conscience. He held his position with the legendary words, "Here I stand; I can do no other." The emperor allowed Luther to leave the Diet, whereupon his supporters spirited him away into hiding. Charles concluded the Diet by declaring Luther an outlaw and by pledging to kill him in order to stamp out his heretical ideas.

Since Emperor Charles V ruled over the most wide-ranging empire in history up to that time, such a threat carried weight. As the head of the Habsburg dynasty, Charles V had inherited the lands of Austria and most of the lands of Burgundy (including much of Flanders) from his grandfather, Emperor Maximilian. From his mother he received Naples and Spain, which by this time also included much of the New World (see below), and soon, possessions in Asia. The sun never set on Charles V's empire.

Surprisingly, this powerful emperor never concentrated enough power to crush Luther and his allies. First, he was weaker in reality than on parchment. The office of Holy Roman emperor had been wasting away during centuries of conflict with the popes and the German princes. Second, Charles faced turmoil in the lands he controlled as a dynast. Both Bohemia and Hungary opposed Habsburg rule. Even some in Spain, although rich from its new colonial possessions, rebelled against Charles's authority. Third, King Francis I of France started a Habsburg-Valois dynastic conflict to weaken Charles's hold on lands hemming in France from southwest and east. Even though he enjoyed the title "Most Christian King," Francis even encouraged the Muslim sultan of the Ottoman Empire to conquer Charles's ally Hungary in 1526 and besiege the Austrian capital of Vienna in 1529.

Meanwhile, the former monk set up a new Christian denomination called **_Lutheranism_**. While in hiding, Luther translated the Bible into simple German. In doing so, he both set the style of modern German and promoted literacy. He simplified the worship ceremonials, emphasizing more preaching, prayer, and music. Luther closed monasteries, ending monasticism in his church. That action complicated his personal life, however. A nun, Katherine von Bora, and several other nuns were both inspired by Luther's writings and disappointed with religious life. They had escaped from their nunnery in fish barrels. Then Katherine complained to Luther that since the single, celibate life of a monastic was no longer an option, nuns needed to be married and have children. So he obliged her. He married Katherine and started a family. Other Lutheran priests and bishops soon married.

For some of the common people, though, Luther's reforming efforts did not go far enough. He reined in many reformers who had started to destroy all images and fancy decorations in churches. The bourgeoisie had long wanted more asceticism from the clergy (although the burghers themselves often spent their wealth on conspicuous consumption). Many German peasants seized on Luther's rhetoric on the defiance of authority and applied it to their social and political obligations. They rebelled against their lords in 1525. As was typical of peasant revolts during the later Middle Ages, the peasants killed a few hundred landlords; the nobles then regrouped and avenged the deaths by hanging many thousands of rebels. Luther disassociated himself from the peasants, calling them "thievish, murderous hordes."

Ultimately, Luther relied on the power of Lutheran princes, both to protect him and to help spread his message. Starting with Luther's own Duke of Saxony, many northern German princes and kings in Scandinavia welcomed the Lutheran Church.

The new structures allowed them to act as popes in their own provinces. The rulers took over the administration of the former Catholic Church property and lands for themselves and had a strong hand in appointing the bishops and priests. The Lutheran Church could devote itself to spiritual matters (which did not involve land reform for peasants).

When the Habsburg Charles V tried to ban Lutheranism at a Diet in 1529, Lutheran princes protested. From that event onward, Christians who are neither Eastern Orthodox nor Roman Catholics have usually been called **Protestants**. Once debate failed, the Protestants resorted to weapons, and wars of religion (1546–1648) sporadically erupted through Europe. Charles never achieved the military victory needed to crush Luther's princely supporters. With the **Treaty of Augsburg** in 1555, Charles V capitulated to the right of princes to maintain their Lutheran churches. He resigned his throne the next year and died shortly thereafter.

Luther's successful defiance of ecclesiastical and political authority raised a question for Christianity: who had the authority to interpret and define faith? The original, traditional answer had been the church councils. Such was still the position of the Orthodox churches in eastern Europe, although they had not held a council since long before the Great Schism with the Western Latin Church in 1054. That latter church had rejected conciliarism and instead granted the papacy a monarchical authority to determine the faith.

In contrast, Luther relied solely on his own conscience, as guided by holy scripture. Yet how was his conscience necessarily better than anyone else's? Could not anyone claim to be guided by the Holy Spirit and use individual judgment to assert doctrine? Such is what happened. Religious leaders formed new sects and denominations. Success in drawing followers validated divergent religious truths. *Protestantism* became a container for multiple Christian groups, each avowing to have the one true interpretation of Christianity.

One variety of sectarians who enjoyed some success in the sixteenth century were collectively known as Anabaptists (not directly related to later "Baptists"). *Anabaptism* consisted of many different groups lumped together by enemies who disagreed with their common refusal to accept infant baptism. For Anabaptists, only mature adults ought to be baptized. These groups often drew their followers from the lower classes, who rejected religious hierarchy and ecclesiastical wealth.

Both Lutherans and Catholics joined in exterminating most of these Anabaptists through such traditional methods as torture and war. The most famous example was the siege and destruction of Münster in 1535. There the allied Lutherans and Catholics killed thousands of Anabaptists as they retook the city. The victors tortured the survivors, executed them, and then hung their remains on a church tower in cages that remain there today. Only a few groups of Anabaptists survived, often by fleeing to the New World, especially Pennsylvania, which was founded in the late seventeenth century on a principle of tolerance. Their successors exist today in such denominations as the Mennonites, Moravians, Hutterites, and the Amish or Pennsylvania Dutch.

Various reform ideas soon spread from Germany to France, one of the most powerful nations in Europe. The kings of the Valois dynasty had little need or interest in supporting any changes. The monarchy had already arranged the Concordat of 1516, which created a convenient royal co-dominion with the church in France. The agreement authorized the French king to appoint most of the bishops, abbots, and abbesses, while the pope got a large cut of the revenues.

One Frenchman, however, found himself more sympathetic to Luther's reforms than the structures of kings and bishops. **Jean (or John) Calvin** (b. 1509–d. 1564) learned of Luther's ideas in school. Inspired by them, he created his own new religious framework, called *Calvinism*, which he solidified after being called to be the leading preacher in Geneva, Switzerland. Geneva became the center of a theocracy, a government based on divine commands. While elected leaders still ran the town council, they passed laws that tried to make the townspeople conform to Calvin's beliefs. From Geneva, Calvin then sent missionaries throughout Europe.

Calvin differed from Luther in two main ways. First, Calvinism focused on **predestination** or *determinism*: the belief that God determined in advance, for all of time, who was saved and who was damned. Nothing any person did could influence God's preordained, omniscient decision. This idea went back to Augustine and had a certain logic to it: if God knows everything, then he surely knows who is going to heaven and who is going to hell. While some complained that this belief removed free will, Calvinism called believers to choose to live the exemplary life of saints, participating in baptism and the Lord's Supper. In doing so, they hoped to re-create heaven on earth.

A second difference in Calvinism was its democratic tendency; members of a church were supposed to be involved in running it. The congregation itself approved ministers or appointed the preacher instead of a distant pope or prince from above. Calvinism expanded through much of the West under the title of Reformed churches in the northern Lowlands (the Netherlands) and much of the Rhineland. In France, Calvinists were called Huguenots. In Scotland they formed Presbyterian churches, and in Wales, Congregationalist churches. In England and its colonies, most Calvinists were labeled Puritans.

When Luther first called for reform, no one thought that the authority of the pope could be overthrown by religious ideas. Yet Lutherans, Calvinists, small groups of Anabaptists, and other sects successfully defied papal control. Papal supremacy would suffer yet another loss before it reorganized and redefined itself. Amid all this religious diversity, killing for reasons of faith continued.

Review: On what issues did the different Protestants carry out reforms?

Response:

SOURCES ON FAMILIES: MARTIN LUTHER, *TABLE TALK* (1566)

While the great reformer Martin Luther preached and wrote about marriage and family, he also talked about it informally with students and visitors around a table in his residence. Many quotes from these informal conversations on a wide variety of subjects were compiled by recorders over the years and eventually published as his Table Talk. *The source presented here collects a variety of quotes. Of his and Katherine, or Katie, von Bora's six children together, Elizabeth died in infancy; their other daughter, Magdalene, or Lena, is featured here at about two years old and at her death at thirteen.*

"My boy Hans is now entering his seventh year. Every seven years a person changes; the first period is infancy, the second childhood. At fourteen they begin to see the world and lay the foundations of education, at twenty-one the young men seek marriage, at twenty-eight they are house-holders and patres-familias, at thirty-five they are magistrates in church and state, until forty-two when they are kings. After that the senses begin to decline. Thus every seven years brings a new condition in body and character, as has happened to me and to us all." . . .

"To have peace and love in marriage is a gift, for a good woman deserves a good husband. To have peace and love in marriage is a gift which is next to the knowledge of the Gospel. There are heartless wretches who love neither their children nor their wives; such beings are not human."

"The greatest blessing is to have a wife to whom you may entrust your affairs and by whom you may have children. Katie, you have a good husband who loves you. Let another be empress, but you give thanks to God."

"The faith and life of young children are the best because they have simply the Word. We old fools have hell and hell-fire; we dispute concerning the Word, which they accept with pure faith without question; and yet at the last we must hold simply to the Word as they do. It is moreover a trick of the devil, that we are drawn by our business affairs away from the Word in such a manner that we do not know ourselves how it happens. There it is best to die young."

To his infant child Luther said: "You are our Lord's little fool. Grace and remission of sins are yours and you fear nothing from the law. Whatever you do is uncorrupted; you are in a state of grace and you have remission of sins, whatever happens."

Playing with his child, Magdalene, he asked her: "Little Lena, what will the Holy Christ give you for Christmas?" and then he added: "The little children have such fine thoughts about God, that he is in heaven and that he is their God and father: for they do not philosophize about him."

As Magdalene lay in the agony of death, her father fell down before the bed on his knees and wept bitterly and prayed that God might free her. Then she departed and fell asleep in her father's arms. Her mother was also in the room but farther from the bed because of her grief. As they laid her in the coffin he said: "Darling Lena, it is well with you. You will rise and shine like a star, yea like the sun. . . . I am happy in spirit but the flesh is sorrowful and will not be content; the departing grieves me beyond measure. It is strange that she is certainly in peace and happy and yet I so sorrowful. . . . I have sent a saint to heaven."

"We should care for our children, and especially for poor little girls. I do not pity boys; they can support themselves in any place if they will only work, and if they are lazy they are rascals. But the poor little race of girls must have a staff to lean upon. A boy can go to school and become a fine man if he will. But a girl cannot learn so much and may go to shame to get bread to eat."

As his wife was still sorrowful and wept and cried aloud, he said to her: "Dear Katie, think how it is with her, and how well off she is. But flesh is flesh and blood blood and they do as their manner is: the spirit lives and is willing. Children doubt not, but believe as we tell them: all is simple with them; they die without pain or anguish or doubt or fear of death just as though they were falling asleep." . . .

When one day Luther's wife was upholding her authority pretty insistently he said to her with feeling: "You may claim for yourself the control over affairs of the house, saving nevertheless, my just rights. Female government has accomplished no good since the world began. When God constituted Adam master of all creatures, they were safe and governed in the best way, but the intervention of woman spoiled all: for that we have you women to thank, and therefore I am not willing to endure your rule."

Questions:

- *What are the differences between males and females within families?*
- *How does faith serve the young and old?*
- *How does husband Luther interact with his wife Katherine?*

Responses:

Citation

Luther, Martin. *Conversations with Luther: Selections from recently published sources of the Table Talk*. Translated by Preserved Smith and Herbert Percival Gallinger. Boston/New York/Chicago: The Pilgrim Press, 1915, pp. 42–55.

For more on this source, go to http://www.concisewesternciv.com/sources/sof9 .html.

FATAL BELIEFS

Although Calvinism gained popularity in England, the **English Reformation** (1534–1559) originated uniquely due to matters of state. The reigning king, **Henry**

VIII (r. 1509–1547), had strongly supported the views of the pope against Luther. The pope had even awarded King Henry the title of "Defender of the Faith," still sported by English monarchs today. A higher priority for Henry, however, was the security of the Tudor dynasty, for which he thought he needed a male heir. After twenty years of marriage to Catherine of Aragon and six births, only one child had survived, a daughter, Mary. Although a daughter could legally inherit the throne in England, Henry believed, like most monarchs of his time, that he needed a son. So he asked the pope to end his marriage, as many kings before and since have done. Contrary to the common version of history, Henry did not want a divorce (the breakup of a genuine marriage). He actually sought an annulment (the declaration that a marriage never had existed). Catherine steadfastly resisted, backed up by her nephew and Luther's overlord, Emperor Charles V. Charles just happened to have an army outside of Rome. Fearing the nearby Holy Roman emperor more than the distant English king, the pope refused to support Henry's annulment.

Still determined to father a legitimate male heir, Henry decided to break with the pope. His Parliament declared him head of the **Church of England**, and his bishops willingly annulled his first marriage and blessed his second with his courtier, Anne Boleyn. Although the pope excommunicated Henry and declared his new marriage void, that little bothered the monarch or the great majority of the English people. Both the king and many of his subjects had long disliked what they saw as Roman interference in English affairs. Moreover, many of the members of Parliament profited nicely from the subsequent dissolution of the monasteries, whose properties they bought up at bargain rates. Despite the schism, Henry remained religiously conservative, so Calvinist and Lutheran ideas gained very little influence.

Unfortunately for Henry, he did not achieve his sought-after heir with his second wife, Anne Boleyn; she managed to give birth only to a healthy daughter, Elizabeth. To make way for a new wife, Henry had Anne executed on trumped-up charges of adultery. The third wife, Jane Seymour, gave birth to his heir, Edward VI (r. 1547–1553), but died soon after. Three more marriages followed. Henry had the fourth marriage annulled and the fifth wife legitimately executed for adultery. His sixth wife managed to outlive him. Despite this rather unseemly string of marriages, most of the English people did not oppose their king. Henry had to chop off the heads of relatively few who resisted his religious transformation.

A genuinely distinctive Church of England, or *Anglicanism*, grew after Henry's death. His son, King Edward VI, came to the throne as a child, and his advisors began to push the Church of England further away from the Church of Rome. They began to alter significantly the interpretations of the sacraments and methods of worship to be more in line with simplifications introduced by Calvinist, Lutheran, and other Protestant reformers from the Continent.

These policies abruptly reversed when the young Edward died after a reign of only six years. A brief effort failed to put his cousin, the Protestant Lady Jane Grey, on the throne. Henry's daughter by his first marriage, Mary I (r. 1553–1558), won the day. Her religious policy forced the English church back under the authority of the pope. To do so, she persecuted clergy and laypeople, many of whom, surprisingly, were willing to die rather than go back to obedience to Rome. She burned several hundred "heretics." For these efforts the English have dubbed her "**Bloody**

Mary." Her disastrous marriage to her cousin King Philip II of Spain did not help, either. Many English hated him as a Spaniard and a Roman Catholic, and he avoided both the country and his wife. When she died without an heir, Henry's daughter by Anne Boleyn, Queen **Elizabeth I** (r. 1558–1603), inherited the crown.

Elizabeth, who had managed to survive the changes of political and religious policy, now faced a choice herself: should she maintain obedient to Rome or revive the Church of England? In 1559, with the Act of Supremacy enacted in Parliament, she chose the latter course. Henceforward, the English monarch occupied a ceremonial role as head of the Church of England. Anglicanism defined itself as Protestant while still Catholic, trying to maintain the best of both versions of Christianity. The *Book of Common Prayer* (1549) laid out how worship was to be carried out, but it said little of belief. One's conscience was up to oneself—a fairly tolerant attitude. Fortunately for Elizabeth, most English embraced her religious compromise.

In fact, Elizabeth became one of England's greatest monarchs. The late sixteenth century saw a number of powerful and effective women on or behind the thrones of Europe, provoking the Calvinist preacher John Knox in Scotland to rail against such a "Monstrous Regiment of Women," as he titled a pamphlet against them. Although the others ruled fairly competently, Elizabeth outshone them all. England flourished during her reign, culturally, economically, and politically. Renaissance culture reached its high point with Shakespeare's plays. Meanwhile, the English navy began to help its countrymen explore and start to dominate the rest of the world, taking the first steps toward founding the British Empire. It is ironic that Henry VIII thought he needed a son, when Elizabeth was "man" enough to surpass her father's accomplishments.

The one force that seriously threatened Elizabeth was *Roman Catholicism*. By the beginning of her reign, Rome had begun what historians call either the "Counter-Reformation" or the "Catholic Reformation." Many people thought the popes had been too distracted by the opulence of the Renaissance. Newly devout and energetic popes now sought to recover lands recently lost from obedience to them. They redefined their leadership over what had become the Roman Catholic Church as a branch of Christianity. Having accepted the inevitability of reform, the papacy called the **Council of Trent** (1545–1563). Leaders chose the obscure cathedral city at the southern edge of the Alps for a general council because it satisfied Charles V (it was in the empire), the king of France (it was not German), and the pope (its residents spoke Italian).

Some clergy at the Council of Trent wanted to compromise or adopt some ideas of the Protestants, but the council rejected that path. Instead, the Roman Catholic Church of the popes insisted on the value of justification by faith supported by good works, combined with the mediating role of the priesthood and the sacraments. The Tridentine Reform (named after the Latin word for Trent) limited some abuses and corruptions and established seminary schools for a better-educated priesthood. The council affirmed that their true church, through the papacy, had the final authority to define belief and interpret scripture—not Luther's conscience, or Anabaptist interpretations, or Calvin's scholarship, or anyone's literal reading of the Bible. The popes increased their interest in organizing and clarifying the smallest details of belief and practice.

New monastic orders and reformations of older ones aided the popes in reform. The Ursulines dedicated themselves to the education of girls and women. Most importantly, the Society of Jesus, or the **Jesuits**, gained sway in European affairs. Ignatius Loyola founded the Jesuits after suffering wounds as a warrior in Charles V's Spanish army. During the painful recovery from a shattered leg, he envisioned a new kind of monastic order. Instead of being confined to the cloister, Jesuits dedicated themselves to religious vocation (formed through the *Spiritual Exercises*), education (becoming teachers and guides), and missionary work (both in Europe and the world). Loyola saw his order as a spiritual army for the Roman Catholic Church, with a so-called fourth vow (after poverty, chastity, and obedience) of absolute dedication to the pope.

The Tridentine Reform set a militant tone for Roman Catholicism during the next two hundred years. Roman Catholicism aimed to recapture the allegiance of lost followers and gain more new ones. A new Roman Inquisition began its work in 1542, partly inspired by the Spanish Inquisition of Ferdinand and Isabella. The Spanish Inquisition policed converted Jews and Muslims; this new version hunted Protestants as heretics since they rejected papal teaching. An ***Index of Forbidden Books*** declared the reading of certain authors to be sinful. First issued in 1559 by the Holy Office in Rome and regularly reissued thereafter for four hundred years, the list restricted the circulation of banned works in Roman Catholic countries and forbade Roman Catholics from reading these prohibited books. This censorship even included all the works of Erasmus, so fearful had Rome become of any criticism.

The Roman Catholic vigor also expressed itself in a series of wars of religion that lasted until 1648. Traditionally, territorial, dynastic, and economic reasons shaped decisions for fighting wars. In this period, ideological differences between adherents of branches of Christianity became significant motives. For a few decades, people were ready to die and kill for Lutheranism, Anabaptism, Calvinism, Anglicanism, or Roman Catholicism. Monarchs thought that their subjects and their neighbors needed to conform to their own dogmas as a matter of both public order and divine virtue. People volunteered for armies in the belief that their neighbors should worship the same way they themselves did. Some also enlisted simply as a way to earn a living—soldiering was a growth industry.

In the vanguard of militant Roman Catholicism was Elizabeth's former brother-in-law, King **Philip II** of Spain (r. 1556–1598). Philip had inherited most of his Habsburg father Charles V's possessions (except the Austrian ones, which, along with the elected title of Holy Roman emperor, went to his uncle Ferdinand). In Philip's domains, Spain had one of the world's best armies; Flanders was the textile manufacturing center of Europe; and the Americas poured silver into his treasuries. Philip also briefly united Spain with Portugal, making him the ruler of the sole global power. He built a new, modern capital for himself in Madrid. Although Madrid was not conveniently connected to the waterways that bound Philip's empire together, it was easily accessible from his palace of El Escorial, a massive, gray religious retreat (see figure 9.5). Philip was hardworking but perhaps too

Figure 9.5.   King Philip II of Spain often retreated to the gray abbey of El Escorial, which served also as a second palace, away from Madrid.

focused on small details. He saw himself as a divinely appointed monarch obliged to attend to every corner of his empire. At the head of a vast bureaucracy, he regulated the lace on court costumes, ordered murders of political enemies, corrected the spelling of secretaries, and held *autos-da-fé* (public burnings of heretics at which he served as master of ceremonies).

Above all, the king of Spain sent armies to fight for his vision of the Roman Catholic faith. His navy's victory over the Ottoman Turks at the Battle of Lepanto (1571) cheered the Christian West, showing that the Ottomans were not invincible. At the time, the Muslim sultan claimed the defeat meant nothing—he would just build another fleet, which he did. Despite this boast, historians have seen the defeat at Lepanto as an obvious turning point toward the long, slow decline of Ottoman dominion. Similarly, Philip's power began to diminish. He could not manage his empire from Madrid, as his territories were far too large for the available means of communication. He could not afford his government either, declaring bankruptcy three times and thereby ruining many of the bankers and merchants he needed so badly.

In particular, some of those capitalists, namely the prosperous Calvinist Dutch in the northern part of the Lowlands, resented paying for Philip's dreams of a Roman Catholic empire. In 1581, they declared independence from his rule and formed the **Dutch Netherlands** (often called Holland after the main province). They even began to construct their own democratic government (see the next chapter). The Dutch fought on and off for eighty years before they gained full independence for themselves. To stop this rebellion, Philip first sent in the Duke of Parma, whose army earned infamy for its brutality against the civilian population. In turn,

Dutch and Huguenot merchants harassed Spanish shipping. Philip next turned his attention to England, which had been supporting the upstart Dutch after the death of Philip's wife Queen Mary I. Hostilities simmered for several years as English sea dogs or privateers (informal pirates with permission from a government to raid shipping) preyed on Spanish possessions. Riches looted by the Spanish from the American natives wound up being plundered by the English instead.

Philip retaliated by instigating plots against Elizabeth's life and throne. The pope declared her an illegitimate, excommunicated heretic and encouraged the faithful to overthrow her rule. Philip and the pope supported Elizabeth's cousin, Mary Stuart, Queen of Scots (not to be confused with Elizabeth's half-sister "Bloody Mary" Tudor, the late queen of England) as the true English monarch. The unfortunate Mary Stuart had lost her Scottish Highlands kingdom through her own folly, falling under a reasonable suspicion of blowing up her husband. She fled from her own people to England. Elizabeth kept her in comfortable confinement until Mary got herself implicated in a treasonous Roman Catholic plot. Elizabeth finally ordered Mary's beheading, although it took the headsman three whacks of his axe to succeed.

Seizing upon Elizabeth's execution of Mary in 1587 as an excuse, Philip assembled the **Spanish Armada**. This fleet of 130 ships aimed to sail from Spain to the Lowlands and then ferry Parma's troops across the North Sea to invade England. It all went terribly wrong. The most famous English sea dog, Sir Francis Drake, destroyed most of the fleet in its harbor before it could set sail. A rebuilt fleet launched in 1588, but adverse weather slowed its progress. That the commanding admiral had never been to sea was not helpful, either. Easily repulsing the English in the Channel, the admiral did finally anchor his fleet off the coast of the Lowlands, only to be told, quite reasonably, that if troops there were diverted to England, the Netherlands might succeed in their rebellion. Then the English broke up the armada by pushing fire ships, empty, burning hulls, among the fleet. The panicked Spanish broke formation and came under English guns. Storms sank most of the rest.

Philip at first wrote off this defeat, much as the Ottoman sultan had his own at Lepanto. Notwithstanding Spain's appearance of strength over the next decades, it sank to a second-rank power. England, however, continued its ascendancy, becoming stronger than ever as its national patriotism became bound with its religion and its burgeoning imperialist ventures.

Meanwhile, France had not been able to help Philip II of Spain fight Spain's traditional enemy, England, since France itself almost broke apart in religious warfare. The Huguenots (the name for French Calvinists) had grown to about 10 percent of the population. Their numbers were particularly strong in the productive artisan and business classes. The Valois dynasty might have moved against them once its long conflict with the Habsburgs ended in 1559. But that same year the Valois dynasty plummeted into crisis with the unexpected death of King Henry II, killed during a joust by a piece of splintered lance that thrust through his eye into his brain. His three young sons and their mother, Queen Catherine de Medici (b. 1519–d. 1589), were trapped between two powerful aristocratic families: the Huguenot Bourbons and the Roman Catholic de Guises. Fighting over the throne using betrayal, assassination, and war, these powerful families nearly destroyed the monarchy and the country.

The Roman Catholic party almost triumphed with the **St. Bartholomew's Day massacre** (14 August 1572), during which they viciously murdered thousands of Protestants, great and small, men, women, and children, in the streets of Paris. Henry of Bourbon survived that slaughter and was soon able to gain military domination over most of the country. After the death of the last Valois in 1589, he became officially recognized as the French king **Henry IV "of Navarre"** (r. 1589–1610), founding the Bourbon dynasty. Hostility to his Protestantism still stood in the way of his acceptance by some Roman Catholics. So, in 1593, he converted to Roman Catholicism, allegedly saying, "Paris is worth a mass." He continued to protect the Protestants, though, with the proclamation of the **Edict of Nantes** (1598). This act mandated a certain level of religious tolerance. It allowed Protestants to worship freely and to fortify fifty-one cities for their own self-defense. Diversity brought some peace and security.

The last of the religious wars, the **Thirty Years War** (1618–1648), engulfed the Holy Roman Empire and drew in the entire continent. The conflict began in Bohemia, as the Austrian branch of the Habsburgs labored to convert that province back to Roman Catholicism. Leaders in Prague "defenestrated" the emperor's representatives—meaning they tossed them out the window. Habsburg armies quickly crushed the rebellious Bohemians, but other German princes who feared a resurgent imperial power soon took up arms against Austria. Two foreign Lutheran monarchs invaded the empire—first the king of Denmark, then the king of Sweden. The Protestant armies gained brief advantages through their use of well-drilled and coordinated cavalry, artillery, and infantry units, setting the tone of military tactics for the next centuries. Regardless, the Austrian Habsburgs continued to win, fortified by the resources of their Spanish cousins.

Eventually, what began as a religious war ended as a purely political conflict. France had long feared being surrounded by the Habsburg territories of Spain in the south and the Holy Roman Empire in the east. So Roman Catholic France entered the war against Roman Catholic Austria. Dynastic and national politics overruled religious fraternity. Thus, religion faded as a motive to go to war in the West.

Indeed, the **Peace of Westphalia**, which was signed in 1648, forced Europe into new, modern, international political relationships (see map 9.1). With religious diversity now irreversible, the medieval ideal of a unified Christendom was completely broken. Instead, the numerous independent states of Europe lived in an uncertain rivalry. Each became a sovereign state, free from the influence of higher authorities, although able to agree on international principles if necessary. The most important principle maintained a ***balance of power***, ensuring that the countries should league together against any single state that tried to dominate Europe. This principle kept the great powers in check and left the middle-ranked and small buffer states free to prosper.

The rest of the treaty redrew some political borders to establish a rough balance of power. Spain held on to the southern "Spanish" part of the Netherlands (soon to be known as Belgium) but lost the northern Dutch Netherlands, which everyone recognized as an independent, sovereign state. The Swiss had their independence

Map 9.1. Europe, 1648.
How does the Spanish Empire dominate the western fringe of Europe?

affirmed. The Holy Roman Empire became a mere geographical expression as a synonym for Germany. The petty principalities within the empire were more sovereign than the empire itself. The Holy Roman emperor became even less relevant, a yet still weaker figurehead. While the Austrian Habsburgs kept control of the imperial office, their varied collection of hereditary territories on the empire's southeastern borders mattered far more to them than the office of emperor. Meanwhile, France chewed away a few bits of the empire, bringing its border to the upper Rhine River. Of course, neither the balance of power nor religious toleration stopped war altogether. States continued to try to expand at the expense of their neighbors.

The lack of total victory for any one side assured that religious diversity remained part of Western civilization. The pope's claim to rule Christendom became irrelevant, his prestige greatly reduced. While nations might continue to fight, hoping for power, pride, or prosperity, religion as a reason for war declined. States became the key binding agent for Europeans. The Reformation weakened the bonds between religion and the state. Many governments continued to impose religious uniformity on their own people. Indeed, many people remained satisfied with whatever tradition they were brought up in. Yet people only had to look across borders to know that others differed on Christianity and that some individuals might even be able to choose their faith or even no belief at all.

Review: How did early modern reforms among Christians culminate in wars over religion?

Response:

GOD, GREED, AND GLORY

Another change from the medieval to the modern in European history was **Western colonial imperialism**, when various kingdoms built empires based on overseas colonies. Historians today argue about what exactly made the Europeans strong enough to take the lead in a new global history after 1500. Answers used to imply, if not outright argue, ***Western exceptionalism***, the idea that Europeans were somehow different from (and better than) peoples in other civilizations. More recent historians object to that characterization, especially considering the brutality with which Europeans "civilized" the world, leading to the loss of lives and liberty. Comparative historians who measure the relative accumulation of wealth, strength of government, level of cultural sophistication, status of technological development, and impulse toward creativity of various civilizations around the world over the centuries note that Europe did not rank near the top.

The Europeans benefited from excellent timing as they began their modern history with their "voyages of discovery." The explorers, of course, only "discovered" what the indigenous peoples in these faraway lands knew all along. The difference was that Europeans could exploit these foreign peoples and places as never before in their history. They declared their own Doctrine of Discovery, making up a law to justify their seizure of these new lands and their indigenous peoples. These expeditions allowed Europeans to take profit from preexisting trade networks that incorporated much of Asia and Africa, adding on the *terra incognita* or unknown lands in the Americas and Pacific. The European national governments in competition with each other over global supremacy seized their overseas empires (see map 9.2).

Europeans had three desires that fed this drive to go abroad. The first came from Christianity's own evangelistic and crusading impulses, which had already driven Western culture beyond the borders of Europe. Even before Latin Christianity began to split apart, westerners wanted to force the gospel of Christ on "heathens," as seen in the Crusades. The Reformation only encouraged the divided

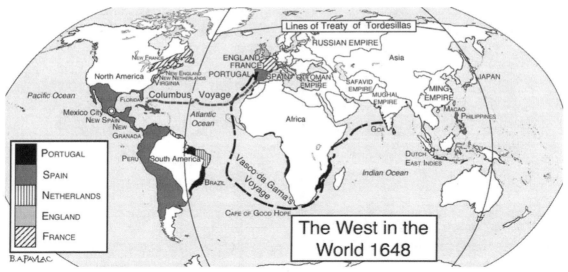

Map 9.2.   The West in the World, 1648.
How did the Europeans begin to divide up the world?

Christians to convert the world, to prove their own version of Christianity as the most successful and, therefore, most divinely sanctioned. Some Europeans ventured on a path of world domination in the name of eternal salvation. Would Jesus, the Prince of Peace, have approved that his message came at the point of a sword and with the price of plundering? His followers thought so, and they had the power to do it.

God provided a spiritual motivation, while money afforded a material one. The capitalism that sprouted from the Commercial Revolution had transformed Europe from a poor offshoot on the fringes of a world trade system centered in Asia to a mainstay of economic dynamism. Financial investments from capitalists further pushed these "voyages of discovery" forward. Instead of being barriers, the deep seas and oceans soon became highways, much as rivers and coastal waters had long been.

A second motive for colonialism, then, was the opportunity for profit. Europeans wanted to travel to "the Indies," regions in distant Asia known to possess fantastic wealth in the form of spices, such as pepper, cinnamon, and nutmeg. What today sits on our shelves in small jars costing pennies was worth more than its weight in gold in 1500.

The main trade routes to the Indies had traditionally run through the Middle East. Only a rare merchant from Europe, such as Marco Polo in the thirteenth century, might travel along the Silk Road through Central Asia all the way to the Chinese Empire. During much of the Middle Ages, most western European merchants bought from the middleman merchants of the Byzantine Empire. After the Byzantine Empire's demise in 1453, the Muslim Ottoman Turks took over supply routes. The idea that the Muslims shut down the trade routes is a myth; they still wanted to trade. Rather, the western Christians resented paying these "infidel" middlemen. Europeans were looking for alternative access to the East.

Pride offered a third motive for imperialism, on both the personal and national levels. At the forefront, monarchs were drawn to the glorification that conquest always brought. New lands meant wider empires and revenues. At the lower social levels, adventuring in foreign lands raised a Renaissance gentleman's reputation and status. Any poor man might acquire treasure or farmland of his own, taken from natives who could not defend it. Thus an obscure man could rise to prominence, whether by lording it over foreigners or bringing immense wealth back home to Europe. All these contradictory motives, winning fame, fortune, and souls for Jesus, tempted Europeans out across the wide oceans.

Surprisingly, the new imperialism began with the little country of **Portugal**, founded in the twelfth century as part of a crusade during the Reconquesta of the Iberian Peninsula (see chapter 8). Over the years, Portugal had fought against the Muslims, but its armies were soon cut off from confronting the enemy by neighboring Castile's successful expansion in the Iberian Peninsula. Unable to combat the Moors in Europe, little Portugal sought another outlet for its crusading zealotry. It channeled its expansionism toward Africa, hoping both to convert the Africans and to profit from trade on that continent. Prince Henry the Navigator (d. 1460), one of the main proponents of African expeditions, also wished to find enough gold to maintain his court in proper style. His sponsored voyages discovered and colonized the islands of the Azores and the Madieras in the Atlantic. Colonists found the latter islands so heavily forested that they set a fire that burned for seven years, leaving the land covered in ash. From this new, fertile soil they grew a new wine, Madiera. Heavily populated Africa was a different matter. Instead of converting and conquering, the Portuguese only wrested away small chunks of African coastline, where they built forts to defend harbors and trading outposts. From these bases, the Portuguese began to deal in slaves, many shipped to work on sugarcane plantations in the Madieras.

Explorers soon thought that it might be possible to sail around the continent of Africa to reach the Indies. Yet sailors faced some serious challenges. First, ocean travel in the Atlantic was far more dangerous than in the Mediterranean and coastal waters. So the Portuguese adapted sailing technology from Muslim civilization in Africa and the Middle East to build ships called caravels, sturdy enough to handle the high seas. Second, navigation was aided by other Muslim achievements, such as the compass, astrolabe, and maps and charts. Thus European voyagers used the Arabs' own ingenuity against them.

On the western edge of Europe, the Portuguese were best located to launch such voyages. In 1468, the Portuguese explorer Diaz succeeded in rounding the optimistically named Cape of Good Hope, the southernmost point of Africa. It took another thirty years before **Vasco da Gama** traveled beyond that cape. In 1498, he sailed up the east coast of Africa and then ventured across the Arabian Sea to reach India, guided by Arabian pilots. He did not have much of value to trade with the Indians, but the spices he brought back profited his expedition thirty times the amount of its cost. On da Gama's next voyage, the Portuguese military technology of guns overpowered the natives. Da Gama plundered foreign merchant cargoes, blew the Arab ships out of the water, shelled cities, exploited rivalries between states, and intimidated princes. Other Portuguese followed. Soon they dominated all seagoing trade and commerce in the Arabian Sea and the Indian Ocean.

Portugal was too small to grab and keep vast territories. For five hundred years, though, the Portuguese held on to many fortified coastal enclaves: Angola, Guinea, and Mozambique in Africa; Goa in India; Timor in the Indies; and Macao in China. Only in Brazil, in the Americas, did they establish a large colony with European immigrants. Despite its overseas imperial success, Portugal itself remained on the periphery of European affairs, only rarely participating in the approaching wars among European states disputing who would dominate the world.

Even before Vasco da Gama had begun exploiting and killing Indians in India, Portugal's neighbor **Spain** had hoped to beat its rival to the Indies. Spain was a young country, founded only in 1479 when King Ferdinand came to the throne of Aragon, while his co-ruler of five years, Isabella, ruled the neighboring Kingdom of Castile. Husband and wife united their two kingdoms to create Spain, centralizing power in both their hands while weakening the nobles and other estates. Spain's hold on southern Italy was secured through Ferdinand's wars on that peninsula.

Ferdinand and Isabella rounded out their immediate realm on the Iberian Peninsula by finishing the Reconquesta crusade begun in the eleventh century. In 1492 they defeated Granada, the last Muslim principality in western Europe. Then, to impose uniformity and conformity on their tidy kingdom, they kicked out of the country all Muslims and Jews who refused to convert to Christianity. The "Sephardic" Jews settled throughout the Mediterranean countries, Christian and Muslim. Meanwhile, Spanish authorities worried about the sincerity of conversions by those Muslims and Jews who stayed behind, called, respectively, Moriscos (after the old term *Moors*) and Marranos (a word for "pig"). The monarchs set up the infamous **Spanish Inquisition** (1478–1834) to deal with their concerns. The Spanish Inquisition investigated and punished cases of people who secretly practiced Islam or Judaism, as well as some cases of sodomy or witchcraft. Over the centuries, the inquisitors ferreted out, tortured, and burned many people to death. By the early 1600s, Spain gave up worrying about whether Moriscos had been converted or not and simply expelled tens of thousands of them to North Africa. Spain's authorities enforced cultural uniformity as they built their new nation.

While Queen Isabella presided over the defeat of Muslim Granada, she gambled on an unusual plan to reach the lavish Indies. In 1492, an eccentric Italian ship captain, **Christopher Columbus**, proposed sailing westward across the Atlantic Ocean, rather than to the south around Africa (which would not succeed for six more years). Isabella's advisors were correct to warn her that Columbus's voyage should fail. Contrary to a popular yet incorrect myth, their advice was not based on a mistaken belief that the world was flat—since the time of the ancient Greeks, every educated person knew that the world was round or, more properly, a globe. Instead, Isabella's advisors were correct to point out that Columbus had underestimated the distance from his last supply point in the Canary Islands to Japan. While Columbus thought that he needed to travel a mere 2,400 miles, Isabella's advisors knew, in fact, the distance to be more than 8,000 miles. Columbus would have died at sea had he not stumbled upon the "New World." For most of his life Columbus believed that what he had claimed for Spain was part of the true Indies of the East, just as he read in Marco Polo's book. He did not want to give up a belief that seemed so close to reality. Instead, other explorers, like Amerigo Vespucci, quickly recognized that the islands of the Caribbean were the "West" Indies and that new continents lay just beyond. Therefore, mapmakers labeled the continents **North** and **South America** after Amerigo Vespucci, not Christopheria or Columbia after Christopher Columbus.

Columbus discovered the Americas at exactly the right moment for Europeans to exploit their advantages. There had been, of course, earlier contacts between the Old World of Eurasia and Africa with the New World of the Americas, going back even to the Vikings. In all these earlier interactions, however, the travelers lacked the interest or ability to dominate the "native" Americans who had been living there for tens of thousands of years. By 1492, however, Spain was ready to commit resources for conquest and lucky enough to have them succeed beyond expectation.

Columbus's own domination of the natives (mistakenly, of course, called Indians after the East Indies) further tarnishes his legacy. He kidnapped natives and killed to seize land at will. In his desire to acquire gold, Columbus cut off the hands of natives who failed to turn in his quotas. Those who fled he had hunted down with huge hounds who tore off their limbs while still alive. His soldiers forcibly took native women for themselves. Following Columbus, other Spanish adventurers called **conquistadors** conquered much of the Americas, supported by a firm conviction in God's blessing for their cause, rich financial backing, and a well-drilled military equipped with horses and guns.

Historians call the European takeover of the Americas and its consequences the Columbian Exchange, a mutual transfer of goods and ideas. It mostly added up to be in the West's favor, however. European settlers rushed into the Americas, grabbing control of vast expanses of land and actually and essentially enslaving native peoples. Wealth in precious metals and food products flowed into Europe, having been produced by the native peoples. Europeans ate better with foods from the New World, including peanuts, maize, potatoes, sunflowers, and tomatoes (although tomatoes were originally suspected of being poisonous because of their bright red color). Tobacco smoking provided a new social pastime. In turn, both native and immigrant Americans fed on cattle, pigs, chickens, sugarcane, coffee, rice, bananas, and even the honey of honeybees brought from the Old World to the new. Along with these new agricultural resources, the American natives gained new rulers and a new religion.

The European conquest came surprisingly easily, within a few decades after Columbus's discovery. Natives on the Caribbean islands could not organize a strong military resistance since they were still at the socioeconomic level of hunter-gatherers or simple agriculturalists. In contrast, millions of American Indians on the mainland were quite civilized and organized. Two recently formed empires maintained societies based in cities as sophisticated as any in the Old World. One of the peoples who ruled the so-called Aztec Empire, the Mexica, gave their name to modern-day Mexico. Their political power reached southward toward Central America. The Aztec capital of Tenochtitlan (today, Mexico City) arguably possessed more comforts, and certainly more people, than any one city in Spain. The Incan

Empire based in Peru controlled much of the west coast of South America. Each empire coordinated agriculture, war, and peace for millions of people, with armies well trained in conquest. These civilized societies were, ironically, even more vulnerable to conquest. They shared three serious disadvantages for competition with the Spanish: deification, ethnic conflicts, and vulnerable immune systems.

First, deification hurt the natives because they expected too much from their own human rulers, who were considered to be gods. The Aztec practice of sacrificing humans for religious reasons, carving out beating hearts with obsidian knives, also upset many subject peoples who did not believe in the Aztec gods. Even worse, the natives too often incorrectly believed the Europeans were gods themselves. The newcomers' pale skins, shiny armor, and unfamiliar horses contributed to this falsehood, which the lying conquistadors exploited to the utmost. This sham allowed Cortés in Mexico and Pizarro in Peru to get close to, capture, and then execute the native emperors (see figure 9.6). Therefore, the embodiment of both church and state collapsed with one blow. Murdered emperors left the natives disorganized and doubting.

Second, the diversity of the Native Americans helped the Spanish defeat the native political states. The Incan and Aztec Empires, like many empires, centered on specific ethnic groups that dominated others. Enemies of these empires, tribes that remained unconquered or had been recently subjugated, readily cooperated

Figure 9.6.   The Spanish conquistadors are the new lords of the palace as they order the Incan ruler Atahualpa strangled by his own people. (NYPL Digital Collection)

with the Spanish against the native imperial supremacy. The Spanish played various tribal groups against one another. Then, conquistadors replaced every native civilized political structure that ruled over good farmland. Only on the fringes of the Spanish Empire did Indians retain some self-rule. They usually survived as hunter-gatherer societies, protected by mountains, deserts, or jungles.

The third and worst problem for the natives was their vulnerability to diseases carried from Europe. We understand now how many diseases are caused by germs (see chapter 11). In the sixteenth century, though, many people felt that disease was a punishment from God. Such had been the case with the Black Death, which killed a third of the European population within a few years. Little knowledge existed on how to prevent or cure illnesses. The Spanish, naturally and unintentionally, brought with them various germs from Europe, from diseases as harmless as the common cold to the more lethal measles and chicken pox and the very deadly smallpox. The Europeans bore substantial immunities to these diseases, but the native Americans had never been exposed to them. In contrast, perhaps the only illness that the Europeans may have brought back from the Americas was the sexually transmitted disease of syphilis. It first appeared in Europe at about this time and for the next few centuries disproportionately afflicted sexually promiscuous people, especially prostitutes, soldiers, and aristocrats.

In comparison, the natives of the Americas were not so fortunate. Millions became sick and died. Spreading rapidly along imperial roads, pandemics (epidemics that range over whole continents and beyond) killed large portions of the population. Large regions were completely depopulated, and native sociopolitical networks broke down.

Through exploitation of political rivalries, military tactics, and disease, Spain quickly came to dominate the Americas, wiping out much of the indigenous cultures and civilization and replacing them with its version of Western civilization. At the time, the Spanish did not realize the complete extent of the devastation or fully comprehend their own role in the plagues. But they knew how to take advantage of the situation. Empty land was theirs for the taking. In the next three centuries, perhaps close to two million Spaniards migrated to what would become known as Latin America (from the linguistic origins of Spanish and Portuguese). The Spanish reduced to servitude and enslavement those natives who survived disease and slaughter. Only insufficient numbers of colonial settlers prevented the Spanish from expanding farther north than they did.

The Spanish masters exploited the defeated. Natives dug in the silver mines (of which there were plenty, but disappointingly few sources of gold). Or they labored in the fields for long hours under the southern sun. Many died from overwork and lack of care, exploited worse than animals. Only a few voices protested, notably Bartolomé de Las Casas, the first priest ordained in the Americas. He spoke out to claim human and Christian dignity for the Indians. He and others won the argument that Indians had souls and were human, capable of entry into heaven after death. But many continued to die. Within a few decades the native population of the Americas fell from what was probably eleven million to only two and a half million.

While the depopulation guaranteed European domination, it also threatened the Western exploitation. Who would produce the silver and food that the Europeans desired and needed? How could they replace all the dead miners and peasants?

The Portuguese offered a solution with the **Atlantic-African slave trade**. In the year 1400, slavery hardly existed in Europe. Soon after, the Portuguese had gained an interest in slavery, which they had seen operating among the Africans. Beginning in 1444 they began to buy and sell black Africans, with the official excuse of the need to convert Muslim prisoners to Christianity. In reality, they wanted cheap, expendable labor. The new plantations for sugarcane, which everyone's sweet tooth craved, promoted harsh labor practices. The crop required hard, nasty, and dangerous harvesting in dank thickets, where workers hacked away at rough, sharp stalks with machetes. So over the next few centuries, Europeans of various nationalities captured and shipped millions of diverse Africans to work as slaves in the Americas. The first boatload arrived by 1510, not even two decades after Columbus's discovery. By the time the Atlantic-African slave trade ended in the nineteenth century, about ten million Africans had been shipped to the Americas, most unloaded in the Caribbean islands and Brazil, but about a fifth going to British colonies (see figure 9.7).

Thus, the new Spanish rulers forcibly converted the native American "Indians" and the imported Africans to the ways of Western civilization, which largely supported and benefited the European masters. Of course, through most of history, in most civilizations, the masses, both free and slave, have supported the few at the top. The institutionalized racism of the Americas, though, has left an especially challenging legacy. "Black" skins were identified as inferior, while "white" skins claimed superiority. The periodic revolts by both the native American and African slaves always ended with the Western masters victorious.

An improved method of investing capital, the bourse or **stock exchange**, soon financed this slave trade and other colonial investments. First appearing in Antwerp

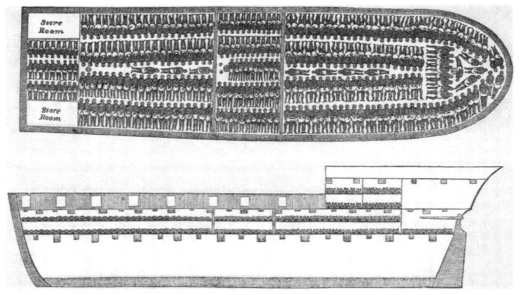

Figure 9.7.   These cross sections of the decks of a slave ship, from above and from the side, show how human beings were packed for transatlantic transport. (NYPL Digital Collection)

in 1485, the stock exchange provided an alternative to banks as a place for capital to be gathered and invested. At first, members pooled their resources for new investment capital. But collective membership risked all of one's own possessions to pay debts if too many of the collective's investments failed. By 1600, joint-stock companies provided a better way to protect investments by restricting losses to only the number of shares any individual owned. This limited liability meant that someone who prudently invested only a portion of his wealth through stock in any one venture could not be ruined. Remember, risk was always part of capitalism.

Although the New World looked like a profitable investment, it had a mixed impact on the European economy. American silver mines added tons of bullion to the treasuries of Spain, which then filtered out to the other nations of Europe and even to China through world trade. But so much silver also led to a quick and devastating inflation. A "price revolution" of swiftly rising costs of goods and services hurt the middle and poorer classes of Spain, eventually weakening the Spanish Empire. The history of capitalism is rife with both growth in wealth and suffering caused by crises in investments.

The simple idea of capitalism, reinvesting profits, offered no real guidelines on how to best keep those profits flowing to everyone's benefit. Some intellectuals attempted to figure out how to prevent economic disaster and promote economic growth. As part of the Commercial Revolution, they began to propose one of the first **economic theories**, sets of ideas that offered comprehensive explanations for how people carried out economic activity (see diagram 15.1). Since then, many theories have tried to suggest plans for action on how best to harness capitalism. Unlike scientific theories (see chapter 10), though, no economic theory has as yet sufficiently explained human economic activity.

The early ***economic theory of mercantilism*** linked the growing early modern nation-states to their new colonial empires. Theorists emphasized that the accumulation of wealth in precious metals within a country's own borders was the best measure of economic success. Mercantilist theory favored government intervention in the economy, since it was in governments' interest that their economies succeed. The theory argued that a regime should cultivate a favorable balance of trade as a sign of economic success. Since most international exchange took place in bullion, actual gold and silver, monarchs tried to make sure that other countries bought more from their country than they bought from other monarchs' countries. By these means, the bullion in a country's treasury continued to increase. Monarchs then obsessed about discovering mines of gold and silver, a practically cost-free method of acquiring bullion.

Because of this tangible wealth, governments frequently intervened by trying to promote enterprises to strengthen the economy. State-sponsored monopolies had clear advantages for a monarch. A state-licensed enterprise, such as importing tea leaves from China or sable furs from Siberia, could easily be supervised and taxed. Diligent inspections and regulation ensured that monopolies' goods and services were of a high quality. The government could then promote and protect that business both overseas and domestically.

Fueled by this burgeoning capital and developing theory, more adventurers sailed off to exploit the riches of Asia, Africa, and the Americas. Unfortunately for imperialists, the world was fairly crowded already with other powerful peoples. Various kingdoms and states in East Asia (the Chinese Empire, Japan), the Indian subcontinent (the Mughal Empire), and Africa (Abyssinia) had long histories, rich economies, sophisticated cultures, and intimidating armies.

Even so, Spain and Portugal boldly divided up the world between them in 1494, even before Vasco da Gama had reached the Indies, with the **Treaty of Tordesillas** (see map 9.2). The pope blessed the proceedings. The treaty demonstrated a certain hubris in those two states. They claimed global domination, notwithstanding their inability to severely damage the existing rich, powerful, well-established, and disease-resistant African and Asian kingdoms and empires. The European powers ruled the oceans but could only nibble at the fringes of Asia and Africa.

People of other Western nations did not let the Spanish and Portuguese enjoy their fat empires in peace for long. Outside the law, pirates in the Caribbean along the Spanish Main (the Central and South American coastline) and in the Indies plundered whatever they could. Some captains became legalized pirates, licensed by governments with "letters of marque." For example, raids by the English Sir Francis Drake and his sea dogs helped provoke the Spanish Armada.

By 1600, the Dutch, the English, and the French had launched their own overseas ventures, with navies and armies grabbing and defending provinces across the oceans. They all began to drive out natives in the Americas, Africa, and Asia. They also turned on one another. In Asia and Africa, the Dutch grabbed Portuguese bases in South Africa and the East Indies. The English, in turn, seized Dutch possessions in Africa, Malaysia, and North America (turning New Holland into New York and New Jersey). The English planted their own colonists along the Atlantic seacoast of North America. The French settled farther inland in Quebec. Likewise, in the Caribbean, India, and the Pacific, the French and English faced each other in disputes about islands and principalities while the native peoples were caught in the middle.

These European "illegal immigrants" seized power from the original native rulers and owners. The colonizers ravaged the native cultures, often with cruelty (scalping was invented by Europeans) and carelessness (smashing sculptures and pulverizing written works). Priceless cultural riches vanished forever. Land grabbing displaced the local farmers, while slavery (whether in body or wages) and displacement of native peoples by Europeans dismantled social structures. Where social bonds did not snap apart, European immigrants ignored and discriminated, trying to weaken the hold of native religions, languages, and even clothing styles. Robbed of their homes and livelihoods, most non-European subjects found resistance to be futile against the weight of European power.

As a result of the westerners' expansion around the world, "Europe" replaced "Christendom" in the popular imagination. Nevertheless, these diverse Europeans continued to hurl insults and launch wars against one another, which they supported through grotesque ethnic stereotypes. While the people of one's own nation were invariably perceived as kind, generous, sober, straight, loyal, honest, and intelligent, they might allege that the Spanish were cruel, the Scots stingy, the Dutch drunk, the French perverted, the Italians deceptive, the English boastful, or the Germans boorish. So Europeans remained pluralistic in their perceptions of one another while united in their desire to dominate the globe.

The elites also recognized certain common bonds in how they practiced their gentlemanly manners in ruling over the lower classes, expanded their many governments, grew their increasingly national economies, and revered the Christian religion (no matter how fractured). Some Europeans adopted a notion of the morally pure "noble savage" as a critique on their own culture. Missionaries preached the alleged love and hope of Christianity, while global natives found themselves confronted by new crimes brought in by the westerners, such as prostitution and vagrancy. The confidence in civilization of Western exceptionalism made Europeans feel that they deserved superiority over all other peoples. These diverse Europeans insisted that they themselves were "civilized" and that their dominated enemies were barbaric "savages." They increasingly viewed humans through racist lenses: "white" Europeans and "colored" others, whether "red" American Indians, "brown" Asian Indians, "yellow" Chinese, or "black" sub-Saharan Africans. All these other "races" by definition were believed to be less intelligent, industrious, and intrepid. Through increasing contacts with other peoples, the rest of the world seemed truly "foreign."

This Eurocentric attitude is reflected in the early maps of the globe. Medieval maps had usually given pride of place in the center to Jerusalem. By the sixteenth century, geographers had a more accurate picture of the globe and could distinguish other continents as connected to one another by at most a narrow isthmus (Panama for the Americas, Sinai between Eurasia and Africa). Nonetheless, they "split" the continent of Eurasia into "Asia" and "Europe," arbitrarily deciding on the Ural Mountains as a dividing point (although these hills hardly created a barrier—as the Huns and Mongols had demonstrated). Westerners saw vast stretches of eastern Europe as hardly civilized at all, a tempting target for building empires. The maps had changed to show that Europeans had moved from being located in one small corner of the map to the center. The explorers who led the voyages of discovery showed audacity and heroism, added to the scientific knowledge of Europeans, and allowed some mutually beneficial cultural exchange. Wielding a newfound global power, Western civilization had conquered much of the world by the seventeenth century. More was to come in the nineteenth century.

Review: *How did the "voyages of discovery" begin colonial imperialism by Europeans?*

Response:

Make your own timeline.

1400   **1648**

Epilogue

Why Western Civilization?

Several hundred years ago, Western civilization took the worldwide lead in politics (often by success in war), economics (by accumulating wealth), and science and technology (by using machines to help with the first two). In each of these areas, states and social groups in the West gained more efficiency and effectiveness than organized societies elsewhere in the world. On the one hand, westerners used the power from these advantages to intimidate and oppress other human cultures and civilizations. On the other hand, westerners brought knowledge to those other societies that, in time, enabled some of them to become powerful in their own right by adopting parts of Western civilization. Cultures around the world are still deciding what to keep from the West and what to use against its dominance. Some would argue that Western values are uniquely essential to those who have inherited them. Others argue that anyone can adopt Western values, that they can be universal. And certainly what some consider to be values can be seen by others as vices. Regardless, the dynamism generated by the West guarantees that tomorrow will be different from today. Therein lie the difficulties of applying historical understanding. In a changing world, what should we ourselves choose to learn from the past of Western civilization?

A couple of decades ago, students at Stanford University chanted the phrase "Western Civ has got to go." They were saying that a Western civilization course requirement in their curriculum was more harmful than helpful. Although the incident was hardly significant, defenders of Western culture sometimes point to this specific incident as a signal of doom for the study of Western Civ. For the West exists only as long as many of its members and opponents say it exists. It becomes real through self-identification or from labeling by others. Without being defined, no civilization has inherent cohesion.

In the last few years people have been arguing about "the West" more than ever. Such is not unexpected, since every civilization has come under attack. The West has confronted external enemies, from Viking, Saracen, and Magyar hordes plundering the Carolingian Empire to al-Qa'ida blowing up commuters in New York, Madrid, and London. The West has also faced internal enemies, who have caused peasant rebellions, civil wars about the role of government, the attempted genocide of Jews, criminal organizations taking the streets, and white supremacists committing mass shootings and blowing up buildings. All civilizations define themselves by the extent of their supremacy over their own subjects or against their neighbors, the "others." All cultures have, at one time or another, confronted new people and ideas and faced the necessity of either absorbing them or eliminating them. Since Western civilization is so widespread today, it cannot help but provoke opposition from those who do not accept the extent of its reach or agree with its values.

It is also important to remember that "the West" has never, at any time, been one single, monolithic entity. As described in this book, a long historical process of human choices about those values, many of them contradictory, have resulted in a divided West. In its belief systems, the West has experienced everything from myths to monotheisms, philosophical speculation to scientific secularism. In its culture, the West has expressed itself in everything from epic poetry to prose history, theatricals and spectacles, novels and newspapers, which have been transmitted on everything from stone and bone, clay and canvas, parchment and paper, to celluloid film and streams of electrons. In its power over nature, the West is historically rooted with all other worldwide cultures in the knife and knapsack of the hunter-gatherers to the plow and pottery of agriculturists. The West progressed further, with the steam engine and steel cruiser to today's computers and cars. But none of these inventions or attitudes necessarily made the West's culture better or superior. Nonetheless, through the power of its militaries, ideas, discoveries, and economies, it is indisputable that the West came to reign supreme over world affairs by the nineteenth century.

Like any powerful civilization in world history, the West achieved its ascendancy most obviously by wielding weapons and wealth. Yet the West has never spoken with one unified voice. Both a strength and a weakness of Western civilization has been its division into many sovereign states. Their rivalries with one another spurred innovation and growth as well as destruction and death. This variety also enabled democratic and republican ideals to survive against prevailing absolutism and authoritarianism. The cooperation of individuals and groups in capitalism financed political growth and further fostered responsive government.

Some people believe that the West is based on freedom of the individual, but its own history shows an ambivalent interaction with that ideal. The nation-state as the primary way to organize people easily subsumes individuals, who only really matter when connected to larger social groups of family, class, and corporation. And when any state goes to war, few support the freedom of the individual to opt out from the collectivism of military service. Nation-states rose to great powers when, ironically, some individual states grew strong enough to create overseas empires. Western guns and galleons gave Europeans a lethal advantage over many other peoples in Asia, Africa, and the Americas. Imperialist Spain and Portugal were joined by France and England, then the Netherlands and Russia, next Germany and Italy, and finally, the United States and even Japan, re-created in the West's own image. The official empires of the West largely collapsed in the twentieth century, partly because the West was drained by three global conflicts: World War I, World War II, and the Cold War.

At the end of these conflicts, the United States of America stood above all others as a superpower. The United States had achieved a unique global superiority through its money, media, and military. An economy and financial system allowed less than 5 percent of the world's population to consume more than 20 percent of its resources. Since World War II, the United States has wielded an influence without precedent. Its ideas have spread in television and movies, games, music, and fashion, while the power of its armed forces reflects a budget larger than about the next seven most-powerful nations combined.

One of the most uncertain directions of Western civilization today is the extent to which the United States of America will either continue to dominate it or separate from it. Some American exceptionalists have suggested that its hegemony should allow the United States alone to define what the world should be in the future, acting unilaterally. To make the USA number one is to focus on its interests at the expense of other nations. Those who critique American exceptionalism wish the United States to work with the nations of Europe, and even the world, funneling war and power through the multilateral international institutions (such as NATO and the UN) created by the West in the second half of the twentieth century. President Obama proposed, "I believe in American exceptionalism, just as I suspect that the Brits believe in British exceptionalism and the Greeks believe in Greek exceptionalism." For true believers, his view was tantamount to a contempt for the West. President Trump has said, "I declare today for the world to hear that the West will never ever be broken; our values will prevail; our people will thrive; and our civilization will triumph." Can the West remain "special," however, without asserting superiority?

The study of the West has thus been undermined due to cultural warfare over which aspect of its past (and present) truly represents its traditional values and virtues. Some who argue for Western exceptionalism like to draw up little lists about what makes this civilization so special, worthy of emulation. This is history written by the victors. But, if the losers have any history of their own at all, they often nurse their grudges until they can try to vanquish their oppressors. Should history remind us of our nobility or force us to acknowledge our crimes? People want their heroes and villains—although usually we want the heroes to resemble us and the villains to appear like some "other." It is hard to cope when the roles are reversed. Christianity had pacifists like Jesus, Saint Francis, and Martin Luther King Jr., as well as murderers like schismatics, crusaders, and inquisitors. Nations had their largely successful, yet flawed, rulers (King Henry II, King Louis XIV, and Chancellor Bismarck), as well as their failure-ridden, yet human, leaders (King John, King Louis XVI, and Adolf Hitler). Each has had, and will have, at least some proponents and some opponents. Good historians try to sort out the greatness and the failures that belong to each of us, recording all facets of events and people, both good and bad.

More important than the leaders of the past may have been the different ideologies that informed their choices. Various factions in our culture identify some beliefs as vices, others as virtues, and vice versa. The Enlightenment consensus of reason and science has never completely overwhelmed religious and superstitious viewpoints. Ongoing resistance to Darwinian evolution by those who assert a literal interpretation of the Bible illustrates this lack of success. Yet Christianity has not been able to beget its "City of God." Neither has rationalism built its utopia, because people have never been able to agree on priorities. Some argue that capitalism should sanctify the pursuit of profit only by corporations, while others call for society to embrace all persons as active economic agents. Elites redefine democracy as the mere holding of elections, in which money makes some voices louder than votes. The masses often seek to be heard but speak in many different voices (quite literally, in the many languages from Basque to Bulgarian still spoken in the European Union). Most people want to win, which means usually that other people lose. Few people seem willing to compromise or forgive.

All these tensions among competing ideas interacted to create Western civilization. Fights over causation, civil rights, capitalism, class, high culture, and Christianity have all driven historical change. Influences from neighboring cultures and civilizations, small and large, from Mesopotamians, Egyptians, Assyrians, Persians, Muslims, North Africans, Byzantines, Slavs, Magyars, East Asians, South Asians, Central Asians, Native Americans, sub-Saharan Africans, Pacific Islanders, and others helped to shape Western civilization over the centuries.

While advocates of *multiculturalism* have attacked Western expressions of power, history shows that the West has always been multicultural. In its earliest phases, Hebrews tried to Judaize their Canaanite neighbors in Palestine; the Greeks began to hellenize the peoples conquered by Alexander; the Romans romanized everyone from the Iberians to the Britains, Germans, Greeks, Mesopotamians, and Egyptians. They also subjugated the Etruscans, Carthaginians, Druids, and others. In the early Middle Ages, the church Christianized the ruling Germans and their neighbors. None of these "-izations" succeeded completely—elements of earlier cultures always survived. The alleged unity of medieval Christendom actually rested on the different "nations" of English, French, Germans, Italians, Spanish, and others. Then, from the Middle Ages into the nineteenth century, the diverse Germanic invaders who had toppled the western half of the Roman Empire melded into their conquered populations, in the process transforming and spreading new cultures. The Gothic Germans and old Romans (and Celts and a few others) diversified into the French, the English, the Italians, the Spanish, the Portuguese, the Scandinavians, the Scots, the Irish, the Dutch, the Swiss, the Belgians, and others, including even Luxembourgers, Liechtensteiners, Andorrans, and Austrians. The Slavic states of eastern Europe connected with the West after the fall of the Byzantines and the Ottomans (although complicated by the Russians and their ambivalent attitude to "westernness"). As many of these westerners trekked into the world, colonizing and colonized peoples organized as Latin Americans, "North" Americans, Australians, New Zealanders, South Africans, and others. All of them reflect multiculturalism; all of them share in Western civilization, insofar as they have appropriated large parts of it. Yet some people claim that Latin America is not "Western," even though the majority of the people believe in Christianity, speak European languages, are organized into industrial-age classes, apply economic theories, use modern science and technology, and live under modern nation-state political systems.

Does Western civilization have a future? At several moments in its past, Western civilization almost did not. Persia might have conquered Greece. The Romans might have self-destructed in their republican civil wars. The Germans might have resisted Christianity. Norse, Magyar, or Saracen invaders might have overwhelmed the Christendom of Charlemagne. The Mongols might have wiped out the West, as they did many societies that opposed them. Asian armies might have conquered Europe anytime up to the seventeenth century. Nuclear war might have ended it all during the Cold War (and still may).

Up to now, Western civilization has become a historical force by surviving numerous challenges and developing overwhelming power, partly because of the revolutions it has experienced and assimilated. It has been held together in the last few decades by a group of institutions such as NATO for a military alliance, and for economics, the International Monetary Fund, the World Bank, many trade agreements, the EU, and the G7. But nothing is stable, ever since the many Western revolutions committed to constant change. The Commercial Revolution, the intellectual revolutions of the Renaissance and Enlightenment, the religious revolution of the Reformation, the Scientific Revolution, the Industrial Revolution, and the political revolutions of England, America, and France all guarantee that tomorrow is different from today. These revolutions encourage human creativity and the application of the "new" to improve people's lives.

Change has not been common to all historical views. Some cultures, such as the Hindu in India or the Mayan in Central America, see a cyclical turn to history, looking to revive or maintain traditional orders, resisting anything new or different. The ancient Egyptian and early Chinese civilizations valued the unchanging permanence of a society that mirrored an eternal heavenly order. The monarchs and nobles ruled from their fine palaces, the priests prayed in their gilded temples, and the peasants shoveled manure in the fields. So it had been; so it always should be. Any disruptions—an invasion by foreigners, the end of a dynasty and civil war, a natural disaster—should be overcome so that the elites could restore the right order of things. These attitudes and concepts are also found in Western civilization.

But from the Jews, through the Greeks and Romans, and to the Germans, the West began to embrace change, even when its leaders would not admit it to themselves. The Jews appealed to the eternal law of God but adapted to changing circumstances as they went from wandering tribes, to kingdoms, to a people scattered across the world. Now, some of them are building the national state of Israel and confronting hostility within and without. The Greeks cleverly expanded outward from their homeland and briefly achieved cultural predominance in the Eastern Mediterranean and the Middle East, only to lose it through their failure to include other cultures. They regained a brief ascendancy with the surviving remnant of Rome known as the Byzantine Empire, only to lose that empire to the Turks. The Romans did so well at learning from the Greeks that they passed on an imperialist legacy to the Byzantine East, Islam, and the West. The Germans who inadvertently destroyed Rome in the fifth century AD bound the cultures of the Greeks and

Romans to their own, tolerated a Jewish presence, and embraced Christianity. Although the Germanic barbarians failed to unite the West under one government, the common appeal to Christianity, Greece, and Rome combined with the eagerness of the states in western Europe to learn from one another, their neighbors, and immigrants to invent the great revolutions in economics, learning, religion, science, and politics.

The themes of supremacy and diversity reveal these ongoing changes. Some leaders and societies have sought domination, which bound allegiances into a unity that strengthened. Arguments over what justified supremacy recast societies: a divine mandate (decided upon by whose God?), tradition (choosing which part of the assorted past?), knowledge (as taught by whom?), power (with what degree of violence?). Over time, though, supremacies have often stifled creativity. They demanded mere obedience and often oppressed. At the same time, humans obviously have sought diversity, fracturing into smaller unities while striving for what is new. Yet emphasis on too many differences, or focusing too much on them, has fragmented people into mutual hostilities, if not armed camps. Recent conflicts show clearly: there are no fundamental assumptions about which everyone agrees. The tendency toward diversity subverts supremacy.

Today, international and multiregional organizations continue to expand, while nationalistic groups persistently cling to their separate constructed identities. As the world economy binds peoples together, nationalists want to restrict immigration; local patriotism resists international solidarity among human beings. Most people still fail to empathize with either the exploited or the enemy, although modern media zap their words, sounds, and images into our living rooms every day. And with anyone able to put information on the Internet, people who look can easily find both facts and falsehoods that confirm their convictions. Our collapsing world seems both smaller and more conflict ridden.

Where does that leave Western civilization? Globalization of all markets and cultures is taking place under pervasive Western methodologies of investment and profit. Superficially, Western culture is everywhere, in the commercial products of food, drink, and clothing, in the machines that make life easier and regulated, in the entertainment of music, games, and visual images. Those countries where Western civilization runs deepest are those whose populations largely descend from western Europe: in North America, both Canada and the United States, and in the South Pacific, Australia, and New Zealand. The states of Latin America through the Caribbean, Central America, and South America are all Western, although with large doses of Native American and some African influences. Substantially westernized countries are also in Eastern Europe, including Russia.

In the Middle East, Israel is largely Western, although increasingly at odds with Arab Palestinians inside and outside its borders. Oil riches have brought Western concepts to many other Muslim countries, provoking the hostility behind much of modern Islamist terrorism. On the African continent, South Africa with its British and Afrikaaner minority is most thoroughly westernized. Yet other African nations bear the scars and retain some of the benefits of Western colonialism while trying to adapt to a global economy run on Western principles. Japan has become largely a Western nation. Contemporary China has exploited Western capitalist policies, while it retains officially a Communist authoritarian system (Western in its mechanisms). In the rest of the world, all former colonial areas of the West, the depth of Western penetration varies. Some nations have strong elements of rejection, while others are eagerly trying to assimilate.

What does it mean to be Western? Take your choice: science or supernaturalism, democracy or dictatorship, socialism or self-interest, class consciousness or ethnic identification, virtuosity or vulgarity, religiosity or rationality. All are rooted in our tradition, and all have flaws, at least according to those who choose one over the other. Perhaps the most significant Western value is a beautiful and dreadful ambiguity (see figure E.1).

I once found a graffito written on a desk in a classroom where I taught history: "If history is so important, how come it is gone?" The writer obviously did not fully understand the point of studying history. The past isn't gone. History is all around us. And not just in dusty museums, crumbling monuments, or misty memories of

Figure E.1. The city of Salzburg represents many of the varied aspects of Western civilization. It uses modern technology of electricity and automobiles, yet encourages pedestrians (with the footbridge across the river); its economy was once centered around its namesake salt, mined in the mountains in the distance, while today tourism dominates; also its river has been canalized to control flooding and increase property. Its politics have gone through many stages since the initial Stone Age settlement: a town under the Celts; a city under the Romans; a town refounded under the German Carolingians after being abandoned in late antiquity; a spiritual principality ruled by prince-bishops in the Holy Roman Empire, who built the powerful fortress; a province fought over by various powers; and finally a federal state today in Austria. Salzburg once had social structures of aristocrats, townspeople, and peasants, and now it has celebrities, professionals, laborers, and the poor. Some of its culture can be seen in the visible churches and their spires and heard in its music festivals. These churches indicate the traditional belief system of Christianity, but they seem increasingly as tourist attractions rather than centers of faith.

old-timers. Could you understand your own self without remembering your childhood? The past is in the baggage of our minds, in the frameworks of our institutions, in the complexity of our problems. We cannot escape history. We may ignore it only at our peril, since it frames all events around us. Our common heritage has shaped the institutions and structures within which we live. Every significant event instantly becomes history the moment it is over.

Because of Western developments, more people have more choices to affect their politics, economics, and culture than ever before in history. The ability to choose is, of course, limited by one's position in society. The rich usually have more options than the middle class, while the poor struggle with even fewer choices. Legitimate authorities (through law enforcement and war) as well as extralegal organized groups (through crime and terrorism) have the ability to restrict choices of disconnected individuals. Nevertheless, many of us have some freedom to decide our own future because of the success of certain Western values.

Our future depends on the choices we make today. Those people who made decisions in the past changed the course of events to restrict our choices. All kinds of people have appeared in the past of the West, whether forward looking or backward leaning, tolerant or closed-minded, humanist or pragmatic, cruel or kind, tyrannical or populist. This diversity allows almost anyone to claim they are defending tradition, whether proposing a liberating innovation or clinging to oppressive preservation.

You should understand what you believe, whether inherited from family, imposed by society, or freely accepted as your own. You should then act according to your beliefs within our global society. This book offers one path to understanding the world's Western heritage. You can either learn more on your own, benefit from study of other scholars and teachers, be satisfied with what has been offered here, or forget it all. You can benefit, or not, from historical examples of wisdom, stupidity, greatness, and failure. It is ultimately up to you. Choose your story and how to live into it.

Review: *How should one shape one's own worldview by picking and choosing from the key legacies of Western civilization?*

Response:

Timelines

Note: The timelines present key names, events, ideas, institutions, and inventions in chronological order, roughly according to their first appearance in history. Numbers along each side of the timelines indicate time segments and the name of the general historical period; older dates are at the top, more recent toward the bottom. Additionally, terms placed within the white and shaded boxes between the horizontal lines are in approximate chronological order. The six vertical columns spread across each timeline divide data according to categories explained in chapter 1. In the Politics column, information from similar geographic areas tends to be grouped together within the cells, aligned left, center, or right. For example, in timeline C, most of the Politics terms aligned at the left relate to Great Britain. Terms given in all capital letters are states or nations when they first appear, important wars, or regimes. Although some terms in the Culture column are not explained in the text, key works, genres, artists, and writers through history are listed to provide context. Book titles are italicized.

Timeline A. The Ancient Middle East and West before 500 BC

Time	SCIENCE & TECHNOLOGY	ECONOMY	POLITICS
Prehistory			
	Paleolithic Age clothing tools	hunter-gatherers	*Homo sapiens*
30,000 Y.A.			
	Neolithic Age	trade/commerce slavery	
7000 B.C.			
	animal domestication agriculture copper Bronze Age	Neolithic Agricultural Revolution property	villages, towns, cities Mesopotamian city states war absolutism monarchy kings kingdoms MIDDLE-EASTERN CIVILIZATIONS Sumerians
2900 B.C.	writing		Egypt
	mathematics astronomy	taxes	pharaohs
	calendar		dynasty
2600 B.C.			
Ancient History			
2300 B.C.			empires
2000 B.C.			Hebrews
			Middle Kingdom of Egypt Amorites/Babylonians
1700 B.C.			
			New Kingdom of Egypt
1400 B.C.			
			Hatshepsut Ahkenaton Exodus "Dark Age"
1100 B.C.	alphabet		Phoenicians Israel & Judea
	Iron Age		colonialism
		money	
800 B.C.			*polis/poleis* Greek Archaic Age Rome
	hoplites-phalanx		ASSYRIAN EMPIRE militarism
	thetes-trireme		Babylonian Captivity of the Hebrews PERSIAN EMPIRE
500 B.C.			

SOCIAL STRUCTURES	CULTURE	PHILOSOPHY & RELIGION	
nomadic tribes community family	language painting sculpture	animism	
			30,000 Y.A.
			7000 B.C.
civilization division of labor upper, urban, lower classes sexism	architecture	polytheism syncretism	
			2900 B.C.
aristocrats artisans peasants	school	priests priestesses fertility rituals	
			2600 B.C.
	epic poetry *Gilgamesh*		
			2300 B.C.
			2000 B.C.
Law Code of Hammurabi		Judaism Monotheism	
			1700 B.C.
			1400 B.C.
	Book of the Dead	Moses' covenant Ten Commandments	
			1100 B.C.
		oracles anthropomorphism Greek civic cults	
			800 B.C.
	Homer, *Illiad*, *Odyssey* Olympic Games	prophets	
			500 B.C.

Prehistory

Ancient History

Timeline B. The Ancient Middle East and West, 550 BC to AD 530

	SCIENCE & TECHNOLOGY	ECONOMY	POLITICS		
	hoplites-phalanx *thetes*-trireme	land reform	aristocracy- -oligarchy- -tyranny- -democracy *polis* citizenship		
			Athenian democracy ostracism ROMAN REPUBLIC		
500 B.C.					
	rationalism		PERSIAN WARS Senate, consuls		
			Delian League, Athenian Empire		
	concrete		PELOPONNESIAN WARS demagogues		
400 B.C.					
	Aristotle		Gauls/Celts sack Rome		
	dialectic logic		Philip II of Macedon tribunes proscription		
	aqueduct		Alexander III "the Great" ROMAN EMPIRE		
300 B.C.	Roman legion Roman roads		Hellenistic kingdoms		
			PUNIC WARS		
200 B.C.					
		latifundia	Hannibal		
			ROMAN CIVIL WARS Tiberius & Gaius Gracchus		
100 B.C.	Julian calendar		Julius Caesar		
			Antony & Cleopatra		
B.C. A.D.			PRINCIPATE		
			Octavian "Augustus" Caesar *princeps, imperator*, Praetorian Guard		
			Pax Romana		
			Goths/Germans		
			natural law, lawyers		
A.D.100	geocentric and heliocentric theories		Five Good Emperors adoption and designation		
A.D.200					
		wage/price freeze	DOMINATE Diocletian		
A.D.300			Constantine I "the Great"		
			Huns Germanic barbarian migrations		
A.D.400			Franks, Merovingians Second Sack of Rome		
			Anglo-Saxons		
			Fall of the Roman Empire in the West		
A.D.500			Justinian Byzantine Empire		

Classical/Ancient History

SOCIAL STRUCTURES	CULTURE	PHILOSOPHY & RELIGION	
GREEK CLASSICAL AGE			
	lyric poetry		
patricians & plebians	Greek Golden Age theater history Parthenon	mystery religious cults philosophy Sophists humanism	500 B.C.
	Lysistrata Oedipus	Socrates	
	Hellenistic Age	Plato idealism Aristotle Jews Diaspora anti-Semitism	400 B.C.
Alexandria			300 B.C.
cosmopolitan		Epicureanism stoicism rabbis	200 B.C.
proletariat			
optimates vs *populares*			
	Gallic War Vergil, *Aeneid*	Hebrew scriptures (Old Testament) deification	100 B.C.
		Yeshua of Nazareth Christianity martyrs Paul of Tarsus gospels councils apostolic succession	B.C. A.D.
		clergy mass saints apologists sacraments excommunication	A.D.100
			A.D.200
Constantinople		Edict of Milan Council of Nicaea Christian Bible (New Testament) orthodoxy heresy	A.D.300
		Augustine of Hippo *City of God* monasticism regular clergy	A.D.400
Justinian's Law Code			A.D.500

Classical/Ancient History

Timeline C. The Medieval West, 500–1640

	SCIENCE & TECHNOLOGY	ECONOMY	POLITICS
			Franks, Merovingians Clovis Justinian
			Justinian's Law Code
600		manorial economics	"Do-nothing kings" Anglo-Saxon kingdoms
700	stirrups		CAROLINGIAN EMPIRE mayors of the palace Pippin "the Short"
800		three-field planting	Charlemagne
	horse collars		Vikings, Magyars, Moslems Alfred "the Great" ENGLAND FRANCE GERMANY FEUDAL POLITICS
900	castles knights		SCOTLAND Otto I "the Great" HOLY ROMAN EMPIRE
1000	reconquest of Toledo Arab science in West	*Domesday Book* commune	HUNGARY DENMARK NORWAY SWEDEN William "the Conqueror" Crusades Henry IV
1100	windmills	revival of towns & trade industrialization putting out/cottage guilds master, journeyman, apprentice	Concordat of Worms Henry II PORTUGAL Philip II "Augustus"
1200	Scholasticism		John Teutonic knights Magna Carta

1300	mini ice age begins
	pikes
	gunpowder, firearms
	        cannons
		COMMERCIAL
		REVOLUTION
			Parliament Philip IV "the Fair"
			Estates-General
			        OTTOMAN EMPIRE
			SWITZERLAND
			Hundred Years War

1400	printing press
	Columbus
	    Vasco da Gama
		capitalism
		banks
		public debt
			Joan of Arc
			        Peace of Lodi
			AUSTRIA
			Habsburg dynasty Ferdinand & Isabella
			        SPAIN
			Western European colonial imperialism

1500		Atlantic/African slave trade bourse, stock exchange mercantilism	Henry VIII Charles V DUTCH NETHERLANDS Elizabeth I St. Bart's Massacre Philip II Spanish Armada Wars of Religion Henry IV
1600			Thirty Years War English Civil War Peace of Westphalia

Vertical axis labels: Early Middle / Dark Ages; High Middle Ages; Later Middle Ages

SOCIAL STRUCTURES	CULTURE	PHILOSOPHY & RELIGION		
clan, kin, tribe, people, folk		monasticism Benedictine Rule		
free-unfree	Gregorian chant	caesaro-papism	600	
personal justice vendetta/feud	Latin literature	Pope Gregory I Islam: Mohammed Qu'ran		
trial by ordeal customary law			700	Early Middle / Dark Ages
	Carolingian Renaissance	Frankish-Papal Alliance Iconoclastic Controversy	800	
	minuscule seven liberal arts			
seigneur & serf feudal society	Romanesque art		900	
	Gothic art	Cluniac Reform Peace & Truce of God	1000	
nobility chivalry courtesy	tournaments rise of vernacular *Chanson de Roland*	"Great Schism" Eastern Orthodox Gregorian Reform Pope Gregory VII Investiture Struggle		
		Crusades	1100	
burghers, bourgeois patrician, artisan, common	universities Romance Goliards	Cistercian Reform canon law Peter Abelard Thomas Becket	1200	High Middle Ages
	colleges	Cathars, dualism Mendicants Francis of Assisi Inquisition Thomas Aquinas	1300	
BLACK DEATH peasant revolts	Dante, *Divine Comedy* Chaucer Christine de Pizan	Pope Boniface VIII "Babylonian Captivity" "Great Western Schism"	1400	
	RENAISSANCE textual criticism humanism Leonardo, Raphael	mysticism witch hunts Christian humanism Erasmus Spanish Inquisition	1500	
	Machiavelli, *The Prince* Michelangelo Shakespeare	REFORMATION Martin Luther Jean Calvin Anabaptists English Reformation	1600	Later Middle Ages
		Counter-Reformation Council of Trent Loyola, Jesuits Inquisition, *Index*		

Timeline D. Early Modern West, 1540–1914

Era / Year	SCIENCE & TECHNOLOGY	ECONOMY	POLITICS
Renaissance & Reformation	Copernicus		Wars of Religion
	heliocentric theory astronomy SCIENTIFIC REVOLUTION	COMMERCIAL REVOLUTION	RUSSIA
	Gregorian calendar		Elizabeth I DUTCH NETHERLANDS Philip II
		mercantilism	REPUBLICANISM divine right
			CONSTITUTIONALISM ABSOLUTISM
1600		joint-stock company	DUTCH REPUBLIC Henry IV "of Navarre"
	scientific method		GREAT BRITAIN Thirty Years War
	empiricism		Cardinal Richelieu
	Galileo		English Civil War
	physics		Cromwell Peace of Westphalia
			sovereign nation-state balance of power
	scientific academies	Scientific Agricultural Revolution	PRUSSIA
	Newton		Louis XIV "the Sun King"
			Glorious Revolution
			ancien régime Peter I "the Great"
Early Modern Europe / 1700	mini ice age ends		cabinet, prime minister
			British Empire
			enlightened despotism
	spinning jenny		Frederick II "the Great"
			War of Austrian Succession Maria Theresa
	canals	INDUSTRIAL REVOLUTION mill/factory system	Seven Years War
			American Revolution partitions of POLAND
		laissez-faire	USA
			federalism, president
	steam engine	Adam Smith	Louis XVI
	encyclopedia	classical liberal economics	FRENCH REVOLUTION
			National Assembly, Bastille, Reign of Terror, Thermidor
			Wars of the Coalitions
1800			Napoleon Bonaparte
			guerrilla warfare Battle of Waterloo Metternich
		"iron law of wages"	Congress of Vienna
			liberalism nationalism conservatism
	railways	Luddites	Monroe Doctrine LATIN AMERICAN STATES
		utopian socialism	
	geology uniformitarianism		British reform bills GREECE Afrikaaners
	evolution	consumerism	neo-imperialism Rev of 1830
			US-Indian removals BELGIUM
	indoor plumbing	corporations	Mexico-US War Opium Wars Rev of 1848
Nineteenth Century			Napoleon III
	biology	Marxism	Crimean War
	Darwin natural selection	trade/labor unions	Sepoy Mutiny Meiji Restoration
			American Civil War
			ITALY Risorgimento Cavour Garibaldi
			Paris Commune
			Bismark 2nd GERMAN EMPIRE
			Third Republic
		social democracy	SERBIA, BULGARIA, RUMANIA
		neo-mercantilism	terrorism anarchism
	oil chemicals electricity		US-Plains Indian Wars
	Pasteur, germ theory	state socialism	Dollar Diplomacy pan-slavism yugo-slavism
	internal combustion engine	Christian socialism	Hawaii partition of Africa
			Spanish American War Zionism
1900	automobile airplane	cartels, trusts	Boer War SOUTH AFRICA
	atomic theory Freud		Boxer Rebellion
			Balkan Wars Franz Ferdinand

SOCIAL STRUCTURES	CULTURE	PHILOSOPHY & RELIGION		
		Roman Catholicism		Renaissance & Reformation
estates		Counter-Reformation		
clergy		Council of Trent		
nobility	Shakespeare			
common-peasant	BAROQUE	Wars of Religion	1600	
	orchestra, opera			
	Rembrandt			
	Rubens			
westernization	Rococo art			
	ENLIGHTENMENT			Early Modern Europe
	philosophes		1700	
	novels	humanitarianism		
	Bach	skepticism Pietism		
		deism		
		agnosticism atheism		
		progress		
	Neoclassicism	Great Awakening		
	newspapers			
Wollstonecraft				
male suffrage	Rousseau			
Declaration of the Rights of Man and the Citizen	Voltaire			
	Mozart symphony			
	ROMANTICISM		1800	
upper/middle/lower classes	Beethoven			
urbanization				
		materialism		Nineteenth Century
police	Goethe, *Faust*			
public sanitation	Turner			
	REALISM			
"family values"	Dickens			
	professional sports	"higher criticism"		
		Social Darwinism		
	naturalism	Christian fundamentalism		
social sciences	Richard Wagner impressionism			
sociology	Monet, Rodin,	Christian modernism		
anthropology	Van Gogh			
concentration camps		Pope Leo XIII	1900	

Timeline E. The Twentieth Century, 1900–present

SCIENCE & TECHNOLOGY	ECONOMY	POLITICS
telegraph, telephone	neo-mercantilism laissez-faire socialism	neo-imperialism conservative, liberal, socialist political parties
Freud's subconscious	consumer economy trade unions	
auto		terrorism militarism Zionism
1900		"open door" policy, Boxer Rebellion
airplane	"robber barons" trusts	Theodore Roosevelt
atomic theory Einstein's relativity	cartels	alliance system
plastic	department stores	progressivism
1910		Balkan crises ALBANIA
gas warfare		WORLD WAR I genocide
U-boats tanks	"war socialism"	Russian Revolution USSR Wafd
bombers/fighters		CZECHO-SLOVAKIA ESTONIA LATVIA LITHUANIA HUNGARY AUSTRIA FINLAND
influenza pandemic		KINGDOM OF SERBS, CROATS, and SLOVENES
1920		
radio	era of big business	IRELAND totalitarianism, authoritarianism
air conditioning	USSR: NEP USSR: 5-year plans	League of Nations TURKEY "Red scare" "Yellow Peril"
	collectivization	Mussolini fascism Jiang, KMT
Heisenberg's Principle		Mao Zedong
	Wall Street Crash	Stalinism YUGOSLAVIA
1930	Great Depression	Hitler Naziism
antibiotics		FDR
	New Deal	Spanish Civil War Atlantic Charter
radar	Keynesian Economics	Munich Conference WORLD WAR II
1940		Blitzkrieg Pearl Harbor
jet computer		United Nations
atomic bomb		Peron Israel
nuclear bomb	Great Leap Forward	Berlin Blockade apartheid Maoism Nehru
1950 television	baby boomers	NATO COLD WAR
genetics		CYPRUS McCarthyism Korean Police Action
Sputnik		Warsaw Pact
space flight Space Race		
		Treaty of Rome Suez Crisis EEC
ICBMs	shopping malls	Castro decolonization
1960		Kennedy Berlin Wall Congo Crisis
laser		Cuban Missile Crisis
transistor		Johnson race riots Vietnam War
	German & Japanese economic "miracles"	Northern Ireland troubles
moon landing		Six-Day War PLO
1970		
Earth Day	OPEC oil embargo	Nixon Allende détente Helsinki Accords Greens
pocket calculators	G7	Sandinistas Solidarity Iranian Revolution
1980		
Three Mile Island	Reaganomics	Reagan Thatcher Iran-Iraq War Falklands War
personal computer Chernobyl	global debt	Gorbachev glasnost End of the COLD WAR
1990		
Internet	globalization	SLOVENIA, CROATIA, BELARUS, UKRAINE, BOSNIA, MACEDONIA MOLDAVIA First Persian Gulf War
cell phones		
	G8	European Union Mandela Chinese Capitalist Revolution
2000		
drones	global recession	9/11 invasion of Afghanistan and Iraq
smartphones		MONTENEGRO, SERBIA, KOSOVO

Twentieth Century

SOCIAL STRUCTURES	CULTURE	PHILOSOPHY & RELIGION	
industrialization urbanization	advertising	Christian fundamentalism	
	fin de siècle	Christian modernism	
suffragettes	ragtime		— 1900
	realism, naturalism		
	primitivism		
	cubism expressionism		— 1910
	abstract art		
	movies		
Ku Klux Klan race riots	dada		
aristocracy depoliticized	Jazz Age	"Lost Generation"	— 1920
	sports	"monkey" trial	
women's suffrage	Roaring Twenties		
Prohibition	surrealism		
Lindbergh		mass evangelists	
	International School		— 1930
gulags	socialist realism	Gandhi	
	Picasso		
	abstract expressionism	Holocaust	— 1940
welfare state	pop art	existentialism	
	television		— 1950
suburbanization desegregation	"Coca-colanization"	Islamic fundamentalism	
civil rights movement	rock'n'roll		
sexual revolution 1968 student protests	The Beatles	Vatican II	— 1960
	op art	Martin Luther King, Jr.	
		drug culture	
women's liberation	rock concerts	cults	
abortion debate			— 1970
NGOs	video games	televangelists	
			— 1980
AIDS	music videos	The "Religious Right" Pope John Paul II	
			— 1990
ethnic cleansing	postmodernism		
homosexual rights			
			— 2000
immigration debate	global climate change debate		

Twentieth Century

Common Abbreviations

AD   anno Domini, in the Year of the Lord (some historians instead use CE, Common Era)

b.   born

BC   Before Christ (some historians instead use BCE, Before the Common Era)

ca.   circa, around or about

cent.   century

d.   died

fl.   flourished

r.   ruled

Glossary

The terms below cover many of the important ideas that Western civilization has either developed on its own, borrowed from others, or interacted with. The terms often end in *-ism* or *-ation* (and are **_boldface italicized_** in the text). Some of these ideas have been discredited by dominant attitudes of political institutions, social pressures, intellectual fashions, or religious organizations. Still, all of these diverse ideas, many of which contradict one another, are options to be adopted and practiced.

absolutism: The idea and practice that one person should dominate in authority and decision making within a state. Historians and political theorists most often apply the term to European monarchs of the seventeenth and eighteenth centuries AD, although the concept does apply to all ages.

agnosticism: The belief that the existence of God or of any supernatural beings is impossible to prove.

American exceptionalism: A point of view that sees Americans as different from their fellow westerners or other peoples, usually as being more virtuous or free. The source of this alleged virtue ranges from a special relationship with God to the unique genius of the Founding Fathers. *See also* **Western exceptionalism**.

Anabaptism: A religious belief that rejects infant baptism, an idea that united diverse groups of Christians during the Reformation. *See also* **Christianity**; **Protestantism**.

anarchism: A political idea that calls for the destruction of industrialized and bureaucratized societies so that a utopian agricultural society can appear. *See also* **terrorism**.

Anglicanism: A branch of Christians formed during the Reformation, first organized as the Church of England, which defines itself as a middle path between Protestantism and Roman Catholicism. British imperialism planted numerous Anglican churches around the world, now loosely connected to one another as the Anglican Communion. *See also* **Christianity**.

animism: The religious belief that nature is alive with spirits and ghosts that affect our natural world. Animism was probably the first religion, and many remaining hunter-gatherers still practice some form of it.

anthropomorphism: The idea that gods and deities look and act like human beings. Much of ancient Greek and Roman mythology was based on this concept.

anti-intellectualism: The criticism of the thoughts and opinions of educated elites as less useful than those of the "common" uneducated masses. *See also* **intellectualism**.

antisemitism: A euphemism for the hatred of Jews. *See also* **Judaism**; **racism**; **Zionism**.

apostolic poverty: The belief that it is virtuous for Christians to live like the poor, since Jesus and his followers did so. The height of its influence was in the Middle Ages with the Waldensians and Francis of Assisi's monasticism of the mendicants. See also **asceticism**.

apostolic succession: The belief in some parts of Christianity that the true church requires its leaders (bishops and priests) to be ordained in a direct line from Jesus and his apostles.

arabization: The process of making people conform to Arabic culture, especially Islam and its associated traditions. *See also* **islamization**.

Arianism: A religious belief in the third century AD that distinguished the human nature of Jesus from the divine. Most denominations of Christianity officially reject this division and see Jesus as fully human and fully divine at the same time. *See also* **heresy**.

aristocracy: The idea and practice that a few families are of a higher status than others and therefore should rule society.

asceticism: The avoidance of worldly pleasures in living one's life.

assassination: The political practice of murdering leaders in order to force change.

atheism: The belief that denies the existence of the supernatural. *See also* **supernaturalism**.

atomic theory: The scientific idea that the smallest indivisible part of a unique substance is an atom (Greek for "not able to be cut"). Ancient Greek philosophers first suggested the idea, which was scientifically verified in the late nineteenth and early twentieth century.

authoritarianism: The modern political practice of a dictatorship, where a ruler and their party significantly control mass communication and bureaucracy while maintaining order through secret police, paramilitary, and military groups. *See also* **absolutism**; **dictatorship**; **fascism**; **Leninism**; **Stalinism**; **totalitarianism**; **tyranny**.

balance of power: A foreign policy idea most popular between 1648 and 1945 that the nations of Europe should league together against any state that tried to dominate the Continent.

balkanization: The practice of carving up larger empires into smaller states, as done after World War I in eastern Europe. Often it is used in a negative sense.

baptism: The religious idea in Christianity that a ritual with water binds one to that belief system.

barbarian: (1) A term used by civilized urban peoples to describe other peoples who are not civilized (that is, living in pastoral or hunter-gatherer economies);

(2) a term used by one people to insult another as unjustifiably cruel, regardless of either's level of socioeconomic development.

Bolshevism: The name for the communist movement in early twentieth-century Russia led by Lenin. *See also* **communism**; **Leninism**.

bureaucracy: The practice of governing by means of written records and offices that issue, administer, and store them.

caesaro-papism: The practice of the medieval Eastern Roman or Byzantine emperors of helping to organize and supervise the hierarchy and belief system of the Christian church in their empire. *See also* **Orthodox Christianity**.

Calvinism: The belief system held by churches formed during the Reformation that followed the theology of Jean Calvin. Predestination, the belief that God has already chosen who is saved or damned, is its most distinctive doctrine. *See also* **determinism**; **Protestantism**.

capitalism: In its simplest form, the practice of reinvesting profits. As part of our modern ideological conflicts, the term often refers to private ownership of the means of production using free markets, as opposed to communism, where the government carries out central planning of the economy. *See also* **communism**; **Marxism**.

catastrophism, theory of: A scientific idea that explains geology or the history and structures of the earth according to rare and unusual events of enormous power, resembling divine intervention. *See also* **uniformitarianism, theory of**.

Catharism: The medieval religion that mixed Christianity and dualism and was therefore identified by the Christian church as a heresy. *See also* **dualism**; **heresy**.

Christianity: The monotheistic religion that asserts that God became incarnate as his son, Jesus of Nazareth. The Romans executed Jesus, but as the Messiah, or Christ, he returned from the dead to offer salvation, or entrance into heaven for his followers. Since the first century, Christians have divided into many groups: a few who did not define Jesus as fully God and human, as well as the vast majority who have. *See also* **Anabaptism**; **Anglicanism**; **Arianism**; **Calvinism**; **heresy**; **Lutheranism**; **Orthodox Christianity**; **Pietism**; **Protestantism**; **Roman Catholicism**; **schism**.

Christian socialism: A socialist idea adopted by Christians, especially Roman Catholics, using religious ideology as a basis to improve conditions for workers while still respecting the private property rights of capitalists.

civilization: The practice of people living in cities, which supported rich political, social, and cultural lifestyles that could spread over vast territories and many peoples. Distinct governments, social structures, art and literature, and belief systems indicate differences among civilizations.

classical liberal economics, theory of: Also called laissez-faire, the idea that the least interference by government provides the best opportunities for economic growth. It was developed in the eighteenth century in opposition to mercantilism. *See also* **mercantilism, economic theory of**; **socialism**.

collectivization: The practice of Stalin during the 1930s, where the state confiscated land from peasants and consolidated the large tracts into communal farms. Communists in other states, such as China and Cambodia/Kampuchea, later undertook similar policies. *See also* **communism**; **Leninism**; **Marxism**; **Stalinism**.

colonialism: The action of one state sending out some of its people to settle in another place. A colony may or may not retain close connections with the homeland. *See also* **imperialism**.

communism: The utopian idea proposed by Karl Marx in the nineteenth century of a perfect society where the means of production would be shared by all. *See also* **Leninism**; **Stalinism**.

conciliarism: The idea and practice that church councils should be the ultimate authority in resolving conflicts among Christians.

conservatism: A political direction, developed into parties during the nineteenth century, that stands for resisting change in order to preserve political, social, and cultural advantages of the elites. Today conservatism often calls for reducing the role of government in the economy.

constitutionalism: The political idea that law limits a government's powers, whether formally written in an explicit document or by the precedent of tradition.

constitutional monarchy: The practice of having a democratically structured government while keeping a royal dynasty as a stabilizing force. *See also* **democracy**; **parliamentarianism**; **republicanism**.

cynicism: A philosophy originating among the ancient Greeks advocating the rejection of common social rules and human comforts. Today it often describes a pessimism that people's intentions are based on self-interest rather than the common good.

deification: The belief that a human being, usually a powerful leader, can be transformed into a god.

deism: The religious belief that God is the creator of the universe, although it deemphasizes the Christian dogma of Jesus's incarnation.

democracy: The political idea and practice that the best form of government involves the largest possible number of citizens making decisions. Democracies usually involve checks and balances upon authority and factions or parties that dispute and compromise about different political viewpoints. Direct democracy in ancient Athens included all male citizens. Modern democracies usually use elected representatives. A democrat is not necessarily to be confused with a member of the modern American political party. *See also* **parliamentarianism**; **republicanism**.

democratic socialism: Also called social democracy, the effort of revisionists of Marxism to work through the political process instead of through a proletarian revolution. The various modern labor and social democratic political parties were the result.

denazification: The policy after World War II to purge members of the Nazi Party from leadership positions in occupied Germany. *See also* **Naziism**.

determinism: A philosophy that asserts humans have very little free will in deciding their fate. *See also* **Calvinism**.

dialectical materialism: The theoretical model of history suggested by Karl Marx, where a dominant class conflicts with an exploited class. *See also* **Marxism**.

dialectic logic: A method of gaining knowledge that uses two pieces of known data to produce or confirm other information. *See also* **Scholasticism**; **syllogism**.

dictatorship: The practice of one person seizing power in a government. While today the term is used in a negative way, the Romans originally used the method during political crises. *See also* **authoritarianism**; **totalitarianism**; **tyranny**.

diversity: The term used in this text to describe the creative impulse as a force in history. New ideas and groupings of people create change.

divine right: The political idea that God has placed kings in power as part of his divine order.

dualism: A religious philosophy that sees the universe as divided between two powerful beings, one a good force inspired by spirit and ideas, the other an evil influence based on matter and flesh. *See also* **Catharism**; **Gnosticism**; **Zoroastrianism**.

ecumenism: The effort by religions, usually those of Christianity, to tolerate one another, work together, and perhaps unify. It was most influential in the mid-twentieth century. *See also* **toleration**.

egalitarianism: The idea that the best society tries to equalize the wealth, influence, and opportunities of all its citizens. It is exemplified by ancient Sparta, the radicals of the French Revolution, and much Marxist ideology.

empiricism: The idea that observations by our senses are both accurate and reasonable. It is the starting point of scientific knowledge. *See also* **rationalism**; **science**.

enlightened despotism: The political idea and practice that asserted that one person, usually a benevolent dynastic monarch, should rule, since unity encouraged simplicity and efficiency.

environmentalism: The idea and practice since the 1960s of reducing human interference with and damage upon the natural world.

Epicureanism: A philosophy that suggests that the best way of life is to avoid pain. The good life lay in withdrawal into a pleasant garden to discuss the meaning of life with friends. Epicureanism originated among the Hellenistic Greeks and was popularized by the Romans.

ethnicity: The idea of grouping humans into categories based on certain physical and behavioral differences. Ethnocentrism means that certain members of ethnic groups view members of other groups as inferior and dangerous. What separates ethnicity from race is the idea that race is unchangeable, while ethnicity is more fluid and open. *See also* **racism**.

evolution: The observed scientific phenomenon about the increasing diversity and complexity of life on earth from millions of years ago to the present. Darwin's theory of natural selection is the framework under which most scientists today understand the process of evolution. *See also* **natural selection, theory of**.

excommunication: The practice of various Christian churches of disciplining members by shunning them from society and cutting them off from the sacraments.

factionalism: The practice of refusing to cooperate with opposing political and social groups.

fascism: A political ideology, most popular in the 1920s and 1930s, where an extreme nationalist dictatorship seemed the best form of government. Fascist authoritarian and totalitarian regimes offered alternatives to socialism, communism, and parliamentary democracy. Many capitalists were able to accept fascist regimes, despite their violent tendencies toward outsiders, since fascism's concept of the corporate state still allowed some private property and profit. *See also* **authoritarianism**; **dictatorship**; **Naziism**; **totalitarianism**.

federalism: The political practice in republics of separating governmental power within a country, where a strong central administration competes and shares power with provincial or state and local governments. It contrasts with a confederate system, where the central administration is weaker than the local governments.

feminism: The idea that women are not inferior to men, but rather should have equal access to education, political participation, and economic independence. Today it is often mischaracterized as hostility or sexism against men. *See also* **women's liberation**.

feudal politics: The system where knights bound one another together by oaths and rituals to rule society after AD 1000. The term *feudalism* should be avoided because of its many confusing meanings.

fundamentalism: A belief that values traditional, often preindustrial customs and attitudes, especially regarding religion. Fundamentalists reject modern ways of knowing based on the skepticism of literary criticism and the scientific and historical methods. In Christianity, it includes those who support an allegedly literal interpretation of the Bible rather than an interpretation through higher criticism. *See also* **higher criticism**; **textual criticism**.

germanization: The policy of making people conform to German culture. Used by some princes in the Holy Roman Empire, bureaucrats in the Second German Empire, and the Nazis of the Third Reich. *See also* **Naziism**; **pan-germanism**.

germ theory of disease: The scientific theory, argued by Pasteur in the nineteenth century, that microscopic organisms, such as bacteria and viruses, cause many sicknesses. While very successful as a means to understand illness, it does not, however, explain all disease.

globalization: The recent practice of the world's economies being tied more closely together, often bypassing the interests of nations, regions, and localities.

Gnosticism: The ancient philosophy or religion that drew on dualism and argued that its followers held secret knowledge about the meaning of life. Gnostics tried to influence early Christianity. *See also* **dualism**.

heathenism: A religion of polytheism. It was once a term of insult in late Rome applied to poor peasants (living in the countryside) who were ignorant of Christianity; since the Early Middle Ages, heathen has meant any non-Christian in or outside Christendom. *See also* **paganism**; **polytheism**.

hedonism: A philosophy originating among the ancient Greeks that suggested success came to those who pursued pleasure as the highest good.

hellenization: The policy of making people under Greek authority conform to Greek institutions and culture. Practiced especially by the Greek rulers of the Hellenistic Age, after the death of Alexander "the Great."

heresy: Literally, a "choice" or a "sect," the term with which winners in a cultural or religious debate label the ideas of the losers. *See also* **orthodoxy**.

higher criticism: The practice of applying modern scholarly techniques to examining the Bible. *See also* **fundamentalism**; **textual criticism**.

history: The idea that the past is a product of human activity that needs to be interpreted. Since the eighteenth century, the historical method practiced by academics has been the most reliable way to produce objective and accurate versions of the past.

humanism: The philosophy begun by the ancient Greeks that the world is to be understood by and for humans. It gained a significant revival in the Renaissance, including a version called Christian humanism, inspired by the faith in Jesus. Recently some Christians attack what they call "secular humanism" which they believe undermines lives based on religion.

humanitarianism: The idea that humans ought to treat one another well. It is sometimes incorporated in Christianity and was promoted by many intellectuals of the Enlightenment.

idealism: Also known as the doctrine of ideas, idealism is a philosophical explanation of reality that proposed that particular things in the observable world are reflections of universal truths. It is famously formulated by Plato in his "Allegory of the Cave."

imperialism: The practice of taking over different peoples in other countries and communities in order to build an empire. Empires often surpass kingdoms or nations in the diversity of their subject peoples. *See also* **colonialism**; **neo-imperialism**.

individualism: The idea that political and social policies should favor opportunities for single human beings over those in collectives or groups. *See also* **collectivization**.

intellectualism: The idea that educated elites should be respected. *See also* **anti-intellectualism**.

Islam: The religion begun by Muhammad in Arabia. Muslims believe that the one, true God has established a special relationship to those who submit to his will, as explained in the Qur'an.

islamization: The policy of making people conform to Islam and live as Muslims.

Judaism: The religion begun by the ancient Hebrews. Jews believe that the one, true God has established a special relationship with them, as revealed in their sacred scriptures (called by Christians the Old Testament). *See also* **antisemitism**; **Zionism**.

Keynesian economic theory: An economic theory, part of which says that massive government spending can rescue a nation's economy from a depression. It is named after its creator, twentieth-century British economist John Maynard Keynes.

kleptocracy: The practice of government public officials using their authority to increase their personal wealth (rule by those who steal).

Leninism: The ideological and political program put in place by Lenin through the Russian Revolution. He established a dictatorship enforced by secret police, had the state take over substantial portions of the economy (a policy called war communism), and carried out land reform. See also **Bolshevism**; **communism**; **Marxism**.

lesbianism: The practice of women being sexually attracted to and involved with other women. The term comes from the island Lesbos, where Sappho, the ancient Greek poet, had her school (although she herself was not strictly lesbian). *See also* **sapphism**.

liberalism: A political direction that developed into parties during the nineteenth century. It generally stands for changing laws in order to broaden political, social, and cultural opportunities for the middle classes. Today liberalism often calls for accepting a role of government in the economy.

liberation theology: A religious idea in Latin America of the twentieth century that called for Christianity to look after the poor in this world and not merely preach about salvation for the next.

Lutheranism: The version of Christianity that originated with Martin Luther during the Reformation emphasizing justification through faith. *See also* **Christianity**; **Protestantism**.

manorial economics: The economic system in which serfs worked the lands of their seigneurial lords in exchange for the use of farmland for themselves; preferred instead of *manorialism*, a term to be avoided because of its confusing meanings.

Marxism: The particular socialist ideology developed by Karl Marx in the mid-nineteenth century that advocated a proletarian revolution to overthrow bourgeois capitalist society. Since then, Marxism has been used as a synonym for communism. *See also* **Bolshevism**; **communism**; **dialectical materialism**; **Leninism**; **socialism**; **Stalinism**.

materialism: The idea that the physical goods and pleasures in this observable world should take priority over any possible spiritual virtues or destinies.

McCarthyism: A belief usually characterized as a paranoid and unfair attempt to persecute innocent people for their allegedly dangerous political views. It is named after a US senator who during the 1950s wanted to purge alleged communists from the government, politics, and the media.

mercantilism, economic theory of: The idea that government intervention provides the best opportunities for economic growth, especially in establishing monopolies and a favorable balance of trade. It was developed in the sixteenth century in order to manage early capitalism. *See also* **classical liberal economics, theory of**; **neo-mercantilism, theory of**.

militarism: The idea and practice that virtues such as discipline, obedience, courage, and willingness to kill for the state are the highest values a civilized society can hold. It is exemplified by the ancient Assyrians, the Spartans, and the modern Prussians.

Mithraism: An ancient religion, originating in Persia but most popular among the Roman military. Its cultic followers believed that Mithras was the son of the sun god, born on December 25, who killed the heavenly bull to bring fertility and whose own death helped human souls to an afterlife. *See also* **Zoroastrianism**.

modernism: A belief that accepts changes brought by the Enlightenment and the Commercial and Industrial Revolutions toward a more secular and materialistic society. In Christianity, it includes those who support rigorous scholarly examination of scripture. *See also* **higher criticism**.

monasticism: A religious way of life in which people live in a cloistered setting under strict rules, usually involving renunciation of property, physical pleasure, and freedom of choice.

monotheism: The religious belief that only one God exists and should be worshipped.

multiculturalism: The idea that knowledge of and appreciation for diverse ways of life is beneficial for society.

nationalism: The political idea that asserts that states should be organized exclusively around ethnic unities. The problem is, few states only have only one ethnic group living within their borders. Nationalists often try to cultivate patriotism, or love of one's country, which can, but does not necessarily, lead to hostility between nations. An extreme form of nationalism is called chauvinism, named after an apocryphal French patriot. The word chauvinism is also applied to male sexism.

nativism: The political movement that promotes fears that foreigners and immigrants threaten the economic opportunities and social positions of the resident population. "Natives" usually means those of European ancestry: not the oppressed native indigenous or aboriginal peoples.

naturalism: (1) The movement in classical sculpture and art since the Renaissance to portray objects exactly as they appear in nature rather than with an abstract interpretation; (2) the movement in literature since the late nineteenth century to focus on suffering caused by modern society. *See also* **realism**.

natural selection, theory of: Also called "survival of the fittest," Darwin's theory explains how the fact of evolution took place. The theory proposes that the struggle of creatures for food and reproduction encouraged change as organisms adapted to their environment, competed with others, and then passed on useful characteristics to offspring. Thus some species went extinct while many living things become increasingly diverse and more complex. *See also* **evolution**.

Naziism or **national socialism:** The uniquely German version of fascism. Formulated by Adolf Hitler and brought into action during the Third Reich (1933–1945), it fulfilled many Germans' need for nationalistic pride. Its extreme germanization, however, aimed for the Nazi domination of Eurasia and the enslavement or extermination of non-German peoples, especially Jews. *See also* **authoritarianism**; **fascism**; **germanization**; **pan-germanism**; **totalitarianism**.

neo-imperialism: The political practice of Western industrialized states that built up overseas colonial empires between 1830 and 1914. *See also* **colonialism**; **imperialism**.

neo-mercantilism, theory of: The economic idea in Western industrialized states between 1830 and 1914 that combined neo-imperialism abroad with laissez-faire practices at home. *See also* **mercantilism, economic theory of**.

nominalism: The medieval philosophy that proposed that only particular material things in the observable world exist, while collective ideas and categories are mere "names" created by the human mind. *See also* **idealism**.

objectivity: The attempt to remain neutral or interpret disagreements from an unbiased point of view. *See also* **subjectivity**.

oligarchy: The political idea that states are best run by the economic and social elites. *See also* **aristocracy**; **plutocracy**.

Orthodox Christianity: The version of Christianity originally centered in the Byzantine Empire. It became a separate branch after the Great Schism with Western Latin Christianity beginning in 1054. *See also* **Christianity**; **Protestantism**; **Roman Catholicism**; **schism**.

orthodoxy: Literally, the "right teaching," it is the label adopted by groups whose ideas win a cultural debate. *See also* **heresy**.

ostracism: The political practice in ancient Athens of exiling politicians who were considered too dangerous. Today it often means a social practice of shunning. *See also* **excommunication**.

pacifism: The political idea that wars are not a proper activity of states. Instead of warmongering, efforts to maintain peace should be prioritized. Some Christians and Christian groups promoted the idea in Western civilization.

paganism: A religion of polytheism. It was once a term of insult in late Rome leveled at poor peasants who were ignorant of Christianity; since the Early Middle Ages it has meant any non-Christian in or outside Christendom. *See also* **heathenism**; **polytheism**.

pan-germanism: The ideology that all German peoples should be ruled together. As a policy of Adolf Hitler and his Third Reich, it had some success in the 1930s until Hitler showed his determination to rule non-Germans also. *See also* **Naziism**.

pan-hellenism: The idea that all Greeks should be united, at least culturally.

pan-slavism: The political idea that called for all Slavs to live together in one nation-state. The Russians, as the dominant Slavic group, were most behind this movement. *See also* **yugo-slavism**.

pan-turkism: A version of Turkish nationalism that sought to promote unity among diverse Turkish peoples. "Young Turks" toward the end of the Ottoman Empire tried to encourage all subject peoples to become more like Turks.

parliamentarianism: The political idea and practice that elected representatives with limited terms are the best means of governing a state. Structurally, the person who leads the majority in the parliament, usually called a prime minister or a chancellor, is the most powerful political official in the government. *See also* **constitutionalism**; **democracy**; **republicanism**.

particularism: The political and social idea that specific local variations in institutions and beliefs are the best way to organize the state and society. *See also* **diversity**; **universalism**.

philosophy: Literally, "love of wisdom," any intellectual system that proposes explanations for the nature of the universe and the purpose of human beings. While a philosophy may or may not have a supernatural dimension, it should rely on rationalism.

Pietism: A form of Christianity that arose during the eighteenth century, especially among Lutherans, in which believers dedicated themselves to prayer and charity.

plutocracy: A government run by and for the interests of the wealthy. *See also* **oligarchy**.

polytheism: The belief in many gods and goddesses. Divine beings usually reflected the values and needs of farming communities. *See also* **heathenism**; **paganism**.

populism: A political ideology that believes the masses of people (usually rural and middle and lower class) have more wisdom and virtue than elites (usually professionals, intellectuals, and capitalists), career politicians, and several social institutions (such as cities, the Roman Catholic Church, and secretive fraternal organizations). Its leaders often resort to demagoguery. *See also* **anti-intellectualism**; **fascism**; **nativism**.

postmodernism: The academic practice of "deconstructing" texts and ideas to understand both how dominant elites perpetuate power and resisting "others" subvert authority. Such postmodernist relativism disputes the Enlightenment effort toward attaining objective truth.

progress: The idea that people should work to improve political, social, and living conditions in this world. It has been an important Western idea since the Enlightenment.

Protestantism: Any version of Christianity that appeared after Luther's Reformation and its break from Roman Catholicism and Orthodox Christianity; the name originates with those who protested the imperial attacks upon Luther. *See also* **Anabaptism**; **Anglicanism**; **Calvinism**; **Christianity**; **Lutheranism**; **Orthodox Christianity**; **Pietism**.

racism: The social and political belief that people inherit immutable characteristics within racial categories as if they were a species and that some "races" are superior to others. There is no good scientific proof of significant differences among these constructed racial groups. Racism developed as an influential political ideology in the nineteenth century.

rationalism: The concept that the human mind can comprehend the natural world.

realism: (1) The movement in art since the Renaissance to make paintings and sculptures portray objects as human eyes see them; (2) the movement in literature since the late nineteenth century to focus on social problems. *See also* **naturalism**.

Realpolitik: The political practice of both pragmatically making compromise and using force to achieve desired ends, usually the strengthening of the state. Conservative nationalists promoted it in the nineteenth century.

regionalism: The political idea that people are best organized within smaller geographic areas rather than the typical large nation-state or centralized empire. *See also* **particularism**; **subsidiarity**.

religion: From the word "to bind," a belief system that proposes a supernatural explanation for the nature of the universe and the purpose of human beings.

republicanism: The political idea and practice that elected representatives with limited terms are the best means of governing a state. Republicanism paired with the checks and balances of constitutionalism are the foundation of most modern democratic states. In its strict form, a republic elects all significant political figures, thus excluding constitutional monarchy. A republican is not necessarily to be confused with a member of the modern American political party. *See also* **constitutional monarchy**; **democracy**; **parliamentarianism**.

Roman Catholicism: The version of Christianity that originally centered in the western portion of the ancient Roman Empire. It is characterized by being under the authority of the bishop of Rome, eventually called the pope. It defined itself as uniquely Roman after the schism from Orthodox Christianity in 1054 and with the rise of Protestantism in the sixteenth century. *See also* **Christianity**; **Orthodox Christianity**; **Protestantism**; **schism**.

romanization: The process carried out by ancient Romans of conforming their subject peoples, institutions, and attitudes to those of the Roman Empire.

Romantic movement: The intellectual movement begun in the nineteenth century that appreciated nature, admired the Middle Ages, and emphasized emotion as a reaction against the rationalism of the Enlightenment.

sapphism: The practice of women being sexually attracted to and involved with other women. The term comes from Sappho, the ancient Greek poet (although she herself was not strictly lesbian). *See also* **lesbianism**.

schism: Literally, a "rip," usually used to describe one religious group splitting away from another. *See also* **heresy**; **Orthodox Christianity**; **orthodoxy**.

Scholasticism: The medieval philosophy "of the schools," which applied Aristotle's dialectic logic to better explain Christianity. *See also* **dialectic logic**; **syllogism**.

science: The idea that knowledge of nature can best be gained through rigorous experimentation and observation according to the scientific method. Scientific theories provide coherent explanations for the facts of natural phenomena. Science's many successes have made it the dominant modern methodology. *See also* **empiricism**.

sexism: The belief that one sex (usually the male) is better than the other (usually the female). *See also* **feminism**; **women's liberation**.

skepticism: The intellectual idea of doubting everything and trusting only what can be tested through reason.

Social Darwinism: The idea of understanding human society through perspectives influenced by the debate over evolution. Social Darwinists usually rationalized the supremacy of rich European elites over the impoverished masses both in the West (through laissez-faire policies) and around the world (through colonialism). *See also* **colonialism**; **classical liberal economics, theory of**; **evolution**; **imperialism**; **natural selection, theory of**; **neo-imperialism**; **racism**.

socialism: Several ideas and practices that have developed since the Industrial Revolution to address the political, social, and economic inequalities between capitalists and workers. In principle, socialism stands for helping the workers. Over time, socialist theories and systems have developed in many directions. *See also* **Christian socialism**; **classical liberal economics, theory of**; **communism**; **democratic socialism**; **Marxism**; **Naziism**; **state socialism**; **trade unionism**; **utopian socialism**; **war socialism**.

sovietization: The practice of the Soviet Union during the Cold War of transforming states under their influence to conform to Stalinism. *See also* **Stalinism**.

Stalinism: The developments in the early Soviet Union that both modernized state and society and created a totalitarian dictatorship based on Stalin's cult of personality. *See also* **Leninism**; **Marxism**.

state socialism: The practice of conservative governments legislating practices to improve the condition of workers. *See also* **socialism**.

stoicism: A philosophy that calls for people to do their duty in difficult circumstances. It originated among the Hellenistic Greeks and was popularized by the Romans.

subjectivity: The inclination to take sides or interpret disagreements from a biased point of view. *See also* objectivity.

subsidiarity: The political idea and practice that decisions should be made at the regional and local levels rather than by a distant national, imperial, or global authority. *See also* **particularism**; **regionalism**.

suburbanization: The process of moving people to live in areas around cities that mixed traditional urban dwellings with rural landscapes. It became common in the late twentieth century with the increasing use of automobiles.

supernaturalism: The belief that another realm exists apart from the reality that can be empirically observed and sensed. Forces or beings in the supernatural realm are often believed to have influence or power within the natural world.

supremacy: A term used in this text to indicate historical change through the enforced domination of ideas or by those with power.

syllogism: An element of dialectic logic as developed by the ancient Greek philosopher Aristotle, where two pieces of known information are compared in order to reach new knowledge. *See also* **dialectic logic**; **Scholasticism**.

syncretism: The process in which elements of an idea, philosophy, or religion are blended with those of another.

terrorism: The political idea and practice of using small-scale violence, usually against civilians, to achieve specific political ends. Large-scale violence becomes guerrilla war, rebellion, or actual war. *See also* **anarchism**.

textual criticism: The intellectual tool developed during the Renaissance of comparing different manuscript versions of an author in order to find the best, most accurate text. *See also* **higher criticism**.

theocracy: The political idea and practice that religious leaders should rule the state.

toleration: The idea that people and society should accept other people who believe in different worldviews, philosophies, or religions. *See also* **diversity**; **ecumenism**.

totalitarianism: The modern political practice of a strong dictatorship, where a ruler and his party substantially control mass communication, bureaucracy, and the economy and maintain order through secret police and a strong military. *See also* **authoritarianism**; **dictatorship**; **fascism**; **Leninism**; **Stalinism**.

trade unionism: The practice of organizing labor unions (trade unions in Britain, syndicalism in France) to help workers. At first illegal, unions often successfully improved conditions for workers to the point that much of the working class blended into the middle class during the twentieth century. *See also* **socialism**.

tyranny: The practice of one person seizing power in a government. While today the term is used in a negative way, tyrants among the ancient Greeks often opened politics to become more egalitarian and democratic. *See also* **dictatorship**.

uniformitarianism, theory of: A scientific theory to explain the history of the earth. It states that the same (uniform) processes that are shaping the earth today have always acted to mold the planet. *See also* **catastrophism, theory of**; **science**.

universalism: The attitude that the same beliefs and practices should be applied or open to everyone. *See also* **particularism**; **supremacy**.

urbanization: The process of moving rural people to live in ever-larger cities, carried out after the Industrial Revolution. Today most people live in urban areas.

utopian socialism: The first version of socialism, which called on capitalists to improve conditions for workers. *See also* **socialism**.

vandalism: The practice of writing on or damaging property, either out of spite or to make a statement. It is named after the Vandal sack of Rome in AD 455, perhaps unfairly since later sacks were worse.

war socialism: A common policy during World War I and World War II when governments took control of large sectors of the economy, creating a new military-industrial complex. In doing so, they often had to appease workers to prevent strikes. *See also* **socialism**.

Western exceptionalism: A point of view that sees Europeans as better than peoples in Asia, Africa, or the Americas. The source of this alleged virtue ranges from the success of Western imperial colonialism, through superior moral upbringing, to divine favor.

westernization: The process of conforming non-European institutions and attitudes to those of Western civilization.

women's liberation: A movement in the 1960s and 1970s that promoted the rights of women to education, political participation, and economic independence. It was largely successful in Western industrialized states. *See also* **feminism**; **sexism**.

yugo-slavism: The political idea that called for all southern (*yugo*) Slavs to live together in one nation-state. The Serbs, as the dominant group of southern Slavs, were most behind this movement. *See also* **pan-slavism**.

zairianization: A political idea of Congolese nationalism, where the authoritarian kleptocrat Mobuto in the 1960s rejected European culture and tried to readapt his country to more native African ways. *See also* **kleptocracy**.

Zionism: Originally the idea of Jewish nationalism, namely that Jews, like any other nationality, should have their own nation-state. Zionism culminated in the modern state of Israel in 1948. Ever since, the term has sometimes been used to describe the alleged racist and imperialist policies of Israel against Arab Palestinians. *See also* **antisemitism**; **Judaism**.

Zoroastrianism: A dualistic religion in ancient Persia founded by the legendary Zoroaster or Zarathustra. *See also* **dualism**.

Index

Letters after page numbers indicate the following: d = diagram; f = figure; m = map; n = note; ps = primary source; sf = sources on families; t = timeline; tb = table. Terms in **boldface** designate a person.

About the Author

Brian A. Pavlac is professor of history at King's College in Wilkes-Barre, Pennsylvania, where he has served as chair of the department, director of the Center for Excellence in Learning and Teaching, and a Herve A. LeBlanc Distinguished Service Professor. He is the author of *Witch Hunts in the Western World: Persecution and Punishment from the Inquisition through the Salem Trials* and articles on Nicholas of Cusa and excommunication, editor of and contributor to *Game of Thrones versus History: Written in Blood*, co-author of the forthcoming *The Holy Roman Empire: A Historical Encyclopedia*, and translator of Balderich's *A Warrior Bishop of the 12th Century: The Deeds of Albero of Trier*.